D1476878

From Abdullah to Hussein

Studies in Middle Eastern History
Bernard Lewis, Itamar Rabinovich, and Roger Savory
GENERAL EDITORS

THE TURBAN FOR THE CROWN
The Islamic Revolution in Iran
Said Amir Arjomand

LANGUAGE AND CHANGE IN THE ARAB MIDDLE EAST
The Evolution of Modern Arabic Political Discourse
Ami Ayalon

IRAN'S FIRST REVOLUTION:
Shi'ism and the Constitutional Revolution of 1905–1909
Mangol Bayat

ISLAMIC REFORM
Politics and Social Change in Late Ottoman Syria
David Dean Commins

KING HUSSEIN AND THE CHALLENGE OF ARAB RADICALISM
Jordan, 1955–1967
Uriel Dann

EGYPT, ISLAM, AND THE ARABS
The Search for Egyptian Nationhood, 1900–1930
Israel Gershoni and James Jankowski

EAST ENCOUNTERS WEST
France and the Ottoman Empire in the Eighteenth Century
Fatma Muge Gocek

NASSER'S "BLESSED MOVEMENT"
Egypt's Free Officers and the July Revolution
Joel Gordon

THE FERTILE CRESCENT, 1800–1914
A Documentary Economic History
Edited by Charles Issawi

THE MAKING OF SAUDI ARABIA, 1916–1936
From Chieftaincy to Monarchical State
Joseph Kostiner

THE IMPERIAL HAREM
Women and Sovereignty in the Ottoman Empire
Leslie Peirce

ESTRANGED BEDFELLOWS
Britain and France in the Middle East during the Second World War
Aviel Roshwald

FROM ABDULLAH TO HUSSEIN
Jordan in Transition
Robert B. Satloff
OTHER VOLUMES ARE IN PREPARATION

From Abdullah to Hussein

Jordan in Transition

ROBERT B. SATLOFF

New York   Oxford
OXFORD UNIVERSITY PRESS
1994

Oxford University Press

Oxford New York Toronto
Delhi Bombay Calcutta Madras Karachi
Kuala Lumpur Singapore Hong Kong Tokyo
Nairobi Dar es Salaam Cape Town
Melbourne Auckland Madrid

and associated companies in
Berlin Ibadan

Copyright © 1994 by Oxford University Press, Inc.

Published by Oxford University Press, Inc.,
200 Madison Avenue, New York, New York 10016

Oxford is a registered trademark of Oxford University Press

Library of Congress Cataloging-in-Publication Data
Satloff, Robert B. (Robert Barry)
From Abdullah to Hussein : Jordan in transition / Robert B. Satloff.
p.   cm. — (Studies in Middle Eastern history)
Includes bibliographical references and index.
ISBN 0-19-508027-0
1. Jordan—Politics and government.
2. Hussein, King of Jordan, 1935–
I. Title.   II. Series Studies in Middle Eastern history
(New York, N.Y.)
DS154.55.S267   1994
956.9504—dc20   92-46562

1 3 5 7 9 8 6 4 2
Printed in the United States of America
on acid-free paper

To Jennie

Preface

Few modern monarchies have been as bound up with the person of their monarch as has the Hashemite Kingdom of Jordan. Indeed, in Jordan itself, biographies of the two kings that have reigned for all but one year of the country's existence often pass for studies of the kingdom's political history. But there was a period in Jordan's history when commoners, not kings, mattered most and when without the lead of a strong monarch, the persistence of a handful of "king's men" were enough to keep the Hashemite monarchy alive.

The purpose of this book is to describe and analyze that period of Jordan's history, the years following the 1951 assassination of Abdullah, the kingdom's founder. By that time, a process was already under way in which there was a considerable widening of the field of power, authority, and influence inside Jordan, and during the subsequent six years, king, palace, government, parliament, army, political parties, and popular opinion all emerged as important players on the political stage. Those years witnessed the country's lone period of weak monarchy, when the king—the sad Talal or the novice Hussein—was not the preeminent political actor in the land and when the fate of the regime was left in the hands of royalists who had never before wielded executive authority inside the kingdom.

Although these royalists often competed among themselves for power and differed with one another on issues of tactics, they were, as a group, intensely loyal to the regime they served and provided the bridge that permitted Hussein to inherit his grandfather's kingdom. Those years also witnessed a series of challenges to the existence of an independent Hashemite regime in Jordan—from both within and without and sometimes self-inflicted. It was when Hussein distanced himself from the "king's men" in the wake of his dismissal of General Glubb in March 1956 that his hold on power was set adrift, and it was only when he turned back to them in April 1957 that the foundation of the Hashemite regime was again secured. That decision set the basis for the restoration of a regime modeled on Abdullah's traditional pattern of rule before the upheaval of the Palestine war.

Jordan's story is, in many ways, just a subplot in the larger saga of Great Power rivalry and ideological fervor that gripped the Middle East in the 1950s. But it is a subplot with significance, for Jordan is the historical exception. Of the principal Arab participants in the Palestine fighting of 1948/49, Jordan's was the only regime that remained intact (albeit shaky) a decade later. Whereas royalist or liberal governments succumbed to military coups d'état in neighboring Syria, Iraq, and Egypt, in Jordan the regime outmaneuvered both its political and military adversaries and endured. How the kingdom resuscitated itself and survived—and especially the changing relationship between king and "king's men" that went far to determine Jordan's fate—is the central theme we explore here.

It is important to note that this is principally a study of Jordanian domestic politics and specifically of the men (and one woman) who ruled the kingdom during its period of uncertainty. Although we touch on Jordan's relations with foreign countries—including Arab states, Israel, Britain, and the United States—those discussions are normally limited to illustrations of policies adopted by particular Jordanian leaders. Similarly, West Bank politics (or, for that matter, peculiarly East Bank politics, too) are addressed only to the extent that they shed light on the central government in Amman, not on their own merits. Such limitations reflect both the major themes of this study and the diplomatic correspondence that comprises its main source of research and documentation.

By way of introduction, three general historiographical observations may be useful. The good news is that a wide range of government archives central to understanding domestic Jordanian politics in this period is open for research. British and American diplomatic traffic is especially valuable, and those charged with declassifying material under the U.S. Freedom of Information Act seem to be reasonably generous when in regard to Jordan. Israeli documents are useful first and foremost for an insight into how Israeli analysts and policymakers perceived events next door, less so for their detail. Jordanian government records have been open for several years, and despite the rudimentary classification system in place, a lode of valuable information can be mined from them, though more so in the social and economic spheres than on political and defense issues. (Many of the sensitive files from the 1950s were destroyed in the bomb blast that killed Prime Minister Hazza' al-Majali in 1960.) Before the opening of these archives in recent years, virtually all studies of Jordanian history in the 1950s relied heavily on parliamentary records and newspaper reportage; such studies are now, for the most part, obsolete.[1]

The bad news is that the full picture will never be known with complete certainty until other archives are also open for research. Most prominent among these are the archives of the Royal Hashemite Court, but they also include French Foreign Ministry archives and that hefty cache of Jordanian government files captured by Israel in the 1967 war that was open to researchers for two decades but has been since closed for "security reasons." Also, Soviet archives should be useful in shedding light on several key episodes. Given what is available, however, collectively these files should fill in gaps only on the margin, not at the heart of the story described here.

Last, a scan of the notes and bibliography reveals that Jordanians do not, on the whole, write post-1948 Jordanian history; rather, Westerners do. Other than biographical and autobiographical works and official, commissioned histories, there are very few works of consequence by Jordanians that touch on the political history of the kingdom during King Hussein's early years.[2] By the same token, it was a Pakistani, not a Jordanian, who was given access to general staff records to compile a massive, royally sanctioned history of the Jordanian army.[3] To be sure, the reticence—government inspired or not—of Jordanians to write on their recent past is not very difficult to understand: Too much of that sensitive past is bound up in the no-less-sensitive present, and the kingdom has not yet developed a strong-enough institutional "thick skin" to stand up under the close inspection of an inquisitive citizenry. As a result, Jordanians are by and large uninformed of their own history, leaving Western historians with the task of answering not only their own questions but the Jordanians', too.[4]

Washington, D.C.   R.B.S.
March 1993

Acknowledgments

This book was conceived in Oxford; researched in Britain, America, Jordan, and Israel; written in the towns and villages of Cameroon; and revised in Washington, DC. Along the way, I have incurred debts of gratitude to many people and institutions.

For their financial and material support, I thank the warden and fellows of St. Antony's College; the Middle East Centre Committee, St. Antony's College; the vice-chancellors of British universities; the Oxford University Committee on Graduate Studies; and the Arnold, Bryce, and Read Modern History Funds. I owe special thanks to Barbi Weinberg and the Board of Trustees of The Washington Institute for Near East Policy, for their confidence and support that enabled me to pursue my doctoral studies.

For their assistance in the course of my research, I thank, in Jordan—the Ministry of Culture and Information, the Department of Documentation, Libraries, and National Archives; the Hashemite Collection, University of Jordan; the Center for Strategic and Hebraic Studies, University of Jordan; the Royal Academy for Islamic Civilization Research (Ahl al-bayt Foundation); and the Department of Statistics, Hashemite Kingdom of Jordan; in Israel—the Israel State Archives; the Jerusalem Municipal Archives; the Moshe Dayan Center for Middle Eastern and African Studies and the Jaffee Center for Strategic Studies, Tel Aviv University; and the Harry S Truman Institution for International Peace, Hebrew University; in Britain—the Public Record Office, London; the Royal Commission on Historical Manuscripts; the Liddell Hart Military Archive, King's

College, University of London; and the Middle East Centre, St. Antony's College; and in the United States—the National Archives and Records Center, Washington, DC, and Suitland, MD; the Harry S Truman Presidential Library, Independence, MO; the Dwight D. Eisenhower Presidential Library, Abilene, KS; the John Foster Dulles Library, Princeton University, Princeton, NJ; the Office of the Historian, U.S. Department of State; and the Widener Library, Harvard University, Cambridge, MA.

For access to documents and private collections, I am grateful to Na'im 'Abd al-Hadi, 'Ali al-Hindawi, Musa Zayd al-Kilani, Mahmud al-Mu'ayta, Sulayman Musa, Saba Qusus, Barry Rubin, Avraham Sela, Moshe Shemesh, and Ghayth Shubaylat. I owe thanks to Saul Smilansky for his help in translating Hebrew documents; to Jhanna Skutelsky for research assistance; to Becky Diamond for swift and expert preparation of the index; and to my friends at The Washington Institute for support throughout this project.

Names, identifications, and dates of those kind enough to sit for interviews appear in the bibliography. I am especially grateful to His Majesty King Hussein ibn Talal, who generously gave me his time on two occasions to discuss his early years on the throne.

I should like particularly to thank Asher Susser for permission to use the fine facilities of the Moshe Dayan Center; Paul Kingston and Paula Thornhill whose camaraderie made PRO research a joy; the families Frenkel and Pick for their generous hospitality; and Bruce Kuniholm and Daniel Pipes who were instrumental in fostering my interest in Jordanian politics and history.

In addition, I extend my gratitude to Roger Owen, who was helpful and encouraging throughout; to Martin Indyk, who built an institution in which ideas matter; to Itamar Rabinovich, who was unstintingly supportive in the publication process; and Bernard Lewis, who generously read this manuscript and offered numerous invaluable suggestions. At Oxford University Press, Nancy Lane and Edward Harcourt were invariably considerate and cooperative.

Elie Kedourie and Uriel Dann died before this book was published. Gentle men of great scholarship, they contributed in fundamental ways to my understanding of both the Middle East and the power and limits of history. Their passing is an irreparable loss.

I owe very special thanks for the love, faith, and support of my family: my parents, Beverly and Morris Satloff; my parents-in-law, Naomi and David Litvack; and my brothers, David and Lewis.

And to Jennie, my wife, this book is dedicated. She has enriched my life with her abiding love and filled it with a world of tenderness, confidence, insight, humor, and adventure.

Contents

Notes on Transliteration and Usage

The only diacriticals included in the transliteration are 'ayns ['] and hamzas ['] in Arabic and 'ayins ['] and alephs ['] in Hebrew. Commonly accepted English forms and, in several cases, the personal preference of the individual concerned, are used for some personal and place names. For example, Hussein, Abdullah, Nasser, Feisal, Abdul Ilah, Ibn Saud, Amman, and Jeddah are used throughout the text, notes, and bibliography.

Only the following security classifications are included in the notes: top secret, secret, emergency, and personal.

During the period under study, the pound sterling and the Jordanian dinar were of equal value. For simplicity's sake, the pound sterling is used throughout.

From Abdullah to Hussein

Introduction

The Passing of an Era Already Past

On Thursday, July 19, 1951, King Abdullah, along with his grandson Hussein and a few courtiers, flew from Amman's small landing strip to Jerusalem's Qalandia Airport in his royal Dove. The next day, he rose at dawn, recited his morning prayers, and was driven off first to visit Ramallah and then Nablus. There the king received the mayor and other local dignitaries and then returned to Jerusalem to prepare himself, as was his custom, for Friday prayers at the al-Aqsa Mosque on the Haram al-Sharif.

The atmosphere in the Old City, normally bustling with activity on a Friday morning, was tense. Just three days before, the former Lebanese prime minister, Riyadh al-Sulh, had scarcely finished a visit with Abdullah when he was shot dead by a team of assassins while en route from the Royal Palace to Amman Airport riding in one of the king's cars. Security for al-Sulh had been lax; he had no police escort and just one aide-de-camp with him in the automobile. Worst of all, one of the three assassins had been a sergeant in the Arab Legion's Criminal Investigation Division (CID). The murder transfixed a country that had hitherto not known political killing, and it shocked the army into a heightened state of readiness and anxiety.[1]

The night Abdullah arrived in Jerusalem, Lieutenant General John Bagot Glubb (Glubb Pasha) telephoned the Jerusalem brigade and warned of a possible assassination attempt on the king. Abdullah himself had fatalistically shrugged off the portentous, if imprecise, warning of the American minister in Amman.[2] Moreover, he refused the offer of Nablus's

3

mayor, Sulayman Tuqan, to remain in his city for Friday prayers.[3] Perhaps it was a clandestine meeting with an Israeli diplomat scheduled for that Friday afternoon that fed Abdullah's eagerness to return to Jerusalem.[4] In any event, his army command took royal security more seriously than he did. Glubb, the Arab Legion's chief of general staff, feared an infiltrator across the no-man's-land with Israel, and so about two hundred soldiers were dispatched to boost border patrols and protection around the king. Abdullah's traditional route through the Old City was changed at the last minute, and later two grenades were found buried inside an overpass under which the king was to have walked.[5] Meanwhile, troops from the Royal Hashemite Regiment, the king's personal guard, swept through the walled city's winding streets, clearing a path for the king as he walked first to the hilltop grave of his father, King Hussein bin 'Ali of the Hijaz, and then to the mosque nearby.

Security was tight but not, however, adequate. Just before noon, as a local shaykh welcomed Abdullah into al-Aqsa, a young man dressed in Western clothes emerged from behind the door to the mosque and stood a few feet from the royal entourage, pistol in hand. He then let off a barrage of shots, hitting the king in the head, wounding the Jerusalem police chief and a Legion officer, and barely missing Prince Hussein. Abdullah died instantly, as did the assassin himself when he was finally shot by a sergeant of the royal guard.

In one sense, Abdullah's death clearly marked the end of an era in Jordanian history. After a quarter-century as amir and then another five years as king, Abdullah's reign was synonymous, not merely coterminous, with Transjordan's consolidation, autonomy, independence, and, ultimately, expansion. For the three decades between 1921 and 1951, he was unquestionably the paramount personality in the land. With great intensity of purpose, Abdullah focused his efforts on the twin objectives of nation- and state-building, and his significant progress toward them was in the end, his greatest achievement. Transjordan bore his indelible mark, not that of either the Sharifian elite he brought with him north from the Hijaz or the Syrians, Palestinians, and Circassians he enlisted over the years to administer the affairs of state.[6]

As the decades passed and the consolidation of the amirate grew firmer, Abdullah's grip over his principality and its government of the day grew even stronger. This process culminated in the 1946 treaty with Great Britain in which the amirate of Transjordan was recognized by the mandatory power as a kindred kingdom, with Abdullah its king. The conventional, almost romantic image of Abdullah is that of a benign despot: "The Emirate of Trans-Jordan," wrote one British servant of the Hashemites, was "a small pastoral duchy of almost primeval simplicity, ruled over with benevolent autocracy by Abdalla, assisted by a British resident."[7] But the autocrat in Abdullah had always chafed under the demands placed on him for constitutional reforms, which Britain had been imposing (if only, as critics pointed out, with periodic resolve) since the amirate was first recognized. The establishment of the monarchy finally loosed the bonds of formal British control and, as British minister and effective proconsul Alec Seath Kirkbride noted, freed Abdullah from "the feeling of inferiority and frustration which had troubled him in the past."[8] When the opportunity presented itself, in the interlude between formal independence and the onset of the Palestine war, Abdullah grasped it to deepen his already-tight grip on domestic political life. By the end of 1947, even a sympathetic observer like Kirkbride, who had known and admired Abdullah for more than a quarter-century, remarked that the newly minted king had "gradually assume[d] power to an extent which was hardly consistent with Transjordan's status of a constitutional monarchy."[9]

Abdullah's rule was never, however, absolute, and his ambitions suffered for it. Throughout his reign, he was hamstrung by tight British financial control, few independent sources of wealth due to prohibitions on land expropriation, and a local political community wary of his territorial ambitions. The history of Hashemite Jordan is as much colored by a continual struggle against dependence on outside financial support as it is by an uphill battle for political recognition and legitimacy. The former is marked by the imposition of a British fiscal "ultimatum" on Abdullah in 1924 and the one-sided agreement of 1928,[10] and the latter consisted largely of the campaign in the 1920s and 1930s to extend central government authority and the pacification of defiant bedouin tribes.[11] Even when Transjordan's internal tension had been relieved, its borders fixed, and Abdullah firmly ensconced in Amman, these two constraints—the lack of financial and political autonomy—deprived him of the economic clout and political backing to carry through with his grandiose schemes for Hashemite territorial aggrandizement. His obsessive need to escape the "wilderness of Transjordania" for the throne of Greater Syria, at times compressed into an ambition for the kingship over all of historic Palestine, was thwarted not least by the recalcitrance and opposition of Abdullah's own subjects and allies. As one British high commissioner of Palestine once wrote regarding Abdullah's ambitions:

> [H]is own Ministers, even those who have felt most loyalty to him . . . are beginning to take the course of alternatively humouring and ignoring him. . . . There is nothing that can be done at present, I think, except to humour the Amir in small matters, treat him with every consideration, and be politely firm with him when he shows a disposition to kick over the traces in matters of principle.[12]

If, as it is said, Abdullah was like "a falcon trapped in a canary's cage," he was pinned there by both his British patrons and his Transjordanian subjects.

On a more immediate level, Abdullah's authority was both secured and circumscribed by the presence of two British officials with whom he shared executive power—the resident (later minister and then ambassador[13]) and the chief of the Legion's general staff. Although the initiative often belonged to Abdullah, resources were usually defined (or denied) and execution supervised, respectively, by these two British officials. It was they who negotiated Jordan's frontiers and decided how best to defend them against such threats as tribal insurrection and Wahhabi aggression. And it was they who had the task of maintaining Jordan within Britain's greater imperial strategy, on both its regional and global levels.[14] In contrast with the rapid rotation of prime ministers—nine men heading twenty-four governments in thirty years—the British presence rarely changed. Only four residents and two army commanders served in Jordan throughout Abdullah's entire reign, with no personnel shifts in either position during its final twelve years. Through them was maintained Jordan's dependence on, and allegiance to, an imperial power. In turn, Jordan developed into the most reliable British ally—bordering on outpost—in the region, what one observer called the "metronome" of British well-being in the Middle East.[15]

Nevertheless, within the boundaries of Britain's imperial strategy and financial constraints, there was a wide playing field within which Abdullah was more or less free to act and maneuver. Outside Transjordan, this usually took the form of scheming for the creation of Greater Syria.[16] The British, however, frowned on Abdullah's ambitions to the throne of Damascus because it exacerbated inter-Arab rivalries, was anathema to the French, and accrued no great countervailing advantage to themselves. As a result, Abdullah was permitted his petty intrigues but, at least until 1948, no tangible progress.[17]

Meanwhile, on the domestic front, Abdullah was normally able to carry the day. As long as he did not affront too blatantly the sensibilities of British auditors (through excessive indebtedness) or Arab nationalists (through his too-clever-by-half dealings with the Zionists, which were often a function of his indebtedness), he was permitted, even encouraged, to bolster his and his family's hold over the kingdom's political life. Abdullah's main domestic challenges sprang from bedouin and other Transjordanian opposition to the extension of central government authority and to their resentment of the predominance of non-Transjordanians in the administration of the state. By the end of the 1930s, both issues had been, for all intents and purposes, settled. First, Glubb, who succeeded to the command of the Arab Legion in 1939, successfully and at times ruthlessly stamped out tribal insurrections and then succeeded in introducing the bedouin into the army itself. Second, in deference to the demands of the local Transjordanian elite, Abdullah rid his government of many veterans of the Syrian independence movement from the 1920s and other itinerant Arab nationalists. But significantly, Abdullah did not allow that Transjordanian elite into the higher echelons of government.[18] Instead, he relied almost exclusively on men with roots outside Transjordan to administer his government. For the most part, these were first-

or second-generation Syrians and Palestinians (i.e., from west of the Jordan River) or second- and third-generation Circassians whose forebears had found, in the ruins of ancient Philadelphia, refuge from czarist Russian expansion in the middle and late nineteenth century.

There were at least two reasons for Abdullah's dependence on outsiders. First, Transjordan boasted just one secondary school, which simply produced too few men capable of manning a bureaucracy and supervising the state machinery. Second, and more central to Abdullah's thinking, delegating authority to expatriates—who, by definition, lacked local political fiefdoms—kept power out of the hands of potential local adversaries. In so doing, Abdullah built up a circle of non-Transjordanians who attained power and privilege solely because they had thrown in their lot with his. Loyalty to the monarchy was the only guarantee of their status; their vested interest in the survival and prosperity of Hashemite Jordan was almost as great as that of the Hashemites themselves. It was a mutually beneficial relationship, so much so that the partnership of Hashemite kings and an expatriate elite of "king's men" survived well beyond Abdullah's demise.[19]

In the years before the Palestine war, therefore, Abdullah ruled Transjordan with a firmer grip than he had in the previous two decades. The three components of Jordan's ruling condominium—Abdullah; the British, operating principally through the British-officered army; and the non-Transjordanian elite that ran the government—so thoroughly controlled the country that the political life there can only be described as sterile and desultory.[20] From 1933 onward, the prime ministry was rotated among four men, three native-born Palestinians and a Circassian, who subsumed any personal political ambition they may have had to Abdullah's own. Governmental crises, such as there were, usually sprang from personality clashes, personal insults, and anteroom intrigues.[21] Only on those rare occasions when Abdullah was too indiscreet with his tactical maneuvering did politics interfere with the machinery of state. Unless Abdullah himself polarized the political situation, by engaging in land deals with Zionist agents or by throwing his full support to the 1939 white paper, for example, even the volatile topic of Palestine itself was not often violently divisive on the internal front.[22] As a result, on the domestic scene, the years of World War II and the subsequent interlude before fighting broke out in Palestine witnessed the apex of Abdullah's power and reign.

All this changed in 1948. Thanks to the tenacity of the Arab Legion, the connivance of British officialdom, and the ambivalence of the Zionist leadership, Abdullah extended Hashemite control into much of that part of Palestine originally assigned by the 1947 UNSCOP (United Nations Special Committee on Palestine) Partition Resolution to become an independent Arab state.[23] In so doing, he was able to take his first steps toward escaping from the confines of Transjordan. But even before the formal act of uniting Hashemite-controlled Palestine (the "West Bank" or *al-dhaffa al-gharbiyya*) and East Jordan (*sharq al-urdunn*) in April 1950,[24] it was readily apparent that the contours of rule established over nearly three decades were changing beyond Abdullah's control. In many ways, Israel was not the only new state to rise from the rubble of mandatory Palestine, for what emerged in Jordan as a result of the 1948/49 war bore little resemblance to what had gone by that name before it.

Although expansion into the West Bank brought only about two thousand square miles to Hashemite control, an increase of less than 7 percent, it added nearly half a million refugees and more than trebled East Jordan's native population. In fact, Abdullah's cabinet conferred full Jordanian citizenship on the people of the West Bank four months before the territory of the West Bank was itself incorporated into the Hashemite kingdom.[25] And it was a different sort of population that the Transjordanians—more literate, more enterprising, and, as a result of its experience of conflict and contest with Britain and the Zionists that went back to World War I, more sophisticated in the ways of politics. In practice, union of the two banks meant the extension of Hashemite rule westward. Conversely, integration of the two populations meant the extension of Palestinian society eastward. In an ironic reversal of Abdullah's original ambition, the Palestinians were, as Kirkbride once noted, "colonising" the Jordanians about as much as Jordan was colonizing Palestine.[26] As a result, the politics of Palestine, which had hitherto been principally an issue of foreign and inter-Arab debate, quickly became the stuff of domestic politics.[27]

To a certain extent, this would have occurred even if Abdullah had not bucked the inter-Arab consensus to pursue his own maverick diplomacy with the new State of Israel. The immutable laws of demography and geography made Palestine, not just the Palestinians, a Jordanian *domestic* problem from the moment the land and people of Cisjordan were amalgamated with those of Transjordan.[28] Even without royal provocation, the Palestinians would before long have made demands on the Jordanian polity—completely unrelated to the conflict with Israel—that would have upset the orderly system that Abdullah, Kirkbride, and Glubb had tried to create over the previous two decades. Indeed, this is what happened in the budget crisis of May 1951, but it probably would have taken longer had not the process been speeded up by Abdullah himself.

In the wake of fighting in Palestine, Abdullah was virtually alone among Arab leaders in believing that stability would come only with a pragmatic attitude toward Israel. In his view, only by reaching an accord with the Zionists could he hope to relieve the economic and political vise in which Jordan found itself in 1950. He envisioned an agreement that would reopen trade routes to the Mediterranean, that would permit the repatriation or compensation of thousands of refugees, and that would, most of all, vindicate some of his more controversial decisions during the war, especially his acceptance of Israel's territorial ultimatum in the secret negotiations for the Rhodes Armistice Agreement.[29]

Most of Abdullah's ministers, however, disagreed. To them would fall the task of undertaking much of the actual negotiations with the Israelis, and few wanted to share Abdullah's reputation as a political iconoclast by dealing with the Jews in secret talks that few were convinced could remain secret for long. It was not that they did not see the potential benefits of peace with Israel. Rather, it was that their political antennae, unlike Abdullah's, were tuned into public opinion in Amman. In just two years, Jordan's capital city had acquired a large Palestinian majority,[30] most of which was in no mood for the compromise and concession that are the heart of diplomatic negotiation. Jordan's ministers knew that Abdullah, a diabetic who, in his late sixties, was the oldest Arab leader of the day, would not and could not last too much longer, and they also knew that with him would pass the urgency of talking peace with Israel. So they played for time, keeping their distance from a diplomatic intrigue that, in their view, could well end up swallowing them in the process.

One by-product, therefore, of the union of the two banks was a deterioration in the relationship between king and government. In 1950, for the first time in years, a government collapsed because the prime minister refused to accede to the monarch's wishes, not once but twice. On both occasions that confrontation was a product of Abdullah's eagerness to reach a deal with Israel. In March 1950, just a month before the first parliamentary election covering both banks of the Jordan, Prime Minister Tawfiq Abu'l Huda resigned rather than go along with Abdullah's efforts to reopen commercial trade with Israel. When replacements either spurned Abdullah's commission or were unable to form a cabinet (technically, the Council of Ministers), Abdullah was forced to back down and agree to forgo trade with Israel. After a checkmated Abdullah promised "no further progress . . . in talks with Israelis until after the election," Abu'l Huda withdrew his original resignation.[31] A second crisis erupted six months later when Abdullah's appetite for a diplomatic breakthrough was whetted by a secret visit to Amman by Walter Eytan, director-general of the Israeli Foreign Ministry. The king pressed for quicker movement in talks with Israel, but the prime minister, Sa'id al-Mufti, balked and resigned.[32] Once again Abdullah shopped around for a successor but found no takers, not even among the lesser lights of Jordan's tiny political constellation. And yet again, Abdullah was compelled to forgo his own political ambitions and ask his prime minister to retract his resignation and carry on.[33]

Year's end saw Samir al-Rifa'i, Abdullah's private emissary to the Zionists in the past, installed as prime minister. But even though he soon did take up the king's demand to renew talks with Israel, little progress was achieved. Al-Rifa'i was more than a tough negotiator; he was also a prudent politician who calculated that in the mood then current in Amman, no deal was better than a deal that could be labeled capitulation. Aware that he had been pinned in the public mind to be a Zionist sympathizer, al-Rifa'i early on took steps to deflect criticism that he was soft on Israel.[34] This included constructing the most progressive cabinet Jordan had known to date, containing at least two outspoken critics of Abdullah's past dealings with the Zionists (Jerusalem Mayor Anwar al-Khatib and Finance Minister Sulayman al-Nabulsi).[35] Al-Rifa'i then acceded to the letter of the king's command in conducting talks with Israel, but his own disinclination toward compromise, coupled with the hard-line composition of his cabinet, meant that the talks were at most *pro forma*.[36] Although tactically more subtle than his predecessors, the outcome of al-Rifa'i's Palestine policy was about the same; that is, he was the third prime minister in a row to deflect, if not reject, Abdullah's determination to reach a deal with Israel.[37]

Driving a wedge between the king and his government[38] was just one of many ways in which the union of the two banks (*wahdat al-dhaffatayn*) changed the foundation of political life in Jordan. The addition of more than 800,000 Palestinians to Hashemite rule (roughly half refugees and half settled residents of the West Bank) fundamentally altered relationships between Palestinians and Transjordanians and among the Palestinians themselves; moreover, it forced continual rethinking about such concepts as "citizenship" and "political participation." Public opinion and political groupings (if not formal parties)—usually, but not exclusively, under Palestinian leadership—let their impact be felt on government decision making, with demands ranging from a halt to Abdullah's negotiations with the Zionists, to preservation of the refugees' full rights to repatriation and compensation, to governmental protection against any attempt by the United Nations Relief and Works Agency (UNRWA) to pare refugee benefits.[39] Militarily, the limited capabilities of the Arab Legion were stretched thin by Palestinian demands for retaliation against Israeli reprisal raids, and the army itself, heretofore almost exclusively a Transjordanian and bedouin mercenary preserve, was pressured to open its ranks to Palestinians.[40] Pressure from his new Palestinian subjects, in the form of a threatened boycott of the April 1950 elections, even forced Abdullah to promise to cede to the new parliament a critical element of his royal prerogative—governmental responsibility.[41] Taken together, these events and trends underscored the extent to which the "happy system of government which obtained in the old Transjordan," as Kirkbride called it, had, within a very short time, become a thing of the past.[42]

If a single date must be offered to mark the passing of the "old Transjordan," it is May 3, 1951, the day the parliamentary budget crisis came to a head. At the time, Jordan's legislature (*majlis al-umma*) was composed of a lower house (*majlis al-nuwwab*), with equal numbers of elected representatives from each of the two banks, and an appointed, and usually lethargic, upper house (*majlis al-a'yan*).[43] At a joint session of both houses immediately following the April 1950 elections, the government pressed parliament to endorse the union of the two banks hastily and with virtually no debate.[44] The opposition learned its lesson, however. From that point on, a skillful bloc of Palestinians and East Bank progressives used their parliamentary platform to harass the government, and indirectly the king, at every turn. Not all of their "considerable number of enlightened and constructive measures," as the American minister termed them,[45] were to the king's liking, and when parliament made too much noise about financial oversight of government ministries, Abdullah lashed out with a stern warning:

> I have learned that some Deputies believe it right that the House should inspect Government departments and handle matters unrelated to legislative duties. I was really surprised that such should be the case. . . . If the House interferes in the action of the Government, it loses its status as a legislative body. This is a very important point which should not be ignored.[46]

With the passage of time, Abdullah's preelection pledge to transfer government responsibility to parliament grew dim, and the gulf between the executive and the legislature widened. Significantly, it was matters of domestic concern, especially the issue of control over the kingdom's finances, at least as much as Palestine-related topics that divided the two. Whereas Abdullah consistently knuckled under when his strategy toward Israel lacked political support, he drew a line in the sand when it came to what he viewed as parliamentary encroachment on his financial prerogatives.

Parliament crossed that line in its critique of the government's budget for fiscal year 1951/52, the first to cover both the East and West Banks. There was surely much to attack; nearly two-thirds of the projected expenditures were targeted toward the Arab Legion and other defense outlays, compared with less than 2 percent on public health, less than 3 percent on education, and less than 5 percent on public works. Deputies were particularly incensed that the Arab Legion should benefit from a £1.5 million increase in the British military subsidy while the government was planning to draw on its limited financial reserves to cover a nearly £2 million deficit. Rather than accede to the government's deadline for approving the budget, parliament referred the budget back to its Financial Committee. Such temerity was too much for Abdullah. Accusing parliament of delaying the budget process unconstitutionally, he dissolved the chamber and scheduled new elections.[47]

Abdullah was assassinated five weeks before those elections were to take place. By then, it was clear that his firm grip over political life inside Jordan had softened. Enfranchising Palestinians and extending equal parliamentary representation to East and West Jordan had been his idea, but the expanded parliament lost its usefulness to Abdullah immediately after it had approved the union of the two banks on the first day it met. "Parliamentary confirmation of the union," wrote one historian, "was the one high water-mark of Abdullah's diplomacy and also a point where political smooth-sailing ended."[48] Parliament and the changes it represented, however, simply would not go away. Abdullah's paternalistic style of rule, fashioned over decades, left no place for the development of domestic challenges to his prestige and authority. The expansion of Hashemite rule into Palestine, however, ensured the development of those very challenges.

What Kirkbride fondly remembered as "old Transjordan"—the tidy, quiet country presided over by the king–government–army condominium—reached its heyday in 1946. It was then at the height of its military strength[49] and was flush with newfound respect (at least in its own eyes) with its status as an "independent kingdom." Tribal resistance was a thing of the past, and the government was in the hands of a non-Transjordanian elite of undoubted loyalty to the throne. Political opposition was marginal; what of it there was centered on individuals and petty interests, not organized parties or ideas. When the politics of Palestine left its mark, it was usually a function of a parochial Transjordanian concern (e.g., Abdullah's controversial land dealings with the Zionists) and not, by and large, a reaction to an existential affront to Arab sensibilities.

By the time of Abdullah's assassination five years later, the edifice that was "old Transjordan" had cracked. Its leadership was disunited on matters of high policy (i.e., relations with Israel); its army, despite having acquitted itself honorably in the Palestine war, was shackled with the ignominy of the forced retreat from the Triangle; its population was inflated with refugees of thread-bare allegiance; and its politics were well on their way to becoming energized and volatile. Abdullah's dismissal of parliament in May 1951, therefore, should not be viewed as a reassertion of royal prerogative cut short by his death three months later. Rather, it is best seen as the penultimate episode in the disintegration of his own patrimonial rule. That process, triggered by the advance of the Arab Legion into Palestine in May 1948, culminated with Abdullah's assassination in July 1951. Therefore, if in one sense, Abdullah's death marked the end of an era in Jordanian history, in another sense it only confirmed the passing of an era that was already largely gone.

1

A Kingdom
Without a King

Abdullah's assassination sent Jerusalem into a frenzy. Police and troops of the Royal Guard went berserk in the Old City, firing indiscriminately into the crowds and rioting through the streets. Dozens were injured; the numbers killed are unknown. The commander of the guards regiment, Lieutenant Colonel Habis al-Majali, assisted Shaykh Muhammad al-Shanqiti in wrapping Abdullah's body in one of the mosque carpets to be carried first to a hospital and then, when death was confirmed, by car to Qalandia to be put on an airplane for Amman. Al-Majali's absence coupled with the wounding of Police Chief Radi 'Innab meant that troops at the Haram al-Sharif were without their two senior officers, thereby fueling the confusion. In any event, the area was cordoned off, and up to five hundred people were herded into the Armenian Quarter and then back into the open space around the mosque for interrogation. Ahmad al-Khalil, governor of Arab Jerusalem, clamped a curfew over the Old City, sealed traffic at the Mandelbaum Gate, and declared martial law. Sam Cooke, a British brigadier stationed in Ramallah, was appointed military governor in his capacity as the senior Arab Legion officer on the West Bank. (Two months later, Cooke was promoted to major general). His own troops, more restrained yet no less outraged than al-Majali's, relieved the Hashemite regiment. In the meantime, gunfire from the Old City triggered sporadic firing across the cease-fire line with Israel, and it was only after some hectic moments that an even more explosive international incident was averted. Almost three hours after the assassination, the body of the slain killer, Mustafa 'Ashu, was identified.[1]

The frenzy in Jerusalem was matched by the daze in Amman. Friday prayers from al-Aqsa were broadcast live over Jordan radio, and the shooting at the Haram al-Sharif came in loud and clear. Minutes later, Abdullah's death was confirmed. In his memoirs, Glubb described hurrying to the house of Prime Minister al-Rifaʿi only to find him whimpering and hysterical and the room "full of men weeping unashamedly with tears streaming down their faces."[2]

The decisions that were to be taken that day by Jordan's elder statesmen—whose number included all former prime ministers, plus the chief of the royal diwan and an Abdullah confidant[3]—marked a watershed in Hashemite history. For the first time, the fate of the monarchy was left in the hands of its subjects. Abdullah's death created a leadership vacuum in Jordan that, for the first time in the young state's history, was filled by men outside the Hashemite family. Consequently, Abdullah's death marked an open season on the competition for power inside the kingdom.

The assassination could not have come at a less propitious moment in the fortune of Abdullah's wing of the Hashemite family. Despite his advanced age and illnesses, Abdullah died with no clear successor. There were, at the time, four possible claimants to his throne: his two sons, Talal and Nayif; his grand-nephew Feisal, the still-underage king of Iraq; and, last, his grandson, Hussein.

Talal's story reads like a Hashemite version of a Greek tragedy. Although he was Abdullah's eldest child, the Hijaz-born Talal (b. 1909)[4] was, from early on, the object of his father's disdain, not his pride. The origin of the rift between father and son is not clear. Contemporary observers commented on Talal's desire to please Abdullah and his overall genial and friendly disposition. His early tutors described him in warm and complimentary terms. His principal supervisor, for example, noted that Talal had even acquired the peculiarly un-Hashemite "art of looking after his money."[5]

Evidently, the "trouble" began during Talal's cadet training at Britain's Royal Military Academy at Sandhurst in 1928—some sort of public school hazing, the records imply—that dampened his appreciation for the British and, by extension, scarred his relationship with his father.[6] For his part, Abdullah seems already to have been an overbearing, domineering parent. At one point, he complained to Kirkbride that despite all the advantages of a prince's upbringing, Talal rarely excelled in any endeavor he undertook.[7] In fact, Talal never did take well to his sundry military postings, but his wandering from post to post—from Cyprus to Baghdad to Jerusalem—was more a means to avoid his father's continual haranguing than an opportunity to hone his military skills. A career in agriculture was mapped out, and Abdullah secured a special spot for Talal at Cambridge, but then the amir abruptly changed his mind and instead preferred to have his son in Amman, where he was soon engaged to his first cousin, Zayn.[8] It was suggested by one close observer that Abdullah saw much of himself in his son—"natural dignity, charm of manner . . . intelligence"—and that this resemblance was the "basic cause of [Abdullah's] parental jealousy."[9] As time passed, Abdullah denied his son any meaningful vocation, and Talal languished in his modest home with literally nothing to do. Over the years, their mutual hostility hardened, and despite episodes of periodic truce, such as the one occasioned by the birth of Hussein, Abdullah's first grandchild, they hardly spoke to each other or could bear to spend time in each other's company.

Abdullah's relationship with his second son was markedly warmer. The child of Abdullah's second wife, an Ottoman princess,[10] Nayif was five years younger than Talal. The two half-brothers had little in common. Whereas Talal received a cosmopolitan education, Nayif's was limited to attending a government school in Jerusalem and then two years at Victoria College in Alexandria. Neither industry nor intellect seems to have been Nayif's hallmark. From the tender age of fourteen, he acquired (among British observers, at least) a reputation for being "rather backward and inclined to be lazy," a characterization that stuck with him for years.[11] As the amir's second son, he had no particular political prospects, and from early on, it was his, not Talal's, susceptibility to political intrigue that worried the Hashemites' British keepers.[12] (In Nayif's case, first impressions proved correct.) Yet throughout those early years, his playful disposition permitted him a more easygoing relationship with his notoriously mischievous father. Indeed, whereas Talal at twenty-five was unwelcome in his own capital city, Nayif at twenty-five was being groomed to replace his half-brother as heir.

Some years before, Turkey's president, Kemal Atatürk, had invited Abdullah to send Nayif to Ankara for military training, and in 1939, the amir took up the offer with Atatürk's successor, Ismet Inönü. For Abdullah, sending Nayif to Turkey was an important element in preparing him for his eventual succession to the throne.

> It gives me the greatest pain [Abdullah wrote Kirkbride] to say that the conduct of my elder son, for sometime past and till the present, compels me to direct my utmost care to my second son, whom I am very anxious to educate and bring up, as far as possible, in such a manner as will make him a man worthy of succeeding his predecessors. . . . I hope I have, now, made my views in connexion with this important matter so clear as to leave no room for ambiguity.[13]

Although the British still thought of Nayif as a man "of small calibre," they went along with Abdullah, because, as the high commissioner commented, "there is no doubt that Na[y]if would be the safer and sounder of the two."[14] In late 1939, a draft law was prepared empowering the amir to exclude potential heirs on the grounds of unsuitability. The idea was that Abdullah would secretly issue an *irade* [royal decree] passing over Talal for the succession, although the decree itself would not be made public until Abdullah's death.[15] Promulgation of the draft law, however, was held up as both Abdullah and Whitehall had second thoughts: Abdullah wavered according to the mood of his relationship with Talal, and Whitehall was never wholly convinced of Nayif's worthiness. In the end, Kirkbride's personal intervention carried the day. In correspondence to the Colonial Office, he damned Talal as "intemperate in his habits, untrustworthy, and at heart deeply anti-British," while whetting London's appetite with the prospect that Nayif, though "not brilliant mentally," might be an adequate ruler "given suitable guidance by the representative of the Mandatory Power."[16]

That clinched the matter. In December 1940, Kirkbride was fearful that Talal might be an object for wartime compromise, and he exploited a violent row between Abdullah and Talal to press for final approval of the succession amendment to the amirate's Organic Law. One month later, Abdullah signed the secret decree excluding Talal from the throne. To Kirkbride's surprise, it was one of the few secrets that Abdullah was able to keep.[17]

Throughout World War II, then, Transjordan's line of succession ran through Nayif, not Talal. At first, the decision seemed vindicated by some of Talal's less judicious statements and actions. He had begun drinking heavily, provoking what British observers called "sottish expressions of pro-German sympathy."[18] Early in 1942, Abdullah was evidently so unnerved by Talal's behavior that he had his son placed under arrest for a time.[19]

Nayif's preeminence in the line of succession was short lived, however. When the war's end occasioned a fresh look at Abdullah's potential successors, Talal was found to have "changed his tune," cut back on his drinking, and become charming and pleasant. Nayif, on the other hand, had transmogrified into a "bonehead" who lacked "sufficient intelligence to play any political role whether it be good or bad." According to Kirkbride, Talal went to great lengths to be "reconciled" with Abdullah and to "make amends" with the British. For his part, Nayif seems to have blackened his prospects by "behaving most irresponsibly in a number of matters not concerned with politics," namely, smuggling and black marketeering. Moreover, by 1945, the regional circumstances had shifted. Rumors that Talal had been passed over for the succession had somehow reached the ears of Syrian nationalists. They, in turn, made much hay with the general unworthiness of Abdullah's sons and spread the tale that Transjordan would be incorporated into a Greater Syrian Republic upon his death. These three facts—Talal's change of heart, Nayif's lack of discipline, and the Syrians' rumormongering—convinced Abdullah to restore Talal as heir and to clear the air about the succession. As a result, the secret *irade* was itself secretly canceled, and in its place, Abdullah issued a public decree in March 1947 formally bestowing on Talal the title of heir apparent. Given that Talal had never publicly been stripped of his inheritance, the net effect of the decree was only to confirm his status. With the war's end, Kirkbride no longer feared for Talal's allegedly pro-German sympathies, and he supported Talal's succession, too. With the succession now secure, Kirkbride noted for the first time his belief that Transjordan could now survive Abdullah's death.[20]

But before long, succession became a volatile topic once again. The reconciliation that led to the revocation of the 1940 *irade* was, as could have been expected, only a lull in the Hashemite family's Forty Years War, and the clashes between Abdullah and Talal continued to erupt. Father forbade son from participating in any way in the fighting in Palestine in 1948/49, and he kept tabs on the comings and goings of visitors to Talal's house.[21] For his part, the once-frugal Talal began running up enormous debts, overspending his £5,000 appanage by £4,000, for example.[22] But most important, it was about this time that the heir began to show visible signs of the mental illness that was to saddle him, and the Hashemite family, for the rest of his life.

As early as 1932, Kirkbride began referring to Talal's "minor idiosyncracies," though he did not elaborate.[23] Such "idiosyncracies," whatever they were, should not have been surprising for a man who led, what successive British observers called, such a "demoralising" life: denigrated by his father and deprived of independent means, housing, livelihood, or activity. As Sir John Shuckburgh, who had wide responsibility for Middle East affairs as deputy undersecretary of state in the Colonial Office, wrote in 1939, "I am sorry for [Talal] and feel that if he has turned out badly, the fault does not rest entirely with himself. Circumstances have been too much for him."[24] Although Talal's mental state at the time of his exclusion from the throne in 1940 is not known, Abdullah did not cite mental illness as grounds for his disbarment, as was his option. Instead, he cited the more amorphous grounds of "unsuitability."

Toward the end of the 1940s, British observers remarked with greater frequency on Talal's mental state. In 1948, Kirkbride noted Talal's "tendency to instability" and his "fits of irritation," and in 1949, Christopher Martin Pirie-Gordon, consul in Amman, commented that Talal's estrangement from his father only exacerbated his natural mental imbalance. Pirie-Gordon also offered the first vivid description of Talal's "unpredictable and violent temper": "Reports allege that it not infrequently reaches carpet-biting proportions," he wrote. At the same time, however, both British and American diplomats referred to such positive traits of Talal's as intelligence, charm, pleasantness, family commitment, and open-mindedness, and they concluded that Talal had the makings of a very successful constitutional monarch, in some ways potentially an improvement on Abdullah himself.[25]

In the year preceding his father's death, however, Talal's condition grew progressively worse. He fluctuated between indecision and docility, on the one hand, and rage and unruliness, on the other. This imbalance—later to be diagnosed as schizophrenia—finally reached a climax on May 15, 1951, the day Abdullah departed for a state visit to Turkey.

Over the previous few months, Talal had evinced "signs of instability and even insanity," and Abdullah did not want to leave the regency in his son's hands during his absence. Kirkbride and Prime Minister al-Rifaʻi, however, thought the prince had been little more than "moody" and convinced the king that a Talal regency was preferable to the political disquiet of appointing in Talal's stead either Nayif or a regency council, on which Nayif might serve. Abdullah acquiesced, but only on condition that Kirkbride postpone taking vacation leave until after his own return from Ankara.

No sooner had Abdullah left than Talal "succumbed to [an] attack of insanity." His outburst was so violent and his paranoia so deep that Kirkbride, al-Rifaʻi, and Minister of Health Dr. Jamil al-Tutunji concluded that Talal had suffered a "mental breakdown." Al-Tutunji volunteered to broach to Talal the idea of leaving Amman to seek medical care in Beirut. In one of his telltale reversals, Talal calmly accepted the suggestion and departed for Beirut the following day.[26] A medical report on Talal prepared at the time by his American University of Beirut psychiatrist, Dr. Ford Robertson, blamed the prince's illness on his sour and repressive relationship with his father and urged a long period of convalescence. Robertson concluded that Talal would never be able to assume "a position of responsibility."[27] In any case, Talal went from Beirut to Europe for medical treatment, but his convalescence proved shorter than expected, and he returned to Amman on June 27. Within days, however, his condition relapsed, and he was again convinced to seek treatment outside Jordan. On July 10, Talal flew to Beirut and then on to Switzerland, where he entered a private sanitarium.

At the time, Gerald Drew, an experienced diplomat who had been appointed as the first U.S. minister to Jordan in 1950, noted that "it is now generally accepted" that Talal "will never completely recover his sanity." Indeed, in Robertson's estimation, Talal "did not have a better than 40 percent chance of recovery."[28] But significantly, no change was made in the line of succession. When Talal first left Amman in May, the cabinet appointed Nayif as regent in his place.[29] Soon after Abdullah's return from Turkey, the palace issued a press release that ascribed Talal's "sudden illness" to "boredom," denied any rift between father and son, and reconfirmed Talal as "still the Heir Apparent and . . . the hope of his exalted father and the Jordan nation."[30] In public, Abdullah and his closest advisers were quick to scotch rumors of any impending change in succession, even at a time when there seemed little chance that the heir apparent would ever be fit to succeed. The reason was that Abdullah was working feverishly behind the scenes on a complete revision of the way the succession would work, not only in Jordan, but within the Hashemite family as a whole.

Scheming for unity among the Arabs of the Mashreq (literally, "East"), an area stretching from the Levant to Mesopotamia, was a fundamental policy of Abdullah's from the early days of his reign. Most often his intrigues took the form of working toward the establishment of Greater Syria, but his version of the plan—a republican Syria subsuming itself to Hashemite rule—was rejected by most Syrians who, not surprisingly, preferred the reverse. Buoyed by his coronation as king in 1946, Abdullah decided to expand his horizons eastward as well as northward, and he tabled several suggestions for closer ties with Iraq. These proposals lacked the scent of territorial aggrandizement of his Greater Syria proposals and, under different circumstances, might have found favor with his Hashemite cousins in Baghdad. But in the mid-1940s, Iraq saw little to gain from aligning so closely with Abdullah, who had already gained a dubious reputation for his relations with the Zionists. Perhaps most important, the Iraqi regent, Abdul Ilah, had no interest in advancing his uncle Abdullah's claims to the throne of Syria at the expense of his own. In any event, Abdullah's effort toward intra-Hashemite unity "culminated" in the April 1947 Treaty of Brotherhood and Alliance, an accord that made up in rhetoric for what it lacked in substance.[31]

Three years later, Abdullah again returned to the question of Jordan's relationship with Iraq. In the interim, his territorial ambitions had been partially realized with the expansion of Hashemite control into Arab Palestine. But at the same time, he had also witnessed his high hopes for Talal deflate. When he hosted the Iraqi regent in Amman in June 1950, Abdullah did not revert to his previous proposals for an evolutionary process of association that might eventually blossom into union. Rather, he spoke directly to the heart of the matter—succession.

According to Abdul Ilah, Abdullah had decided that neither of his sons would make "suitable" heirs: Talal was "unbalanced," and Nayif, "lazy." Abdullah, the regent later reported, offered to appoint him as his successor, but (probably to Abdullah's relief) the regent declined. Then, with the preliminaries concluded, Abdullah set out his vision of the future relationship between the two Hashemite kingdoms. The "only solution," he argued, was the creation upon his death of a Hashemite federation under Feisal II, the still-minor king of Iraq.[32]

When first broached, Abdullah's plan was not taken too seriously. Its details were hazy, ill defined, and sometimes based on erroneous assumptions. (Abdullah was apparently mistaken about Feisal's true age, thinking him older than he actually was.) Kirkbride, for one, dismissed Abdullah's proposals as one of his "impetuous ideas which are launched without any serious thought being given to the matter of their implementation or to their consequences."[33] Moreover, neither the Iraqi regent nor the Jordanian ministers seem to have taken Abdullah's plan too seriously. When one of the periodic reconciliations between Abdullah and Talal took place later that summer, the matter was, in effect, dropped.[34]

Less than a year later, Abdullah again spoke to the Iraqis about the issue of unity and succession. In the interim, Talal's situation had worsened, and as noted, Abdullah had suggested that his son be passed over for the regency during his absence in Turkey. In a conversation with the Iraqi minister in Amman in May 1951, Abdullah sketched his idea of "some loose confederation" that would leave the structures of the two independent states fundamentally intact. However, succession—the issue that appealed most to Baghdad—was not mentioned, so the regent asked for a more "specific" proposal.[35] Abdullah responded with a nine-point plan that included suggestions for the creation of a High Federal Council, with the chairmanship alternating between the two countries' prime ministers; development of "a single foreign policy"; and consolidation of diplomatic representation.[36] The plan fell far short of outright unification; for example, Abdullah had been careful to add that nothing should infringe on either kingdom's "present rights and constitution in full." But on the pivotal issue of succession, his suggestion held enough enticement for the Iraqis to begin to take the matter more seriously.

In his most vaguely worded paragraph, Abdullah proposed: "The Royal Family shall be given similar rights in both kingdoms so that, if a King dies without heirs, he shall be succeeded by the most suitable from amongst the descendants of Hussein bin 'Ali." The implication was clear; that is, if the elderly Abdullah were to die with no Jordanian heir other than Talal or Nayif, his throne would pass to Feisal II. This was the first time Abdullah formally raised the possibility of surrendering his inheritance to his brother's heirs. The wording of the paragraph, however, suggests that he was reluctant to close the door once and for all on his own offspring. Perhaps that is why he reverted to the idea of "kingship by suitability"—the same formula, which has extensive precedent in Islamic history, that he originally employed to disinherit Talal in 1940. Evidently, hope sprang eternal that one of Abdullah's two sons might yet prove himself "suitable" to succeed him. Perhaps it was to gauge for themselves Talal's "suitability" that Abdullah, the regent, and Iraqi Prime Minister Nuri al-Sa'id together visited Talal in Beirut in early June.[37]

Sensing his uncle's quandary, Abdul Ilah decided that all loopholes needed to be closed before Iraq would assume the burden of federating with Jordan. His response to Abdullah was brazen. Federation, he demanded, should begin, not culminate, in the union of the two crowns. Abdullah would have to announce Feisal's appointment as heir before any constitutional measures to implement the federation could be enacted. Such insolence was too much for Abdullah; by moving so forcefully, the Iraqi regent had overplayed his hand. His demand that Abdullah peremptorily waive his children's (and grandchildren's) right to inherit the throne, especially before the details of federation had been finalized, was received with stony silence in Amman. No formal reply was sent to the Iraqi counterproposals, and this is where the matter stood at the time of Abdullah's assassination.[38]

The fourth potential candidate to succeed Abdullah was Talal's son, Hussein. Abdullah had taken a special interest in his eldest grandson, including supervising his private tuition and subsidizing his education at Victoria College in Alexandria. The young prince (b. 1935) was often at his grandfather's side, acting as unofficial aide-de-camp or court interpreter (Abdullah understood English but purported not to speak it). The warmth and affection between the two were mutual[39] and in marked contrast with the relationship between Talal and his father. Abdullah certainly had high hopes for Hussein, and though the evidence is scanty, there are intimations that he considered the idea of naming him as heir. Indeed, the "suitability" clause in Abdullah's confederation proposal might have been envisioned with just that possibility in mind. This line of thinking was not lost on Drew, the American minister, who just two weeks before Abdullah's death, inferred from several of the king's comments that he "may look to young Prince Hussain as eventual successor to the throne."[40] As events unfolded after July 20, it is clear that Drew was not alone in entertaining such notions.

After the initial shock of the assassination, the ministers and elder statesmen who met in Amman on the afternoon of the al-Aqsa shooting soon recovered their composure.[41] Although the challenges of the moment loomed large, they seemed to realize that not all of them demanded an immediate response. Internal security matters were left to Glubb, who, within ninety minutes of the assassination, took preventive steps to quell the minor clashes that soon were to break out between Palestinians and Transjordanians in Amman, Salt, Suweilah, Mafraq, and Aqaba. Furthermore, the imposition of a curfew in Jerusalem and Amman and the appointment of Brigadier Cooke as martial law administrator in Jerusalem cooled passions in the kingdom's two largest cities.[42] Although there were fears that Israel might exploit the situation to launch an offensive that would iron out the meandering armistice line, there was little that the Jordanians could do. They were bolstered, though, in their knowledge that Israeli troops had not returned the sporadic gunshots the frenzied bedouin fired over the border and that the governors of the two halves of Jerusalem maintained efficient lines of communication that would help limit the dangers of miscalculation.[43] And to fill the need for sound British counsel at this critical juncture—Kirkbride was then enjoying the leave that Abdullah had asked him to postpone two months earlier—Prime Minister al-Rifa'i passed an understated request to the British chargé d'affaires that "it would be very useful" to have Kirkbride back in Amman.[44]

Even on the glaring issue of succession, the leadership decided not to decide. To have hastily crowned Talal, Nayif, or Hussein would have divided the royal family, and given the anti-British and pro-British reputations, respectively, of Abdullah's sons, it could have sent the wrong signals to Jordan's allies and neighbors. "Complete agreement" was therefore given to a proposal to leave the throne temporarily vacant and to proclaim Nayif as regent in his brother's absence.[45] In essence, the government dealt with the matter as though Abdullah had departed the country for a visit abroad, not departed the world altogether.

One thorny problem remained. According to local convention and the spirit of the kingdom's constitution, a change in regime required the resignation of the sitting government and the formation of a new one. All knew that with Abdullah gone, the powers of the cabinet would be appreciably enhanced. No longer would the prime minister serve as the buffer between an increasingly boisterous parliament and a similarly strong-willed king; rather, given the weakness of character of both Nayif and Talal, the next prime minister was sure to wield executive power in his own right. As a result, more than any other issue that arose as a result of Abdullah's assassination, the prime ministerial succession brought out the passions and ambitions of the men who would now rule Jordan.

In at least two ways, the imagery of the prime ministerial succession mirrored that of the royal succession. There were, for example, four candidates, namely, the four men who had previously served as prime minister.[46] Two of them stood at center stage, like heirs to the throne, whereas the other two were less politically charged and hence more peripheral. But there the similarity ended, for whereas the contest for the kingship was an unprecedented event in Jordanian history, the competition for the premiership was, at its core, only the most recent engagement in a long tug-of-war between two old warriors who knew each other well.

The two secondary candidates were the Nablus-born elder statesman Ibrahim Hashim and the wealthy Circassian Sa'id al-Mufti. Both men were celebrated for their honesty and integrity; neither, though, was a political heavyweight. Indeed, each made vital contributions to safeguarding the monarchy in the tense months that followed Abdullah's assassination, but at that critical moment, neither mounted a serious challenge for the premiership.

That contest was left to Samir al-Rifa'i and Tawfiq Abu'l Huda, Jordan's leading political antagonists. Their backgrounds were strikingly similar. Both men hailed from territory in Palestine that in 1948 became part of Israel.[47] And both men rejected those roots (al-Rifa'i from Safed, Abu'l Huda from Acre) and identified themselves fully and completely with the Transjordanian nationality that each had embraced in the early 1920s.[48] They took different routes to Abdullah's court: Samir had been a clerk with the British army and then in the Palestine Civil Service, whereas Tawfiq was an Istanbul-trained lawyer who had served in King Feisal's short-lived government in Damascus. Yet they arrived in Amman with similar briefs—they were administrators, men capable of making bureaucracies function in a place that had never known bureaucracy before. Within several years of their respective arrivals, both rose to ministerial ranks, with Tawfiq joining the cabinet in 1929 as secretary-general and Samir, who was six years younger, as minister of education and interior in 1941.[49] They both were forty-three years old when first elevated by

Abdullah to the premiership, Tawfiq in 1938 and Samir in 1944.[50] Between them, they would hold the premiership eighteen times (Tawfiq, twelve; Samir, six).

Once in office, they both matured from bureaucrats into political operatives on whom Abdullah relied to carry out sensitive missions and to implement difficult policies. It was Abu'l Huda, for example, who secured Britain's agreement to Jordan's expansion into Palestine during the 1948 war[51] and who signed the armistice agreement on Jordan's behalf at the war's end; for his part, it was al-Rifa'i who maneuvered his way into the Oval Office in an effort to win American diplomatic recognition in 1949[52] and who carried the burden of being Abdullah's principal negotiator in peace talks with Israel. Perhaps because they owed all to Abdullah, they could be trusted with such combustible assignments.

Except for one other characteristic—ambition—any resemblance between the two ends there. Separating fact from legend in this regard is difficult, but it is clear that they shared neither similar politics (other than the loyalty to the concept of a Hashemite monarchy) nor personalities. Over the years, Abu'l Huda acquired a reputation for softness toward the British; al-Rifa'i, for a tilt toward the Americans. In fact, neither characterization is particularly true or useful. What is more important is that they held differing visions of Jordan's fundamental security requirements. Whereas most states do not have to deal with issues of vital national survival on a regular basis, Abu'l Huda and al-Rifa'i understood that Jordan's peculiar demographic and geographic position meant that such issues were daily fare. What separated them was that they approached solutions to those problems from opposite directions.

In strategic terms, Abu'l Huda equated status quo with stability; change, he believed, inherently engendered risk and thereby threatened stability. To procrastinate was to gain time, and time was the essence of survival. Tawfiq was said to give the following advice to his ministerial colleagues: "The British are always eager to widen the treaty between us. So, if ever you see something that looks like that, just throw it away and write on it that it's 'under consideration.' Keep writing 'under consideration' and they'll get used to it and then they'll stop asking."[53] He championed the politics of the lowest common denominator and opposed all initiatives that might have found Jordan outside the Arab consensus on basic political issues, a position that often put him at odds with his maverick king. Abu'l Huda did not solve problems, he (in the positive sense) avoided them.[54]

Al-Rifa'i, on the other hand, had a more nuanced approach. Stability (or instability) was not a variable: By its very nature, Jordan was an unstable entity fraught with fundamental security problems that could not simply be wished away. The key variable in his strategy was the relationship between risk and gain. Al-Rifa'i knew that there were prices to be paid for even successful gambits; for him, what mattered was the likelihood of success and the potential for countervailing drawbacks and disadvantages. His was a strategy of brinkmanship, subterfuge, and cunning; options had always to be maintained, never closed. It could be said that Samir, too, did not solve problems, he finessed them.[55]

On a personal level, the two could not have been more different. Samir was an expansive, humorous, emotional man, with a large family and a wide coterie of friends, associates, and hangers-on. After enumerating such "admirable qualities" as Samir's openness, frankness, and excellent command of English, one American diplomat went on to describe him as simply "good fun. He drinks, smokes and is the soul of urbanity."[56] One British ambassador depicted al-Rifa'i as "deceptively jolly and Pickwickian. His eyes twinkled behind heavy spectacles, but below there was a mouth like a steel trap and the top joints of his thumbs had an extraordinary, prehensile outward bend to them like claws in reverse. In short, a hawk in owl's plumage."[57] The one character flaw of which most critics accused him was "impulsiveness."[58] Hazza' al-Majali remarked that if Samir had not been so hasty in making decisions, he could have "used his intelligence to solve problems [now] rather than have to correct his mistakes later."[59]

Abu'l Huda was al-Rifa'i's social opposite. He was widely respected but rarely befriended. Admirers and detractors alike refer to his aloofness, detachment, correctness, self-restraint, firmness, and personal loneliness.[60] Glubb, in one of his more descriptive passages, portrayed him as "a quiet, neat, methodical little man, who should have spent his life as an auditor or a chartered accountant."

> Poor Taufiq Pasha! He lived a life of routine. He went to the office at the same minute every morning and returned to his house at precisely the same time every afternoon. He enjoyed detail, particularly financial detail. He delighted in finding some minor irregularity in financial procedure. He loathed all things military, as if by instinct. He detested emergencies, he loathed hasty improvisations. He even disliked people. He lived between his house and his office. He enjoyed handling impersonal problems, minuting files, looking up regulations and checking accounts. Few men could have been more unsuited to rule the storms of a world rapidly sliding into chaos.[61]

If Tawfiq really did "dislike people," it was largely the result of his painful family life. He compensated for a failed marriage through devotion to his only child, Su'ad, who, in turn, was his First Lady and closest friend. Su'ad, however, suffered from a severe depression that took a devastating toll on her father. Abu'l Huda finally committed suicide in 1956, possibly brought on by his own depression over cancer or possibly the culmination of personal family anguish.[62]

From the early 1940s onward, these two men were Jordan's premier political rivals. After 1944, they never served together in the same government. Perhaps it was their similarity of background that heightened their dissimilarities of style and political strategy. Or perhaps, as one of al-Rifa'i's sons-in-law suggested, Abdullah himself stoked their respective fires of ambition and competition, so that he would always have one ready to assume the reins of office if the other were to falter or fall temporarily out of favor.[63] In any event, theirs was a personal as well as a political antagonism. As al-Rifa'i's son recalled:

> I know [my father] did not like Abu'l Huda at all. He did not respect him. He considered him to be a civil servant, a bureaucrat, not a statesman. [Abu'l Huda] was the manipulating type of person, who just tried to further his own interest, very slimy sort of character, without any scruples. They were just different characters, it was a clash of personalities.[64]

It was against this backdrop that al-Rifa'i, the incumbent, and Abu'l Huda, the challenger, competed for the premiership.

Jordan's elder statesmen did not meet a second time until after Abdullah's funeral, three days after the assassination. In the interim, several developments occurred that were to affect the course of events. First, the Jordanian government was reassured by various Israeli actions, including reports of "official mourning" for Abdullah, that Israel would not exploit the assassination to its own advantage.[65] Second, Kirkbride returned to Jordan and provided political ballast for what seemed to be a foundering ship of state. Third, Abdul Ilah, Nuri, and Salih Jabr all flew to Amman, their grief over Abdullah's death barely masking their zest for Hashemite union.[66] Last, Nayif assumed the regency and started displaying a greater interest in politics than the politicians themselves had reckoned for.

Upon his return, Kirkbride quickly realized how entwined were the three issues of Iraqi union, royal succession, and ministerial changes. He soon learned that Prime Minister al-Rifa'i thought the "best solution" would be for Talal to step aside formally in favor of Hussein and to have Nayif serve as regent until Hussein reached the age of majority; that Abdul Ilah held a similar position, though within the framework of Hashemite union; and that Nayif opposed any change of government until the royal succession had been settled. None of them thought that Talal was—or ever would be—in a position to rule.[67] Two stumbling blocks, though, lay in the way of a neat consensus among the three that would have left al-Rifa'i as premier, Nayif as regent, and young Hussein crowned in his father's stead. One was al-Rifa'i's opposition to any closer unity with Iraq, stemming largely from his long-standing personal animosity toward the Iraqi leadership.[68] Another was the opposition of influential members of the royal family to both al-Rifa'i's retention (given Abdullah's and al-Sulh's assassinations and a recent drought that had ravaged the country, al-Rifa'i had earned a reputation for bad luck) and the idea of a long Nayif regency (Hussein would not turn eighteen, the age of majority, for more than a year and a half). The combined opposition of the Iraqis and the royal family—including Talal's freethinking wife, Zayn—rendered al-Rifa'i's outwardly solid position less tenable and Nayif's only marginally less so.[69] The wild card for all involved was that Abu'l Huda, al-Rifa'i's main rival for the premiership, coyly refused to disclose his real position on Iraqi unity.

Soon after Abdullah's funeral, politicking among the claimants to the various prizes gathered intensity. Kirkbride was approached in quick succession by al-Rifaʿi, Nayif, and Abu'l Huda, who all seemed to view Kirkbride as the final arbiter of Jordan's politics, inheriting the mantle of monarch more than any of the true aspirants possibly could. Al-Rifaʿi asked Kirkbride, in the name of stability, to "work in a word of support" for the maintenance of his government in discussion with Nayif; evidently the premier was aware of the movement to unseat him. Nayif, for his part, showed himself already convinced that al-Rifaʿi was a harbinger of bad luck—"no rain and two murders"—and asked Kirkbride to be excused of his prior agreement not to alter the composition of the government until the issue of royal succession had been settled. Apparently Nayif believed that his best chance of gaining the monarchy was to align himself with the Iraqis, and the Iraqis, he knew, were out to get rid of Samir.

Then Abu'l Huda weighed in with a request that Kirkbride withdraw his opposition to a change in government. Public opinion and the Iraqis were working against al-Rifaʿi, he argued, and it would be better for the country if parliamentary elections, due in a month's time, were held under a new prime minister. Abu'l Huda, of course, viewed himself as the most likely candidate, and with good reason. His positions on royal succession and Iraqi unity did not differ markedly from Samir's: He opposed the latter and expected a doctor's report to confirm Talal's incapacity to rule, thereby opening the door to a Hussein monarchy and a Nayif regency. What the wily Abu'l Huda had most in his favor was that in contrast with al-Rifaʿi, he was wise enough to mask his opposition to Iraqi union beneath an accommodating public demeanor, and of no little importance, no one thought he was cursed with bad luck.[70]

In the three days after the assassination, al-Rifaʿi's political stock dropped precipitously. Nayif, whom he had backed for the regency, turned on him. The Iraqis were feverishly conspiring against him. The royal family had little confidence in him. And Abu'l Huda was openly campaigning for the premiership himself. With few options remaining, al-Rifaʿi opted for statesmanship over gamesmanship. The morning after Abdullah's funeral, he told Kirkbride that he had decided to resign and would make an announcement to that effect on the following day. Kirkbride immediately telephoned Abu'l Huda with the news and offered his hope that he would take over the premiership.[71] Abu'l Huda had won without a fight the first political battle in post-Abdullah Jordan.

Before that was settled, however, the scene immediately shifted to the contest for the monarchy and Nayif's bungled efforts to claim the kingship for himself. Despite public declarations of allegiance to Talal, Nayif evidently involved himself in behind-the-scenes schemes to have himself named king in his half-brother's place. The same day that Kirkbride learned of al-Rifaʿi's impending resignation, both Abu'l Huda and elder statesman Ibrahim Hashim warned Kirkbride that two of Abdullah's personal retainers were canvassing support for Nayif and "egging [him] on" to have himself named heir.[72] In the whirlwind of activity and rumor that surrounded the assassination, Abdullah's old confidants probably saw in Nayif their last chance to retain the power and privilege they had come to enjoy under the late king. After all, Nayif, who had grown up on the hearth of the royal household, was certainly more controllable than the mercurial Talal. Moreover, given Nayif's pro-British reputation, Abdullah's courtiers may have calculated that London (or, more precisely, Kirkbride) would back their scheme so as to preserve as much as possible of the friendly and accommodating ancien régime.[73]

Kirkbride, however, would not play. Not only was he keen to avoid any accusation that Britain had manipulated Jordan's royal succession for its own imperial interests, but he also knew that politically, Nayif was no great improvement on his brother. Therefore, when it became clear to Nayif that even the British would not support his claim, he changed tack and sought to ally himself with Samir, the very man whom he had just helped ease out of the premier's office. When al-Rifa'i formally offered his resignation on July 25, Nayif refused to accept it. Instead, he appealed to Samir's sense of ambition and intimated that he (Nayif) would support Samir's retention of the premiership if the latter would arrange a cabinet decision backing Nayif's claims to the throne. By this time, al-Rifa'i had already come to terms with his own personal shock at being maneuvered out of power[74] and refused to bite at Nayif's bait. Samir later reported to Kirkbride that Nayif was "surprised and pained" when he told him that it would take a constitutional amendment, not just a government decision, to alter the line of succession.[75] With no options left (for the time being, at least), Nayif recognized defeat, accepted Rifa'i's resignation, and offered the premiership to Abu'l Huda.

By day's end, Abu'l Huda was ready to present his cabinet to Nayif. Wisely avoiding the temptation to pack it with cronies, Abu'l Huda formed a government that included associates of both Nayif and al-Rifa'i, defeated in their respective bids for the kingship and the premiership.[76] To a great extent, honesty and efficiency were sacrificed to political expediency.[77] But it must be recalled that Abu'l Huda was playing high-stakes politics under extraordinary circumstances. Sa'id al-Mufti's participation as deputy premier and interior minister, a position from which he would supervise the upcoming parliamentary elections, went far to redress the government's reputation for corruption; al-Mufti was believed (correctly or not) to be too wealthy to be bribed. And to soften the political pill of presenting a cabinet with the fewest Palestinians since the union of the two banks, Abu'l Huda promised to replace this "temporary" government after the elections.[78]

The last party to be heard from was Iraq. Abdul Ilah was in London when the news of the assassination broke, and before flying to Amman, he briefed the Foreign Office on the details of Abdullah's federation suggestions and his own counterproposals. Perhaps unnerved by his uncle's violent demise, the Iraqi regent said meekly that he would not pursue the matter without the "advice and approval" of Whitehall, a far cry from his earlier brazenness.[79] Once in Amman, Abdul Ilah left Iraq's civilian leaders, Nuri and Salih Jabr, to carry the torch for Hashemite unity, but neither had a very clear notion of what kind of union they wanted.[80] Nuri seemed to lobby for the sort of dynastic union envisioned in the abortive Abdullah–Abdul Ilah discussions, whereas Jabr emphasized military cooperation and the need for strong administrative links.[81] On a more practical level, both understood that either the accession of Talal (who had harbored no secret of his dislike for Abdul Ilah or Iraq in general) or the retention of al-Rifa'i as premier would have sounded a death knell to their plans. In surmounting both obstacles within five days of Abdullah's death, the Iraqis had good reason to congratulate themselves.

But they could progress no further. Although Iraq's unity offers grew more enticing, with Nuri offering to Jordan significant financial support and a wide degree of autonomy (e.g., a Canada-like "dominion status"), Amman's new civilian leadership refused to be tempted. Indeed, by the time Abu'l Huda assumed the premiership, Nuri realized that he had little hope of "rushing matters through" while Jordan's throne was still vacant, and he resigned himself to a longer-term plan of working for the election of deputies who would support union in Jordan's parliamentary vote at the end of August.[82]

Forcing this retrenchment in Iraqi policy was the culmination of a week-long series of political victories by Jordan's new prime minister. In the aftermath of Abdullah's murder, Tawfiq Abu'l Huda proved himself a master of political legerdemain. His goal was to regain the premiership, and he skillfully maneuvered his way to achieve it. His policy was to take no firm positions on the issues of the day, preferring to make and shed alliances, not commitments. Nayif and the Iraqis helped him defeat Samir because they interpreted his silence as support—but they were wrong. Abu'l Huda opposed Nayif's accession to the throne as well as Iraq–Jordan unity because both were flashpoints of internal and inter-Arab contention, and Jordan's stability, he believed, was to be secured only through consensus, not contention. He simply refused to be drawn on the issues until he was in a position not to suffer politically for them.

Once in office, Abu'l Huda raised "risk aversion" to a fundamental policy of state. His public stance on royal succession was to put off any decision until Talal's doctors issued a report on his health in five weeks' time. His policy on Iraqi unity was to permit external pressures—from Britain, Israel, and the other Arab states—to build against any unity scheme, "forcing" him to bow to the opposition. In reality, his preference was for Hussein to be named king with the support of a regency council; not until the end of July did he even entertain the idea that Talal could be a candidate.[83] In addition, Abu'l Huda opposed any formal link with Iraq. However, to stake out those positions, rather than permit matters to take their own course, would have been to invite controversy, divisiveness, and dissension. Eight previous terms as prime minister, plus Abdullah's own assassination, had given Abu'l Huda an acute appreciation of the transience of political power and of Jordan's particular vulnerability. It was, therefore, a function of a cold calculation of his and Jordan's potential and limitations that Abu'l Huda assumed the premiership in late July with a political platform that had only two policy planks: Avoid all risks and preserve the monarchy, though not necessarily any particular monarch.[84]

2

Kingpins, Kingmakers, and Would-be Kings

The weeks following Abdullah's murder were among the most pivotal in the kingdom's short history. Tawfiq Abu'l Huda's victory in the battle for the premiership resolved only one of four pressing political issues. Royal succession, parliamentary elections, and the trial of Abdullah's assassins remained ahead. What is perhaps most remarkable about Abdullah's death is that each one of those hurdles was surmounted by the end of the first week of September. The kingdom did not, as was widely feared, collapse with the demise of its founder. As the *New York Times* correspondent in Jerusalem noted: "What apparently has astounded the colony of diplomatic observers here, as well as a good many Jordanian subjects, has been the degree of stability that the little kingdom has shown under extraordinary circumstances."[1]

After the roundup of suspects on July 20, hundreds were remanded into custody for questioning, observation, and, in some cases, intimidation. The police even checked the *bona fides* of Jerusalem's most prominent citizens, including Anwar al-Khatib and Anwar Nusaybah.[2] Although no one was above suspicion, the Arab Legionnaires did not, as legend would have it, exact revenge on the Palestinians. After an initial outburst, their patrols through the streets of Jerusalem were strict, though not spiteful. Within ten days, the number detained was down to less than one hundred, and the curfew was progressively lifted.[3]

Only a handful of journalists—a few Arabs, just one American, and, surprisingly, no Europeans[4]—were on hand for the trial of Abdullah's assassins, but the new regime went to great lengths to ensure at least the appearance of propriety in the investigation and adjudication of his murder. Jerusalem Attorney-General Walid Salah was given wide leeway to prepare his case. He was a close friend of the chief conspirator, Musa al-Husayni, but when convinced of the latter's guilt, Salah pursued the case with vigor.[5] The defendants were represented by the finest counsel in Jordan, including the noted Ramallah attorney 'Aziz Shehadeh and Yahya Hammudeh, later to succeed Ahmad Shuqayri as chairman of the Palestine Liberation Organization. Ibrahim Hashim, the kingdom's senior jurist, was present to serve as special judicial adviser to the court.[6] And despite the misgivings of some ministers, the trial was held in open court, with the proceedings broadcast by loudspeaker to the waiting crowds outside.

Although conscious of public relations, neither Abu'l Huda nor Kirkbride wanted too lengthy an investigation or too prolonged a trial. Rather, they preferred to have Abdullah's murder resolved before the parliamentary elections and the appointment of a new monarch. As luck would have it, soon after the investigation began, the son of one of the conspirators identified the murder weapon as belonging to his father, and the evidence quickly piled up from there.[7] A speedy trial with cooperative judges was ensured by the decision, taken privately by Abu'l Huda and Kirkbride and confirmed by a decree by Nayif, to bypass the existing civilian courts and convene instead a special military tribunal whose judgment could not be appealed.[8] In all, it took less than one month to complete the inquiry, take all depositions, prepare the evidence, and bring ten men, including two *in absentia*, before the court. It took only ten more days to close the case and reach a verdict.

The speedy completion of the proceedings was in direct proportion to the explosive potential of the case. With three of the ten offering confessions, there was no pretense that Mustafa 'Ashu had been acting alone when he shot Abdullah. On the contrary, the extent of the conspiracy suggested in the prosecution's indictment struck at the very fiber of Jordanian, Jordanian–Palestinian, and inter-Arab politics. The presence in the docket of three members of the prominent al-Husayni family—Tawfiq, Da'ud, and Musa—confirmed to many that Abdullah's murder was a venomous plot by Hajj Amin to settle old scores left from the Palestine war; 'Ashu, after all, had allegedly participated in an illegal "dynamite squad" subsidized by the ex-mufti.[9] Indicted as one of the plot's ringleaders was Colonel Abdullah al-Tall, former wartime governor of Arab Jerusalem. Safely ensconced in Cairo, al-Tall responded to the allegations by releasing to the press a pile of incriminating photocopies he had made two years earlier when serving as one of the late king's intermediaries in secret negotiations with Israel. The charges against Ibrahim Iyad, a Palestinian Catholic priest well known for his nationalist connections, gave vent to accusations by many Muslims that the Christians in their midst were disloyal "fifth columnists."[10] It was because of these potentially incendiary complications that the trial was dispatched with such haste.

It is important to note that the tribunal did not accept the prosecution's case in full. Four of the ten accused, including Tawfiq and
Da'ud al-Husayni, Iyad, and one of the lesser conspirators, were acquitted, significantly blurring the implications of the verdict.[11] Neither of the
two chief conspirators was said to have had a political motive. Musa, the
lone al-Husayni convicted, had been at odds with the ex-mufti for years
and was among the most pro-Hashemite of the clan. Although he had
followed Hajj Amin to Hitler's Germany, he apparently split with his
cousin in 1941 but still received two years in the Seychelles for his collaboration and then went on to serve as an official Jordanian adviser to
the Palestinian Conciliation Commission and to run (unsuccessfully) for
the Hashemite parliament.[12] Greed, not politics, was Musa's alleged stimu-
lus; prosecutor Salah summed up his incentive as "money . . . pure
money." As for Abdullah al-Tall, the man behind Musa, his goal was said
to be revenge, not, however, for the late king's connivance with the
Zionists, but for his own thwarted ambition.[13] The ex-mufti and Abdullah
al-Tall raved at the proceedings from their Cairo redoubt, but the tribunal itself refused to stoke their fires further by accepting the theory of a
grand *political* conspiracy.

In the end, the trial did not lay to rest the question of "who killed
King Abdullah."[14] By its verdict, the tribunal refused to extend the conspiracy beyond Musa al-Husayni and Abdullah al-Tall, but so little money
had changed hands by the time of the murder—just £70—as to insult
the cosmopolitan Musa, educated in London, Berlin, and Jena, by charging him with the sole motive of greed. Moreover, it is highly unlikely
that al-Tall, who was residing in Cairo as the guest of the Egyptian government, could have masterminded the operation without at least the
knowledge of his hosts. Indeed, Glubb went so far as to accuse the Egyptian legation in Amman of cooperating in the plot.[15] Prosecutor Salah
was convinced that "it was the King of Egypt that was behind it."
Although historians have routinely referred to "the shadow of Hajj Amin
[that] loomed behind the plot,"[16] a figure no less than Kirkbride himself rejected any notion of the ex-mufti's complicity and seemed to accept
the idea of a free-lance operation controlled solely by al-Tall.[17] More
fanciful theorists have accused Britain, America, Israel, the Soviet Union,
Saudi Arabia, and Syria (and various combinations thereof) of plotting
Abdullah's demise.[18]

From the government's point of view, the measured verdict handed
down on August 28 accomplished three practical goals. First, the acquittal of half (four of eight) of the West Bank defendants permitted the
government to reject allegations that it had been driven by a vendetta
against Palestinians by establishing the special tribunal in the first place.
Second, by the court's refusal to accept a grand conspiracy theory, the
government was free to embark on a policy of inter-Arab and Palestinian–Jordanian fence-mending that it was to launch the following month.
Third, with the case completed so swiftly, it was the mixed verdict, and

not the trial itself, that was on the minds of voters when they went to the polls on the following day, August 29.

When Abdullah dissolved parliament in May 1951, the idea was to engineer elections that would produce a less troublesome, more compliant group of legislators. But his assassination, six weeks before the vote, radically changed the significance of the elections. No longer would the campaign be fought on the limited, though important, issue of the relationship between crown and parliament; rather, it was the very shape of post-Abdullah Jordan that was now at stake. All the options were placed on the table, from the radical-nationalists' spectrum of anticolonial demands (ranging from the dismissal of Glubb to taking up arms against Israel to the abrogation of the Anglo-Jordanian treaty) to the Iraqi unionists' desire for closer ties with Baghdad. To secure their desired outcomes, the Arab states employed local agents and their own resident diplomats to influence the vote. Of course, no one could be sure that the new parliament would play a greater role in governance than it did under the ancien régime, but it behooved them to hedge their bets.

Among foreign powers, the most active was Iraq. Although the Iraqis had succeeded in isolating what they viewed as the main opponents of Hashemite union—Talal and Samir al-Rifa'i—they could make no further progress with the new civilian leadership. Parliament was their next target. In mid-August, Nuri al-Sa'id dispatched a three-man committee to Jordan to lobby parliamentary candidates, and the electorate in general, on behalf of closer Jordan–Iraq ties.[19] Its goal was to win over Arab nationalists, mainly Palestinians but some East Bankers as well, who would create a ground swell of support for union that would carry the idea in parliament.[20]

So as to ensure that their efforts did not provoke the active opposition of the political establishment, the Iraqi minister in Amman was also said to enlist the paid support of Sulayman Tuqan and Sa'id al-Mufti, the ministers of defense and interior, respectively. Having "bought" the most powerful pro-Hashemite in the West Bank (Tuqan) and the minister responsible for the elections themselves (the allegedly "unbribable" al-Mufti), the Iraqis were convinced that their efforts would guarantee the return of sympathetic candidates to parliament.[21] Exactly what kind of union Iraq and its local supporters had in mind is not clear, as the term *union* often masked substantive differences among confederation, federation, association under a single crown, and outright merger. In defense of their acceptance of Iraqi largesse, for example, Kirkbride noted that al-Mufti and Tuqan wanted nothing more than federation of the two states, with the latter motivated principally by a desire to thwart the political resurrection of the ex-mufti.[22]

Iraqi unity efforts did not go unchallenged by Baghdad's Arab competitors. The leaders of both Saudi Arabia and Syria viewed any scheme at Hashemite unity as threatening irredentist challenges to themselves.

For his part, Ibn Saud was fearful that a Hashemite kingdom that stretched from Jerusalem to Baghdad might set again its sights on the Hijaz, whereas Syria's rulers did not fancy the prospect of an emboldened Abdul Ilah setting his own sights on Damascus. This confluence of interests gave rise to a flurry of curious and sometimes contradictory initiatives: an appeal by Ibn Saud to Washington to "maintain the status quo" because it is "unjust to deprive [King Abdullah's sons] of their rights";[23] a Syrian proposal for a plebiscite in Jordan to determine the kingdom's future;[24] Saudi support for a Syrian countercampaign encouraging Jordan's annexation into a Damascus-based Greater Syria;[25] and even a joint Saudi–Syrian effort to carve up Jordan between them. With irony, Kirkbride noted that "Greater Syria as conceived by King Abdullah is dead but Greater Syria in reverse (Syria absorbing Jordan) is alive and being supported by Egyptian and Saudi influence."[26] Added to this was Egyptian agitation, in concert with supporters of the ex-mufti, to remove the West Bank from Jordanian control and place it under direct Arab League mandate.[27]

The parliament itself, though, was rarely the object of such scheming by the other Arabs. None of these outside powers tried to the same degree as the Iraqis did to build (or buy) electoral support. In addition, the anti-Iraqi bloc spread itself thin by its inability to agree on a single alternative strategy. Arab diplomats and journalists were active on behalf of these various intrigues, but the multiplicity of suggestions tended to dilute the attraction of any one. As a result, the appeal of these options tended to cancel out one another and, in the end, had little impact on the vote.[28]

Abu'l Huda's response to these sundry stratagems was to fine-tune the elections though a mix of diplomacy, magnanimity, and strength. His goal, as with his stage managing of the trial of Abdullah's assassins, was to project a liberal image with the assurance of a predetermined outcome. When he took office, Abu'l Huda promised "to safeguard the freedom of the voters" and "not to ignore the promise of the late majesty to widen constitutional life."[29] Political parties remained banned, but the authorities did little to prevent the formation of informal groupings and electoral alliances.[30] Decisions that had been taken jointly by Abdullah and the then-premier al-Rifa'i to ensure the defeat of the more outspoken deputies were countermanded: Only one candidate was blacklisted, and even cabinet ministers were not "guaranteed" victory.[31] Abu'l Huda went so far as to release two Ba'thist candidates jailed in the roundup of the late king's assassins (Abdullah al-Rimawi and Abdullah Na'was) in time for them to campaign—and win—on the slogan "From Prison to Parliament."[32]

On the regional front, Abu'l Huda distanced himself from the confrontational policies of the late king. Specifically, he publicly renounced any attempt at either a separate peace with Israel or a Hashemite-focused Greater Syria plan, and he let it be known that his was a policy of live-and-let-live with the rest of the Arab world. When Cairo, Damascus, or

Riyadh threatened to dismember Jordan in any one of a variety of ways, he turned the other cheek. Indeed, if any neighbor earned his particular disdain, it was Iraq, which further helped mollify Baghdad's Arab competitors. He handled Iraqi scheming by simply letting it take its course. Abu'l Huda's policy seemed to work. Kirkbride noted that despite Baghdad's importuning, Jordanian public opinion (such as it was) cooled to the idea of being swallowed up by Iraq. Instead, as election day drew nearer, it warmed to the possibility that Jordan might have a go at it alone.[33]

In the end, the election produced a parliament not unlike the one that Abdullah had dismissed four months earlier. Analyses by foreign journalists, temporarily stationed in Jerusalem, that emphasized the "anti-British" character of the new chamber were exaggerated and wide of the mark.[34] More than half the members of the dissolved parliament—twenty-three of forty—were returned, and no political party gained or lost more than one seat.[35] Indeed, there was significantly more turnover among East Bank deputies (60 percent) than among West Bankers (35 percent), a sign that politics was not just a Palestinian concern.[36] Despite predictions of electoral gains by candidates of the proto-Communist Popular Bloc, they fared no better than in the 1950 election; Munif al-Razzaz, a founder of Jordan's Ba'th party, received the fewest votes of all the candidates. By the same token, two of the four cabinet ministers running for parliament lost, lending an air of propriety to the entire proceeding.[37]

In retrospect, the election was a fairly lackluster affair. Voter indifference was high and especially marked on the West Bank, a surprising development given the relative liberalism under which the campaign was waged and, in the wake of Abdullah's death, the significance of the electoral stakes. Whereas there was a 23 percent rise in East Bank voter registration from the April 1950 election, there was only an increase of one-half of 1 percent on the West Bank. Similarly, Kirkbride estimated the overall voter participation at 37 percent for the East Bank and only 30 percent for the West Bank. Based on his statistics, the East Bank provided a large majority (58 percent) of the total votes cast. Taken together with his observation that there was a "complete lack of interest among the citizens of Amman," this meant that voters from Transjordan's smaller cities had to have gone to the polls in very high numbers.[38]

On the surface, the Iraqis had reason to be pleased with the result. Most of the candidates they backed, from Palestinian Ba'thists like al-Rimawi to East Bank conservatives like al-Mufti, won with convincing pluralities. Even Israeli Foreign Ministry analysts, who had earlier belittled the chances of an Iraq–Jordan union, now admitted to themselves that a parliamentary vote in its favor loomed likely.[39]

But in the end, the issue was never even broached in parliament. What the Iraqis (and the Israelis) failed to anticipate was Abu'l Huda's ability to engineer the one scenario that neutralized the prounion lobby, disarmed the nationalists, and captured the popular imagination. Alone he could not have prevented parliament from voting for some form of closer affiliation with Iraq. But even the most prounionist deputy would not press the issue should Abdullah's rightful heir return to Amman to claim his legacy.

For nearly a week after Abdullah's murder, Crown Prince Talal remained incommunicado in his Swiss sanitarium. Al-Rifaʿi asked that news of the assassination be kept from Talal until thirty-six hours after the fact and that the British vice-consul in Geneva prevent Talal from returning to Amman without the Jordanian government's approval. The prince's whereabouts were kept secret until reported in a Geneva newspaper on July 26. In the meantime, there was a swirl of press stories, some datelined Geneva but none based on factual reporting, fueling rumors that Talal was furious at Jordanian politicians and British diplomats for conspiring to designate his half-brother as regent.[40]

Back in Amman, Nayif's appointment bought the central players much needed time to consolidate their positions. For Abu'l Huda, this meant waiting the full five weeks for the doctor's report on Talal's condition. He told Kirkbride that he "did not doubt" the report would find Talal mentally unfit to rule, opening the way for the crown to pass to Hussein. Nayif's consolation prize would then be retention of the regency until Hussein came of age. To the Americans, Abu'l Huda maintained a stolid impartiality, expressing loyalty to both Nayif and Talal and "guarded optimism" about the latter's health, but to Kirkbride, whom he evidently viewed as a virtual coconspirator, he confided his visceral opposition to a Nayif monarchy. Characteristically, Abu'l Huda opposed taking any initiative to induce Talal to waive his rights to the throne and simply preferred to let matters take their course.[41]

Similarly, the Talal–Nayif split left the British in an awkward position, and Kirkbride was in no hurry to press a decision on succession. Talal's alleged Anglophobia provoked claims that London was plotting to deprive him of the throne. In the polarized politics of the moment, Talal came to represent Arab independence, and Nayif, capitulation to Western colonialism; that neither characterization was true was of little importance. Safe in Cairo, Abdullah al-Tall, the self-styled defender of Arabism, audaciously called for an Arab medical mission to examine Talal: "It is not right to leave Talal in the hands of a British doctor," he proclaimed.[42] The best course of action, in Kirkbride's view, was to take no action at all and to permit the Jordanian government to take the lead on succession. He concurred with Abu'l Huda's political prognosis but would not actively campaign for either Talal or Hussein. But to ensure that Nayif would not entangle him and British policy in a scheme not of his own doing, Kirkbride took several behind-the-scenes steps to defuse Nayif's own pretensions to the throne.

By the end of July, those pretensions had grown very great. Nayif was apparently not satisfied with his interim appointment as regent.

Despite denying as "absolute lies" the allegations that he had robbed Talal of the latter's inheritance, there are a variety of reports—American, British, and Israeli—that he had secretly begun plotting to gain the kingship for himself, most likely at the instigation of several of the late king's retainers.[43]

Within just a few days, however, the pressure on Abu'l Huda to bring the matter of succession to a head had evidently intensified. Perhaps the reason was some sign of success on the part of Iraq's agents or progress by Nayif's handlers, or perhaps it was just the recognition by Abu'l Huda that Talal's presence would solve a host of political problems. On July 29, Talal's personal physician, Ford Robertson, arrived in Amman to brief (in order) Nayif, Abu'l Huda, Minister of Health al-Tutunji, Talal's wife Zayn, and then Kirkbride on the crown prince's progress. Whether or not he gave them enough hope (or, in Nayif's case, despair) that Talal might indeed be on the verge of medical recovery was not disclosed. What he did relate, in a personal letter to the acting British consul-general in Geneva, was that the Jordanian ministers were very anxious to have Talal returned to Amman and installed on the throne: "There is no doubt here that H.R.H.'s presence in Jordan is needed; he is popular with all," he wrote. Indeed, he suggested that the cabinet was so eager for Talal's return that, as he warned, "it could provide an excuse to cut and run from [Talal's] treatment." He apparently acquiesced to a proposal that he and al-Tutunji travel to Geneva to assess Talal's status several days ahead of the original schedule.[44]

Talal first entered the drama as an active character in early August. After being informed of his father's death, he was kept almost completely in the dark, and on about August 6, he finally demanded that "some responsible person" be sent from Amman to brief him on the political state of play. Sa'id al-Mufti—who might otherwise have been busy attending to preelection (or, perhaps, pro-Iraqi) duties—left for Geneva the following day.[45] No record of al-Mufti's meeting with Talal is available, but his debriefing in Amman caused quite a stir. Talal, he said, appeared eminently sane, making his the most important vote so far weighing in for the crown prince's accession. He also relayed Talal's suspicions, evidently fed by letters from Talal's wife, that Nayif had his own designs on the throne.[46]

Nayif, who may have been informed of al-Mufti's report, took this moment to make his bid for the throne. In a conversation with Kirkbride, he laid down his threat. His position as regent, he said, had become "false" (ostensibly because his claim to the throne was being stymied at every turn). Therefore, he vowed never to assume the responsibility for confirming death sentences on any of his father's assassins (this still being a week before the conclusion of their trial). Furthermore, he hinted that he might instead resign the regency and throw the kingdom into what he hoped would be a constitutional crisis.[47]

In retrospect, Nayif's gambit to cow the Jordanian establishment into taking his royal pretensions seriously was foolish. Until that point, Abu'l Huda had been supportive of Talal but was willing to await the doctors' report; Kirkbride had his own personal preference but had publicly retained his impartiality. However, once Nayif threatened to endanger their best-laid plans in regard to the execution of Abdullah's assassins, he became politically expendable. Kirkbride and Abu'l Huda together agreed to call Nayif's bluff: Should Nayif insist on resigning, the government would accept his resignation and appoint a Regency Council in his stead; should he remain as regent but "continue to make difficulties," the government would consider bringing Talal immediately back to Amman, if only for a short visit, "to settle the matter of succession finally."[48]

Events then moved swiftly. Robertson and al-Tutunji left for Geneva, according to plan, on August 21.[49] They examined Talal and released a medical report, bearing the additional names of three Swiss specialists, four days later. In it, they pointedly dismissed claims that Talal had *ever* been mentally ill. Although they admitted that the crown prince had been under treatment for "an extraordinary case of mental depression," they described "the cause" of Talal's illness as "entirely bodily and not mental."[50] They then declared his recovery "very satisfactory" and removed all barriers to his return to Amman in two weeks' time. According to al-Tutunji, Talal was in better "physical [and] psychological condition" than he had seen him in fifteen years.[51]

The last week of August, therefore, witnessed Jordanian history being written with lightning speed. In just five days, Talal was issued a clean bill of health to assume the kingship; his father's assassins were convicted and condemned to death; and the electorate chose a new parliament. Each event softened the reverberations of the subsequent one. The announcement of Talal's imminent return, and the general sense of optimism it engendered (even among many Palestinians), was the penultimate act in closing the case against Abdullah's killers; with those loose ends tied, much of the potential tension of parliamentary elections was defused. In the process, both Iraqi designs and Nayif's ambitions were checked.

Or so it seemed. For some reason—vanity, stubbornness, or maybe just poor counsel—Nayif still refused to accept his lot. Even with his half-brother preparing to return to Amman, he embarked on his third and most ill considered bid for the throne.[52] A coup plot was hatched, allegedly by Muhammad al-Shurayqi (Abdullah's foreign minister and minister of court) and Farhan al-Shubaylat (Abdullah's chief of diwan), for troops of the Hashemite Regiment to encircle parliament when the deputies were due to meet in their first postelection session on September 3. The plan, it seems, was to imprison the cabinet, forcibly dissolve parliament, and proclaim Nayif the king. A critical player in the conspiracy was the regimental commander, Habis al-Majali, who evidently found time to prepare the "putsch" while serving as judge at the trial of Abdullah's assassins.[53]

As with his earlier plotting, Nayif's coup making was sloppy and easily circumvented. Glubb's information network got wind of al-Majali's projected troop movements, and on September 1, thirty-six hours before the projected coup, a series of precautionary measures were implemented: A crack bedouin company was deployed near the parliament building; two mechanized regiments were placed on alert; roadblocks were set up on Amman's main highways; and much of the Hashemite Regiment was ordered out on maneuvers. In the end, the coup was never attempted.[54] With little publicity (and no lasting detriment to his career), al-Majali was quietly removed from his post and eventually banished to the command of the Ma'an police; none of the other conspirators was ever arrested or tried.[55]

Nayif's options were now exhausted. On September 3, he opened parliament with a brief "speech from the throne" (read by Abu'l Huda); after last-minute stonewalling, he was finally compelled to sign the death warrants for his father's convicted assassins later that day. Before the sentences could be carried out, Nayif left Amman to join the official Jordanian delegation that was to accompany Talal from Geneva back to Jordan.[56]

On September 6, Jordan had a new king. Talal flew to Beirut and immediately on to Amman, where he proceeded by cavalcade to the parliament building to take the oath of office. By all reports, his arrival and accession were well received among virtually all segments of the population.

There were a variety of reasons for Talal's popularity. For many Palestinians and the regime's East Bank critics, Talal represented the closest that the Hashemites could muster in terms of a political "new deal." He was thought to ascribe to some vague Arab nationalism, not his father's Hashemite parochialism, and his reputation for confronting his father and Glubb had earned wide sympathy.[57] Perhaps the apocryphal story about his having shot Glubb in the arm in a fit of anger four months earlier had something to do with this, or perhaps Palestinians simply recognized the fact that Talal had played no role in the calamitous war against Israel.[58] For whatever reason, the political "opposition" was hopeful that Talal would sweep out of power his father's leftover cronies, invigorate the regime's commitment to constitutional government, and place Jordan's foreign policy in step with the Arab mainstream.

Ironically, the traditional political elite, and especially Abu'l Huda, shared much of the same agenda. First, Abdullah's maverick inter-Arab politics had long been the main bone of contention between the late king and his retinue of supporters. With Talal on the throne, Abu'l Huda would be able to find the security he so fervently sought in blending in, not deviating from, the Arab consensus. Under the new regime, Jordan might not take the battle directly to Israel, as some Palestinians might have wanted, but it would not enter peace talks with Israel either.

Second, the "king's men" and the opposition found common ground again on the potential benefits of constitutional reform. Talal's presence brought such welcome relief from the machinations of the regent that, according to Kirkbride, "the experience of [rule] by an inexperienced and irresponsible person" hastened the process of constitutional change.[59] With Abdullah's death, the new executive elite no longer had any quarrel with the principle of constitutional reform, as long as it meant a greater increase in the power of the government vis-à-vis the crown than in the increase in the power of the parliament vis-à-vis the government.

Third, much of the elite (including both Abu'l Huda and al-Rifa'i) had no compunction in joining the opposition in wanting to see the government and the palace cleansed of the more sordid and reactionary of the late king's hangers-on. Among these were many of the leftover Hijazis who had schemed vainly with Nayif in order to maintain their ancien régime prestige. In addition, the ruling elite welcomed Talal's accession as a rallying point to defuse the push for union with Iraq. When a pro-Iraqi diehard broached the topic in parliament later that autumn, his colleagues shouted him down.[60]

More generally, Talal's presence brought welcome relief to seven weeks of anxiety and uncertainty. Since the Palestine war and the union of the two banks, Hashemite rule in Jordan had undergone radical change. The most vivid symptom of this was the creeping diminution of Abdullah's power and authority. As noted earlier, Abdullah's murder did not mark the abrupt end to three decades of patrimonial rule but, rather, was the final act in the decay of royal absolutism that was already well under way.

Even before Abdullah's murder, the potential political effect of the elderly king's eventual demise was a source of much concern, but the manner of his death lent it an additional sense of gravity and foreboding. Few observers believed the shooting on the Haram al-Sharif would be the last shots fired before the future of Jordan was settled. Kirkbride warned Whitehall that his "principal fear" was of a "murder campaign" directed against leading regime supporters. In a stunning admission of how swiftly he believed the Jordanian tides could turn, he counseled London that the security of the British position in Jordan "depends almost entirely on the attitude of the new Parliament that is to be elected."[61] Meeting within hours of the assassination, Israel's top strategists decided on the need to "work against the event of bitter Palestinians taking control of the country and inviting the Mufti to Jerusalem and against Syrian and Iraqi entry into Jordan."[62]

In the end, none of these fears came to pass. There was no Palestinian insurrection, no "murder campaign," no public clamoring for the return of the mufti, no Israeli land-grab on the West Bank, no follow-up attempts by Iraq to engineer a union, and no Syrian–Saudi pincer movement to divide Jordan between themselves. Rather, what occurred instead was the acceleration of the transition of power that was already under way. In retrospect, order, speed, and relative harmony marked the way in which Abdullah's political (though not biological) heirs—the "king's men"—claimed their legacy. In less than two months, the former administrators of government confirmed their hold on executive authority and began to wield it (under the watchful eyes of Kirkbride and Glubb) with poise and confidence. They felt strong enough to discard some of the lone-wolf initiatives that had earned Abdullah enemies abroad and to shore up their own domestic position through a series of popular decisions that also departed from the late king's policy and temperament.

Talal's accession underscored the resourcefulness of the men who (figuratively and literally) brought him back from Geneva to place him on the throne. As a group, they took the monarchy seriously because only the monarchy secured their position; there would be no place for them in a system without the king. They realized all too clearly that the range of challenges facing the independence of the kingdom threatened them directly, and they responded by arranging the one scenario that would defuse those challenges, disarm the opponents of the monarchy, and thereby preserve their own status. "The public," reported the American minister, "feel that there is not much to choose between the mad Tallal, the venal Naif and the child Hussain," but Abu'l Huda and his colleagues thought differently.[63] They knew that only Talal's return to Amman would meet their requirements, and when the decision was taken that the crown prince's presence was needed to safeguard the monarchy, his "recovery" was quick. In the end, Talal's accession proved to be the "crowning" act in the transition of power from Abdullah to a group of men whose understanding of the twin pillars of the Hashemite monarchy—survival and endurance—was no less than his own.

3

The Short Unhappy
Reign of King Talal

The first few months of Talal's rule were an extended political honeymoon for the king and his prime minister. It was, for both of them, a time to replace Abdullah's fading authoritarianism with a new way of governing inside Jordan and a new basis for relations with the outside world. For Talal, the kingship was a refuge in which he could finally escape his father's domineering reach, withdraw from public life, and be everything but his father's son. That, in turn, offered Abu'l Huda an opportunity to build his own structures of more substantive political security, which involved pacifying adversaries, quieting critics, and, when possible, keeping competitors and rivals at bay. The relationship between king and prime minister, which remained the only constant fixture in Talal's life during his eleven-month reign, was founded on a simple, shared goal—peace of mind.

The first element of Abu'l Huda's "peace offensive" was to scatter the regime's domestic opposition. After Talal's accession, Abu'l Huda constructed a new cabinet that was markedly more liberal than the one cobbled together in the aftermath of Abdullah's murder. Not only did he drop a lightning rod of Palestinian hostility, Justice Minister Felah al-Madadha,[1] but he also recruited a widely respected opposition leader, 'Abd al-Halim al-Nimr, to take the vexatious finance portfolio. In that one swift maneuver, Abu'l Huda neutralized criticism of the budget that had prompted Abdullah to dissolve parliament in the first place. Talal, too, got into the act when he dissolved the upper house of parliament that Nayif had appointed during his short regency and reconstituted it with more Palestinians and fewer of his half-brother's appointees.[2] In October, Abu'l Huda ordered the release of forty-five political detainees, most of whom had never been brought to trial, and promised still more releases to come.[3] He lifted censorship on international cable traffic, in place since the 1948 war, and eased suspensions on a few banned publications. He even permitted several peaceful political demonstrations.[4]

The major thrust of the conciliation effort, however, was constitutional reform. By all accounts, Talal was wedded to the notion of reigning as a constitutional monarch, an idea that most likely grew as much out of his driving need to be what Abdullah was not as it did out of his liberal inclination. For Abu'l Huda, the question was one of political expediency. Given Abdullah's still-unfulfilled promises and the continual howling of parliamentary wolves, Abu'l Huda concluded that there was no sense in trying to "beat" the reformist trend if he could "join" it and turn it to his advantage.[5]

The trick was in defining "reform." Under Jordan's 1946 constitution, there were virtually no checks and balances delineating the relationship among king, government, and parliament. "All authority," the constitution stated, "is vested in King Abdullah ibn al-Hussein." Governments served at the sovereign's pleasure, and the legislature was little more than a deliberative body. It was Abu'l Huda's task to offer a new division of political authority that would satisfy parliament's thirst for change but that would, in fact, tilt the balance of power from the monarchy to the new ruling elite. What he came up with was a new constitution whose lack of substantive change belied its high-sounding rhetoric.

The rhetoric was certainly stirring. In its final form, the constitution included provisions banning discrimination based on race, language, or religion (Article 6i); ensuring work, education, and equal opportunity (Article 6ii); guaranteeing freedom of opinion in speech, writing, "photographic representation," and the press (Article 15i/ii); offering asylum for political refugees (Article 21i); and protecting labor and the rights of workers (Article 23ii). Most noteworthy of all was the declaration that the "nation"—not the king—"is the source of all power."[6] In return for this litany of liberal commitments, Abu'l Huda won from parliament a rider making virtually each of these rights contingent on "the limits of the law," a catchall phrase that, as one historian noted, gave "the authorities considerable latitude in restricting or suspending the actual enjoyment of rights."[7]

Major controversies arose over the issues of no-confidence motions and administrative detention. The loftiness of the rights and duties clauses notwithstanding, these were the key determinants of how political power would be apportioned in the new Jordan. Abu'l Huda's objective was to limit parliament's ability to exercise these powers in practice.

In his draft text of the constitution, submitted on September 30, Abu'l Huda proposed that motions of no confidence require a two-thirds vote of both houses of parliament. This would have meant that just seven members of the appointed upper house—probably cabinet members themselves—could have thwarted any motion. As could be expected, the reformers offered a counterproposal, but Abu'l Huda's opening bid had the effect of laying down the outer limits of the bargaining on the prime minister's terms. The reformers suggested that a simple majority of the lower house alone should be enough to bring down a government, and the two sides compromised at a requirement of two-thirds of the lower house. At the time, Abu'l Huda had little doubt that he could command the support of at least fourteen deputies (one-third plus one) and, as a result, was able to gain credit for a concession that actually cost very little.[8]

On administrative detention, Abu'l Huda would not yield. He insisted that the government have the freedom to act as swiftly as possible on matters of public security and rejected any suggestion that might have circumscribed that freedom. The relevant paragraph may have sounded progressive—"No person may be detained or imprisoned except in accordance with the provisions of the law" (Article 8)—but the final phrase gave the state enough leeway to continue dispatching troublemakers to desert detention camps without the necessity of a trial.[9] Ambiguity was also an important element in other key passages of the constitution, such as articles that permitted the promulgation by royal decree of Defense Regulations "in the event of an [undefined] emergency necessitating the defence of the Kingdom" (Article 124) and that outlined the similarly ill defined circumstances in which the king might declare martial law (Article 125).[10]

Both houses of parliament approved the constitution's final text on December 29, and Talal gave his royal assent on New Year's Day, 1952. In terms of the separation of powers and the protection of individual liberties, the new constitution was a significant advance on its 1946 predecessor. It did not, however, merit the American minister's praise as going "far to adopt democratic processes as we know them" or its acclaim by a historian of the period as "a bold experiment in democracy."[11] The essence of the new constitution, as the British legation noted insightfully, was the "notable curtailment of the power of the King," not, by implication, a great enhancement of the power of the legislature.[12] The most that Abdullah's death and the promulgation of a new constitution had done was to "transform" Jordan into what a British diplomat termed a "pseudodemocracy."[13]

Abu'l Huda's policy of mollifying domestic critics carried over to foreign relations as well. Although this may have entailed a certain amount of swallowed pride, no concessions of strategic importance were made. In fact, improving ties with the Arab world helped cement the kingdom's acquisition of the West Bank, and Abdullah's death itself removed one of the root causes of Jordan's estrangement from most of the Arab world.

In practice, Abu'l Huda's inter-Arab policy involved snubbing established friends (Iraq) and accommodating erstwhile adversaries (Saudi

Arabia, Egypt, and Syria). It ran so against the grain of Abdullah's traditional approach that Abu'l Huda found in Talal a most willing partner. In November, Talal embarked with his family (on Saudi airplanes, no less) on the first return to the Hijaz for a Hashemite prince in almost three decades when he visited Mecca, Medina, and then Ibn Saud in Riyadh.[14] In January 1952, Abu'l Huda buried the lingering animosity between Jordan and Egypt (and between Abdullah and Faruq) by agreeing to sign the Arab League Collective Security Pact.[15] And by distancing himself from Abdullah's Greater Syria machinations and affecting a nationalist pose, Abu'l Huda succeeded in engineering a reconciliation with Damascus as well.[16]

Together, these initiatives helped lay to rest latent tensions with the kingdom's former rivals, at little political cost. Abdullah had originally refused to sign the Collective Security Pact, for example, because of Egypt's (and, in general, the Arab League's) refusal to recognize the union of the two banks. By the time Abu'l Huda agreed to join the pact, the Palestinian government in exile was dormant and there was little other Arab states could do about Jordan's control of the West Bank. In typical fashion, Abu'l Huda pocketed the diplomatic gain of signing the pact without sacrificing much in return. As he said at the time, "While the pact could do no good, it could do no serious harm."[17]

By the same token, rapprochements with Egypt, Syria, and Saudi Arabia did not pay out much in the way of immediate political dividends either.[18] In fact, their main objective seemed to lay elsewhere, namely, in distancing Jordan from its historic relationship with Iraq.[19] On a personal level, Talal's dislike for the Iraqi regent was no secret. He held a deep grudge against Abdul Ilah both for some decade-old affront and for what he considered the Iraqis' sinister attempt to deprive him of his throne. Even after Talal's accession, Abdul Ilah continued to provide fodder for the new king's ire, ranging from disagreements over Abdullah's remaining *waqf* property in Egypt[20] to rumors about the regent's relationship with Nayif.[21] For Abu'l Huda, antagonizing Iraq was a matter of politics, not personality. First, frosty relations between the two monarchies provided an extra hurdle to any attempt at Iraqi–Jordanian unity, a movement that had subsided but not altogether expired.[22] Second and more important, he calculated that Iraq needed Jordan's deference more than Jordan needed Iraq's patronage.[23]

In this regard, Abu'l Huda was the first Jordanian statesman to appreciate that Jordan's structural weaknesses—its need for outside protection, its swollen refugee population, its inadequate economic base, its long frontier with Israel, and, of course, its control of only part of the land west of the Jordan River—could be turned into valuable political (and economic) assets. The monies that foreign donors, UNRWA (United Nations Relief and Works Agency for Palestine Refugees), and, eventually, other Arab states paid to Jordan were, after all, a function of Jordan's frailty, not its strength. Abu'l Huda knew that Jordan's market value would be maximized in the inter-Arab arena if it were not too closely linked with any single Arab power, so distancing from Baghdad's embrace was an essential step in merchandising the country's limited wares.[24]

Abu'l Huda's lack of interest in making peace with Israel mirrored his opposition to union with Iraq. In this regard, he was not driven by some visceral anti-Zionism or anti-Semitism; he, in fact, praised German reparations to Israel as "unexpectedly reasonable."[25] Nor was he motivated by some lingering connection to his Palestinian roots; on the contrary, during his first nine months of office, Abu'l Huda only once visited the West Bank.[26] (Neither, for that fact, was Talal eager to champion the Palestinians after he narrowly avoided his father's fate when an assassin's bomb attempt failed during his first visit to Jerusalem as king.)[27] Rather, Abu'l Huda resisted dealing with Israel out of his aversion to anything that might upset Jordan's strategy of rapprochement with the Arab League and its major players (outside Iraq). When important decisions needed to be taken on Arab–Israeli matters, Abu'l Huda seems to have been guided principally by how he felt such decisions would play in the public's mind. The record shows that he kept men in his cabinet who, in private at least, held quite liberal notions about the idea of peace with Israel.[28] Moreover, Abu'l Huda showed himself willing to extend diplomatic feelers to Israel. But he always held back, even when the response was positive, for fear that any movement would involve the sort of risk taking that his personal character and political doctrine would not permit.

Ahmad Tuqan's near-breakthrough in informal talks with Israel in early 1952 is a good example. A former foreign minister, Tuqan was serving at the time as Jordan's senior representative on the Jordan–Israel Mixed Armistice Commission (MAC). He was one of the most moderate and forward-thinking politicians in Jordan, a man that the American embassy later praised for his "incisive mind . . . pragmatic approach [and] . . . firm but enlightened hand."[29] Since November, when the postassassination military alert had been lifted, border infiltration had risen significantly, and Israelis and Jordanians were being killed at the rate of about one per day.[30] After a particularly violent Israeli retaliatory raid in January 1952, Tuqan was reportedly instructed by Abu'l Huda to seek direct contact with the Israeli Foreign Ministry in the hopes of "getting a brake put on the [Israeli] Army." According to Tuqan, Abu'l Huda told him "to stay in Tel Aviv a month if you want." Tuqan first met with one of Abdullah's former interlocutors, Moshe Sasson, and was said to relay a message dictated by Abu'l Huda "to the effect that nothing had changed in Jordan's policy towards Israel . . . since King Abdullah's death, [and] that Jordan was the only state with whom Israel was likely to be able to conclude an agreement in the foreseeable future."[31] Then at the end of February, Tuqan had an "informal talk" with the acting director of the Israeli Foreign Ministry's Middle East Division, Ziama Divon, during which he gave him a slightly different message from Abu'l Huda.

The prime minister, he said, had "expressed interest in the possibility of some change of attitude of the Arab League toward Israel." That "interest" was evidently based on the more moderate tone of recent Egyptian statements and, more important, on the absence of any "public disapproval" of the idea inside Jordan itself.[32] Nevertheless, Tuqan told an American diplomat that Abu'l Huda had been "receptive to consideration of [his] idea" that Jordan's interest lay in reaching a broader settlement with Israel, "if necessary without [the] participation [of] other Arab states."[33]

The crunch came several days later when Tuqan presented Abu'l Huda with a proposal worked out with his Israeli MAC counterparts for an exchange of territory along the armistice line. The transfer entailed the relinquishing to Jordan of several villages and farms in the Qalqilya area in return for some territory near the Dead Sea for use by Israel to expand its potash works. For Amman, the plan was a good deal in that it would receive hundreds of acres more than it would surrender; for Jerusalem, the plan held out the precedent of territorial rectifications with Arab states individually, not collectively. Although a peace settlement was not on the agenda, agreement to Tuqan's proposal would have been no small step in that direction.[34]

But Abu'l Huda, wary of getting too far ahead of public opinion, left the proposal languishing on his desk. He did not reject it; he merely, as was his custom, avoided it. Amman was (and remains) in many ways a small city, and it was not long before the local press got wind of the gist of the plan. The reaction was belligerent, with editors violently attacking any policy that implied peace with Israel.[35] By this time, Abu'l Huda's political honeymoon had reached an end, and he was facing a series of thorny problems ranging from a recalcitrant parliament to a gradually deteriorating king.

Tuqan's proposal was a victim of Abu'l Huda's effort to gain some ground with public opinion. On May 21, one day after reports of a pending deal with Israel sparked some minor unrest on the West Bank, Abu'l Huda issued a statement denying all rumors of an agreement and reaffirming Jordan's commitment to a pan-Arab policy toward Israel. In addition, he stated categorically that his government would never relinquish "one square inch" of territory to the Zionists. Tension along the frontier heightened, and Tuqan resigned a bitter man.[36]

Just as he sought to balance Jordan's ties in the Arab world, Abu'l Huda, often acting through Talal, also put Jordan's relations with Britain and America on a more even keel. The prime minister evidently believed that Jordan could benefit by building some tension between the great power in decline and the superpower in ascent.[37] At the very least, cooling ties with Britain would earn Jordan some political kudos in the Arab world, and it was explained and justified to British diplomats in that context alone. Indeed, inasmuch as Abdullah suffered from the reputation of toadying to Whitehall, it was smart politics for Abu'l Huda to put as much distance as possible between himself and Abdullah's legacy, especially when Cairo and London were locked in a struggle over Britain's base at Suez.

This "arm's-length" policy toward Britain was manifest in a variety of measures, but most of them—like preventing Jordanian workers from traveling to the Canal Zone to take the place of striking Egyptian laborers—were public-relations gambits designed to tweak the British but not leave any lasting damage to the bilateral relationship.[38] The reason is that Abu'l Huda's policy did not grow out of any developing doubts in his mind that Jordan's ultimate source of protection rested in its mutual defense treaty with Britain or that its economic health depended on Britain's subsidy (then £6.5 million) to the Arab Legion. Rather, he thought that some judicious adjustments in Jordan's diplomatic posture might be enough to forestall the circumstances that might force him to turn to the treaty as a last resort. As the British minister noted:

> It seems evident that [Abu'l Huda] is now concerned to represent Jordan as being a loyal member of the League and on good relations with all the other Arab states indifferently, i.e., having no particular ties with Iraq. . . . We ought, in his view, to regard this situation as being in our interests as well as Jordan's. In any important issue, we could rest assured that Jordan would be faithful to her alliance with the UK, but in matters of lesser importance we should recognise, and make allowances for, Jordan's need to align her policy with that of the League.[39]

One factor that undoubtedly worked in Abu'l Huda's favor in his policy toward Britain was Alec Kirkbride's departure from Jordan in December 1951. After thirty-one years of almost continuous service that predated the arrival of Abdullah himself, Kirkbride requested a transfer and was posted as Britain's minister (and then first ambassador) to Libya. Abdullah's death—and, in a larger sense, the expansion into Palestine—had sapped Jordan of the allure that had kept Kirkbride there so long. His chargé d'affaires may have exaggerated the emotive power of Kirkbride's departure, but probably not its political significance, when he stated that his transfer had provoked "widespread and genuine sorrow at his going among all classes of Jordanians who regarded him, with King Abdullah, as the father of their country. Coming as it did within six months of the death of King Abdullah," he wrote, "there could no longer be any doubt that the old order had changed."[40]

The gravity of Kirkbride's departure was magnified by the contrast in personality of his successor, Geoffrey Furlonge. Amman was Furlonge's first post as chief of mission, and even though it would have been next to impossible for any diplomat to assume fully Kirkbride's mantle in the eyes of the Jordanians, Furlonge was clearly not up to it. A dour, undemonstrative man,[41] Furlonge lacked Kirkbride's uncanny ability to strike the proper balance between asserting Britain's position and ushering Jordan toward maturity; instead, he naively accepted Jordan's own rhetorical positions as his own.[42] Perhaps one of the reasons for the failure of Tuqan's initiative with Israel was Furlonge's self-fulfilling prophecy that "no matter what the Arabs might say, they didn't want peace with Israel."[43] At the same time, Furlonge had such blind faith in the British position in Jordan that he failed in his task of outlining the potential circumstances under which that position might be undermined.[44] Because of his faulty counsel, Furlonge bears a not insignificant amount of blame for the poor state of readiness in which London found itself when that position was later threatened.[45]

January 1952 was the high-water mark of Talal's reign. After four relatively tranquil months on the throne, the kingdom's new constitution was promulgated and approval granted for Jordan's accession to the Arab League Collective Security Pact. It was the symbolism, not the substance, of these developments that was particularly important. In both domestic and foreign policy, a new set of "rules of order" was seen to take the place of Abdullah's old ways. Abu'l Huda's genius, as described earlier, was in preserving the kernel of the ancien régime while dispensing with its outmoded and often-problematic husk.

This tranquillity was not to last. In the first half of 1952, both Talal and Abu'l Huda failed to live up to the carefully scripted roles they had prescribed for themselves. The former succumbed to a relapse of mental illness that stripped him of the ability to reign in the detached, dispassionate manner of a constitutional sovereign; the latter dropped the guise of the king's *éminence grise* and began to assume the trappings of a civilian despot. Together, these developments prodded the parliamentary opposition into renewed activity. The balance of this chapter discusses the dynastic turmoil of Talal's remaining months on the throne, and the following chapter examines the emergence of political confrontation between Abu'l Huda and his domestic critics.

For the first six months of his reign, Talal acquitted himself like the constitutional monarch he aspired to be. Diplomats praised his "aplomb and dignity," and on those occasions when he had a hand in policy decisions, he seems to have been lucid, well informed, and even tempered. As late as March 1952, Furlonge could write categorically that "Talal is at present displaying no signs of abnormality."[46] In fact, signs of Talal's mental illness had begun to reappear in January 1952 when he and his family were on a European vacation, although Zayn had loyally kept the secret to herself.[47] Later that spring, when she was abroad for medical treatment, Talal suffered a relapse, and it was left to Abu'l Huda to conceal the king's creeping instability.[48]

To the outside world, the first sign of any change in Talal's behavior was when he began to assert his prerogative in personnel matters. The king had long harbored grudges against politicians known to be his father's favorites (such as Shari'a Chief Justice al-Shanqiti) and against those he believed had campaigned to have him declared insane (such as Minister of Health al-Tutunji), and he periodically asked Abu'l Huda to sack them. Each time, Abu'l Huda's response was to wait for the king's mood to pass, but after his March outburst, Talal's anger was unremitting, and Abu'l Huda was forced to accede to the king's wishes and dismiss al-Shanqiti and al-Tutunji. The real cause of the dismissals, however, was hidden from public view, because Abu'l Huda undertook other cabinet shuffles at the same time. In fact, some of Abu'l Huda's own appointments were so contentious, and his lack of consultation with other cabinet colleagues so flagrant, that public debate often revolved around questions of his own competence, not Talal's.[49]

By early May, however, Talal's situation had deteriorated considerably, with Zayn's return from Europe itself provoking the king into more frequent and more violent attacks against her and their children.[50] Abu'l Huda decided to take preemptive action. After summoning psychiatrists from Beirut and Switzerland, he finally informed his fellow ministers about the gravity of Talal's illness. At first, he planned to force Talal into medical care but was stymied by his inability to find two Jordanian doctors willing to certify Talal's illness. (The real cause of al-Tutunji's dismissal had by then become known.)[51] Then Abu'l Huda went the political route, and the cabinet empowered its three most senior ministers—Interior Minister Sa'id al-Mufti, Defense Minister Sulayman Tuqan, and Abu'l Huda himself—to try to persuade Talal to go abroad for treatment. The king, in a moment of lucidity, agreed to a family "holiday" in Europe but would hear nothing of hospitalization. With Whitehall's help, a charter aircraft was found, and Talal, Zayn, and their family left for Paris on May 18.[52] Just before his departure, Talal signed a royal decree establishing a Throne Council, of Abu'l Huda, Ibrahim Hashim, and 'Abd al-Rahman al-Rushaydat (presidents of the upper and lower houses, respectively), to exercise his powers in his absence. Several hours earlier, the two foreign physicians had signed a joint statement strongly recommending medical treatment for Talal, but they never, in fact, had had a chance to examine him themselves. Four days later, the cabinet accepted the doctors' report and decided to seek Talal's hospitalization with or without his consent. On May 22, al-Mufti and Tuqan left for Paris to try to do just that.[53]

The next two weeks were among the darkest the Hashemite family had witnessed since the loss of the Hijaz. Talal's (and, equally, Zayn's) personal tragedy was played out in full on the streets and newsstands of Paris, Geneva, and Lausanne. The two branches of the family, Amman and Baghdad, quarreled as they had never done before; sympathy for the king degenerated into ridicule of the royal house. In the heat of the moment, Abu'l Huda himself quipped that to prevent one particularly ruinous outcome—Nayif's return to sit on a Regency Council—he would rather dismantle the monarchy altogether and establish a republic in its place.[54]

In Europe, one calamitous event briskly followed another. The ministerial mission to Paris was an abysmal failure. Talal feared that al-Mufti and Tuqan had come to force his abdication and virtually refused to see them. Zayn, meanwhile, grew fearful of Talal's violent outbursts and took refuge in the British embassy in Paris; she was joined there by her son, Hussein. Talal, though, had other ideas. He cabled Abu'l Huda for sufficient funds to set sail aboard the *Queen Mary*—destination, America.[55]

Back in Amman, important political developments were taking place. News of Talal's departure and the formation of the Throne Council had caused considerable anxiety. On the West Bank, the hasty exit of the popular king was seen as confirmation of the rumors of Abu'l Huda's territorial deal with Israel (the Tuqan episode), and the prime minister was forced to disavow any negotiation with Israel and to explain the reasons for Talal's European tour.[56]

Even before Talal left the country, the composition of the Throne Council had aroused much consternation among Amman politicians. It was widely believed that the king's absence might this time be permanent, and there was anxiety that the council would rule until Hussein came of age twelve months later, a long time by Jordanian standards. Especially controversial was the lack of Palestinian representation on the council and the unseemliness of Abu'l Huda's dual role as prime minister and council member. According to one West Bank minister, both issues had been "hotly discussed" by the cabinet, but "nothing would dissuade Tawfiq from such [a] course."[57]

But even Abu'l Huda could be humbled. When the spirit moved them, Jordan's contentious politicians could, on rare occasions, unite in common cause, and opposition to Abu'l Huda's titular monopoly on power was one such occasion. Before the matter got too out of hand, Abu'l Huda realized that the opposition was on a symbolic, not a substantive, crusade. Both he and they knew that his replacement on the Throne Council would not alter the balance of power in the kingdom by one iota.

Therefore, to clear the air, Abu'l Huda convened a special, closed session of parliament on June 3. After outlining Talal's condition, he reportedly made two surprise announcements. First, he accepted the fact that his dual appointment was "not entirely regular" and agreed to reconstitute the Throne Council with neither himself nor any other minister on it. The following day, the council was disbanded and a new one appointed under the constitutional article providing for the king's incapacity due to illness. Sulayman Tuqan, that most loyalist of Palestinians, resigned as minister of defense and was named to the council in Abu'l Huda's place.[58]

Abu'l Huda's second announcement to parliament was that he had invited the Iraqi regent to Amman to discuss Jordan's dynastic predicament. Given Abu'l Huda's long-standing animus toward Iraq, this came as a particular surprise. As it turned out, Abu'l Huda's invitation was less a request for Abdul Ilah's participation in deciding Talal's fate than it was a maneuver to neutralize his potential interference in that process.[59]

The Iraqi regent and the Jordanian prime minister held fundamentally different conceptions of the situation. Whereas Abu'l Huda viewed Jordan "as an independent country," Abdul Ilah (noted the British envoy in Baghdad) regarded "it as an appendage of the Hashemite house." Specifically, Abu'l Huda wanted to restrict the power of the monarchy by keeping Talal as a weak, titular ruler—even if he were declared mentally unfit—and having the Throne Council continue to govern in his name. Abdul Ilah, on the other hand, suspected Abu'l Huda of having "sinister designs on the throne" and wanted to install a member of the Hashemite family either as regent or as a member of a Regency Council. After crossing Nayif's name off the list—even Abdul Ilah was wise enough to recognize that Nayif would not do—the only suitable candidate left was Amir Zayd, the Iraqi ambassador in London and the last surviving son of King Hussein bin 'Ali of the Hijaz.[60]

When Abdul Ilah arrived on June 3, Abu'l Huda tried to allay his fears about the fate of the Jordan branch of the Hashemites. He explained that if Talal could not be compelled to undergo treatment in Europe, he would be immediately returned to Amman and kept away from the scurrilous European and American press. Abu'l Huda also confirmed his intention to resign from the Throne Council while at the same time gently rejecting Abdul Ilah's notion of appointing a Hashemite regent.[61] But Abdul Ilah was neither pacified nor deterred. The following day, he pressed his suggestion of a Zayd regency on "tearful royal ladies and opposition politicians" who were receptive to any idea that would circumscribe Abu'l Huda's monopoly on power. Then he took the unprecedented step of inviting the entire Jordanian cabinet to a meeting at the Iraqi legation, and to add insult to injury, he requested that they postpone a scheduled cabinet session until after they met with him. That, according to Furlonge, precipitated a full-scale row between the Iraqi regent and the Jordanian premier, with Abu'l Huda ridiculing Abdul Ilah—himself no great democrat—for appealing for support to local politicians who, the prime minister said, "thought one way yesterday, another today and probably another tomorrow." When Abu'l Huda flatly rejected any suggestion of appointing "an Iraqi Emir to a position of ultimate control," their conversation turned particularly nasty. In a thinly veiled threat, the regent told Abu'l Huda that he reserved the right to intervene in Jordan if its government "did something [he] regarded as liable to affect the country's safety." The prime minister snapped back that Jordan had both an "excellent army" and a treaty with Britain with which to defend itself. The regent held his tongue, but when he returned to Baghdad the following morning, he delivered a blistering attack against Abu'l Huda's management of the Talal affair and alleged that in Abu'l Huda's hands, the monarchy was in serious danger. When the Iraqi press called on the Arab states to foil what it termed Abu'l Huda's "conspiracy" with the Zionists to surrender Jerusalem to Israel, Iraqi–Jordanian relations had reached their lowest ebb yet.[62]

Meanwhile, the situation in Europe continued to worsen. On June 5, Talal sent Abu'l Huda a telegram stating that he was not off to America but "on his way back" to Amman and that he had considered himself in the meantime to be on "vacation." Abu'l Huda had earlier vowed that should Talal return without a "clean bill of health," he would strip him of his royal prerogative and rule through a Regency Council,[63] but now, when the situation had presented itself, Abu'l Huda wavered. His troubles did not end there, however. When Talal learned that his wife had left Paris for Lausanne two days earlier, the king headed for Switzerland, not Jordan.[64]

All the loose strands of the Talal affair then came together in Lausanne. It was, in the words of one Whitehall official, a "painful . . . comic opera," with the tragic saga of the wandering king and queen of Jordan played out sensationally in the international media.[65] In the end, Zayn took the lead in forging a solution. It was she who suggested that either the Swiss authorities be convinced to commit Talal or, even better, that Talal be brought back to Jordan and kept under medical supervision. Abu'l Huda concurred, and London, wary of taking "the Queen's part against her husband," reluctantly agreed to contact Berne on Amman's behalf. Anastas Hanania, Jordan's minister of social welfare, was dispatched to the Swiss capital to handle the delicate negotiations.[66]

At that critical juncture, a gambit by the Iraqis forced Abu'l Huda to take the matter into his own hands. Having convinced himself that a direct appeal to Zayn would neutralize Abu'l Huda's opposition to Amir Zayd's participation on a Regency Council,[67] Abdul Ilah prepared to set out for Lausanne himself to see his cousin. Only Nuri's offer to go to Switzerland in his stead kept Abdul Ilah in Baghdad (though not for long). When Zayn heard that Nuri was on his way, she immediately summoned Abu'l Huda to join her in Switzerland.[68]

By the time he left Amman, Abu'l Huda knew what needed to be done. Hanania had informed him on June 20 that Swiss officials refused to order Talal's hospitalization.[69] Abu'l Huda's task, therefore, was to convince Talal to return to Jordan and submit to medical care there. Nuri's visit presented an unwelcome complication: To Abu'l Huda, the proposal to include Zayd on the Regency Council was a backhanded way of bringing about an Iraqi–Jordanian union.[70] To frustrate the Iraqis, he sent Talal a telegram playing on the king's natural antipathy to Abdul Ilah and warning that if Talal refused this time to return to Amman, his government would resign.[71]

The following week's theatrics fell short of the Foreign Office's nightmare of "the prime ministers of Iraq and Jordan racing to Geneva [sic] to vie for Queen [Zayn's] attention," but not too far short.[72] Nuri arrived in Lausanne on about June 20; by chance, he checked into the same hotel in which Talal was staying. Zayn's original plan had been to postpone seeing Nuri until she conferred with Abu'l Huda, but she agreed to receive the Iraqi premier early on June 22. Abu'l Huda, with his daughter Su'ad, arrived on the following day and proceeded immediately to meetings with the British consul, Hanania, Talal, and Zayn. Nuri departed for London on June 25.[73]

What actually transpired during the intervening forty-eight hours is not clear. British, American, and Swiss diplomats were so skittish about possible charges of interference that they even refrained from asking most of the principals what had happened.[74] Only Nuri's account is recorded in the archives. Nuri said that he had met with Zayn, Abu'l Huda, and twice with Talal. The queen, he reported, was highly critical of Abu'l Huda's handling of the crisis and blamed him for bringing "the Hashemite house into public derision." Nuri stated that he convinced Zayn that Iraq had no designs on Jordan's independence and that the sole purpose of his visit was to suggest that Crown Prince Hussein be proclaimed king as soon as possible. But, he added, he still thought a Hashemite ought to sit on a Regency Council that would serve until Hussein's majority and that even though he believed that Amir Zayd would refuse the regency if asked, the offer itself would "go far to assuage the Regent." According to Nuri, the queen agreed to this proposal. In his meeting with Abu'l Huda, Nuri said he again pressed his idea of offering to Zayd a seat on the Regency Council; in reply, Abu'l Huda had told him that the idea of an Iraqi–Jordanian union "had died with King Abdullah" but that he would consider the proposal once he had returned to Amman. Nuri added that his meetings with Talal convinced him that the king was truly ill and that the best solution would be for him to abdicate in favor of Hussein.[75]

Whether or not Nuri's account is wholly or partly true, Abu'l Huda did get what he came for. On June 25, he announced to the press that Talal would leave for Jordan in two days. Once there, said Abu'l Huda, Talal's responsibilities would continue to be carried out by the Throne Council acting in his name. According to Hanania, Abu'l Huda's strategy was to keep Talal out of harm's way until Hussein came of age, at which time the king's abdication could then be arranged. He noted that Abu'l Huda had twice rejected Talal's offers of abdication while in Switzerland but that a photostatic copy had been made of the second letter for potential future use.[76]

On July 3, Talal arrived in Amman to "the warmest possible welcome from his subjects." The story of his reign thereafter staggered toward its conclusion.[77] To stymie rumors of a British-inspired plot to get rid of the popular king, Jordan asked King Faruq's court to dispatch Egyptian psychiatric specialists to consult on Talal's treatment. A team of two arrived on July 15, examined Talal twice, and returned to Cairo five days later. In their report, they noted the gravity of Talal's illness and urged strongly that the king be moved to Egypt where proper treatment could be administered.[78]

This proposal jibed nicely with developments in both Zayn's and Abu'l Huda's thinking, but for different reasons. Though she was due to leave Lausanne on July 7, Zayn repeatedly postponed her return to Amman for fear of one of her husband's fits of violence. Even a special cabinet decision empowering Abu'l Huda to "undertake all measures" to guarantee her safety failed to pacify her; she now wanted Talal either moved out of Amman or out of the country altogether—she suggested Cyprus or Egypt—before she would come home. In the meantime, she began to have misgivings about Abu'l Huda's handling of the affair. These were no doubt fueled by conversations she eventually did have in Lausanne with the regent of Iraq, who, in the end, could not be dissuaded from one final attempt to win over Zayn to the idea of a Hashemite regent and therefore decided at that time to take a Swiss vacation.

When Abu'l Huda learned that Abdul Ilah had reentered the picture and that Zayn was poised to fly to London with the regent to discuss the situation with the Foreign Office, he moved quickly. Armed with the psychiatrists' report, Abu'l Huda was determined to send Talal to Egypt and to bring Zayn back to Amman. These developments in Zayn's and Abu'l Huda's reasoning are noteworthy in that what began solely as an altruistic effort to secure the best treatment for Talal was resolved under the cloud of less noble political motivations.[79]

So far, the idea of deposing Talal had not been broached. In Abu'l Huda's mind, even if Talal were committed to medical care in Egypt, he would have remained king in name, with the Throne Council operating in his absence. What forced the matter were actions by Talal himself. On July 27, Talal told Abu'l Huda that he absolutely refused to undergo any medical treatment whatsoever and had decided instead to abdicate, return to his native Hijaz, and devote himself to prayer. This pronouncement only further confounded the confusion caused by the July 23 coup d'état in Egypt. Faruq had previously promised to provide for Talal's medical needs should he seek care in Egypt, but now Abu'l Huda had no idea whether the coup's military leaders would honor that commitment. With the Egyptian option apparently closed and Talal insisting on abdication, Abu'l Huda sent a message to Ibn Saud asking him to assume responsibility for Talal. He also decided not to inform Zayn of this turn of events until he could present to her—and to Abdul Ilah, who, the Foreign Office opined, would "go off the deep end"—with a *fait accompli*.[80]

By the time Ibn Saud sent word that he would accept Talal as his ward, the situation had again shifted. On August 2, Abu'l Huda received a message from Talal, this time denying any intention to abdicate; the prime minister learned from several sources that Talal had, in the meantime, been contacted by disaffected elements in the army who feared a pro-British conspiracy against the king. At that point, when it was clear he no longer wielded any influence over Talal, Abu'l Huda decided to depose him. On August 5, on his instructions, the cabinet ordered an extraordinary session of parliament to meet in six days to implement Article 28m of the constitution, which provides for the king's deposition on the grounds of insanity. What would happen to Talal thereafter was still not clear, but that decision would be made easier once the king was a private person.[81]

By the early morning of August 11, squads of soldiers took up positions around Amman. The previous three days had witnessed both leftist and Islamist protests denouncing Abu'l Huda for planning to dethrone the king, and several opposition figures had already been placed in preventive detention in anticipation of the parliamentary session.[82] At 10 A.M., both houses of parliament convened in a secret, joint session. Abu'l Huda immediately moved Article 28m, but many deputies protested that they needed "conclusive proof" of the king's illness before they could vote for deposition. Their attitude was aptly summed up by the newly arrived American minister, Joseph C. Green: Talal "might come back again some day and hang them all," he wrote in his memoirs.[83] A special committee of three senators and six deputies was then formed to review the recommendations of the Egyptian and Jordanian doctors (the latter of which had not examined Talal for several months) and to call witnesses, including Abu'l Huda himself.[84] Early that afternoon, the committee declared itself convinced of Talal's illness, and after a half-hour debate, parliament voted unanimously to depose the king and to name Hussein in his place. The scene was not without tension. Green noted that when some of the "more obstreperous members of the opposition" voted for the motion, Abu'l Huda reportedly called out to each of them, "And you!" "And you!," obliging them to repeat their vote so as "to make it perfectly clear to all how they were voting."[85] Immediately thereafter, the Throne Council confirmed Talal's deposition and then dissolved itself, only to be reconstituted by the cabinet as a Regency Council to serve until Hussein's majority.[86] Abu'l Huda, it seems, did not want to bear the ill tidings of the deposition to Talal personally so he sent Major General Ahmad Sidqi Pasha al-Jundi, the Arab Legion's deputy chief of staff, in his place. The dethroned king accepted the news calmly and gracefully.[87]

Even after his deposition, Talal continued to attract political attention, focused mostly on the question of where he would be sent for medical treatment. Given the uncertainty of the Egyptian situation and the implications of the Saudi proposal, Abu'l Huda thought it best that Talal remain in Jordan, and so he was installed in a house in Irbid with his mother, Abdullah's widow. When word came from Egypt that Talal would be welcome under the new regime, Abu'l Huda set the wheels in motion for the king's relocation to a private home in Hilwan.[88] Despite Iraqi objections, Talal left quietly for Cairo on September 16, and his role as a political actor came to an end.[89]

Talal remained in Egypt for only eleven months. On July 3, 1953, he was involved in a serious accident when his chauffeur-driven automobile overturned at high speed on the Cairo–Alexandria road; his aide-de-camp was killed. When the accident raised the prospect of undesirable publicity, the Jordanian government took the occasion to move him to a site farther from the Arab political limelight. On August 15, 1953, with the approval of the Turkish government, Talal was relocated to a private home on the Bosphorus. Two weeks later, King Hussein and his mother paid their first visit to him there, beginning a ritual they would follow for the next nineteen years. Talal died in Istanbul on July 8, 1972. As his obituary in *The Times* noted, "his death closes a tragic episode in the history of the Hashemite dynasty."[90]

4

Abu'l Huda in Command

During the early weeks of Talal's rule, Abu'l Huda's strategy was to deal with parliament on its terms, not his. When some particularly prickly matter roused the opposition's ire, he would spend long hours, often in secret session, talking with parliament as though it were an equal partner in the affairs of state. He reportedly struck a "friendly pact" with the more outspoken deputies so that they would be free to attack the government on domestic policy but would hold their collective tongues on foreign affairs.[1]

This "honeymoon" lasted only about three months. Emboldened by the stunning (and serendipitous) arrest of virtually the entire leadership of the Jordanian Communist party in December 1951, Abu'l Huda began to put his authoritarian stamp on the constitution's liberal ideals. He imprisoned without trial a number of prominent government critics and requested American assistance to "establish a large concentration camp" in the eastern desert; he apparently wanted to extend the practice to what the American chargé d'affaires called "Commie agitators and sympathizers." Although Washington declined his request, Abu'l Huda kept sending prisoners to already existing detention camps.[2] In April 1952, the prime minister gained for himself the power to cancel the license of any publication that "attempts to spread sedition, breach of good order, security, and tranquility" and to interdict a labor strike in any "institution serving the public interest."[3] Such moves stripped both the constitution's commitment to free speech and workers' rights from any meaning in practice.

One of the factors that permitted Abu'l Huda to amass so much power was the lack of a unified opposition. Throughout at least the first six months of Talal's reign, the opposition (such that it was) was divided among anti-Hashemite militants and proregime, but anti-Abu'l Huda, traditionalists. The latter were rendered ineffectual owing to the political eclipse of their natural leader, Samir al-Rifa'i. From Samir's arrival in Transjordan in 1924 until his son's dismissal from the prime ministry in 1989, Talal's reign marked the only time that the al-Rifa'i family had no role whatsoever—formal or informal—in the governing of Jordan. Al-Rifa'i had the bad luck not only to suffer at the hands of his rival, Abu'l Huda, but also to incur the "active dislike" of Talal on account of injudicious leaks to the press he made regarding the king's mental illness. Together, the king and his prime minister made the al-Rifa'i family one of their favorite whipping posts—ostracizing Samir; sacking his brother, Munir, from a government job; and forcing his brother-in-law, Haidar Shukri, to resign as manager of the Ottoman Bank, by threatening to take the kingdom's account elsewhere.[4]

In many ways, this double-gauged attack on al-Rifa'i was to the overall detriment of the kingdom's political stability. Samir represented the loyal Hashemite opposition, whose criticism focused on the government, not on the regime. His exile to the political wilderness ran against the grain of Abdullah's strategy of fostering creative political tension, that is, ensuring that politicians of comparable stature were always competing to take one another's place. Talal was too removed from politics to follow his father's policy, and Abu'l Huda eagerly took advantage of the king's animosity toward al-Rifa'i to inflict as much political damage as he could. In the meantime, the most that Samir could do was guarantee that no other politician emerged to assume his mantle. As Furlonge noted, in the absence of the traditional Abu'l Huda/al-Rifa'i rivalry, Jordan ran the risk of building up "an undue head of political steam" without its "natural safety valve"—the rotation of political power.[5]

The result was that politics grew increasingly polarized between the regimentation of Abu'l Huda's rule and the agitation of the more militant opposition. Through the early months of Talal's reign, the parliamentary militants (mainly Ba'thists and a handful of supporters of the ex-mufti) were cowed by Abu'l Huda's "peace offensive," whereas the ones outside parliament (Communists and their sympathizers) were rather easily dealt with through the heavy hand of the internal security apparatus.[6] When parliamentary criticism of Abu'l Huda began to grow, the prime minister dropped all pretense of conciliation and met the challenge head-on. This was exemplified in the April 1952 budget debate.

There had always been prophecies of doom about the "unviability" of Jordan's economy, but Talal's reign was a particularly difficult time.[7] The combination of drought, high customs tariffs, the loss of coastal markets, capital flight, the exhaustion of savings by Palestinian refugees, and the burden of a largely unproductive (and unemployed) population combined to produce a near-depression. Hardest hit were the "economic refugees," Palestinians whose homes lay east but whose sources of livelihood lay west of the serpentine armistice line. One British report estimated that one-quarter of the West Bank population was "slowly starving," with another quarter "not far from the same level"; about 120,000 Palestinians were labeled "wholly destitute."[8] Although less well documented, such deprivation was no less menacing in many of the East Bank's southern towns, whose inhabitants lacked recourse to international aid and relief agencies. Only foreign assistance, mainly in the form of UNRWA support, Point IV aid, and British subsidies to the Arab Legion, kept the kingdom from total collapse.[9]

For Abu'l Huda, arresting the drain on the government's cash reserves—which had fallen by more than 75 percent to less than £1 million—took priority over priming the economy through increased government spending. He therefore persuaded his finance minister, former opposition deputy al-Nimr, to prepare an austerity budget that reduced overall expenditures by 11 percent. The allotments for health and social welfare (down 27 percent) and public works (down 20 percent) were slashed by even larger amounts, and the Amman municipal budget fell by nearly one-third. In contrast, because the Arab Legion subsidy remained unchanged from the previous year, overall defense spending dropped by only a nominal 4 percent.[10]

When the budget was debated on April 15, parliamentary hostility focused on two particular measures, curtailing the cost-of-living allowances for government employees and trimming the civil service through dismissals and mandatory retirement. Opposition ran deep. Before the budget came up for a vote, civil servants went on strike and even forcibly occupied the parliament building. But Abu'l Huda would not budge, preferring to push—or, rather, arm-twist—for his original, unamended budget, and he won. Interestingly, Abu'l Huda relented four months later, allocating a supplementary £200,000 for cost-of-living allowances. But in April he had to prove his point. His refusal to truck with either the striking functionaries or his legislative critics was a clear sign that on domestic matters he expected his decisions to be accepted as fiat. Moreover, his stubborn persistence showed that he was not so easily goaded into precipitate reprisal against recalcitrant deputies as Abdullah had been when he suspended parliament one year earlier.[11]

As noted earlier, Abu'l Huda's hoarding of power during Talal's illness was particularly irksome to many deputies, and he eventually bowed to the universal criticism of his dual role as prime minister and member of the Throne Council. The impact of Talal's infirmity on Jordanian politics was felt in an even more fundamental way, however. On the eve of Talal's departure for Europe, Samir al-Rifa'i had warned that the king's absence would deprive the people of "a final appeal against the dictatorial methods of the government" and would assuredly lead to a "great increase of tension in the country." Much of what al-Rifa'i said proved accurate (although he failed to mention that he himself would be the source of much of the tension he prophesied).[12]

While Abu'l Huda was busy dealing with dynastic matters, critics of his blunt authoritarianism grew louder and more numerous. Their principal complaints were against his frequent recourse to the Defense Regulations, his arbitrary dismissal of long-serving government employees, and his calculated negligence of West Bank development. Opposition focused on three, not wholly separate, groups: one headed by al-Rifa'i that included mostly East Bankers who had served in his previous governments; a second group of moderate Palestinians that was headed by Sulayman Tuqan; and a third group of Ba'thists and other militants that was largely, though not exclusively, Palestinian.[13] These three groups overlapped with one another and, except for the Ba'thists and Communists, were more like fluid political alliances and associations than formal parties.[14]

Palestinian deputies affiliated with each of these trends—moderates and radicals alike—found common ground in their criticism of Abu'l Huda's indifference to the West Bank. Their platform was summed up in a petition to Abu'l Huda approved by ten MPs meeting in Nablus on July 26. After the obligatory statement of homage to the "unity of the two banks," the deputies went on to denounce the government's inaction against Israeli border incursions; its continual recourse to "despotic" Defense Regulations; its neglect of Jerusalem as a political, administrative, and spiritual center;[15] its discouragement of Palestinian enlistment in the Arab Legion;[16] its economic and commercial bias against the West Bank; and its discrimination against Palestinians in hiring, firing, and promotions. Six other MPs sent telegrams associating themselves with this petition, and two of Abu'l Huda's Palestinian ministers (Hashim al-Jayyousi, communications; and Khulusi al-Khayri, health) even sent polite messages apologizing for their absence. The wording of the petition could have been even more incendiary if two of the most radical deputies— Ba'thists al-Rimawi and Na'was—had not been warned against attending the meeting by the mutesarrif of Jerusalem. The mutesarrif reportedly told a British diplomat that he had threatened al-Rimawi and Na'was with "the sort of measures which he learned were so useful with objectionable people," which the diplomat understood to mean torture. The two did not attend.[17]

Then just a week before Abu'l Huda went before parliament to seek Talal's deposition, the prime minister faced a direct challenge to his authority when the Throne Council, wielding its royal prerogative, for the first time rejected a cabinet decision. The issue itself was minor—personnel transfers—but in the words of the British legation, the refusal to endorse the cabinet signaled "the first sign of a show-down between [Abu'l Huda] and Suleiman Touqan." When Tuqan was first appointed defense minister in July 1951, he was not expected to be one of the cabinet's stronger personalities. Indeed, at the time, the American mis-

sion commented that as "a good friend of the British, [he] can doubtless be counted upon to follow Glubb's instructions to the letter."[18] Those
expectations proved premature. Although he retained his affinity for the
British connection, Tuqan soon evolved into the cabinet's second most
powerful member, and he thereafter became the most outspoken voice
on the Throne Council. That he owed both his cabinet and his Throne
Council appointments to Abu'l Huda did little to hamper his own aspirations for the prime minister's job. He had no deep political differences
with Abu'l Huda; he was at least as much a Hashemite stalwart as the
prime minister was.[19] His only grudge against the government was that
its parsimony toward the West Bank prevented him from showering much
government largesse on his own Nablus constituency. Rather, he seems
to have moved solely by ambition. During his long term of office, Abu'l
Huda had certainly angered enough people for Tuqan to believe that he
could parlay his unique position as the longtime mayor of Nablus and
loyal champion of the Hashemites into a West Bank/East Bank coalition
that would lead him to the prime minister's chair.[20]

Abu'l Huda's decision to convene the special parliamentary session
to vote on deposition was, therefore, not made lightly. Since its adjourn-
ment in April, Abu'l Huda had not needed formal parliamentary support for his policy toward Talal. Now, when that approval was necessary,
he was forced to go to parliament at a time when relations between the
executive branch and the legislative branch were at their lowest since the
1951 election.

In any event, the deposition session was not, as feared, the setting
for the showdown between Abu'l Huda and his critics. Perhaps humbled
by the gravity of the decision at hand, all sides seemed to have comported
themselves with appropriate dignity and restraint. Moreover, Abu'l Huda's
reappointment of Tuqan to the Regency Council showed that he was
not going to permit local politics to muddle the dynastic question, and
it put off, at least for the time being, a confrontation with his main Palestinian rival.

The resolution of the Talal saga marked a new stage in Abu'l Huda's
virtual one-man rule over Jordan. "For the first time in many months,"
he told Furlonge, he felt himself "free to concentrate on the real task of
governing the country."[21] It was also the last chance Abu'l Huda would
have to brandish a few political carrots before resorting, if necessary, to
his heavy stick.

First, he dealt with Palestinian discontent. In a mid-August press
conference, Abu'l Huda rejected the notion that the parliamentary authors
of the Nablus petition were motivated by separatist sentiments and said
he believed they were merely doing their duty to their constituents by
airing such grievances. Furthermore, he noted that he was "most interested in studying the problems" the deputies raised.[22] Soon thereafter,
he followed this generous demarche by convening a series of open meet-

ings with Palestinian deputies to discuss their complaints in detail. Abu'l Huda had no intention of acting on the more substantive opposition demands; instead, his strategy was to defuse political tension through continuous talk, and it did seem to buy him several weeks of additional calm. Furlonge noted that Abu'l Huda's tactic was "sound psychology where Arabs are concerned, as they dislike not being able to expound a grievance more than they dislike a grievance itself."[23]

In late September, Abu'l Huda formed a new cabinet whose composition represented a further attempt to placate his political opponents. This was one of Abu'l Huda's favorite tactics: Personnel, unlike policies, were flexible and Abu'l Huda moved them like pieces on a chessboard. After the budget confrontation in April, for example, he had named Palestinian refugee Khulusi al-Khayri, one of his harshest critics, to be minister of health and social welfare, and he had appointed Hazza' al-Majali's main hometown rival, Ahmad Tarawneh of Kerak, as minister of agriculture. The September 1952 reshuffle was an even more daring attempt to defuse the opposition with a velvet glove. Three new West Bank ministers were brought into the government, including prominent nationalists Musa Naser and Anwar Nusaybah.

Naser had been a minister in one of Abu'l Huda's earlier governments but had since become a staunch critic of both Abdullah and Abu'l Huda.[24] Nusaybah had served as a member of the ill-fated All-Palestine Government, set up in Egyptian-administered Gaza in September 1948, and for this he bore the reputation of being a sympathizer of the ex-mufti. In fact, he had long since reconciled himself to Hashemite control of the West Bank and had performed ably as Jordan's chief MAC representative.[25] Both men were appointed to ministries that dealt primarily with Palestinian concerns. At Finance, Naser had to answer charges of the government's spending bias against the West Bank; at Reconstruction and Development, Nusaybah was responsible for Jordan's often-testy relations with UNRWA. Ten days later, Nusaybah was given the defense portfolio as well, assuming the added responsibility for dealing with Israeli raids in retaliation against cross-border infiltration. Together with the assignment of al-Khayri as the minister of economy, these appointments of Palestinians to cabinet posts were a shrewd maneuver by Abu'l Huda to deflect further Palestinian opposition. Their presence also restored equality in terms of East Bank/West Bank representation in the cabinet. In contrast with these forceful Palestinian personalities, the East Bank ministers were a lackluster lot. Acre-born Abu'l Huda was the strongest "Transjordanian" among them.[26]

Abu'l Huda also sought to pacify his critics in other ways. In early October, he released all prisoners detained under the Defense Regulations (except the most extreme Communists)[27] and suspended the use of special detention rights enforceable only on the West Bank that were a lingering reminder of the British Mandate. As a further sop to Palestinians, he also created a new post of deputy ministry of the interior to be resident in Jerusalem and filled it with a West Banker of cabinet rank, Justice Minister 'Ali Hasna.[28] These sorts of stratagems—dialogue with the opposition, ministerial changes, prisoner releases, promises of policy reviews—were vintage Abu'l Huda. They never led to real change, because they were not meant to lead anywhere. Rather, their goal was to provide a fiction of activity that would delay as much and as far as possible any substantive political reckoning. But in a rare moment of political immaturity, Abu'l Huda attempted a risky maneuver without the strength to see it through and, in the process, confirmed the charges of "despotism" that his detractors had so frequently lobbed against him.

Despite the ministerial shake-up, criticism of Abu'l Huda's long (by Jordanian standards) tenure in office continued to grow. He, in turn, feared that a combination of Palestinian hostility and the restlessness of many East Bank politicians, for whom a change of government would hold the prospect of ministerial spoils, might prove a potent enough mix to paralyze parliament, if not actually bring his government down through a no-confidence vote. He decided, therefore, to try to postpone the next parliamentary session from November to January and, if necessary, to dissolve parliament altogether. "So many urgent tasks confronted the Administration," Furlonge reported, that Abu'l Huda wanted "to get on with the work without Parliament's preoccupations."[29]

The problem was that Abu'l Huda needed the Regency Council's approval to postpone parliament, and the council refused. On October 6, Abu'l Huda tried to persuade the council to endorse his plan as well as to confirm the arrests of a large number of the regime's political opponents. Two of the three regents—Sulayman Tuqan and Ibrahim Hashim—immediately voiced their opposition but agreed to defer a final decision for one week. In that time they sought ought the opinions of various deputies and even went so far as to query Queen Zayn. Most important, they asked Glubb whether he could ensure public security if the postponement led to a general strike; Glubb said he could not give such a guarantee. They then formally rejected Abu'l Huda's petition for postponement and ordered parliament to convene as scheduled, on November 1.[30]

Abu'l Huda's error was in not fully realizing that politicians—not a distant and distracted king—now exercised the powers of the throne. For Hashim, the jurist, the issue was clearly constitutional, but for the ambitious Tuqan, the issue was politics. Given al-Rifa'i's political exile, Tuqan viewed himself as Abu'l Huda's natural successor, and he was not prepared to lend royal legitimacy to a plan that would confirm what he called the premier's "dictatorial" methods.[31]

Abu'l Huda, therefore, was forced to withdraw his proposal for postponement. It was a humiliating episode, all the more surprising in that Abu'l Huda evidently thought he could not muster the mere fourteen votes needed to defeat a no-confidence motion. In retrospect, it looks as though Abu'l Huda grossly miscalculated. Hashim later told Furlonge that although he strongly opposed the postponement idea, he was "equally convinced that there was no alternative to Abu'l Huda as prime minister." He also believed that Abu'l Huda would "in all probability" have received a "substantial majority" of confidence votes. But the failed attempt to dispense with parliament and rule by executive decree had the unintended consequence of emboldening Abu'l Huda's parliamentary critics into open confrontation.

Parliament's opening on November 1 proved an ominous beginning for the prime minister, as the government immediately suffered two successive setbacks. First, its candidate for speaker of the house, the wealthy Circassian Wasfi Mirza, was soundly defeated, twenty-five to fifteen, by the similarly wealthy Nablus deputy, Hikmat al-Masri. Then, before the session adjourned, Abu'l Huda attempted to deliver the government's own statement of policy (as distinct from the speech from the throne), so as to avoid the necessity of holding separate opposition debates on each address. When Hazza' al-Majali, speaking for the opposition, protested, Abu'l Huda left the chamber in disgust. Three days later, Abu'l Huda finally read his ministerial statement—an uninspiring recitation that contained no substantive initiatives—and the chamber scheduled the confidence debate for the following week.[32]

In the interim, Abu'l Huda made his second parliamentary mistake. Evidently shaken by the margin of Mirza's defeat, which was only two votes short of the two-thirds necessary to bring down his government, he tried once again to have parliament suspended. The prime minister laid out his strategy at a meeting with Furlonge and Glubb on November 4. According to him, Sulayman Tuqan had been doling out bribes to deputies to ensure their opposition to the government. Although he had no hard evidence, he said he was "morally certain" that the source of the money was Iraq and that Baghdad was intent on finishing the job it had started a year earlier when it had first used Tuqan to buy electoral support for Iraqi–Jordanian union. Abu'l Huda said he had solicited a confession from the Amman merchant who claimed to have passed money from Tuqan to the deputies, and the last-minute shift of five votes from Mirza to al-Masri confirmed the merchant's story. Tuqan, he said, was likely to attempt the same ruse with the no-confidence motion, and though he expected to hold on to the fourteen votes he needed to stay in office, he would find parliament "impossible to control." Therefore, Abu'l Huda said he "would be obliged" to ask the Regency Council once again to dissolve parliament and permit him to rule by decree pending new elections.

This time, Abu'l Huda had given considerably more thought to the problem of neutralizing Tuqan. He told Furlonge and Glubb that he expected Hashim to support his request rather than face the instability that might result from the government's collapse. If that were the case, then Hashim and fellow regent al-Rushaydat (a close confidant of Abu'l

Huda's deputy premier, Sa'id al-Mufti) could overrule Tuqan in the Regency Council and perhaps even force the latter's resignation. Although that might result in some public disturbances, Abu'l Huda said he believed they could be handled without much difficulty; Glubb kept silent. But if Hashim were to continue to oppose dissolution, Abu'l Huda pointed out that he had two other options. First, he noted that the cabinet, which had appointed the Regency Council in the first place, could sack Tuqan; the constitutional propriety of such a move did not interest him. And second, if all else failed, Abu'l Huda declared that he would himself resign, confident that in the ensuing scramble, the opposition would probably be too splintered to agree on an alternative.[33]

Again Abu'l Huda miscalculated. When he took his proposal to the Regency Council, Hashim stood firm. Not only would the council "under no circumstances" approve dissolution, but (he later said) if Abu'l Huda attempted to manipulate the council to achieve his aims, Hashim himself would resign. For Hashim—lauded by the American ambassador as "without question the First Man of the Kingdom"[34]—to resign from the council would almost certainly guarantee a vote of no confidence in Abu'l Huda, if it did not actually provoke widespread rioting. Moreover, Hashim said that though he thought Abu'l Huda was still the best man to lead the government, there were still several others—al-Mufti, Tuqan, al-Rifa'i, and al-Nimr, he suggested—who could do a satisfactory job without destabilizing the country in the process. Outflanked and stymied, Abu'l Huda was forced to back down for the second time and face a confidence debate on November 11.[35]

It turned out to be an utter fiasco. After several reasonably constructive critiques, Abdullah al-Rimawi launched into a blistering, ninety-minute diatribe against the government, followed by a direct attack on the prime minister himself by al-Rimawi's Ba'thist colleague, Abdullah Na'was. When Wasfi Mirza asked Na'was to stop his *ad hominem* invective, two tribal deputies began to lob epithets at the Palestinian representatives, charging them with "feminine" cowardice in the 1948 war. These outbursts solicited equally provocative ripostes from the West Bank MPs, and the chamber turned to bedlam. Daggers were "fingered," and the police had to intervene. When the house was finally called to order, opposition spokesman Anwar al-Khatib charged Abu'l Huda with colluding to stage the outburst—the premier had been seen whispering intently to the main instigator, bedouin MP Hamid Bin Jazi—and demanded apologies from both Bin Jazi and the government. Abu'l Huda refused, and the eighteen opposition deputies (sixteen Palestinians, two Transjordanians) left the chamber for the nearby Park Hotel, where they formed an opposition "bureau" and drafted a statement of protest.[36] Meanwhile, one of the two remaining West Bank deputies, 'Abd al-Rahim Jarrar, moved the vote of confidence, which the government then received with the unanimous support of the twenty-two members still in the chamber.[37]

The vote of confidence reportedly filled Abu'l Huda with "buoyant self-confidence." He told Furlonge that there was no longer any need for dissolution, since he could now depend on those twenty-two deputies either to support the government with their votes or to absent themselves from the chamber and thereby deny the opposition a quorum. Furlonge noted that Abu'l Huda had relied on a "judicious expenditure of funds placed at his disposal by Ibn Saud" to ensure his parliamentary victory, a form of foreign aid apparently sanctioned by Iraq's alleged assistance to the opposition.[38]

On the following day, the entire opposition caucus presented its protest to the Regency Council. In it, they demanded Abu'l Huda's resignation, the abolition of the Emergency Laws,[39] the legalization of political parties, and a constitutional amendment lowering the threshold for no-confidence motions to a simple majority. Even though Hashim sympathized with the gist of their complaint—he had little doubt that Abu'l Huda was guilty of provoking the opposition—he stalled to let passions cool. But he did warn the deputies that the regents would not hesitate to deploy the army to suppress any civil disturbances.[40] Nevertheless, demonstrations did break out on November 14 and 15 throughout the West Bank, symbolizing what the British consul in Jerusalem called the "real hatred which exists . . . for the Amman Government." They were, he also noted, the first since the end of the Mandate to take an anti-British flavor and, as such, would "hardly have been conceivable a year ago." As Hashim promised, the army was called out to quell the protests.[41]

Abu'l Huda was ebullient. The demonstrations had given him an excuse to employ force against the opposition, and he even spoke of dispatching the more obstreperous deputies to desert detention camps. Furthermore, the crisis had divided the Regency Council. On the one hand, Tuqan had opposed the army's deployment and had instead wanted the council to sack the prime minister. Hashim, on the other hand, not only insisted on dealing firmly with the rioters but also believed that Abu'l Huda should remain in office, if only for a short while, so as not to give the impression of having been forced out; he was, al-Majali alleged, playing both sides. (The third regent, al-Rushaydat, generally deferred to Hashim.) Tuqan and Hashim did concur on two points: They were adamantly opposed to the idea of imprisoning members of parliament, and they agreed that Abu'l Huda would, before long, have to go. Their compromise candidate for prime minister: Sa'id al-Mufti.[42]

On the morning of November 18, with parliament due to reconvene later that day, Hashim called a general meeting of pro- and antigovernment deputies to try to repair the previous week's damage. Among those who attended were fourteen oppositionists, eight loyalists, and Sulayman Tuqan; Abu'l Huda, who had little interest in mending fences with the opposition, stayed away. The meeting was a tentative success. Hashim urged his guests to confine their differences to the "legitimate channels of parliamentary debate," and both sides reportedly agreed "to sink their differences and parted in amity."

But the truce lasted less than six hours. When the opposition deputies showed up at parliament that afternoon, they learned that Abu'l Huda's men had refused to attend, thereby depriving them of a quorum. The prime minister's plan to circumvent parliament had passed its first hurdle. With the support of twenty-two deputies thus confirmed, Abu'l Huda permitted parliament to convene the following week. When the progovernment majority defeated opposition motions protesting the legality of the previous vote of confidence, Abu'l Huda finally knew he had the upper hand. The opposition could do no damage in parliament, and the Arab Legion was taking steps to prevent any public demonstrations. As Furlonge noted, Abu'l Huda's position had improved "to an extent which would have been inconceivable a fortnight ago." Two weeks later, he reported that Abu'l Huda was "on the top of the world."[43]

Although he had won the battle, Abu'l Huda had not, in fact, won the war. His success at slapping a lid on parliament did little to defuse the underlying tensions that fueled opposition to his heavy-handed rule. Throughout the winter, he continued to employ his preferred tactics— delay a session, postpone a decision, and obfuscate an issue—rather than address the very real economic and political grievances that provoked the opposition. Parliament, to be sure, was at times a nettlesome political sideshow, but shorn of its theatrics, there were concrete issues at stake that the prime minister chose to avoid.

It was, in retrospect, a lost opportunity. Abu'l Huda's government enjoyed the participation of several of the kingdom's most widely respected Palestinians—Nusaybah, al-Khayri, Naser, and Hasna. Their presence in his cabinet offered prima facie proof that there was nothing inevitable about the eventual breach between the two banks, which was, in essence, a breach over conflicting visions of Jordan itself. Unlike old Abdullah supporters like Sulayman Tuqan and Hebron's Muhammad 'Ali al-Ja'bari, these men were nationalists who had reached the eminently reasonable conclusion that union with the East Bank was the best of the bad options available to the Palestinians after the 1948/49 war. Together, Abu'l Huda and his Palestinian ministers could have helped fashion a more symbiotic relationship between the two banks. But Abu'l Huda preferred to keep his critics at bay rather than confront the source of their criticism. In the process, he alienated not just Palestinians but many Transjordanians as well.[44] As a result, his satisfaction at outmaneuvering the opposition proved short lived.

After outwitting his parliamentary critics, Abu'l Huda, in vintage form, did extend an olive branch or two. In mid-December, for example, he proposed the formation of a joint governmental–parliamentary committee to prepare legislation to amend the Defense Regulations. Even though he had promised to do away with the regulations several months earlier, the opposition nevertheless agreed to his offer as a conciliatory step in the right direction.[45] Similarly, he permitted parliamentary debates on civil service corruption, nepotism, and even his own role in the negotiations of the Rhodes Armistice Agreement three years earlier, each time confident that his parliamentary majority would reject any motions of no confidence.[46] In February, Abu'l Huda approved a visit of a parliamentary delegation to East Bank detention camps to find out whether prisoners were being held illegally. (To the opposition's dismay, twenty-six of the twenty-seven prisoners interviewed reaffirmed their Communist sympathies, the legal basis of their incarceration.)[47] In point of fact, Abu'l Huda's previous strong-arm handling of parliament magnified the importance of these concessions beyond their actual significance. Not surprisingly, the parliamentary session closed with only one of the Emergency Laws abolished and the Defense Regulations still intact.[48]

Offering such petty concessions was only one reason that domestic politics passed more peaceably during the winter of 1952/53 than during the previous few months. The other main factor was the renewed tension along the Israeli frontier that consumed public interest even more than did popular frustration with the prime minister. In January 1953, there was a sharp rise in cross-border attacks and infiltration following the expiration of the Local Commanders Agreement designed to build cooperation between Jordanian and Israeli border police.[49] In accordance with Jordan's doctrine of trying to avoid direct clashes with the Israeli army, the Arab Legion took little part in the defense of villages subjected to Israeli retaliatory raids. This left the task almost entirely in the hands of the ill-armed, ill-trained, and undermanned National Guard. Because of its seeming indifference to West Bank defense, the central government came in for about as much abuse as Israel did. Frustration spread even to the Arab Legion, with Glubb reporting for the first time anti-British (and, by extension, antigovernment) "murmurings" among the Arab officers.[50]

Ever the politician, Abu'l Huda's strategy was to claim some undisclosed "indisposition" and to deflect the criticism onto his defense minister, Anwar Nusaybah. It was a shrewd maneuver. Nusaybah had earlier won praise for initiating military training for frontline villages,[51] and he responded to this challenge by implementing several vigorous remedial measures that improved both the West Bank's defense and the government's public approval.[52]

But he went too far. Convinced that the Anglo-Jordanian treaty was the only effective deterrent to Israel, Nusaybah not only invoked the treaty's mutual defense clauses, but, speaking for the government, he also invited Britain to station an armored brigade group in Jordan to safeguard the frontier. London was delighted; for months its military planners had been trying to find a way to deploy in Jordan a sizable number of troops it planned to withdraw from Suez.[53] Abu'l Huda, on the other hand, was aghast, as the establishment of a large British base in Jordan would undermine his strategy of conciliation with Egypt, Syria, and Saudi Arabia. He quickly intervened to quash the initiative in his usual way, by suggesting to postpone any decision until after King Hussein's formal accession in May. Several weeks later, Abu'l Huda resorted to the same tactic when in a contentious mood, parliament (including several of his erstwhile supporters) threatened to reject his proposed government budget for the 1953/54 fiscal year.[54]

Abu'l Huda, therefore, ended his prime ministry on a rather muted note. Having forcefully and adroitly controlled parliament in the autumn, he seemed unusually meek and withdrawn in the weeks preceding the end of his term the following spring. As the date approached for Hussein's formal assumption of powers, Abu'l Huda informed his colleagues of his intention to resign. He would not retire from public life altogether, he was reported to say, but would establish himself as the young king's *éminence grise,* as he had with Talal.[55] Furlonge suspected that Abu'l Huda's firm and frequent declarations not to seek reappointment were really a ruse to elicit pleas that he stay on for the good of the country. But none was forthcoming, not from London, the palace, or his fellow Amman politicians.[56] After his unusually long tenure in office, few tears were shed over his departure, even by his political allies. Given the fact that Abu'l Huda intended to remain a political force from sidelines, his hangers-on—caustically nicknamed the "Mau Mau"—did not expect to suffer greatly by his return to private life.[57]

When Hussein formally assumed the kingship on May 2, 1953, Abu'l Huda was in for a disappointment. The young monarch rarely turned to the old warhorse for advice. Perhaps it was because Abu'l Huda was too closely associated with the crisis surrounding his grandfather's assassination. Or perhaps the palace's arm-length attitude toward Abu'l Huda was the doing of the new prime minister, Fawzi al-Mulqi. Al-Mulqi had previously served as Abu'l Huda's subordinate, and they both were linked to the Rhodes Armistice Agreement. Whatever the reason, the ex–prime minister was, for the first time in nearly two years, a political outsider.[58]

During that time, Abu'l Huda had made two strategic errors. First, he failed to distinguish among the various phases of his prime ministerial career. Over time, he wore three different hats: Abdullah's chief administrator, Talal's *éminence grise,* and his own autocratic prime minister. Although each role required more political savvy, sagacity, and restraint than the previous one had, Abu'l Huda did not seem to mature with each new situation. Indeed, after Talal's deposition, Abu'l Huda never seemed to grasp the fact that the absence of a monarch did not endow him with any special royal prerogatives. He had worked well when he had only Abdullah to answer to or when Talal, in his debilitated state, answered to him. But the idea that he might be only *primus inter pares* was not something Abu'l Huda easily accepted. As time passed, he mistook the endorsement of his fellows as an expression of their personal loyalty to him; in fact, it was only his defense of the Hashemite system that had earned their support.

Abu'l Huda's failing stemmed fundamentally from his inability to deal with people as anything but superiors or subordinates; he seemed to lack an understanding of the concept of peer. Very few of the men around him were his intellectual match. The East Bankers in his cabinets were viewed as either political operatives (such as Felah al-Madadha) or prestige appointments (like the ineffectual Sa'id al-Mufti). The West Bankers were, on the whole, more impressive, but they had only titles and not power. Abu'l Huda was, in Glubb's characterization, a "super effendi."[59]

Abu'l Huda's second shortcoming was his predilection to avoid problems rather than face them directly. He was not, of course, the only politician to postpone difficult decisions, but for him procrastination was strategy, not tactics. Despite a term in office that was longer than any other prime minister had served in more than a decade, he ruled as though he were leading only a caretaker government. Long-term problems were given short-term solutions; Abu'l Huda reacted only to crises, never offering initiatives to avert them. To him, Palestinian discontent was only a security matter. A quick deployment of troops, combined perhaps with a symbolic appointment of a Palestinian to his cabinet, was about the sum of his West Bank policy. There is no evidence that Abu'l Huda ever considered the possibility that left alone, Palestinian indignation might fester and eventually threaten the "unity of the two banks." Similarly, he rarely devoted any energy to Jordan's economic well-being. His idea of development, summed up in his ministerial statement in November 1952, was little more than "the construction of roads all over the kingdom."[60]

Abu'l Huda was by nature an insular man. He kept his own counsel and rarely delegated authority to subordinates or even his ministers. At one time, he simultaneously held the posts of prime minister, foreign minister, and defense minister. Such consolidation of power skewed his appreciation of the political, economic, and social problems facing the kingdom and gave him an unduly narrow understanding of Jordan's security requirements. On several occasions, Abu'l Huda explained to Furlonge that he ruled with a heavy hand because parliamentary democracy had failed in Jordan just as it had in Syria and Egypt. Furthermore, he explained, the British character of the Arab Legion prevented Jordan from resorting to the sort of military dictatorship that those other countries had created. Therefore, he had developed his own brand of authoritarianism, a police state with a civilian face. He termed it "a middle course."[61]

It was, admittedly, a policy not without benefit. With single-minded intensity, Abu'l Huda almost single-handedly ensured the survival of Hashemite rule in Jordan. His tactics—ranging from his inter-Arab "peace offensive" to his speedy drafting of a new constitution—may have seemed contrary to the late king's, but his fundamental objective remained profoundly loyalist. It was, very simply, to preserve: to preserve the kingdom's independence, to preserve the contours of the "unity of the two banks" (no matter how artificial it may have been in practice), and to preserve the interests of both Abdullah's nominal and political heirs. His stewardship of the kingdom in the uneasy period between Abdullah's death and Hussein's assumption of power proved that it was loyalty to an idea, not to royal blood, that marked one as a Hashemite. As one historian noted: "The regency proves that at a certain time, ages ago in terms of Middle East political history, the establishment could keep on top in the rough-and-tumble of domestic challenges, without the Hashemite ruler as a continuous prime mover."[62]

In this context, Abu'l Huda mistook all criticism for opposition and viewed any substantive change as inherently dangerous. An article in the *Christian Science Monitor* could not have been further off the mark than when it praised the prime minister's "vast program of reform, rehabilitation and democratization" and his "anxious haste for radical change."[63] It is doubtful that Abu'l Huda even recognized missed opportunities to extend the umbrella of the regime beyond its most traditional supporters. After the November 11 parliamentary fiasco, for example, Ibrahim Hashim drew a distinction between the government's militant and moderate critics: It would be a mistake, he warned, to "tar all [opposition deputies] with the same brush."[64] It was the sort of observation that Abu'l Huda would never have made. And it was for that reason that Fawzi al-Mulqi took office in May 1953, intent on replacing Abu'l Huda's "middle course" with a reform-minded course of his own.

5

From Liberty to License

Abdullah's assassination was at least as much a turning point in the life of his grandson Hussein as it had been for the kingdom as a whole.[1] It thrust the young prince into the political limelight for the first time and ushered in twenty-two months of continuous, almost dizzying, change. Forced to discard plans to return to Alexandria's Victoria College, Hussein was sent instead to Harrow. There, Whitehall first began to take interest in the education, both scholastic and political, of the heir to the throne of its closest Middle East ally. Shortly before Talal's deposition, when Fawzi al-Mulqi, Jordan's ambassador in London, suggested that Hussein enroll in a training course at the Royal Military Academy, Sandhurst, the idea caught the prince's fancy, and over Abu'l Huda's initial objections, he departed in September 1952 for a condensed, six-month course.[2] Again, London attached great importance to Hussein's training and took steps to ensure that he "profited not only in his military instruction" but also from his exposure to "aspects of British life." In particular, Sandhurst's commandant took pains to strike the proper balance between cushioning Hussein from the "rigour of Sandhurst" and avoiding an excess of "privileged treatment" that could, in the long run, "backfire" against both Hussein and Britain.[3] After Sandhurst's passing-out parade and a month-long, cross-country automobile tour, organized by the Foreign Office, Hussein returned to Amman in early April 1953. On May 2, his lunar birthday, Hussein took the oath of office, assumed his constitutional prerogatives, and became Jordan's king in fact as well as in name.

It is difficult to gauge Hussein's thinking at the time. A reading of his memoirs suggests it was at once both a heady and a bittersweet moment for the seventeen-year-old monarch. At his grandfather's side in Jerusalem and his mother's side in Lausanne, he had been an eyewitness to both the violence and the tragedy that had befallen his family. But instead of cursing the fates, Hussein defined both occasions almost solely in terms of the contempt with which he viewed the men around his father and grandfather.

> It was with relief that I learned that my father, who was being treated in Switzerland, appeared to be recovering. On his return I hoped I could go back to Victoria [College], away from the power lust and avarice that followed my grandfather's death as rapacious politicians fought for the crumbs of office, sullen, determined, hating each other, like the money-hungry relatives who gather at the reading of the will.[4]

Their betrayal, Hussein stated, was a "constant reminder of the frailty of political devotion."[5] His accession to the throne, therefore, was an opportunity to wipe "the opportunists" from office and install men of his own choosing.

But *Uneasy Lies the Head,* published in 1962, was as much a professional publicist's attempt to fashion a "lonely-at-the-top" image for the king as it was an exploration of Hussein's inner feelings and beliefs.[6] "Politicians" are depicted by Hussein as enemies of Jordanian independence virtually on a par with Communists and Nasserites. In his various memoirs, Glubb played on the same theme, charging that "anybody who enters politics does so with the sole aim of achieving personal gain or advancement."[7] Both Hussein and Glubb inflated the role of Jordanian "politicians" to exaggerate the "us-versus-them" aspect of their personal stories. In neither case does the record bear out the memoirs: After a decade at the helm of the Arab Legion, Glubb was no less a politician than a soldier, and a year after his accession, Hussein called on the men he would later label "opportunists" to run his government and salvage a deteriorating domestic situation. Indeed, in an interview, Hussein stated that he was "never against" the politicians of his grandfather's day and that he "always respected them," a far cry from the invective of his autobiography.[8] It is particularly noteworthy that nine of Hussein's first ten prime ministers had served as a minister to Abdullah, including four (Abu'l Huda, al-Mufti, Hashim, and al-Rifa'i) who had served previously as prime minister.

Nevertheless, Hussein's return to Jordan clearly ushered in a new era. His youthful enthusiasm and buoyant energy electrified the rather staid government of the day. "The future is ours," Hussein was wont to say, readily earning himself the label of "a young man in a hurry."[9] But in practical terms, accession did not immediately permit Hussein to wield all the powers he theoretically enjoyed; although a catalyst of Jordan's new era, he was not yet its main protagonist.[10] He was, of course, just a teenager and, having spent little of the previous two years in Jordan, was largely unknown to the Jordanian public.[11] Even though he undoubtedly had the goodwill of both his subjects and the kingdom's political elite, he did not yet have their respect. This was reflected in the American embassy's incredulity when the State Department requested that he arrange an audience with Hussein during Secretary of State John Foster Dulles's whirlwind Middle East tour in May 1953. "After all," Ambassador Green wrote, "the King is only a boy and while anything he may say may be interesting, it can't be of any importance."[12]

If anyone could be said to claim both the respect and the powers of the kingship it was Hussein's mother, Queen Zayn. Politically astute, intensely loyal to her family and its legacy, and, at times, the ultimate source of strength in times of despair, Zayn was for many years the legendary power behind the throne. Throughout Talal's reign, the subsequent regency, and beyond, Zayn quietly asserted herself on all levels of politics and was recognized as a force to be reckoned with by government, parliament, Regency Council, and opposition alike. Jordan's leaders, Green noted, were "very careful to take her desires into account."[13] For its part, London thoroughly appreciated that Zayn—a "woman of great intelligence and force of character"—was destined to be "a powerful influence for some time to come" and therefore jealously guarded its special relationship with her.[14] Indeed, on the eve of Hussein's departure from England in 1953, Whitehall concluded that Zayn's was perhaps the most powerful voice in the kingdom: "The choice [of Abu'l Huda's successor] will be made by King Hussein's mother, Queen Zayn, who is a lady of strong character and, as the senior member of the Royal Family resident in Jordan, has exercised considerable influence behind the scenes although constitutionally the power has lain with the Regency Council."[15] In fact, Zayn's influence extended far beyond the appointment of Abu'l Huda's successor. Throughout Hussein's early years on the throne, she played a role of heretofore undocumented significance as confidante, adviser, and protector of her eldest son.[16]

By the time of Hussein's accession, the choice of Dr. Fawzi al-Mulqi as Abu'l Huda's successor was a foregone conclusion. In many ways, he was a new breed of Jordanian politician. Born in Irbid of Damascene parentage, the forty-one-year-old al-Mulqi was Jordan's first native-born prime minister. He was, by training, a veterinarian, with degrees from the American University of Beirut and the University of Edinburgh, but he had never practiced. Instead, he entered government service, first as a teacher but then as a diplomat, and he spent most of his career in posts outside Jordan, as consul-general in Cairo, then foreign minister, minister in France, and, most recently, ambassador to Britain. As a result, al-Mulqi was a man of the world, but he lacked much in the way of a political following at home. His detachment from local politics and his lack of a strong power base might very well have been factors that commended him for the prime ministry. For Zayn, there was political advantage in having as premier a relatively weak political outsider who could not easily overwhelm and suffocate her son. What clinched the matter was al-Mulqi's close personal relationship with Hussein, struck up during the latter's tenure at Harrow and Sandhurst. Hussein was keen on having al-Mulqi return to Jordan, both because he was someone the king "knew very well" and because he "had a whole fresh approach" to popular participation in government that appealed to the king's youthful vigor and budding Anglophilia.[17]

Al-Mulqi's advantages bespoke drawbacks as well. On a personal level, he was ambitious, vain, and self-congratulatory. After only their second meeting, American Ambassador Green believed the new prime minister to be "an egregious ass": "He showed no signs of intoxication," Green wrote, "but such asinine conduct is hardly to be expected of a sober man."[18] Politically, al-Mulqi had no grand strategy for his government; the prime ministry was an end in itself, and maintaining it became his mission. By nature, he was not a strong leader, and after twenty-two months of Abu'l Huda's virtual one-man rule, al-Mulqi's natural indecision was put in sharp relief. His cabinet colleagues knew how to exploit al-Mulqi's preference for lowest-common denominator agreement to their own parochial advantage. He was, in many ways, their captive, dependent on his ministers' local power bases to ensure popular support for the government.[19] London recognized the danger of an al-Mulqi ministry early on: "A strong man who is our friend would be an asset; and a weak man who was regarded as our enemy might not be too bad," read a letter to Furlonge. "But a man who was weak and was looked on as pro-British would soon fall victim to opposition, with harmful effects on our position in Jordan." But in a mistake Whitehall made repeatedly, it was left it to the ineffectual Furlonge to "keep him on the right lines."[20]

What al-Mulqi's true political colors were remains something of an enigma. History has portrayed him as a frustrated liberal, handcuffed by circumstances from implementing a program of progressive reform that would have transformed Jordan into a British-style constitutional monarchy.[21] Thirty-five years after the fact, Hussein described his and al-Mulqi's philosophy upon taking office as follows:

> [Al-Mulqi] wanted people to partake in deciding their future. He wanted the young generation to be involved in building Jordan. He had very liberal ideas in mind. So as far as the king was concerned, my idea was that if we could develop a system in which he [i.e., the prime minister] could assume the responsibilities, then the king would be maybe an advisor or an ear—certainly a symbol of continuity more than being involved too much in the details of how things were run.[22]

Although that may very well have been the intention of the young and impressionable Hussein, it smacks of a roseate, almost eulogistic description of al-Mulqi's political design. Al-Mulqi was hardly the noble crusader for progressive reform that he has often been made out to be. He was, rather, a politician who endeavored to turn his liabilities into virtues. His absence from Jordan during the critical years after Abdullah's death bestowed on him a certain political cleanliness, as his lack of a single political constituency forced him into embracing all constituencies. There was no benefit to be gained in emulating Abu'l Huda's autocratic policies when it earned him little political gain and when there were far better practitioners available. For al-Mulqi, liberalism—but, even more important, conciliation—was the answer.

After Hussein assumed the throne on May 2, al-Mulqi set about to construct what he called a "coalition government," one that would include both Abu'l Huda men and prominent opposition personalities. His goal, though, seems to have been less an effort at national reconciliation than an attempt to defuse criticism by bringing as many potential troublemakers under his political tent. Indeed, even though he widened press freedoms and pardoned dozens of political prisoners early in his ministry, al-Mulqi later pushed through parliament tough press and anti-communist legislation and even resorted to his predecessor's authoritarian tactics when popular pressures began to mount.[23] This, of course, rendered al-Mulqi expendable; it made little sense for a weak man to employ strong-arm tactics when the strongest arm himself, Abu'l Huda, was waiting in the wings.

Al-Mulqi's plans for a "coalition government" were derailed from the start. In a tête-à-tête before Hussein's formal enthronement, Sulayman al-Nabulsi, leader of the Transjordanian branch of the moderate opposition, spelled out to al-Mulqi two conditions as the price of the opposition's support: that al-Mulqi embrace the anti-Abu'l Huda platform drafted after the November 1952 parliamentary fiasco and that he not reappoint any member of Abu'l Huda's government except 'Abd al-Halim al-Nimr, who had been one of their own all along. At first, al-Mulqi rejected al-Nabulsi's ultimatum, but when al-Nabulsi made his demands public, al-Mulqi changed his mind. Expediency, not principle, lay behind his original goal of a "national" government, and there was no reason to begin his ministry by inviting the opposition's ire.[24] To salvage his own pride, al-Mulqi retained one minister from the previous government, but he, the indolent Sa'id al-Mufti, was little more than a fig leaf. Of the other nine, five had never before served in a cabinet, and three had been active members of the parliamentary opposition (Anwar al-Khatib, Hikmat al-Masri, and Shafiq al-Rushaydat). The most notable addition was the appointment as foreign minister of the viscerally anti-Israel Hussein Fakhri al-Khalidi. Al-Khalidi, former secretary of the Arab Higher Committee and minister in the All-Palestine Government, at one time had been interned by the British in the Seychelles Islands. Al-Mulqi's ten colleagues were equally divided between Palestinians and Transjordanians, but not so in talent; as in Abu'l Huda's cabinet, the former were a much more formidable group.[25]

Al-Mulqi's cabinet choices were popular from the start. Although half the cabinet had served as ministers under Abdullah, they were viewed as the young, modern generation of Jordanian leaders. King Hussein's letter appointing al-Mulqi emphasized the twin principles of political reform and Arab solidarity, and al-Mulqi gave substance to those popular themes in his own ministerial statement three weeks later.[26] Specifically, he promised legislation to enforce and expand the individual and collective rights outlined in the constitution, including freedom of the press and the right to form unions and political parties; he promised diligence in frontier security and extra pay for National Guardsmen; he promised large-scale public works projects; and he promised solidarity with the Arab struggle "against imperialism and foreign influence in all its forms." Furlonge noted caustically that "it would be highly satisfactory if there were any chance of the Government being able to carry out even a fair proportion of" what it promised, but that, he said, was "unlikely." With little debate, al-Mulqi won his vote of confidence with just four dissenting votes.[27]

Almost immediately, the press tested al-Mulqi's sincerity by unleashing a series of virulent attacks on former prime minister Abu'l Huda and by taking up the Ba'thist criticism of Anglo-American "imperialist" control of Jordan.[28] Lest he fall into the same mold as Abu'l Huda, who also had promised press freedom but reinstituted censorship when the freedom did not suit him, al-Mulqi turned a blind eye to the media's excesses. That, in turn, emboldened the opposition even more. When their newspapers continued to test the limits of al-Mulqi's tolerance, they found it to be virtually inexhaustible.[29]

Al-Mulqi also bowed to opposition pressure when he tried to extract himself from the budget morass that his predecessor had so unceremoniously left him. The controversy revolved around a £750,000 British grant-in-aid to cover the budget deficit. Whereas British aid normally took the form of military subsidies or development assistance, this was the first grant targeted to the general government expenditure pool (specifically to the police budget). As such, it opened the government to charges that its day-to-day spending was actually controlled by the British exchequer. Only when London agreed to manipulate the budget accounts to make them appear less odious to parliament was al-Mulqi able to accommodate the government's critics.[30]

One bright spot during the early months of al-Mulqi's tenure was the signs of political maturity on the part of several of the Palestinian ministers. Despite fears to the contrary, the move from the opposition to the government benches proved, for most, to be a sobering experience. For example, Anwar al-Khatib, minister of development and reconstruction, took the courageous step of bucking the Palestinian refugees' unequivocal demand for repatriation by encouraging refugee resettlement projects such as the scaled-down Yarmuk River plan.[31] Indeed, the cabinet's most militant activist on behalf of the refugees turned out to be an East Bank minister, Mustafa Khalifa (health and social welfare), who single-handedly led a campaign against UNRWA's efforts to trim what it viewed as wasteful spending.[32]

Domestically, therefore, al-Mulqi considered his first six months in office a success. He carried through on a good measure of his promises, especially those relaxing press controls and releasing political prisoners, and he started the legislative process toward constitutional reform and the softening of the Defense Regulations. Just one journalist was imprisoned and only because he had been foolish enough to make personal attacks on the queen mother and her brother, Sharif Nasser bin Jamil.[33] Otherwise, al-Mulqi retained good relations with the press, who saved their most vicious slurs for Abu'l Huda. The relative calm that Jordan (and al-Mulqi) enjoyed during this period was, of course, bought at the expense of the government's acceding to opposition demands on both personnel and policy issues. At the time, though, only a few voices in the wind—notably that of Abu'l Huda himself—were warning that the "excessive liberty" countenanced by al-Mulqi could only lead to "grave damage" being done to the kingdom as a whole.[34]

Also contributing to the domestic calm during these early months was the flurry of diplomatic activity that kept Hussein and his prime minister occupied almost to the exclusion of all other business. Between May and July 1953, Amman came to a halt to accommodate visits by Saudi Crown Prince Saud, the Iraqi regent, Lebanese President Camille Chamoun, and Syrian strongman Adib al-Shishakli. During that time, Hussein also made his own return visits to Baghdad and Riyadh. Despite al-Mulqi's effort to play on Iraqi and Saudi animosity by inviting them to "compete for Jordan's favours," his diplomatic endeavors came to naught. Neither of the two states took up the role of courtier by offering Jordan any economic assistance, unless one can include in that category the lavish gift giving by the visiting Saudi prince.[35]

Although inter-Arab affairs remained fairly stable, tension along the frontier with Israel did not. Indeed, if any issue threatened to mar al-Mulqi's first six months at the helm, it was the danger that the cycle of infiltration and retribution could degenerate into war. Two weeks before Hussein's inauguration, gunfire between Israeli and Jordanian troops in Jerusalem had again focused popular attention on the unstable border situation. At the time, Defense Minister Nusaybah reportedly gained the king's assent to his suggestion to invite British troops into Jordan as a deterrent to Israel. The time seemed ripe for Britain to push for deployment: Fear was running high, the king was sympathetic, and, perhaps most important of all, Israeli Premier David Ben-Gurion offered no strong objection to the plan.[36]

Furlonge, however, counseled caution and put off a demarche to al-Mulqi first for "a week or two" and then until "the end of May." Meanwhile, London deferred to its local envoy.[37] In the end, al-Mulqi was

not pressed for an answer until late June, by which time the border tension—and the urgency to invite the British troops—had temporarily subsided.[38] As a result, Furlonge was forced to make his pitch not just in
terms of bolstering Jordan's defense but also by highlighting the economic dividends of an expanded British presence.[39] The issue, even in
al-Mulqi's eyes, was therefore reduced to money and politics. His response
was that even though Jordan welcomed the prepositioning of stores for
British reinforcements and wanted plans to be drawn up for the "rapid
deployment" of British troops, it "was not politically possible" to invite
those troops into Jordan at the present time. The most his government
could do, al-Mulqi declared, was to permit some expansion of the British "O" Force garrisoned at Aqaba since the Palestine war.[40] Privately,
he told Furlonge that there would be "no hope of overcoming local
political resistance" to the idea until two conditions were met: that the
Jordanian public accepted the gravity of the kingdom's financial situation and that it could be convinced that fellow Arab states had refused
to supply Jordan with significant economic aid.[41]

Two months later, al-Mulqi had a change of mind. On August 25,
he sent a secret letter to the British embassy formally requesting London
to "afford all possible assistance required for the defense of Jordan." One
week later he clarified, in his inimitably oblique way, his request to
Furlonge. Unless Jordan received commitments of "real, effective military help" at the upcoming Arab League Defense Council meeting in
Cairo, then, in Furlonge's words, al-Mulqi "thought that [the cabinet]
might conceivably be convinced that arrangements for pre-positioning of
British units in Jordan ought to be pursued."[42]

What caused al-Mulqi to reverse himself is not known. Several days
earlier, the British embassy reported that the Queen Mother—"and *ipso
facto*, King Hussein"—were "perturbed" about the frontier situation and
were "doubtful" of the army's ability to withstand an Israeli attack. But,
the embassy noted, al-Mulqi held a more sanguine view of the likelihood
of conflict with Israel.[43] In addition, three days before al-Mulqi's secret
letter, evidently sent without cabinet approval, Israel agreed to extend
the Local Commanders Agreement and also proposed a border rectifica-
tion that the acting MAC chairman termed "generous."[44] There was little,
therefore, to justify the fear of an impending Israeli attack in force that
apparently prompted al-Mulqi to risk the opposition of his nationalist
colleagues by inviting large numbers of British troops into the kingdom.
Certainly, there is no reason to believe that the two conditions he outlined to Furlonge in June had somehow been met by August. The only
possible explanation is that al-Mulqi somehow planned to use the prospect of British deployment in Jordan as a way to cajole military aid out
of the Arab League.

If that was indeed al-Mulqi's intention, he was sorely disappointed.
Al-Mulqi's fellow Arab leaders turned the tables on him. On his return
from the Cairo meeting, he reported that they "all seemed to regard it

as natural that Jordan should rely" on Britain for military assistance. Syria, he said, "expressed surprise" that with such a strong ally in Britain, Jordan should even have raised the matter in the first place.[45] But given the fact that Britain and Egypt were at a delicate moment in their negotiations over the Suez base, the Arab League did not give formal consent for Jordan to request British troops and instead offered some meager support for the kingdom's quasi-military frontier patrol, the National Guard. For al-Mulqi to have gone ahead with his request for British troops would have then meant flouting the league's wishes (at least officially) and incurring the wrath of vital domestic constituencies. Therefore, he backtracked. When a British military commander came to Amman to deliver London's approval of al-Mulqi's request, the premier told him that "the threat from Israel now appeared less imminent than some weeks back." The most he could do, he said, was to "not oppose" the dispatch to Zerqa of a small armored unit and only on condition that "it could be represented as being there for training with the Arab Legion."[46] Although disappointed with al-Mulqi's vacillation, Britain accepted his counterproposal "in the hopes," wrote Furlonge, "that we shall thus be getting a foot in the door."[47]

In retrospect, al-Mulqi's assessment of Israeli intentions was abysmal. His sudden request for troops in August was, at the time, unwarranted; his abrupt about-face in September was precipitate.[48] It is, of course, impossible to presume what might have occurred if al-Mulqi had followed through with his original request for British support. But it can be safely assumed that once Ben-Gurion's tacit approval for the deployment was solicited, the subsequent lack of movement could reasonably have been interpreted by Israel as a sign of British irresolution and Jordanian weakness. Such inaction eroded the deterrent power of the Anglo-Jordanian treaty, which the Jordanians, perhaps too credulously, relied on for their defense even more than the Arab Legion itself. Many factors contributed to Israel's decision to take military action against Jordan—ranging from the armed provocation of Jordanian infiltrators to conflict over the proposed Yarmuk River scheme to policy clashes between Ben Gurion and Moshe Sharett[49]—but the inconsistency of al-Mulqi's own security policy should not be left off the list. On October 14, the British cabinet finally endorsed the move of a squadron of tanks to Zerqa. For al-Mulqi, it was too little, too late. Less than twelve hours later, Israeli troops attacked the West Bank village of Qibya.

Early on October 13, three Israelis were killed in a bomb attack in the village of Tirat Yehuda, near Lydda. It was the first serious border incident in more than a month. Israeli and Jordanian police cooperated in the search for the infiltrators, but their trail was lost on the Jordan side of the frontier. Israel's retaliation came the following evening, as a squad of crack Israeli troops under the command of a dynamic, young officer named Ariel Sharon attacked and then demolished the medium-sized village of Qibya.[50] They had little trouble overcoming the thirty-man National Guard platoon defending Qibya; reinforcements from the Arab Legion's Third Brigade were never sent. In the end, thirty-nine houses were razed; more than fifty people were killed; and dozens more were wounded in Qibya and nearby villages. It was one of the most lethal nights in the long, numbing, and inconclusive border war that defined the Arab-Israeli conflict throughout much of the 1950s and 1960s.[51]

Qibya was the watershed event of al-Mulqi's ministry, the beginning of the end. From that point on, al-Mulqi was consumed with criticism from inside and outside his government, ranging from outrage at the Arab Legion's apparently lax approach to the West Bank's defense to the government's naive belief in the deterrent power of the Anglo-Jordanian treaty. Calls for Glubb's ouster, once restricted to the militant fringe, suddenly found a ready appeal among many government supporters. On a personal level, al-Mulqi was stung by charges of weakness and Anglophilia. His opponents saw his response—which, even when it appeared strong, was at its core timorous—and smelled blood. Before the end of his term, al-Mulqi was to rue the liberalism that gave his critics virtually unbridled license to turn their attacks on their benefactor.[52]

The Jordanian cabinet's immediate reaction was to interpret the Qibya incursion as the opening stage of an Israeli invasion. In an unprecedented act, it ordered virtually the entire Arab Legion to take up positions on the West Bank.[53] This, in turn, did provoke an Israeli mobilization, and the two countries were, for a brief moment, at risk of stumbling through sheer miscalculation into war.[54] But al-Mulqi was wise enough not to invite further Israeli retaliation. He told Furlonge that the army would not act unless "in direct response to Israeli actions" and opted instead for a diplomatic riposte. He invoked British military assistance under the Anglo-Jordanian treaty[55] and called in the American and French envoys to invoke the 1950 Tripartite Declaration as well.[56] While Jordan awaited the response of the Tripartite signatories, its cabinet invited the Arab League Political Committee to meet in emergency session in Amman to discuss ways to bolster frontier security. Qibya was already a political, not just a military event, and al-Mulqi's strategy was to deflect attention from his government's apparent inadequacies to the hollow commitments of its Western and Arab allies. As one American diplomat caustically noted, al-Mulqi's insistence on bringing the Arab delegates to Amman "was motivated by a reason which was pure and simple: the saving of his own skin."[57]

But within hours of the attack on Qibya, the initiative slipped from al-Mulqi to his parliamentary and extraparliamentary opponents. Street demonstrations broke out on both the East and West Bank's on October 16, the day after the Qibya attack. They transcended political affiliation; Muslim Brothers, Ba'thists, and Communists together called for retaliation against Israel and the expulsion of British officers from the Arab Legion. But before long the leftist-nationalists began to monopolize the criticism of Qibya. Ba'thist deputy al-Rimawi arrived at Qibya shortly after a visit by al-Mulqi and started "stirring up" sentiment against the army's failure to intervene. On October 18, about twenty deputies, both East and West Bankers, met in Ramallah, where they argued the merits of court-martialing Glubb and dismissing the army's entire British officer corps. In the end, their inflammatory draft resolutions were significantly diluted, but among those the caucus did approve was a demand for a parliamentary inquiry into the Arab Legion's conduct at Qibya that al-Mulqi was able to circumvent only by authorizing a full-scale ministerial investigation.[58] Eight deputies circulated a statement, censored by the government, alleging that Glubb was in "Jewish pay." Its sentiments were summed up by an unnamed Arab Legion officer quoted by a London newspaper:

> We hate our government for not allowing us to take a gun and go into Israel to shoot Jews. We know that the Government only acts because it is paid money by Britain and America. The money Britain pays might just as well be paid to the Jews because it bribes the Legion not to attack.[59]

Then, on October 21, the day the Arab League Political Committee convened in Amman, a group terming itself the Nablus Committee for a National Arab Conference called for a nationwide strike "as an expression of indignation toward the attitude of the Arab states and their armies." In a display of conciliation the government was soon to regret, it agreed to issue a permit for a "peaceful demonstration." The demonstration turned into a riot; the crowd stoned the French embassy, tried to storm the American cultural center, and pelted a car carrying two visiting American congressmen. The local police had neither the will nor the means to disperse the protesters, and only the deployment of an army battalion finally broke up the mob.[60]

If the rioters' intention was to cow the visiting Arab League delegations into offering more for the Palestinian cause than their usual parlor rhetoric, they were at least partially successful. The Political Committee approved resolutions to supply arms and ammunition to border villages, establish an emergency "defense fund" to respond to future frontier attacks, and rebuild Qibya at the Arab League's expense. In its premier resolution, the committee voted a £2 million contribution to the Jordanian National Guard, in addition, it was said at the time, to the £500,000 promised in September.[61]

For al-Mulqi, the Arab League meeting provided some measure of political relief. First, it removed the danger of royal dismissal. Hussein returned from London hours before the meeting convened and, apparently impressed with his prime minister's ingenuity in convincing the League to meet on short notice, publicly expressed confidence in al-Mulqi.[62] Second, the meeting also deflected, temporarily at least, accusations that al-Mulqi's government had neglected the inter-Arab component of Jordan's defense, especially by failing to elicit financial aid from

Iraq and Saudi Arabia. "Rulers of Jordan must realize," *Falastin* editori-
alized on October 18, "that if they cannot defend the country and the
people, let them not assume power." After the League meeting, al-Mulqi
was finally able to point to the promised National Guard contribution as
tangible evidence of his earnestness in providing for the kingdom's
defense.[63]

Al-Mulqi, however, did not fare as well on the international front.
Initially, the Great Power response was promising. On October 18, the
Tripartite signatories requested an emergency United Nations Security
Council session, and Washington and London together demanded that
"those who are responsible" for the Qibya attack "be brought to account."
As a protest against Israel's raid on Qibya and its construction of water-
works on the upper Jordan River, the Eisenhower administration took
the unusual step of suspending all economic assistance to Israel.[64] Inside
Jordan, though, these events were seen through a clouded lens. The
Security Council's mandate to discuss border security *in general,* rather
than restrict its focus to the Israeli retaliatory raid, was viewed as a way
to dilute the significance of Qibya. Similarly, the suspension of Israel's
economic aid as a punishment for violating UN decisions—coming six
years after the UNSCOP Partition Resolution—was derided as a halfhearted, soon-to-be-forgotten measure.[65]

Having already ruled out military action, however, al-Mulqi had little
choice but to await the outcome of the UN debate. In the meantime, he
was occupied with fending off challenges to his government from both
right and left. Militant nationalists accused the government of backtracking on its liberal program and kowtowing to Britain and America; Abu'l
Huda, his political ambition now revitalized, lent his support to the militants in a tactical alliance geared to bring down al-Mulqi's ministry.

Like his predecessor, al-Mulqi tried to divide the opposition by en-
listing several of its members into the government. Even before Qibya,
he had appointed two men close to Samir al-Rifa'i to Jordan's most
important diplomatic posts: Sulayman al-Nabulsi as ambassador to London and Samir's brother, 'Abd al-Mun'im al-Rifa'i, as ambassador to
Washington. Then, in the weeks following Qibya, he tried to shore up
his government's position by having Sulayman Tuqan named King
Hussein's minister of court and by bringing Hazza' al-Majali into the
cabinet as minister of interior. These moves enabled the prime minister
to muster a majority for the vote of confidence, but just barely and only
after his opponents had gained passage of a resolution condemning his
government's continued use of the Defense Regulations and terming
Jordan's relations "with States called 'Allied'"—that is, Britain—"as un-
natural and calculated to serve the interests of the foreigner." Pressure
from parliament was unrelenting. In mid-October, Abu'l Huda tried to
exploit the post-Qibya hysteria by threatening to expose al-Mulqi's
involvement in secret talks with Israel during his term as defense minister in 1950. Only al-Mulqi's appeal to King Hussein to intercede with

Abu'l Huda kept the item off the upper house's agenda. Then parliament forced al-Mulqi to submit to questioning in secret session as to why he had failed to solicit financial aid from Iraq and Saudi Arabia.

It was at this point that the spectacle of competition for power among Jordan's politicians first soured Hussein on the idea of a limited constitutional monarchy. According to Furlonge, the young king "spoke wistfully of [Syrian leader Adib] Shishakli's success in sending the Syrian politicians packing." For the moment, though, he stood behind his premier.[66]

On November 23, the day before the Security Council was to vote on a Qibya resolution, Israel shrewdly invoked Article XII of the General Armistice Agreement (GAA), and al-Mulqi's diplomatic strategy unraveled. Under that article, the secretary-general was obligated to convene a conference between Jordan and Israel to discuss reviewing, revising, or suspending provisions of the armistice, and most important, Jordan and Israel were obligated to attend. The Security Council had no choice but to defer to the terms of the GAA. Therefore, when UNSC Resolution 101 was adopted on the following day, its "strong censure" of Israeli actions at Qibya was tempered by a demand that both countries "achieve progress by peaceful means toward a lasting settlement." In one swift maneuver, Israel turned the tables on Jordan and upped the political stakes for al-Mulqi. As conceived, the meeting would not constitute a "peace conference" as such, but in the highly charged post-Qibya atmosphere, any public meeting between Jordanian and Israeli representatives would be portrayed in the Arab press as capitulation. Al-Mulqi was faced with two distasteful options: to reject the Article XII conference and thereby invite accusations that Jordan was flouting the GAA and possibly give Israel cause to denounce the armistice altogether; or to attend the conference and thereby provoke intense public protest that Jordan was rewarding Israel's retaliation policy, divide his cabinet, and probably force his own resignation. Al-Mulqi reportedly told the American chargé that he and his cabinet colleagues "feared not only for [the] tenure of [the] present government but also for their lives."[67]

Finding a solution to the Article XII dilemma hounded al-Mulqi for the rest of his ministry. At first, he was inclined to accept the invitation, given assurances that the conference would be held solely "within the framework" of the armistice and that discussions would be limited to technical issues. But after several days, he announced his government's opposition to any meeting with Israel outside the MAC machinery, a position that was later endorsed by the Arab League.[68] Al-Mulqi reportedly bowed to pressure from Foreign Minister al-Khalidi, who threatened to resign, and thereby bring down the government, if the cabinet agreed to attend the conference.[69] Despite prodding from London and Washington and promises from Dag Hammarskjöld to restrict the agenda, al-Mulqi held his ground. He was even willing to court dismissal by refusing King Hussein's requests to accept the invitation, and on at least one occasion, only Furlonge's personal intervention saved the prime minister

from being sacked.[70] A not insignificant factor in al-Mulqi's stand against
the conference was the good publicity it generated among his detractors
in parliament and the press. He exploited a short interlude of popularity
to gain parliamentary passage for several controversial measures (e.g.,
restricting communist activity and approving tight regulations for the
licensing of political parties) and at least to dilute several constitutional
amendments proposed by the al-Rimawi/Na'was group.[71]

In reality, though, al-Mulqi's rejection of the Article XII conference
grew out of political weakness, not from the strength of his nationalist
convictions. He wanted to find a diplomatic means to accept the invitation but lacked the political vigor to persuade his own cabinet, let alone
parliament and informed public opinion. Instead of shaping the "politics of the street" that he had promoted during the early months of his
government, he was reacting to it. In the end, it was that element of
weakness that led to his government's demise anyway.[72]

While al-Mulqi was preoccupied with parliament and his quarrelsome
ministerial colleagues, King Hussein began to "inject himself more and
more into the affairs of state," as one American diplomat put it.[73] In the
process, he added a dimension to the local political calculus that had been
absent since the death of Abdullah.

In the first few months of his reign, Hussein contented himself with
observing the government at work. He received weekly briefings from
his prime minister and pressed his "pet strong opinions" on issues ranging from ways to bolster frontier security to his obsession with striking
oil. Occasionally, he was rankled by the excessive constraints the ministers placed on his personal activities, such as cabinet decisions—emanat-
ing from Whitehall, no less—to prohibit his learning to pilot aircraft and
then to fly solo.[74] But for the most part, the months preceding Qibya
were a learning experience for the young monarch.

After Qibya, when Hussein's public vote of confidence was an important element in keeping al-Mulqi in office, the king became more "a
prime mover than an onlooker" in political matters. He began expressing his views directly to foreign diplomats, without even a minister in
attendance; he started dispensing his opinions in the form of commands,
not advice.[75] Part of his assertiveness might be ascribed to the appointment of a strong personal adviser, Sulayman Tuqan, but it seems to have
resulted mostly from a combination of growing personal confidence and
deepening disillusionment with the political bickering that was consum-
ing Jordan. Hussein was evidently convinced by British and American
arguments that it was in Jordan's best interests to accept the Article XII
invitation and thereby return the onus of diplomatic responsibility to
Israel, and he was particularly annoyed with al-Mulqi's pandering to the
press and his vulnerability to pressure from his ministerial colleagues.[76]
Hussein was similarly incensed that al-Mulqi would permit—or, more
specifically, lacked the power to prevent—parliament from voting amend-

ments to the constitution that had been drafted by opposition deputies and not by the government itself.[77]

Hussein's disillusionment with parliamentary democracy in Jordan was real and deeply felt, but exactly how he envisioned the development of Jordanian institutions (if he envisioned their development at all) was not clear. "Any final picture wasn't in mind," he later said. "We had to go through a process leading to it. And we tried it and we weren't successful, because I believe we tried too quickly."[78] At times, he seemed to wish that parliament would just behave more responsibly (i.e., in a more British way); at other times, he seemed to long for the simplicity of governing Jordan with a strong prime minister and no parliament at all (i.e., more like his grandfather's rule). Meanwhile, he grew increasingly exasperated with al-Mulqi's inability to lead Jordan in either direction.

Hussein reportedly first resolved to sack al-Mulqi over the latter's laissez-faire attitude toward the constitutional amendments. He went so far as to inform Samir al-Rifa'i of his plans and subsequently received a "thorough headwashing" from the queen mother for his "impulsiveness."[79] As mentioned, Furlonge's intercession pulled al-Mulqi back from the brink of dismissal a second time the following month. Despite two clear warnings, the prime minister would not, or perhaps, could not, mend his ways. In May 1954, when al-Mulqi showed himself incapable of reining in Jordan's increasingly obstreperous press, parliament, and even his own ministers, Hussein finally let him go. The fall of the al-Mulqi government had been rumored by several months, but not until Hussein actually fired his prime minister did he establish himself as a force and not just a factor in Jordanian politics. That the protégé would finally sack his mentor was an important turning point in Hussein's own political development.

The origins of al-Mulqi's ultimate fall from grace can be traced to a December 1953 bargain he made with parliamentary deputies whereby he promised to release most of Jordan's remaining political prisoners in exchange for passage of the Law for Combating Communism.[80] Although most of those freed were (by their own admission) Communists, their release provided a fillip to militant oppositionists across the political spectrum: Ba'thists, Qawmiyun al-'Arab, and the like. Soon al-Mulqi's laxity toward the opposition seeped into the cabinet itself. Anwar al-Khatib, for example, who had earlier won plaudits from British and American diplomats, suddenly adopted two planks from the opposition platform, including a threat to forgo all Point IV aid unless Jordan received support in direct proportion to American assistance to Israel.[81] By late March, even Furlonge urged the prime minister to take a harder line against opposition attacks on Glubb and the British CID (Criminal Investigation Division) chief, Sir Patrick Coghill, but he still handled al-Mulqi with kid gloves. "Obviously, we do not want to force the latter out of office on such issues if it can be avoided," he wrote.[82]

Al-Mulqi's strategy—conciliating the opposition while deflecting demands from the palace to clamp down on the opposition's excesses—proved impossible to maintain once the emotional issue of frontier security returned to public prominence following the March 17 attack on an Israeli bus at Scorpion's Pass in the eastern Negev. When the MAC failed to condemn Jordan for the attack, retaliation seemed, at least to the Jordanians, imminent.[83] Inexplicably, Whitehall chose that moment to launch a political initiative to "maintain peace" between Jordan and Israel. The Article XII idea had foundered, according to Minister of State Selwyn Lloyd, because it was too public an arena for the two countries to negotiate in earnest. "If we can get these two together without the other Arab countries," he urged, "I think we might hammer out better arrangements for maintaining peace."[84] Lloyd's proposal was for a private meeting between Jordanian and Israeli representatives under solely British auspices. Al-Mulqi would have nothing to do with Lloyd's plan. Not only did he reject any meeting outside the Arab League, but he also pointedly noted that the very suggestion of a meeting with Israel at a time when Jordan expected an Israeli retaliatory raid could threaten both his government and its relations with London. To al-Mulqi, Britain seemed to be behaving less like an ally than an impartial mediator.[85]

Al-Mulqi's prophecy proved true. Just before midnight on March 28, Israeli troops attacked the West Bank village of Nahhalin. This time, Arab Legion troops reinforced the local National Guard unit and ably defended the village; casualties were kept fairly low.[86] Even though there was little public criticism of the army's response at Nahhalin, government opponents stepped up their rhetoric against the British connection and London's efforts to expand the subsequent Security Council debate from an investigation of individual border incidents to a more general discussion of the armistice. The parliamentary budget debate on March 30, for example, focused almost exclusively on Coghill's tenure as CID chief.[87] Three weeks later, the lower house unanimously voted a resolution thanking the Soviet UN delegate for exercising his veto in support of the Arab position in Security Council debates. Foreign Minister al-Khalidi declared: "A veto by [Soviet delegate Andrei] Vishinsky is worth all the aid of America and Britain." Al-Mulqi reportedly sat "reddened and in angry silence" during the vote praising Vishinsky, but he nevertheless offered his own "appreciation and satisfaction" at Moscow's UN stance.[88]

By then, al-Mulqi was powerless to influence the king, the parliament, the press, or even his own cabinet. His policy, reported the American ambassador, was to "be all things to all people":

> The embassy does not complain so much of the present government in this country as of the absence of government. . . . [T]he present experiment in a free press and democratic government, as we know it, is a failure, and . . . unless early steps are taken to re-establish a strong government, even though unpopular, chaos will eventually develop.[89]

At the end of April, al-Mulqi's position was virtually untenable. He was being harangued by the leftist press and also by a new journal, *al-Nidal*, edited by two Abu'l Huda loyalists, Ahmad al-Tarawneh and Riyadh al-Mifleh, that attacked his government from the conservative right.

Finally, al-Mulqi tried to salvage his position through a last-ditch show of strength. He had come to realize, he told the British embassy, that his progressive policies had resulted in the "increasing abuse of liberty by subversive elements," and so he had decided to change course. He ordered the suspension of three weeklies, two leftist and *al-Nidal*, and then sought a private vote of confidence from Hussein for a plan to dissolve parliament so that he could rule with a "firm hand." By this time, however, the king's patience had run out, and Furlonge was no longer around to plead al-Mulqi's case.[90] When Hussein declined to support his prime minister, al-Mulqi was forced to resign. Even his exit lacked grace; al-Mulqi encouraged press reports suggesting that his resignation was the result of pressure from London to agree to a compromise in the UN debate on Nahhalin, an echo of his earlier prophecy regarding Lloyd's proposed meeting with Israel. He left a diplomatic mess that his successor had to spend the first month in office cleaning up.[91]

Al-Mulqi was his own undoing. Under his ministry, commented one informed observer, "liberty had turned to license."[92] There is no doubt that al-Mulqi was a Hashemite loyalist, for which he was awarded with high posts—foreign minister, defense minister, minister of court—throughout the rest of his career. But never again was he entrusted with the premiership, because al-Mulqi committed the cardinal sin of confusing the means with which he sought to safeguard the Hashemite regime—parliamentary supremacy, constitutional freedoms, allegiance to the Arab League—with the ends in and of themselves. By sacking al-Mulqi, Hussein sought to restore balance to Jordanian politics and, in so doing, displayed signs of a mature understanding of Hashemite fundamentals.

6

Abu'l Huda's
Last Hurrah

Immediately after dismissing al-Mulqi, Hussein appointed Tawfiq Abu'l Huda to form a government once again. It was a move not without its irony. Abu'l Huda was exactly the sort of man Hussein would decry in his autobiography as one of those "rapacious politicians [who] fought for the crumbs of office" after Abdullah's death three years earlier.[1] Only once did Hussein refer in those memoirs to Abu'l Huda by name, and incorrectly, no less; no mention is made of Abu'l Huda's replacement of al-Mulqi in May 1954.[2] But when the young monarch needed a firm hand to restore balance to Jordanian politics, it was to the ten-time prime minister that he turned.[3] Hussein was later to say that after al-Mulqi, he "had to go back to the older generation. I believe," he admitted, "they gave us the chance to continue."[4]

Abu'l Huda's new cabinet was composed entirely of Hashemite loyalists. It was largely a throwback to the days of the regency, with five ministers who had served in Abu'l Huda's previous government and only one, the largely apolitical Anastas Hanania, retained from al-Mulqi's. The most notable addition was Foreign Minister Jamal Tuqan of Nablus, who brought a more supple, moderate, and imaginative mind to his post than did his predecessor. The cabinet's demographic composition was loyal to convention: two Christians, one Circassian, at least one minister representing every geographic division in the kingdom, and what by now had become the ritualistic even split between East and West Bankers.

Again, in terms of strength of personalities, the Palestinians overwhelmed the Transjordanians.[5]

Abu'l Huda's immediate tasks were to restore order and to clean up the diplomatic mess left by al-Mulqi's resignation. Al-Mulqi's legacy greatly complicated both assignments. His permissive attitude toward the strikes, riots, demonstrations, and political activity that had bedeviled the kingdom limited Abu'l Huda's freedom to apply the strong-arm tactics in 1954 that he had so readily employed in 1952. Similarly, by portraying himself as a martyr against British pressure, al-Mulqi tied Abu'l Huda's hands on the Article XII issue and Palestine in general. Abu'l Huda had to find a way to restore confidence in Jordan's British connection without appearing to be any less uncompromising than his predecessor.

Because Abu'l Huda was armed with a well-earned reputation for firmness, he had the freedom to make a generous first approach to his political adversaries, and he early on presented himself as the model of conciliation on domestic matters and of steadfastness on the Palestine issue. Specifically, he reaffirmed al-Mulqi's rejection of the Article XII conference and vowed that "peace with Israel will never be discussed." He also disingenuously endorsed al-Mulqi's progressive reforms, vowed to respect constitutional rights, and promised to follow normal procedure in seeking a parliamentary vote of confidence.[6]

The only promise that Abu'l Huda kept was his commitment not to talk peace with Israel, and it was not long before he moved out from under al-Mulqi's shadow on virtually all other issues. For example, he and his foreign and defense ministers proved themselves much more flexible than their predecessors had been in considering practical, and less publicized, ways t fortify frontier security. As long as an initiative could not even remote'/ be construed as leading to peacemaking, they lent a receptive ear.[7] That was the case on May 23, when Britain's new ambassador to Jordan, Charles Duke,[8] acting on behalf of the Tripartite powers, secretly proposed eleven steps to promote the armistice's border arrangements.[9] In contrast with al-Mulqi's flat rejection of Lloyd's ideas two month's earlier, Foreign Minister Tuqan immediately promised his government's support "for any practical measures to reduce incidents," and with uncharacteristic swiftness, Abu'l Huda brought the matter before the entire cabinet within a week. On June 13, Tuqan told Duke that five of the eleven suggestions had been approved. In fact, the government had endorsed only "those suggestions which require no action by them" and had resisted any proposal that might have required textual modification of the GAA. But what was significant was the government's willingness to consider the Tripartite initiative in a sober, businesslike fashion and, no less important, its success in preventing any leakage of the proposals to the mischievous local press.[10]

Similarly, Abu'l Huda's government ushered in a new era of warm relations with the United States. Al-Khatib's (and al-Farhan's) anti-American posturing largely disappeared; ultimata regarding U.S. aid levels were

forgotten. Just a week after taking office, the cabinet approved an $8 mil-
lion economic aid agreement that had been languishing for two months.[11]

On the domestic front, Abu'l Huda tried to cast a liberal image for
himself and urged Jordanians to "forget the past."[12] Because al-Mulqi
had so graciously suspended the licenses of several opposition journals
before his government collapsed, Abu'l Huda did not have to sully himself with the task. Although he did take steps to prevent street demonstrations by local Communists, the rest of the political spectrum was relatively
free to organize. His ministerial statement reaffirmed his commitment to
"an atmosphere of liberty" and promised reforms of laws governing elections, trade unions, and the Defense Regulations. Given its surprisingly
conciliatory tenor, the prime minister boasted that he expected parliament
to accord him a "thumping vote of confidence."[13]

A large swath of Jordan's politicians, many of whom had languished
in jail under previous Abu'l Huda ministries, were not to be fooled,
however. They decided to take advantage of Abu'l Huda's apparent magnanimity to press forward with the licensing of political parties under the
party law approved by al-Mulqi the previous January. Their goal was to
present the prime minister with a dilemma: He could either agree to the
formation of political parties and thereby institutionalize opposition to
his regime, or he could reject party applications and thereby put the lie
to his progressive protestations.

By mid-June, four parties filed requests for official recognition: the
Nation (Umma) party, which consisted of Samir al-Rifa'i and his circle
of supporters;[14] the unfortunately named National Socialist party (al-Hizb
al-Watani al-Ishtiraki, NSP), a grouping of moderate and well-to-do
government critics;[15] the proto-Communist National Front (al-Jabha
al-Wataniyya), headed by 'Abd al-Rahman Shuqayr;[16] and Jordan's branch
of the Ba'th party (al-Hizb al-'Arabi al-Ba'thi al-Ishtiraki, the Arab
Socialist Renaissance party), whose application listed al-Rimawi as its secretary-general.[17] The first two parties were composed of men who had
once held at least some power and wanted it back; their party manifestos
pledged support for king and country and did not depart much from
existing government policy. In contrast, the latter two parties contained
only dyed-in-the-wool oppositionists and boasted platforms that were blatantly republican and avowedly anti-West. In addition, two Muslim religious groupings entered the political arena: the militant Liberation
(Tahrir) party, founded by Shaykh Taqi' al-Din al-Nabahani, and the more
establishment Muslim Brotherhood.[18]

Although the parties pressed for immediate consideration of their
license applications, Abu'l Huda's strategy was to defer all decisions until
after the parliamentary vote of confidence, when he expected to be in a
stronger position to reject the applications of the leftist parties. The fact
that he did not feel strong enough to dismiss their applications earlier
was taken as a sign of weakness that only emboldened the opposition.
Nevertheless, Abu'l Huda still remained confident that a large majority

of deputies would support his government in the confidence vote, and indeed, the Jerusalem newspaper *al-Difa'* forecast a comfortable twenty-five-to-fifteen margin in the government's favor.[19]

But in the final twenty-four hours before the scheduled vote, frenetic political activity completely altered the political landscape. Technically, the government needed only fourteen votes (one-third plus one) to remain in office; a constitutional amendment passed during al-Mulqi's tenure that raised the requirement to a simple majority was not due to take effect until November 1955. Anything less than a majority, however, would have been a hammer blow to the prime minister's prestige and would have provided a tremendous fillip to the opposition. On the morning of the vote, the government awoke to find itself assured of at most nineteen supporters, one short of a majority. Sometime during the previous day, the twelve National Socialist deputies and the four pro-Rifa'i deputies had met in secret and agreed to a scheme to force Abu'l Huda's resignation and the appointment of a coalition government under Speaker of the House 'Abd al-Halim al-Nimr. When added to the five leftists in parliament, the alliance arrayed against Abu'l Huda could number as many as twenty-one votes.[20]

Even though some deputies showed themselves to be wavering—one reportedly put his vote up for the bargain price of £400—Abu'l Huda was not confident of a majority. Therefore, at a hurriedly convened cabinet meeting, his government decided (as the American embassy reported in high literary style) "that discretion was the better part of valor and that the currently well-organized oppositional movement should be nipped in the bud." Their plan was to dissolve parliament and schedule new elections in four months' time. As early as that first cabinet meeting, the ministers discussed the need for "strong Government backing and discreet pressure in certain electoral areas" to ensure the election of a "considerably more sympathetic" parliament.[21]

Abu'l Huda then presented his plan to the king, the second time in six weeks that a prime minister had asked him to dissolve parliament. The young monarch must have despaired, as al-Mulqi and Abu'l Huda had virtually nothing in common other than their inability to win parliament's confidence, a parliament freely elected in the aftermath of the death of the king's grandfather.[22] At first, the king refused, but an hour later, Abu'l Huda returned to the diwan, this time with Glubb in attendance, and put his own ultimatum to the king: Either dissolve parliament or face the government's resignation. Hussein relented and issued the dissolution decree just three hours before parliament was due to convene. That afternoon, as a precaution against opposition demonstrations, Arab Legionnaires took up positions throughout the city and set up roadblocks on the Allenby Bridge; the day passed quietly.[23] Over the next five days, the cabinet took a series of preemptive decisions to unsettle the opposition further, including rejecting the National Front's and the Ba'th's license applications and issuing suspension orders for four opposition newspapers.[24]

With many of the media cowed into silence, the confrontation between Abu'l Huda and his political opponents focused on the palace itself. Leaders of the moderate opposition, namely, Samir al-Rifa'i and Hazza' al-Majali, lobbied the king to appoint a caretaker government. They wielded a strong argument: One of the constitutional amendments that the king had recently signed into law but that was not due to take effect for a year required the government of the day to resign whenever parliament was dissolved. Although Abu'l Huda was not technically required to step down, they argued, Hussein should be governed by the spirit of the constitution. Moreover, they told Hussein that the kingdom's parties, including their own loyal opposition, were likely to boycott any election in which Abu'l Huda had a controlling hand. The result, they warned ominously, would be anarchy.[25]

The "unfortunate young king," as Duke called Hussein, was subjected to intense pressure from all sides, and evidently it proved too much for him. After receiving an assurance from Glubb that the army could handle all foreseeable domestic disturbances, Hussein departed on July 11 for a month-long European vacation. Al-Rifa'i and al-Majali thought they had won a commitment from Hussein to appoint a caretaker government, but in fact the political situation he left behind was shaky and uncertain. A firm decision on whether Abu'l Huda would still be prime minister come election day awaited the king's return.[26]

Electioneering did not come naturally to Abu'l Huda. An intensely private man, he never once stood for parliament. A sly, cunning political operator, Abu'l Huda practiced his trade in the corridors of government rather than the streets of Amman. For a brief moment, however, Abu'l Huda decided to play the political game. His goal was to disarm and divide the opposition, so as to ensure Hussein's support upon his return from Europe.

On July 7, the cabinet approved licenses for the Nation party and the National Socialists. Although there was nothing objectionable in their platforms, the real reason Abu'l Huda chose not to reject their applications had more to do with politics than constitutional propriety. By legalizing the parties, Abu'l Huda gave their respective leaderships a stake in the October election. After all, if the parties planned to participate in, rather than boycott, the election, their demands for a caretaker government would be sorely weakened. And as al-Majali noted, approving both applications instead of just one guaranteed competition between them.[27] Abu'l Huda then lifted suspensions against the four opposition journals proscribed in June and ordered the release of two opposition leaders, Shafiq al-Rushaydat and 'Abd al-Qadir al-Salih, arrested at the Amman airport for smuggling fifteen thousand antigovernment leaflets in from Beirut. (The leaflets were, of course, confiscated.)[28]

These high-profile moves were designed to lower the opposition's guard. Less publicized were some personnel changes by which Abu'l

Huda moved his loyalists into key positions from which to control the elections. Most notable among these was the appointment of Sa'ad Jum'a, a Kurd and future prime minister, as undersecretary of interior. Having served as private secretary to four successive prime ministers, Jum'a was the political insider par excellence, and he fervently supported Abu'l Huda's election plan to ensure the defeat of opposition candidates. When al-Rifa'i learned of the appointment, he feared that his supporters would bear the brunt of Jum'a's machinations no less than the Ba'thists and Communists would and so appealed directly to the king while the latter was still in Britain. Hussein, unable to escape local politics even on vacation, sent Abu'l Huda a telegram from London ordering a freeze on all personnel changes until his return. Abu'l Huda, in turn, was livid. That the neophyte monarch would interfere with the day-to-day administration of government from thousands of miles away was particularly galling. Abu'l Huda let it be known to all within earshot that he planned a "showdown" with Hussein when he returned from Europe like the one that forced the king to agree to parliament's dissolution: Either give Abu'l Huda a free hand to conduct the elections as he sees fit or find a new prime minister.[29]

Immediately upon Hussein's return on August 8, partisans of the various political trends descended on the palace to plead their case. A delegation of Samir al-Rifa'i, Fawzi al-Mulqi, and Sa'id al-Mufti was deputized by the Nation and National Socialist parties to lobby for the appointment of a caretaker government under al-Mufti to supervise the elections; Hussein temporized. At the same time, the NSP/Nation opposition prepared a backup plan should Hussein reject their pleas. They approached Abu'l Huda with an offer to drop demands for his resignation in return for the appointment of six of their number to cabinet portfolios. The prime minister countered with an offer to accept two, and then four, of the opposition nominees, but he refused their demand for six, which would have given the NSP/Nation alliance a cabinet majority. The delegation again petitioned the king, this time armed with the argument that Abu'l Huda was too greedy for power to accept a coalition cabinet. Finally, on August 16, Abu'l Huda had his "showdown" with the king. Something—perhaps counsel from the British ambassador, perhaps advice from the queen mother—convinced Hussein that he needed Abu'l Huda's strong hand more than the combined talents of the loyalist opposition alliance, and accordingly, he guaranteed Abu'l Huda the palace's full support.[30]

Armed with the royal carte blanche, Abu'l Huda reverted to form. On August 18, he issued three new Defense Regulations empowering the government to cancel newspaper licenses without the necessity of showing cause (DR 3), to dissolve political parties (DR 4), and to prohibit political assemblies (DR 5). The cabinet immediately invoked its new powers to suspend six opposition journals, including the four whose suspensions it had just recently lifted. "The Prime Minister," noted

American ambassador Lester Mallory, Green's astute and highly regarded successor, "is for the time being firmly in the saddle and riding with tight rein."[31]

During the run-up to the October 16 election, Abu'l Huda further tightened his grip on the opposition. For example, he gave district governors wide latitude to ban any open meetings deemed not in the public interest and warned teachers in government schools against politicking in the classroom. In addition, the Interior Ministry greatly inflated the numbers of registered voters in the kingdom, giving the government a sophisticated way to manipulate the elections should the need arise.[32]

Most worrying to the opposition was the army's role in the elections. Abu'l Huda won Glubb's agreement on a plan to instruct soldiers of the Arab Legion how to cast ballots for government candidates, to have soldiers vote inside their own army camps and not in regular polling booths, and, if necessary, to redeploy army units on election day to constituencies where the opposition stood a chance of winning. Such a move was designed not only to intimidate the electorate but also to permit the government to add army votes to the local ballot box. When one British officer asked local election officials what he should do about men on leave, he was reportedly told that he (the Briton) should himself cast a vote for each man absent. In the estimation of the American embassy, the army vote was "the [government's] most decisive instrument of direct control [in the elections]."[33]

For the loyalist opposition, the most pressing question was whether to take part in the election at all. When they had lobbied the king for a caretaker government during the summer, al-Rifa'i, al-Mufti, and al-Nabulsi had warned of an electoral boycott, but their bluff was called. In the end, the Nation and National Socialist party leaderships reached a face-saving compromise: Party members were to participate in the election on an individual, not a party, basis. In most constituencies, the two parties failed to reach agreement on combined slates that would have maximized their joint electoral strength.[34]

Meanwhile, the militant opposition campaigned vigorously. Candidates of both the National Front and Ba'th waged strong campaigns in Amman, Irbid, Salt, and throughout the West Bank. But like the loyalist opposition, the leftist parties could not agree on an electoral alliance, with the result that their candidates sometimes split the antigovernment vote between them. In total, 117 candidates vied for parliament's 40 seats.[35]

Until election day itself, it was not clear whether the government would target only leftist candidates or moderates and leftists alike. Election-day violence quickly overshadowed that question. The vote went awry almost as soon as the polls opened, as riots broke out in all the kingdom's major cities. In Amman, a mob attacked the American cultural center and stoned police and Arab Legion troops; for the first time in Jordan's history, soldiers opened fire on civilians, killing three. Disturbances continued for the following two days, reaching their peak on October 18. That day, a crowd of about 1,000 Ramallah students—National Front candidate Qadri Tuqan was headmaster of a Ramallah college—attacked an American Quaker school and set fire to the British Council reading room, and before they were overwhelmed, the building guards shot and killed one protester. By the end of the day, most of the country was under curfew, and many of the Ba'th and National Front leaders were in detention; even Sulayman al-Nabulsi, Anwar al-Khatib, and 'Akif al-Fa'iz, scion of the one of the kingdom's leading tribal families, were placed under house arrest. In most trouble spots, army troops took over from undermanned and overwhelmed local police. All told, at least 15 people were killed, more than 150 wounded, and, in Amman alone, 165 arrested during the three days of violence.[36]

The disturbances, it seems, were neither wholly premeditated nor completely spontaneous. The fact that the American cultural center was located directly across the street from the home of a Ba'th central committee member, from which protesters emerged to attack the building, was certainly not propitious. (Also, perhaps the Americans proved a less fearsome target than the more locally influential British, who, after all, still held sway over the Arab Legion.) There were several incidents in which government forces allegedly turned a blind eye to violence among opposition partisans and between opposition loyalists and progovernment thugs. When kinsmen of Sulayman al-Nabulsi and Sa'id al-Mufti were roughed up as policemen stood idly by, the two withdrew from the elections and fired off protest telegrams to the king and the prime minister. Turning electoral defeat into virtue, Ba'thist and National Front candidates withdrew in protest as well.[37]

What had evidently prompted the violence was the prospect of a near clean sweep for the government. By the time the ballots were counted, it was clear that Abu'l Huda's supporters had garnered an overwhelming majority of votes and could count on at least twenty-eight and perhaps as many as thirty-four seats in the new parliament. All seven cabinet ministers on the ballot won; progovernment candidates swept all seats in Amman, Salt, and Jerusalem, with opposition candidates winning only ultranationalist Nablus. As it turned out, the moderate and the radical opposition both fared miserably. The Nation party and the National Socialists each took two seats; the National Front and the Liberation party, one each. The Ba'th's withdrawal meant that Abu'l Huda was finally rid of "the two Abdullahs," ex-Deputies al-Rimawi and Na'was. In sum, if Abu'l Huda had set out to remake parliament in his image, he had succeeded.[38]

Indeed, fears quickly arose that Abu'l Huda may have "overdone" it. As Duke reported, the progovernment candidates "triumphed completely and in the completeness of the triumph have become a target for the accusations that the results were manifestly rigged."[39] For example, thanks to four thousand Arab Legion votes in Jerusalem, Defense Minister Nusaybah trounced his archrival Anwar al-Khatib (who had previously beaten Nusaybah handily) by a margin of nearly four to one.[40] Indeed, the magnitude of the government landslide caught observers by surprise. Duke, for example, protested that he had been told that though the government would not permit leftists to win, the rest of "the elections would be free." That was manifestly not the case. "There is no doubt in my mind," he wrote, "that this did not happen and that administrative interference was blatantly used to keep out independent or opposition candidates who could not in any way be suspected of communist or Ba'thi sympathies." Perhaps in a graver indictment of Abu'l Huda's handling of the vote, Duke reported that "the manipulation of the election was carried out extremely clumsily."[41]

Finesse, though, had never been one of Abu'l Huda's hallmarks. He never once evinced any second thoughts about having bulldozed loyalist and militant opposition alike; it simply was not his style. The morning after the last riots were quelled, he told Duke he was "satisfied with the result . . . and full of confidence."[42]

In the immediate aftermath of the election, numerous politicians appealed to the palace not to reappoint Abu'l Huda as premier. By then, of course, it was too late. In order to keep Abu'l Huda at the helm, Hussein had already dismissed parliament and rejected pleas for a caretaker government. Now that the prime minister had done what he set out to do—that is, produce a "completely subservient" parliament—it made little sense to sack him.[43] The king, however, was sensitive to the fact that the election had either alienated or discredited virtually all prospective successors to Abu'l Huda. Sa'id al-Mufti and Fawzi al-Mulqi let it be known that they rejected the new parliament's legitimacy and would never request from it a vote of confidence. Samir al-Rifa'i was so embarrassed by his party's abysmal electoral showing that his Nation party soon disbanded itself, and he never again forayed into electoral politics.[44] But the galaxy of Hashemite loyalists of prime ministerial stature was not wide enough for Hussein to let their disaffection fester for long. He, therefore, urged Abu'l Huda to form a coalition government.

At first, it looked as though he might be successful. At the king's personal request, al-Mufti agreed to join the cabinet if al-Mulqi plus Hazza' al-Majali and Hikmat al-Masri, the two successful NSP candidates, were appointed as well; Hussein, and Abu'l Huda, accepted. But then the plan unraveled. According to al-Majali's account, the weak link was al-Masri, who withdrew in the face of adverse reaction from his Nablus constituency. Then al-Mufti reportedly demanded new elections as his price for joining the government, and when Abu'l Huda refused, al-Mufti pulled out of the deal, taking Fawzi al-Mulqi with him. In the end, al-Majali was the only opposition deputy to accept a ministerial portfolio.[45] The cabinet that Abu'l Huda eventually patched together on October 24 was a coalition government, of sorts. In addition to al-Majali, it included as its foreign minister the former prosecutor-general Walid Salah, an al-Rifaʿi supporter, as well as one of the few independent candidates to outpoll a progovernment nominee, Dhayfullah al-Hmoud of Irbid. Six of the ministers, though, were holdovers from Abu'l Huda's previous government.[46]

Before long, even Abu'l Huda recognized that his manipulation of the vote could backfire against him. What was particularly stinging were allegations, confirmed by the army's role in the elections, that he was being maintained in power solely at the behest of British interests. On October 27, forty of Jordan's leading politicians petitioned the king, charging Abu'l Huda with "falsifying the will of the people" and "creating an armed terroristic atmosphere during the elections." The second charge, with its implicit condemnation of the Arab Legion and Abu'l Huda's reliance on it for his election triumph, rankled more than the first.[47] Throughout his public life, Abu'l Huda had tried to avoid being identified with Jordan's British connection, but ironically, on the morrow of what might have been his greatest political achievement, he was tagged with a pro-British label. In the atmosphere then prevailing in Jordan, when virtually all parliamentary candidates campaigned on platforms of greater Arab self-reliance, being pro-British was only marginally less damnable than being stamped soft on Israel. To correct that impression and thereby defuse the last remaining impediment to his rule, Abu'l Huda presented a ministerial statement to parliament on November 7 in which he announced his intention to seek the revision of the Anglo-Jordanian treaty. It was one of the most impetuous decisions of his long career, and in the end, it proved to be his undoing.[48]

Treaty revision had been a banner under which Jordanians of various political stripes had marched almost since the revised text of the treaty had been worked out between Abu'l Huda and Ernest Bevin in 1948.[49] Various aspects of the treaty were considered to be galling to Jordan's national pride, including the base rights awarded to Britain in Amman and Mafraq and the complete reliance on Britain for financing the Arab Legion. Perhaps most insulting was something that did not even appear in the treaty text at all but grew out of obscure wording in a letter of understanding between the signatories annexed to the treaty. This was the arrangement in which the British subsidy was paid not to the Jordan government but to an Arab Legion account in London under Glubb's control.[50] By circumventing the Jordan's own exchequer, Whitehall believed that it had ensured the accurate accounting and proper disbursement of the subsidy, that is, less graft and theft. London consistently rejected any suggestion that the procedure might have been an affront to Jordanian sensibilities and therefore deserved to be modified. The most it would concede was a *pro forma* consultation process. As one War Office official explained: "[Glubb] is really an eighteenth century colonel given a lump sum to raise a regiment. He is an efficient colonel of his time and in our view the effectiveness of the Arab Legion depends very largely on his control remaining impaired."[51]

The immediate background to Abu'l Huda's revision declaration takes as its starting point the Israeli retaliatory raids in the Jerusalem area in early July 1954. At the time, Jordan had invoked the Anglo-Jordanian treaty as a deterrent against Israel, but the strength of that deterrent was called into question by the signing of the Anglo-Egyptian Heads of Agreement later that month. Both London and Amman recognized the difficulty of Britain's fulfilling its treaty commitments once its troops withdrew from the Canal Zone.[52] At the same time, though, it would have been unseemly for Amman to accept the redeployment of British forces inside the kingdom so soon after Egypt had just succeeded in its long crusade to get rid of them. One possible solution, Abu'l Huda told Duke, was to change the treaty's terms of reference so as to make the idea of an eventual expansion of British armor and troop levels inside Jordan more palatable to local public opinion.[53] It was in this context that King Hussein evidently introduced the idea of treaty revision to Selwyn Lloyd during his summer vacation in London.[54]

In September 1954, rumors first began to swirl around Amman that the government was considering raising the issue of treaty revision with London. As the election campaign began to heat up, Abu'l Huda broached the topic with Duke directly, saying he expected to travel to London before the year's end to discuss treaty revision face to face with the Foreign Office. Jordan had to keep in step with the new developments in the region, he said, including the initialing of the Anglo-Egyptian Heads of Agreement and the prospective replacement of the Anglo-Iraqi treaty with a special bilateral agreement. But he went on to say (as Duke reported), that treaty "modification might be of form rather than of substance." Through it all, the prime minister refused to assume personal responsibility for the initiative, reminding Duke that it was King Hussein who had first spoken about the matter with Selwyn Lloyd. Similar approaches to Duke were made by Defense Minister Nusaybah and, interestingly, Sulayman al-Nabulsi. Both evidently advocated what Duke called "form over substance," suggesting that the Arab Legion subsidy be paid directly to the Jordan government in the form of rent for the use of bases at Amman and Mafraq. These conversations left Duke with the gnawing feeling that the Jordanians had little idea what they really wanted out of a treaty revision, other than the political kudos of having achieved it.[55]

Abu'l Huda did not bring up the issue again until after the October election. In the interim, the army had played its prominent part in manipulating the vote, and Abu'l Huda wanted to put some distance between himself and the British connection. On October 30, the prime minister told Duke that Hussein would be spending Christmas in Europe and would like to discuss treaty revision with the relevant British ministers. The king, he went on to say, "was personally interested in" treaty revision and was "anxious to discuss it with [Eden himself]." For his part, Abu'l Huda stated that he would merely accompany the king. Once again, Duke disparaged Abu'l Huda's intentions, noting caustically that he believed Abu'l Huda was only "anxious to obtain a reasonable excuse for the king and himself to visit London."[56] Duke's instructions were to stall the Jordanians. He told Abu'l Huda that it was not possible to review the entire treaty relationship in a short, hastily prepared visit. The truth was that after Egypt and Iraq, Eden had no stomach for a third round of treaty negotiations; "I plan to have a break . . . which neither kings nor princes shall disturb," he wrote in a margin note. But before Duke could warn Abu'l Huda against any "premature" action, the prime minister publicly declared his intention to seek revision, and it was thenceforth formally on the political agenda.[57]

Abu'l Huda made treaty revision the featured plank of his government's policy. To cover his tracks, he made sure to highlight the king's role in the initiative:

> [The government is] considering the fact that what is extended to us in the form of a subsidy or a grant-in-aid represents nothing more but a payment in return for privileges enjoyed by the friendly or allied State. We wish to declare our thanks for this are due to His Majesty the King who took the opportunity of his journey last summer to express the desire to discuss the matter. His Majesty's wish received a ready response. Discussions may start shortly. The Government wishes to announce and confirm that, if these discussions take place, she will not accept anything which fails to serve the interests of the country and the aspirations of its citizens.[58]

It was a rare attempt by Abu'l Huda at diplomatic brinkmanship. By describing the subsidy as "nothing more" than rent, by stating that Whitehall had given a "ready response" to whatever Hussein may have said about revision, and by saying up front that he would brook no compromise, Abu'l Huda left himself little room for maneuver. When this policy received an overwhelming vote of confidence, thirty-five to three, there was no turning back.[59]

Abu'l Huda evidently thought he held a strong bargaining position. Internationally Britain had already renegotiated its ties with two of Jordan's neighbors and therefore, he believed, was most likely expecting Jordan to request the same; domestically, Britain had acquiesced in (or perhaps even counseled) the dissolution of the old parliament and the electoral manipulation of the new one. If ever there was a time to revise the treaty with the least amount of concession from Britain and the greatest amount of benefit to Britain's friends in Jordan, it would be in the opening months of the new parliament.

If that indeed was Abu'l Huda's thinking, he sorely misread British intentions. Precisely *because* Britain had loosened its ties with Egypt and Iraq, it was in no mood to give ground in Jordan, too. Whitehall already felt that it "gave more than it got" from Amman, and the bullheaded

way in which Abu'l Huda demanded revision only fueled London's
indignation. If all the Jordanians had in mind was a one-sided exchange
to salve Jordan's nationalist consciences, the British government would
be unyielding. "For once," minuted Ivone Kirkpatrick, "I feel we may
have the whip in dealing with an Arab State."[60]

Abu'l Huda, King Hussein, Anwar Nusaybah, Chief of Diwan Bahjat
al-Talhuni, and a handful of Arab Legion officers left for London in the
second week of December. Formal talks opened on December 21, with
Minister of State Anthony Nutting heading the British delegation.
Hussein, in fact, took no part in the actual discussions, leaving that task
to his prime minister. He and Abu'l Huda had one uneventful meeting
with Winston Churchill on December 22.

From the moment the first session began, Abu'l Huda was in
trouble.[61] He began by backtracking from previous public statements,
admitting that Selwyn Lloyd had not, in fact, given a "ready response"
to Hussein's summertime suggestion to discuss revision but had only
"given the impression that Her Majesty's Government would consider
the question." Then he quickly stated that he had not come to London
to discuss revision at all. "The matter was not particularly pressing," he
told Nutting. The real reason he had sought this meeting, he said, was
to deal with "two more urgent questions": paying the Arab Legion subsidy directly to the Jordan government and strengthening the National
Guard.[62]

Abu'l Huda's opening statement showed that the Jordanians lacked
any real bargaining advantage. They might have come to London in what
one of Hussein's biographers called "a suitably pugnacious mood," but
the talks quickly degenerated from negotiation into supplication.[63] Nutting immediately sensed his interlocutor's basic weakness and exploited
it. He first reconfirmed for the record that treaty revision was not to be
on the agenda. Then he outlined his government's policy on the two
items that Abu'l Huda did want to discuss. First, the British government
considered the current procedure for paying the subsidy as "convenient
administratively" and would not be changed. Second, Nutting said there
was no more money available for the National Guard. Case closed. Twist-
ing the knife a bit more, he pressed Abu'l Huda for a decision on the
requested move of the British armored regiment to north Jordan. Abu'l
Huda meekly replied that though the proposal needed more study, he
did not think it would present "any difficulty." Then, because Nutting
had gotten much of what he wanted—and Abu'l Huda none of what he
wanted—Nutting closed the meeting on a more conciliatory note. The
British government, he said, would study the idea of converting a por-
tion of the subsidy into rent.

If Abu'l Huda saw a glimmer of hope, it was extinguished when the
second session of talks opened the following afternoon. The question of
rent, Nutting said, had been studied and found wanting.[64] Not only was

the subsidy "out of all proportion" to the value of potential rent for British bases, but also, he added, the payment of such rent would create a "very difficult precedent" for London. The meeting ended with Nutting's reaffirming the British government's refusal to increase National Guard funding.

Eden attended the talks' final session, December 23, as much to mollify the bruised egos of the Jordanian delegation as anything else. By this time, a disconsolate Abu'l Huda would search vainly for something he could take back to Amman as a victory. Instead, he ended up giving Eden an unexpected bonus. When Eden expressed the wish that a full-fledged treaty revision might be possible after "the development of general Middle East defence arrangements," Abu'l Huda interjected to say that he hoped that Jordan "would not be left out" of any regional defense plan that might be drawn up, a promise that Eden graciously and happily pocketed. In return, though, he held out no more concessions than Nutting had. As a final effort, Abu'l Huda left behind an aide-mémoire outlining his previous proposals, in the hope that with the passage of time, Eden might soften enough to allow him to save face at home.[65]

The London talks were Abu'l Huda's Qibya. A foreign power—in this case, allied Britain instead of enemy Israel—proved the Jordanian leadership impotent to defend its national integrity. Abu'l Huda showed himself to be a pitiable negotiator; he thoroughly miscalculated British intentions, and he dared to play high-stakes poker without a single trump card in his hand. What made his London performance even more mortifying was that he had billed himself as the man who guaranteed success. If, as a Whitehall official remarked, Abu'l Huda was "concerned to demonstrate that he is not a British puppet," his plan failed miserably.[66] By forcing the subsidy issue when he had no leverage over Britain, Abu'l Huda sacrificed in one swift maneuver much of the political gain he had accumulated over the previous six months.

Understandably, Abu'l Huda was in no hurry to face the local political scene in Amman. When he arrived in Jordan, he came down with one of his periodic bouts of "political" illness and, after a few days, left for Beirut. In the meantime, rumors were rampant that Hussein was embarrassed by Abu'l Huda's performance in Britain and would soon ask for his resignation. A press leak from the minutes of the London talks suggesting that Abu'l Huda had pleaded with Eden for some sort of political gesture to save his political career was seized as a sign of his tenuous hold on the job. According to al-Majali, Abu'l Huda was "furious" that Britain let him down.[67]

Until Abu'l Huda received Whitehall's response to his aide-mémoire in early February, he hoped against hope for a change of Eden's heart. In the meantime, he refused to respond to Britain's request for a decision to redeploy the armored regiment. In the end, Britain did offer Jordan a five-year, £1.75 million aid package for the National Guard, in the belief that it would ensure acceptance of the tank redeployment, but

Abu'l Huda refused to budge. Redeployment, he knew, was his only leverage, yet even that proved lacking.[68] When he finally received the British government's rejection of the aide-mémoire, Abu'l Huda's bubble burst. Nevertheless, he gamely put as bright a gloss on his disappointment as was possible. The Jordanian delegation, he explained in a press statement, had won both extra support for the National Guard and London's agreement to discuss treaty revision once the Anglo-Iraqi treaty issue was settled. He added, with more than a hint of guile, that London's reply had not been decisive, when it was, in fact, crystal clear. During the five remaining months of his ministry, Abu'l Huda never did give a definite yes or no answer to Whitehall's repeated requests regarding the tank move, and the treaty's deterrent posture remained unchanged.[69]

On February 24, 1955, Iraq and Turkey signed a mutual defense treaty that was to become the Baghdad Pact. It marked the beginning of a fateful year in which the Arab League would be polarized into competing camps, Egypt would shock the West by turning to Moscow for military aid; large-scale *fedayeen* and retaliatory raids would dramatically raise tensions along the Arab–Israeli frontier; and the Hashemite kingdom itself would be stricken with political turmoil that would, in Hussein's words, "all but split Jordan in two." It was a year in which international and regional politics dwarfed domestic affairs, a year in which little Jordan would show itself vulnerable to the spread of infectious ideologies and competing visions of military alignments.[70]

After his disastrous performance in London, the political challenge posed by the Baghdad Pact in particular and the new internationalist age of Arab politics in general were too much for Abu'l Huda. He, it must be remembered, had already been scored by nationalists for his role in negotiating the 1948 Anglo-Jordanian treaty and the 1949 General Armistice Agreement. To the public, the 1954 London talks confirmed his deficiency as a diplomat. His strength was as an administrator or, perhaps, as a conservator of the Hashemite regime, but 1955 was a year of "taking sides" in the Arab world, and that sort of polarization ran against the grain of his political philosophy. Just seven weeks after Britain's April 1955 accession to the Iraqi–Turco Pact, Abu'l Huda left the prime ministry for the final time.

Abu'l Huda was still in Lebanon when Iraq and Turkey announced their intention to sign a mutual defense treaty, and he was hastily summoned back to Amman by his agitated cabinet colleagues. According to al-Majali, the cabinet eventually agreed to take a "moderate" line at a special Arab League meeting in Cairo to discuss the pact, namely, that Jordan would side with neither Iraq nor its opponents. That Britain would concede the demands of his longtime antagonist, Nuri al-Sa'id, in renegotiating its treaty with Iraq only added insult to Abu'l Huda's injury, but in public at least, he held his tongue.[71]

Discerning Jordan's true attitude toward the question of its own accession to the pact in early 1955 is difficult; indeed, even defining who spoke for Jordan at that time is not simple. During this period, Hussein grew steadily more confident of himself and his authority to speak out on affairs of state, whereas Abu'l Huda did what he could to minimize the loss of power and prestige that resulted from his London debacle. The influence that he previously wielded over the king was clearly slipping away, and he chose carefully when to exercise what little of it remained. Both men had strong personalities, and during this phase of flux in their relationship, the kingdom no longer spoke with one voice.

At first, it seems, Hussein was "sold on the Egyptian viewpoint" that Iraq's iconoclastic accord with Turkey undercut whatever collective security the Arab League provided on the Arab–Israeli front. He evidently believed that the goal of joint Arab–Western defense, which he supported, would have been best achieved via the Arab League own's machinery. But at the same time, Hussein opposed Cairo's attempt to counter the Iraqis by forming its own Arab military alliance (with Syria and Saudi Arabia) as a move that would only exacerbate inter-Arab tensions.[72] As late as March 2, he reportedly told Duke that Jordan would side with neither Egypt nor Iraq, a neutralist position that the U.S. embassy unsympathetically labeled as "timid."[73]

By mid-March, however, Hussein's attitude changed dramatically. In place of his earlier coolness to the pact was a "ready acceptance and appreciation" of the Western powers' point of view. Specifically, he told Mallory that "Jordan [was] prepared to listen to any request from [the] U.S. to join in agreements," and he wanted to know exactly what military benefits Jordan would stand to gain. Apparently, a visit Hussein made to Pakistan impressed on him the potential military advantages of close alignment with the West. In particular, Mallory seems to have been instrumental in enticing Hussein with ideas of bolstering Jordan's infant air force.[74]

For his part, Abu'l Huda said different things to different people. In early February, he reportedly told the Turkish minister in Amman that he expected other Arab states to join the Baghdad Pact and that Jordan would "certainly not [be] the last."[75] He took a different tack in discussions with the American ambassador, observing that pact membership was superfluous because Jordan's treaties with Britain and Iraq had already rendered "any question [of its] basic orientation academic."[76] When Hussein returned from Pakistan with a lively interest in the pact's military benefits, Abu'l Huda dutifully queried the British and Americans on what Jordan could expect to receive "over and above" the Arab Legion subsidy.[77] He went so far as to tell the Turkish minister that Jordan's eventual accession to the pact was "likely," prompting Mallory to report that "everything considered, very satisfactory progress is being made here on [the] Northern Tier concept."[78] Even then, however, Abu'l Huda's words seemed to have been carefully chosen to lend the impression of a commitment without actually giving one.

Unlike Hussein, Abu'l Huda's main interest throughout seems to have been political, not military. His goal was to play off Britain and American patronage, with an eye toward achieving the elusive prize of treaty revision. As the Iraqi chargé in Amman pointed out, the "chief Jordanian interest" in the pact was only to modify the Anglo-Jordanian treaty "after the Iraqi fashion." Whereas Britain promised modification after Jordan's accession, Abu'l Huda, he said, demanded modification first.[79] Indeed, in words strikingly similar to those he used when the British first pressed for the redeployment of armored units in the summer of 1954, Abu'l Huda told Duke and Mallory that although he personally supported joining the pact, he had a difficult problem with public opinion. Unless there was "manifest advantage"—money and matériel—to show the populace, Jordan would not likely join "for some time to come."[80] It was in that light that Abu'l Huda delivered a statement to a secret session of parliament on March 29 in which he was said to have confirmed his government's neutrality toward Iraq and Egypt.[81]

If Abu'l Huda's true intentions had been to invite Anglo-American competition for Jordan's favor, he was once again far off the mark. He had no inkling that Washington and London did not see eye to eye on the Baghdad Pact and especially on the wisdom of recruiting new Arab members for it. He had no idea that Dulles feared that Eden's efforts to enlarge the pact would undermine Washington's tentative plans at brokering an Egyptian–Israeli peace agreement, known as Project ALPHA.[82] And he did not know that London acquiesced in an American proposal "neither to encourage nor discourage" other Arab states to join the pact while Dulles was engaged in his peacemaking effort.[83]

Once Abu'l Huda did learn that the door to treaty revision had been shut a second time, he lost all interest in the pact and reverted to his natural aversion to "taking sides."[84] But the Great Powers' "hands-off" policy did not stop Iraq from urging accession on its Hashemite cousins in Amman, and in Hussein they found a receptive partner. While spending the 'Id al-Fitr holidays in Sarsank, Hussein was pressed by his hosts to sack Abu'l Huda and appoint a government more agreeable to joining the pact.[85] Prominent Jordanian politicians were courted by Baghdad, too. When a private delegation, led by Sa'id al-Mufti and including such National Socialist luminaries as Sulayman al-Nabulsi and Hikmat al-Masri, attended ceremonies celebrating the handing over of the RAF's Habbaniya air base to Iraq, they delivered a series of financial aid requests to Nuri al-Sa'id. The Iraqi premier reportedly replied with a single sentence: "Not one cent to Jordan so long as Tawfiq Abu'l Huda heads the government." On his return to Jordan, al-Nabulsi spoke privately of his belief that Jordan should join the pact if it could be assured of adequate inducements from its Western and Arab allies.[86]

With such opposition figures giving their (albeit lukewarm) support to Jordan's accession, Abu'l Huda's public neutralism was, to Hussein, an unnecessary irritant. The king, therefore, prepared the ground to dismiss his prime minister. First, he appointed Abu'l Huda's rival, Fawzi al-Mulqi, as minister of court, and then he sided with Hazza' al-Majali in the latter's resignation in protest against Abu'l Huda's high-handed methods.[87] Finally, on May 28, Hussein demanded that Abu'l Huda sack three of his most loyal cabinet supporters—Salah, al-Mifleh, and al-Khayri —and when Abu'l Huda temporized, the king asked him to resign. According to Duke, Hussein's firm stand in dismissing Abu'l Huda "took everyone by surprise."[88]

By the end of May, Abu'l Huda had outlived his usefulness as premier. He had violated his personal philosophy of risk aversion by insisting on the London talks, and when he reverted to his neutralist policy vis-à-vis the Baghdad Pact, Hussein was already of a different mind. Moreover, by May, the king was beginning to display more than a passing restlessness with advisers that belonged more to his grandfather's generation than his own, and it was during this period that Hussein first showed his disgruntlement with Glubb's command of the army and the slow pace of advancement of Arab officers.[89]

The old order in Jordan was clearly changing, and Abu'l Huda had become, in the words of one of Hussein's aides-de-camp at the time, "an ancient dinosaur."[90] That Hussein would force the dismissal of a loyalist prime minister in order to push his own agenda was an unmistakable sign that the balance of power inside the kingdom had shifted from the government back to the palace. Abu'l Huda, who emerged from Abdullah's shadow to epitomize the powerful premier, never again held office and played no role at all during the pivotal Baghdad Pact crisis of winter 1955/56. He died in July 1956.[91]

7

Hussein and
the Baghdad Pact

If Hussein's dismissal of Fawzi al-Mulqi in May 1954 was a sign of political maturity, his dismissal of Tawfiq Abu'l Huda one year later was a sign of political independence. And the way he handled Sa'id al-Mufti's subsequent appointment confirmed that the young king was determined to have the final say in running his country.

Al-Mufti (b. 1898), a Circassian, occupied a special spot in the pantheon of "king's men." His politics, like that of some other ethnic or religious minorities in predominantly Arab Muslim countries, was "more Arab than the Arabs'" in its anti-Zionism. As an independently wealthy landowner, he was seen to be uncharacteristically incorruptible, notwithstanding his Iraqi ties; as one of the first to welcome Abdullah to Amman in 1921, he was viewed as devoutly loyal, despite infrequent disagreements with the amir.[1] Thanks to his generally exemplary personal and political credentials, al-Mufti was often tapped to fill cabinet slots, and he served in eleven different governments from 1929 to 1955. The high esteem in which he was widely held owed, however, more to the virtues he represented than to any particular deeds with which his name was associated. He was, the American embassy reported in 1954, "exceedingly popular, a good hand-shaker," but not industrious, imaginative, or of "real practical value."[2] Al-Mufti had been appointed by Abdullah to his lone previous term as prime minister, in 1950, to exploit his vote-getting ability in that year's elections. When he refused to sully his reputation by negotiating with the Zionists, Abdullah dismissed him eight months later. Although he was still a relatively young man, al-Mufti contented himself in the aftermath of Abdullah's death with the unburdensome status of elder statesman, serving in each of the first four post-Abdullah governments in the figurehead post of deputy premier.[3] Days before his May 1955 appointment, al-Mufti was described as anything but prime minister material. "His health is reported poor," one diplomat noted, "as a result of excesses of alcohol and women."[4]

More than any available politician, though, al-Mufti mixed popular appeal with unswerving loyalty. His firm stance against Abu'l Huda's manipulation of the 1954 elections and in support of Palestinian and Arab rights were popular with most Jordanians. In fact, the impropriety of the 1954 vote was less a political issue for al-Mufti than a matter of personal honor, for as a lifelong Hashemite loyalist, he shared little of the radical nationalist criticism of Jordan's British connection. On the Baghdad Pact, al-Mufti was more pliable than Abu'l Huda. Although he was reticent to support any venture that might be characterized as "anti-Arab" and thereby call into question the loyalties of his fellow Circassians, he certainly did not share Abu'l Huda's antipathy toward Iraq and was receptive to arguments for the pact made by two of his closest friends, Hazza' al-Majali and Farhan al-Shubaylat. Perhaps most important, Hussein opted for al-Mufti—whom he described in his memoirs as "a good man, but old"[5]—because he wanted a premier who would not put up too stiff a challenge to his own growing sense of authority. As events were to show, naming a timid and deferential premier in the place of one who too jealously guarded his powers may have solved one problem for Hussein, but it brought on a host of others.

From the very beginning of al-Mufti's ministry, Hussein was determined to have a greater say in government. He spurned al-Mufti's demand to dissolve parliament and schedule new elections; indeed, Hussein had never been particularly perturbed by the way Abu'l Huda and Glubb handled the 1954 vote.[6] The king also took an active role in vetting cabinet members, and al-Mufti apparently put up little fight when Hussein vetoed several of his preferred choices.[7] Hussein also became involved in parliamentary politics for the first time by meeting with groups of deputies to urge them to support the government, and on August 24, the chamber awarded al-Mufti an overwhelming vote of confidence.[8]

The cabinet that al-Mufti eventually formed was decidedly more East Bank in orientation than were any of its post-1949 predecessors. For the first time since Abdullah's death, a Palestinian did not serve as foreign minister,[9] and a Transjordanian (other than the sitting prime minister) was named defense minister: Farhan al-Shubaylat of Tafileh, the former chief of Abdullah's court who had been implicated in Nayif's plots for the throne four years earlier. Al-Shubaylat and Hazza' al-Majali, minister of the interior, formed a potent pro-Iraqi/pro-British bloc. Of the five Palestinian ministers, only two—'Azmi al-Nashashibi, former chairman of Jordan's MAC delegation, and Na'im 'Abd al-Hadi, a leader of Nablus's anti-Tuqan faction—were politicians of any standing. Perhaps the most popular minister among Palestinians was al-Mufti himself.

Throughout the spring and summer of 1955, Jordan was consumed with the issue that dominated Arab politics: the threat of war between Egypt and Israel. Since February, a series of *fedayeen* raids and Israeli retaliations had radically raised tensions along the Gaza frontier. The regional polarization signaled by the signing of the Turkish–Iraqi (later to be known as the Baghdad) Pact on February 24, Egypt's subsequent condemnation of the alliance, and Britain's own accession to it six weeks later raised the war fever even more. Whereas Abu'l Huda had avoided any entangling Jordanian commitment to Egypt, al-Mufti was far more forthcoming in promising to join in common defense against Israel. Indeed, his dedication to Arab unity helped compensate for the lack of strong Palestinian personalities in his government. As popular sympathy for Egypt swelled throughout Jordan, al-Mufti offered Cairo his complete and unequivocal support: "Jordan would not stand with its hands tied in the face of the repeated attacks carried out by Jewish forces against Gaza," he told the Egyptian chargé d'affaires. Al-Mufti went so far as to intimate that Jordan's solidarity with Egypt outweighed its treaty obligations to Britain. "They are unusually serious," reported American envoy Mallory.[10] Following an Israeli retaliatory raid in Gaza in August, Hussein declared that "the Armistice Line constituted a single defense line." On the same day, al-Mufti announced that Jordan would join other Arab states in providing immediate military assistance to Egypt in the event of war with Israel.[11]

When Egypt stunned the world with its announcement of the "Czech" (in fact, Soviet) arms deal on September 27, Arab nationalist pride and anti-Western ardor reached new heights. In Jordan, banner headlines hailed Egypt's success in breaking the Western stranglehold on the flow of weapons to the Middle East, and the press followed, on almost a daily basis, the progress of Soviet arms to Cairo. Jordan's parliament enthusiastically cabled its congratulations to Egyptian President Gamal Abdel Nasser, and Jordan's ambassador to Egypt went so far as to describe the deal as the "greatest Arab step in decades." Despite his Circassian wariness of all things Russian, even al-Mufti welcomed Nasser's move as a boost to Arab self-defense.[12]

"In an instant," King Hussein later recalled, "everything changed."[13] Egypt's purchase of Soviet arms fundamentally altered the West's understanding of the Communist danger in the Middle East and transformed the Baghdad Pact from a prospective "strategic concept" into a response to an "actual challenge."[14] Inside Jordan, the Czech arms deal rekindled the debate on whether or not to join the anti-Soviet Baghdad Pact.

By September 1955, the issue of Jordan's accession to the pact was on hold. Although he had a lively interest in the pact's potential military benefits, Hussein had witnessed the mutual vilification between Iraq and

Egypt and was not yet convinced that the political costs of accession were worth its military rewards. Al-Mufti, whose family had fled czarist Russia, was certainly sympathetic to fears of Russian intentions. However, after seeing how Iraq's membership had so polarized the Arab world, he shied away from any strong position on the specific question of Jordan's accession.[15] He also lacked his predecessor's obsession with treaty revision that had first prompted Abu'l Huda to consider joining the pact. The combined effect of Hussein's hesitation, al-Mufti's agnosticism, and the Anglo-American agreement "neither to encourage nor discourage" Arab recruits for the pact kept the accession issue off the local political agenda. Abu'l Huda's resignation had removed a large obstacle to Jordan's accession should the time have been ripe, but it was not. Despite the enthusiastic support of several cabinet members, al-Mufti's government did not at any time during its first four months entertain the idea of joining the pact.[16]

Indeed, Hussein showed himself curiously reticent even to discuss the pact. He never once, for example, raised the issue during trips he made to London in June and October 1955. Whitehall thought that the king might want to take the occasion of his June visit, his first since Abu'l Huda's debacle six months earlier, to negotiate the parameters of Jordan's accession,[17] but it was left to Anthony Nutting to broach the subject. Hussein's response was not enthusiastic.

> The King replied that he was trying to avoid getting committed to either of the rival groups in the Arab world. He was trying to use his influence to bring them together. He made it plain that for these reasons an early decision by Jordan to accede to the Pact was unlikely.[18]

The topic did not come up during Hussein's October visit at all. This was particularly strange given that Whitehall knew that Turkey shortly planned to launch an all-out effort to secure Jordan's accession to the pact. Instead, London's agenda for the October talks was strictly mercenary. Its prime "objective" at the time was to exploit Hussein's obsession with building a Jordanian air force "to mop up the money [£250,000]" that the Jordanian parliament had allocated for aircraft, hardly the stuff of Great Power strategic thinking.[19]

The only party that consistently and energetically urged accession on Jordan was Turkey. It was an uphill battle. In March 1955, Ankara presented Amman with a batch of training aircraft as a "no-strings" gift, but not until the Czech arms sale did the Turks finally seem to make any headway. Five days after the deal was made public, Hussein left Amman for a European tour, stopping first to see his father in Istanbul. After talks with Turkey's premier, Adnan Menderes, Hussein left the "impression" of being "much more favourably disposed" to Jordan's "eventual" adherence to the pact than ever before.[20] Encouraged by Hussein's attitude, Ankara tried to convince London and Washington to pursue Jordan's accession more vigorously. For its part, Turkey promised to use all means at its disposal to win over the Jordanians during President Jelal Bayar's state visit to Amman in early November.[21]

Britain and America, however, were far less sanguine than were their Turkish allies. While Hussein was in Europe, Duke reported "no sign of any inclination" by the Jordanians to alter their "neutral attitude towards this pact."[22] An American appraisal of public opinion was even more pessimistic: "There is universal [and] popular Jordanian enthusiasm for [the] flame of Arab political liberation ignited by Nasser's arms deal with Soviet bloc. . . . Government cannot or will not carry through 'unpopular' policies. . . . Mass pressure now so sways [the] Amman authorities [that] they fear mob action if [the] government tried to move against current Arab thinking."[23] Greatly moved by Mallory's gloomy report, Washington expressed little optimism that Bayar's visit might end in success and did little to promote it. The most that Secretary of State John Foster Dulles would do was to instruct diplomats to "not advise Jordan not to accede" to the pact.[24]

Meanwhile, all other parties stepped up their own activity in anticipation of Bayar's visit. Egyptian radio and media heaped abuse on Turkey, Iraq, and Britain and warned Jordan to stay away from the "imperialist" Baghdad Pact. On a more clandestine level, Glubb reported that Egyptian diplomats and agents actively courted Arab Legion officers and Jerusalem editors to oppose accession.[25] Saudi Arabia, for its part, relied on its traditional conduits to power in Jordan and hosted visits by Hussein, Sharif Nasser, and—more secretly—Queen Zayn to discuss the regional situation firsthand with the Saudi leadership. The Saudis' tactic was to distance themselves from Cairo's meddling in Jordan's internal affairs while still cautioning their guests against joining the Baghdad Pact. To warm up a relationship that had cooled markedly over the previous six months,[26] the Saudis passed to the Jordanians some information regarding Egyptian infiltration in the Arab Legion and offered some derogatory remarks about Nasser.[27]

Even the Russians took steps to win over the Jordanians. During his European tour in October, Hussein was contacted by Soviet diplomats in Paris and offered economic and military assistance. The king neither gave the Soviets a firm response nor mentioned the proposal to his British allies.[28] Two weeks later, the Soviet ambassador in Cairo approached his Jordanian counterpart with a less contentious offer to exchange diplomatic representation. Again, the offer was not rejected, but the British embassy in Cairo was informed of the contact.[29] It remains unclear whether the Jordanians, and particularly Hussein, were actively engaged in brinkmanship, playing East and West off against each other, or whether they just found themselves overwhelmed by a high-stakes diplomatic game with which they had little experience.

Inside Jordan, al-Mufti's government adopted a wait-and-see attitude toward the Turkish visit, and its tentative policy was reflected in the contradictory signals emitted by the local media. On successive days, for example, a normally royalist newspaper ran banner headlines announcing Russia's "Readiness to Supply the Arabs with Weapons and Economic Assistance" and the arrival of "Planes and Other New Weapons from Britain to Iraq."[30] Of the small number of popular figures backing Jordan's membership in the Baghdad Pact, virtually none was confident enough to base his support on the pact's anticommunist rationale. Instead, these supporters had to argue that pact membership would strengthen Jordan in its confrontation against Israel. With even partisans of the pact focusing on the Arab–Israeli, not the East–West, conflict, pact opponents had a clear field in shaping public opinion.

On November 2, Turkish President Bayar and Foreign Minister Fatin Zorlu arrived in Jordan to a "sullen" and "uneasy" reception. Despite a police roundup of what the British embassy termed "all the well-known trouble makers who could be found," a commercial strike went ahead as planned, and virtually the only Jordanians visible on Amman's streets were Arab Legion troops. Over the previous few days, anti-Turkish leaflets had been distributed throughout the kingdom by such groups as the Muslim Brotherhood, the Communists, and a shadowy organization calling itself the League of the Officers' Struggle, which Glubb believed was an Egyptian front. "Return to your country, o' Jelal Bayar," proclaimed the brotherhood's leaflet. "You will not find in Jordan a single man who agrees to put his hand in yours or to link his fate with yours." The government ordered local newspapers to welcome Bayar's visit, but their expressions of greetings were at best lukewarm.[31]

Nonplussed by the hostile reception, the Turks thrust themselves headlong into the task of convincing their hosts to join the Baghdad Pact. Their goal was to persuade Hussein to sign on to the pact before the end of their visit,[32] and their strategy was to hammer away at Jordan's anxieties about joining the pact, one by one. Turkey's close ties with Israel were a thing of the past, they vowed, and pact membership would secure Ankara as an "on the spot" ally against Israeli aggression.[33] Similarly, Jordan should not fear Syrian retaliation if it joined the pact, because, they promised, Turkey "could take action which would be crippling" to Damascus. Finally, the Turks reiterated their most persuasive argument, that only by adhering to the pact could Jordan convince Britain to revise the treaty and win unprecedented levels of military aid.[34]

Although they were impressed with the Turks' arguments, the Jordanians realized that Britain was the key to arms and treaty revision. Therefore, Duke should not have been surprised to be asked in the midst of the Bayar talks for a clear enunciation of the British government's position regarding Jordan's adherence to the pact. But instead of taking a strong line, as the Turks urged, London hesitated. Duke was instructed that "it would be wise to leave things and not to initiate further pressure on the Jordanians."[35]

Ironically, the source of British indecision was Prime Minister

Anthony Eden himself. "I am somewhat apprehensive that the effect on Egypt of Jordan joining *at this time* might be unfortunate," Eden minuted on November 6. "On the other hand Jordan's membership of the Pact might make the Egyptians hesitate to react violently." It was left to an assistant undersecretary, Evelyn Shuckburgh, to forge policy on this important issue. "I see no reason why we should invite for ourselves a share in Turkish unpopularity," Shuckburgh urged his superiors. "In particular, our aid to the Jordan Air Force and in other respects should not be made conditional on their joining the Baghdad Pact, at any rate not until the Americans are prepared to join it." That was the gist of the policy directive later telegraphed to Duke.[36]

Bayar and Zorlu left Amman on November 8 without having won Jordan's immediate accession, but their importuning had not been for naught. The Jordanians, they believed, were convinced that they "would like to join the Pact but are now trying to obtain the maximum benefit from doing so." The sort of military demands Amman was contemplating—including a threefold increase in ground forces and a "corresponding" expansion of the air force—were clearly "unrealistic," Zorlu admitted, but "it would probably turn the balance" if Britain could make an "immediate offer of some substantial amount of equipment and some expansion of the Legion if they joined the Pact." Glubb seconded Zorlu's suggestion and emphasized that "time," not substance, "was of the essence." Glubb termed Hussein's ideas for the Legion's expansion "a bribe for his consent" to join the pact.[37] The cogency of this advice was confirmed later the same day, when Sa'id al-Mufti informed Duke, with uncharacteristic resolve, that he would soon be wanting "to talk business." The following day, Hussein himself told Duke that Jordan "was ready to join the Baghdad Pact now," provided that it received "the necessary backing."[38]

In less than forty-eight hours, Britain's "leave things" policy had become outdated. The pace of events so outstripped the pace of British policymaking that London could no longer afford a passive attitude toward Jordan's accession. Duke, for one, virtually begged Whitehall to move quickly. "I am convinced that we must act very soon if we are to do any good," he pleaded. "Even a few days might make all the difference." Specifically, Duke believed that a speedy commitment of more military aid, including the prompt supply of ten Vampire jets discussed during Hussein's October visit to London, would be "the deciding factor."[39]

Nevertheless, London hesitated once again. Foreign Secretary Harold Macmillan, in Geneva for summit talks, was jolted by Dulles's blunt comments that Jordan's accession "would make it difficult for the U.S. to support the Pact," ostensibly because of the complications of having a defense treaty with a country at war with Israel.[40] The lack of formal American membership in the pact was burdensome but manageable for Macmillan. But for Washington to threaten to withdraw all support for the pact was a different matter altogether. Until he could decide which was more valuable—Jordan's immediate accession (a surety, he thought) or America's tepid support—Macmillan instructed Duke merely to play "the role of the sympathetic listener."[41]

The next three weeks witnessed a crystallization of attitudes all around. Inside Jordan, popular opposition to the pact intensified. Although Egyptian propaganda was active in this regard, most Jordanians were genuinely opposed to accession; even Glubb admitted that "majority public opinion is strong on side of Egypt."[42] Given the public mood and the absence of British lobbying for the pact, Hussein and his ministers refused to come out openly in favor of accession. Indeed, the only ministers involved in the Bayar–Zorlu talks were al-Mufti, al-Shubaylat, and al-Majali, plus Court Minister Fawzi al-Mulqi and Chief of the Royal Court Bahjat al-Talhuni; the cabinet as a whole was kept in the dark. This had the consequence of ceding further ground in the battle for public opinion to the antipact forces: Without arguing publicly *for* the pact, there was little the government could do to curb propaganda *against* it. As al-Majali told Glubb, Jordan could not very well expel the Egyptian military attaché for espionage without first deciding which side, London's or Cairo's, it wanted to be on.[43]

Slowly but surely, however, Hussein showed himself to be more confident in his inclination to join the pact, and this confidence spilled over to some of his ministers. On November 16, al-Mufti presented Duke with an informal aide-mémoire outlining Jordan's "ideas" about what it expected to receive in compensation for joining the pact. On the following day, a secret session of parliament heard al-Majali present "a frank account" of the Bayar–Zorlu talks. (Evidently, al-Mufti and al-Majali thought it wiser to appeal directly to parliament, whose election had been manipulated so effectively by Abu'l Huda the year before, rather than the cabinet, which contained at least two visceral opponents of Jordan's accession.) It was then that the government for the first time announced its intention to pursue pact membership should it receive the requisite "advantages." Significantly, parliament was reported to have passed a motion of confidence in the government's policy, raising a glimmer of hope that public opinion, too, might be swayed by some concrete proposals of British military assistance. "What would impress the Jordanians more than anything else," Duke wrote, was if Macmillan could visit Amman on his way back from the November 22–23 Pact Council meetings in Iraq.[44]

With the battle lines drawn between a government willing to join the pact and a populace virulently opposed to it, the missing ingredient was a firm British offer, which Whitehall was still not ready to make. On the eve of the Pact Council meetings, the most that Macmillan could instruct Duke was to inform the Jordanians that the British government would "welcome" Jordan's membership and that it promised to revise the treaty "upon accession." London did offer to transform a loan of ten Vampire jets into an outright gift, but this was a subtle difference that paled in light of the Jordanians' grand designs. Macmillan found Duke's request to visit Amman premature and begged off.[45]

In Baghdad, the pact members strongly urged Macmillan to recruit Jordan to their side. Again, the Turks took the lead. The "right course for Britain," Zorlu argued, "would be to let the Jordanians have a list of what they were prepared to supply to them and then to stand firmly on that list."[46] That position was seconded by Duke, who flew to Baghdad to give Macmillan a memo outlining the "specific undertakings" that he believed would "bring Jordan into the Pact if they can be made very soon." Duke's suggestions were much more moderate than al-Mufti's demands and, indeed, formed the basis of Britain's offer to Jordan two weeks later.[47]

Macmillan was won over during the Baghdad talks. On his return to London, he wrote Eden that "as an immediate step we must get some other Arab States to join . . . The first must be Jordan."

> I very much fear that if we do not get Jordan into the Baghdad Pact now, she will drift out of our control. . . . I think we can work out a package offer. . . . present it to them and more or less compel them to come in. In the final resort, we may have to say that we cannot continue our financial and military support for a country which will not stay on our side in grave issues; and then the Israelis will get them.

As for the Americans, the bullish Macmillan stridently argued that the choice was theirs: Either "shore-up the tottering Middle East area or . . . risk losing it all to Communism."[48] On December 2, the Cabinet Defense Committee approved a package along the lines of Duke's Baghdad memo, calling for an increase in the British subsidy from £10 million in 1955 to £16.5 million in 1956 and £12.5 million per year thereafter. In retrospect, it is difficult to understand the hesitation that marked the Foreign Office's policymaking. The package offer was neither particularly substantial nor very innovative. Whitehall officials admitted that "about half" of its initial cost was "in some measure fictitious" and that much of the rest was just a repackaging of previous but unfulfilled commitments.[49]

The suggestion (originally Shuckburgh's) to dispatch the chief of the imperial general staff, General Sir Gerald Templer, to present the package to the Jordanians underscored Whitehall's belief that Hussein could be won over with an appeal in which style, speed, and flair greatly outweighed substance.[50] Indeed, it highlighted a noteworthy shift in British attitudes, namely, that the key to Jordanian accession was the king and the king alone. In the buildup to the Templer mission, Hussein's state of mind concerned Whitehall above all else: "Assure the king"; "speak to the king," Duke was repeatedly instructed. This is also the background of the idea of awarding Hussein the honorary rank of RAF vice-marshal should an "appropriate moment" arise during the negotiations. (It never did.)[51] There was, conversely, virtually no effort to canvass support among other important political elements in Jordan—the cabinet, the court, or the parliament—and British officials exhibited virtually blanket indifference to Jordanian public opinion. Only hours before Templer's arrival in Amman did London finally consider the need, belatedly articulated by Duke, for "some advanced lobbying" to overcome ministerial and parliamentary opposition.[52]

Inside Jordan, the weeks before Templer's arrival were marked by intense political volatility. After having sided with the propact camp in mid-November, al-Mufti spent the latter half of the month trying to find a graceful way to extricate himself from the prime ministry. Never one to handle responsibility well in the best of times, the Circassian premier was overwhelmed by the conflicting pressures of pro- and antipact forces and wanted to have nothing to do with what his brother Rifa't termed a "purely Arab dispute." Twice al-Mufti reportedly offered his resignation, only to be talked out of it by Hussein and (to his later regret) Duke.[53] With that avenue closed, al-Mufti found another way to unburden himself of the ordeals of office—he avoided them. For ten critical days, November 16 to 27, al-Mufti claimed "illness" and divided his time between his bed and his winter home in Jericho; his "indisposition," brother Rifa't said, was "not altogether physical." Al-Mufti was eventually prodded into resuming his duties at the end of November, but his return instilled little confidence that he was strong enough to carry Jordan into the pact. That there was no robust, experienced, and well-respected leader to take al-Mufti's place said much about the quality of support for the pact among Jordan's political elite.[54]

Egypt sought to capitalize on the chasm that separated Jordan's propact official policy from its strongly antipact public opinion, by sending to Amman its minister of war, 'Abd al-Hakim Amer. Having just recently been appointed commander in chief of the combined Egyptian and Syrian armed forces, Amer was a visible symbol of both Egypt's claim to Arab self-reliance and its defiance of the Baghdad Pact. His arrival on November 30 was heralded in banner press headlines, and throughout his four-day visit, Amer was accorded exactly the sort of gracious welcome from the Jordanian public that it had denied to Turkish President Bayar one month earlier.[55]

Ironically, on the same day that Amer's plane touched down in Amman, two Vampire jets, the first of ten, arrived at Mafraq, Britain's own visible symbol of its intention to woo Jordan into the Baghdad Pact. This confluence of events set the stage for one of the murkiest aspects of the Baghdad Pact affair, King Hussein's attempt to secure Egypt's support for Jordan's accession. Evidently expecting London to try to entice Jordan into the pact,[56] Hussein took advantage of Amer's visit to outline Jordan's conditions for joining the pact, to explain his reasons for not adhering to the rival Egyptian–Syrian–Saudi pact, and to ask for a commitment from Egypt not to destabilize his regime in retaliation. According to the king's account, he received not only Amer's blessing but a message of support from Nasser himself soon thereafter. When, a few days later, Egypt's media led a chorus of denunciation against Jordan that provoked mass violence and rioting, Hussein cried foul. "What on earth made Nasser change his mind?" the king later exclaimed. Nasser's "*volte-face,*" Hussein argued, caught him completely by surprise and was the cleaver that "all but split Jordan in two."[57]

On December 3, Duke informed Sa'id al-Mufti that Templer and Michael Rose, head of the Foreign Office's Levant Department, were flying to Amman in two days to present Britain's proposals for Jordan's accession to the pact, and on the morning of December 7, Templer held his first talks with al-Mufti, al-Shubaylat, and Foreign Ministry Undersecretary Baha' al-Din Tuqan. All seemed to be proceeding smoothly. Although al-Mufti said he still had "doubts about the tactics" of securing "public acceptance" of Jordan's accession, he praised the British proposals as "very acceptable." Templer was hopeful that further sessions with the whole cabinet and the king would suffice to "carry the Prime Minister"—and, by extension, Jordan itself—into the pact.[58]

By the end of the day, however, Templer's optimism had dimmed. At a palace meeting that evening, he was surprised to find King Hussein, whom he had been led to believe was a firm supporter of immediate accession, taking the lead in expressing anxiety about Egyptian and Saudi "subversive propaganda" and the near-complete lack of propact sentiment among the Jordanian public. (That Hussein had done little to promote the pact publicly was not mentioned.) Faced with such reticence, Templer opted not to press his hosts for a firm, public commitment on accession. Instead, he suggested that Hussein and his ministers consider entering into a "private agreement" to accede at a later date, not to be published until the Jordanians saw fit. As he reported to London, he believed this option had "a good chance" of success—"*inshallah.*"[59]

Over the following week, events spiraled out of Templer's control, and Britain's chances for achieving even that second-best scenario steadily faded from view. By a fluke, four key ministers were out of the country when Templer first arrived. Hazza' al-Majali and Na'im 'Abd al-Hadi were in Baghdad, negotiating an economic aid package that would comprise Iraq's contribution to the pact recruitment effort; Bishara Ghaseeb (Finance) and Sa'id 'Ala' al-din (Economy), the cabinet's fifth Palestinian member, were in London for the annual subsidy talks, also framed to provide a few bonuses to the Jordanians.[60] Because the two ministers in Iraq were, respectively, the leaders of the cabinet's pro- and antipact factions, no real progress in the Templer talks could be made until their return late on the night of December 8.[61] With every passing day, the urgency of Templer's offer and the impact of his presence dissipated, and the ministers' apprehension at the prospect of flouting public and Arab opinion by joining the pact only deepened. Templer himself grew "increasingly frustrated" with just about everybody. Al-Mufti, he wrote in a celebrated remark, "is a jelly who is frightened of his own shadow"; pact opponents "bleat continuously" about Israel; and even King Hussein prefers "to spend the afternoon driving his fast cars on a sand track" rather than make time to see him.[62]

On December 10, the entire cabinet (minus those still in London) met throughout the day and found itself deadlocked. The five East Bankers present (including al-Mufti) were in favor of accession, but the four West Bank ministers demanded more time to consult with what were called "leading personalities outside the Government."[63] At what he hoped would be a final session at the British embassy the following day, Templer met the ministers (minus al-Mufti and al-Majali) and seemed to make the needed breakthrough. Two of the four Palestinians gave him a tentative agreement in principle to Jordan's accession, though they insisted on a fourteen-day delay "to consult leaders of opinion and prepare the ground." That left just Na'im 'Abd al-Hadi and 'Azmi al-Nashashibi as the lone holdouts. When Templer arranged for Hussein to lobby 'Abd al-Hadi personally and Whitehall telegraphed its approval of a series of semantic concessions to Palestinian sensitivities, the chances for success looked brighter. Of course, by that time, London's definition of success had been significantly whittled down. By then, Whitehall would have considered a "letter of intent," or even just a personal letter from al-Mufti committing himself to work for Jordan's accession, as an unqualified triumph.[64]

But even that was beyond Templer's reach. Over the next forty-eight hours, the two Palestinian waverers, Sam'an Da'ud and 'Ali Hasna, slid back into total opposition, and on the morning of December 13, all four West Bankers resigned. Al-Mufti, though, refused to accept their resignations, pending Templer's response to a "counterproposal" that had been drawn up by a ministerial committee that included, among others, 'Azmi al-Nashashibi. This "counterproposal" contained provisions that completely vitiated any strategic rationale for Jordan's membership in the pact, such as limiting Jordan's obligations under the pact to the kingdom's own territory. But Whitehall was willing, in principle, to accede to all the Jordanians' demands, save one; even at that late date, the idea of paying the Arab Legion's subsidy directly to the Jordanian treasury was still "wholly unacceptable."[65]

At a meeting with Hussein, al-Mufti, al-Majali, and al-Mulqi on the afternoon of December 13, Templer tried one last time to salvage his visit. Even though the government's collapse was imminent, it was a moment of high drama. Templer first presented al-Mufti with a "heads of agreement" on which future negotiations would be based; however, citing the cabinet crisis, the premier refused to sign. Then Templer placed before him a more general "letter of intent," and to the disbelief of those present, again al-Mufti balked. Despite the harangues of King Hussein and his own fellow ministers, al-Mufti held his ground; without cabinet support, al-Mufti refused to budge.[66] Hussein then offered to sign the letter himself but was advised against it by Duke and Templer. Six hours later, al-Mufti rejected a final plea "to sign any letter" and resigned. "I am afraid I have shot my bolt," Templer telegraphed London. "I am sorry I have failed."[67] The general left Amman early the following day, leaving behind a goodwill note to al-Mufti's successor, Hazza' al-Majali, and an assurance that London would consider sending another mission to Amman in a week "to find out [as he told Whitehall] whether [the Jordanians] have come to their senses." The call for a second mission never came.[68]

The *raison d'être* of al-Majali's government was to bring—"drag" may be more accurate—Jordan into the pact. It was doomed from the start. Al-Majali himself made a game effort at achieving the virtually impossible and earned for his efforts a reputation as a "king's man" par excellence.

This had not always been the case. Al-Majali's career had so far been marked by several radical shifts of allegiance that stamped him as something of an opportunist. After a stint as court chamberlain, Hazza' had been appointed by King Abdullah to be mayor of Amman in 1949. Over the next five years, he served in cabinets under every subsequent prime minister. Always a popular figure in his native Kerak, al-Majali was adept at keeping himself in the public eye and at maintaining an aura of indispensability. When criticism of Abu'l Huda's autocratic methods mounted in 1952, al-Majali became a leading light of the Parliamentary Opposition Bureau; when al-Mulqi drifted too far in the opposite direction, al-Majali again led the chorus of disapproval and, for his efforts, was begged to join the government to shore up its popular support. The following year, he switched gears again when he sacrificed both his liberal protestations and his position as secretary-general of the National Socialist party to participate in Abu'l Huda's coalition cabinet after the 1954 election scandal. But when Abu'l Huda ran afoul of the king in the spring of 1955, al-Majali resigned early enough to be ready for a new assignment under a new prime minister.

On each of these occasions, al-Majali accurately read the mood of the times and of the king, which were normally one and the same. In that light, his decision to assume the premiership on December 13 ran counter to form, for by vowing to bring Jordan into the Baghdad Pact, al-Majali sided for the first time with the king against the times. It may have earned him the government's highest post, but his decision cannot justly be labeled opportunistic. In the heat of December 1955, it was no simple step for even the most loyalist of politicians to declare himself so boldly against the Nasserite tide and for the Baghdad Pact.

Forming a government on that basis was no simple matter. Although three of al-Mufti's East Bank ministers—al-Shubaylat, al-Tutunji, and Ghaseeb—agreed to remain in office and 'Abbas Mirza, a Jerash native and a lesser light in the Circassian hierarchy, accepted the Interior Ministry, recruiting Palestinians proved extremely difficult. Sa'id 'Ala' al-din, who was in London and therefore was the lone Palestinian not to resign from al-Mufti's government, rejected al-Majali's offer to join his cabinet, as did Jordan's ambassador to Britain, the onetime mayor of Haifa, Yusef Haykal. In the end, al-Majali appointed five men who had strong home-town support but no previous cabinet experience: the mayors of Hebron (Muhammad 'Ali al-Ja'bari) and Ramallah (Jalil Badran); a former mayor of Jerusalem ('Arif al-'Arif); a family boss from Jenin (Farid Irshayd); and a popular independent from Ramallah ('Umar al-Bargouti). The lack of representation from nationalist Nablus was conspicuous. Before their appointment, every minister was asked to sign an undertaking to sup-port Jordan's accession to the pact.[69]

Al-Majali's strategy was to shift the accession decision from the cabi-net to the parliament. It was a shrewd political gamble. The chamber, it must be recalled, was still filled with Abu'l Huda's handpicked deputies, illegitimate in the eyes of many and far more conservative as a whole than the public at large. Al-Majali's plan was to present the deputies with all the facts regarding the Templer mission and force them to make the choice. He assumed that most deputies would chose king (accession) over country (rejection), since most had so sullied their political prospects via the 1954 election that they had no chance of reelection anyway. Within hours of his appointment, al-Majali had met with about twenty depu-ties, and the initial response was encouraging. He told Duke he would need about two weeks to prepare for a vote of confidence, after which he hoped to continue the accession negotiations in London. In the meantime, he said, "a combination of inducements and threats" to the local media would ensure more assertive publicity on behalf of the pact. That ominous note was echoed in his first public statement upon taking office: "I have undertaken to resist any ill-disposed intentions which aim at sowing the seeds of dissension among the people. I shall take strong action against anyone who chooses to follow this difficult course."[70]

But al-Majali never had a chance to put his plan into motion. Riot-ing and protests broke out throughout Jordan on December 17, the worst the kingdom had ever witnessed. Normally quiet towns like Hebron, Jericho, Bethlehem, and Aqaba erupted for the first time in memory; traditional hotbeds of opposition like Amman, Nablus, Irbid, and Salt shook as never before; refugee camps, usually docile and well controlled, exploded, too.[71] Foreign missions and institutions, public and private, were favorite targets; Duke, the French consul-general in Jerusalem, and the American military attaché all were stoned as they drove through city streets. Preventive arrests and large-scale troop deployments did little to temper the daily demonstrations. Instead, poor communication between local police and Arab Legion contingents only exacerbated tensions and led to unnecessary death. The American embassy's "conservative" casu-alty estimate for the five days of rioting was fifteen dead and one hun-dred wounded.[72]

Although both the East and the West Bank quaked under the rioting, it was, demographically, primarily a Palestinian affair. East of the Jordan, violence flared mostly among the Palestinian communities of Amman and Irbid and their surrounding refugee camps; west of the river, the protests were nearly ubiquitous. Indeed, one of the pact's few prominent Palestinian supporters conceded that "95 percent of the populace" firmly opposed Jordan's accession.[73] Many Palestinians were driven by a very real but almost irrational fear that Hussein and al-Majali were conniving with London at their expense, and even though they lacked the strength to avenge their loss of Palestine, they did have the wherewithal to stymie what they viewed as a new Transjordanian–British conspiracy of betrayal. (That Israel opposed Jordan's accession, because of the military benefits that pact membership would bring, did not normally figure into this calculus.)

At first, the king held firm. "Things were going as well as could be expected," Hussein told Duke on December 17. Al-Majali had his "full support." For his part, the prime minister seemed to revel in the protests. "He showed no sign of being intimidated at all," Duke reported. Instead, al-Majali ordered Saudi and Egyptian diplomats dressed down for their "machinations," banned all public gatherings, and readied a general declaration of martial law. It looked as though he was intent on seeing his policy, and his government, through to the end.[74]

But after three days of rioting, Hussein gave way to the opposition's demands for al-Majali's resignation. A variety of factors led to this decision. First, despite a nationwide radio address appealing for calm, the rioting showed little sign of abating.[75] Second, a group of senior civil servants had threatened to resign and grind the government to a halt. And most important, al-Majali's own cabinet had cracked. After swearing loyalty to the government's propact policy, two ministers, Mirza and al-'Arif, presented al-Majali with their own ultimatum on December 19: Unless he broadcast a statement repudiating efforts to join the pact, they would resign and bring down the cabinet with them. Under the weight of these multiple challenges, Hussein gave way. The nation was so divided, he told Duke, that "the only thing to do" was to dissolve parliament and conduct elections "on the question of whether Jordan should or should not join the Baghdad Pact." Al-Majali, he said, would resign within the week, in accordance with the constitution, and Minister of Court al-Mulqi would form a caretaker government to supervise the elections. Buoyant to the end, al-Majali told Duke he was "sure" he could secure the election of a parliament that would bring Jordan into the pact. That evening, parliament was dissolved.[76]

Even that, however, did not silence the rioters. In the face of continued protests on December 20, al-Majali decided to resign immediately, rather than wait out the week. That day, Hussein bypassed Fawzi al-Mulqi and called instead on the kingdom's eldest (and "cleanest") statesman, the upper house president Ibrahim Hashim, to form a government. Still the demonstrations continued. The "only bright news," reported Mallory in a bit of gallows humor, was that Amman's lawyers were on strike. As its last act of capitulation, the government issued an order on December 21 releasing most of those arrested during the five days of violence. By the following day, Amman and other major cities had "returned more or less to normal." Al-Majali's ministry, begun in great expectation, had proved to be just a violent affirmation of the failure of the Templer mission.[77]

In ascribing blame for that failure, every party has its favorite villain. For Templer, the chief culprits were the "intransigent attitude of the Palestinian" ministers and the "spineless pusillanimity of the Prime Minister."[78] For Hazza' al-Majali, the Palestinians were the main problem, too. In a celebrated pamphlet, he not only accused the four Palestinian ministers who opposed the pact of suffering from a "mental disorder" but also extended his indictment to virtually the entire Palestinian leadership. The four ministers, he charged, labored under "an inclination to negativeness which they doubtless have inherited as a principle of 'negation for negation's sake' from the days of the mandate in Palestine."[79]

For Hussein, whose memoirs sidestep a discussion of domestic opposition to the pact, Egypt—and especially Nasser's alleged about-face—was the root cause of the mission's failure. Within days, his courtiers began to spread rumors of specific incidents of Egyptian subversion and Saudi bribery, including the story that three of the West Bank ministers benefited from Saudi largesse to secure their opposition to the pact. A key figure in this regard was Colonel Anwar al-Sadat, Egyptian minister without portfolio, said to be the "evil genius" who offered 'Abd al-Hadi, al-Nashashibi, and Hasna £9,000 each for their resignations.[80]

The Americans bear their share of the blame, too. At a critical moment (December 12), Washington was asked for an unambiguous statement of backing, coupled with some vague assurances of economic aid, that Whitehall believed would secure Jordan's agreement to a secret letter of intent. Turkey, Iran, Iraq, and even Lebanon all responded without delay to Whitehall's pleas for declaratory support, but the State Department shunted London's request off to the side; it did not reach Dulles until December 15, by which time al-Mufti had already fallen. Britain's ambassador in Washington, Sir Roger Makins, later placed the blame for the Baghdad Pact fiasco squarely on the Americans. "The United States," Makins said in his understated way, "hadn't gone down the whole way with this idea."[81]

Opponents of Jordan's accession have a different list of villains. According to 'Abd al-Hadi, the central issue was not accession itself but, rather, the need for consultation with fellow "frontline states" Egypt and Syria.

> Had we had no objection from Egypt and Syria, we would have had no
> objection to joining the pact. Our main point was that we shouldn't split
> the forces surrounding Israel—Egypt, Jordan, and Syria. It was not as much
> a question of "yes" or "no" to the pact as it was to the question of encir-
> cling Israel.

At a cabinet meeting on December 10, he claimed that it had been
decided that he and al-Majali would visit Cairo to discuss Jordan's pact
membership with Nasser and that Sa'id al-Mufti would go to Damascus
to see Syrian Prime Minister Sa'id al-Ghazzi. King Hussein, he said, had
blessed these two missions, and Templer, he claimed, had agreed to a
two-week delay in the cabinet's deliberations. The following day, however, 'Abd al-Hadi stated that Templer had pressed the cabinet for an
immediate decision on accession. According to 'Abd al-Hadi, the main
culprit was Glubb, who allegedly convinced Templer to demand an answer
without regard for consultations with Cairo and Damascus. The West
Bankers, he claimed, had no choice but to resign.[82]

Both pact critics and supporters cite other factors contributing to the
collapse of the Templer mission, including the "impatience" and general
high-handedness of Templer himself[83] and the complete absence of public
education about the details of the British proposal.[84] To focus on these
and other secondary issues, however, is to obscure the root cause of
Templer's failure and al-Mufti's fall. And that, it seems, was the unpolished
politics of the young king and the absence of sound advice from those
who ought to have known better.

The decision to join the Baghdad Pact was Hussein's first attempt
to lead his kingdom in a direction of his choosing, and it went miserably
awry. By fluctuating between hesitant ambivalence toward the pact and
precipitate action on its behalf, Hussein exhibited serious faults of judgment and leadership. By failing to line up a team committed to seeing
accession through once the decision had been taken in principle, Hussein
showed himself lacking in political perspicacity. And by blithely accepting Egyptian promises of support for Jordan's accession—if indeed such
promises were made—Hussein displayed a stunning naiveté. None of this
is particularly surprising in a monarch who had turned twenty just three
weeks before Templer's arrival. And indeed, each of these faults was cor-
rected in a matter of weeks. Hussein recovered from letting Jordan sink
into the Baghdad Pact morass in December by playing a large role in
pulling it back from the brink of anarchy in January.

What is surprising is that Hussein was allowed to apprentice—or, more
appropriately, "fly solo"—at that crucial juncture. Neither the traditional
elite nor Hussein's palace counselors (royal and otherwise) seem to have
provided the sort of ballast to which the kingdom had grown accustomed
since Abdullah's death. "The street," said al-Mufti's justice minister, 'Ali
al-Hindawi, "was with Nasser, right or wrong"—but nobody told Hussein
what that meant or how to change it.[85] As noted, this problem was

exacerbated by London's lobbying efforts that focused on the king himself. Exactly why such an abdication of responsibility by Jordan's elder statesmen and the kingdom's British ally occurred at such a critical moment is unclear, but the kingdom surely suffered for it. Out of the Baghdad Pact debacle, Hussein drew important lessons about the need for careful preparation, reliable intelligence, and unswerving loyalty. But it would be a trying sixteen months before he would apply those lessons with the full backing of the "king's men" and the support of outside patrons. In the meantime, he continued to strike out alone.

8

Charting a New Course

The fall of Hazza' al-Majali's government, the second to collapse in less than a week, underscored to Hussein the risk of charging ahead with policies and politicians so wildly out of touch with the public mood. The much-sobered monarch therefore retreated from the exposed position in which his support for the Baghdad Pact had left him. Instead, he took cover under the cloak of the dissolution announcement and the formation of a coalition government as broadly based as the tense situation would allow.

Ibrahim Hashim, appointed as the caretaker prime minister on December 21, earned his title as Jordan's senior statesman not only because of his age—he was born in 1888—but also because he held solid credentials as both an early Arab nationalist and a Hashemite loyalist. Born in Nablus, the Istanbul-trained lawyer abandoned the Ottoman civil service in the mid-1910s to join the Istiqlal (Independence) party, a decision for which the Turks sentenced him to death during the World War I. Hashim escaped from a Turkish jail in the Jebel Druze and sat out the war in hiding in his hometown. In 1918, he joined King Feisal in Syria, only to return to Nablus when the nationalist government collapsed. Soon thereafter, Hashim was recruited by Feisal's brother, Abdullah, to supervise the creation of a judiciary in the newly established amirate of Transjordan. Hashim left Nablus again, this time leaving behind any "Palestinian" political or national identity he may have had, to become Abdullah's "faithful servant," the archetypal "king's man." From 1922 onward, he served in no fewer than eight different governments, including two as prime minister. Like other Palestinians coopted into Abdullah's service, Hashim had no base of popular support inside Transjordan. Rather, he owed his status to loyalty and a reputation (rightly deserved, it seems) for personal integrity.[1] Like other nationalists of the old school, Hashim had over the years been disabused of his youthful notions of Arab military or economic self-sufficiency, and he had an abiding appreciation of Britain's historic contribution to Arab independence. "In spite of everything," his son later recalled, Hashim believed that Britain was the "best ally" the Hashemites, and the Arabs in general, ever had.[2]

Having never himself participated in electoral politics, Hashim was appointed to lend a measure of judicial propriety to the upcoming election campaign. In contrast, the men who joined his cabinet were politicians of a more expedient nature. The two most powerful were Samir al-Rifaʻi (deputy premier and foreign minister) and Fawzi al-Mulqi (defense and education), tarnished former prime ministers attempting political comebacks. To the credit of each, both could claim a political following, though not popular support, and neither had left a clear record of his position on the Baghdad Pact. Hashim's cabinet was a piece of political artwork, encompassing either directly or indirectly each of the three main loyalist power brokers—al-Rifaʻi, al-Mulqi, and Tawfiq Abu'l Huda. Two ministries were allotted to each. Al-Rifaʻi was joined by political ally ʻUmar Matar; al-Mulqi was joined by Palestinian Hussein Fakhri al-Khalidi; and Abu'l Huda had his still consequential voice heard via the appointments of Felah al-Madadha and Hashim al-Jayyousi. Two Palestinian technocrats, Anastas Hanania and Khulusi al-Khayri, rounded out the cabinet. As a caretaker government, it was carefully balanced to represent the various and competing streams of "king's men." It was indeed a coalition, but one that excluded the very forces that had felled al-Mufti and al-Majali—the moderate (National Socialist) and radical (Baʻthist and Communist) opposition.

To make up for that obvious deficiency, Hashim immediately set out to distance his ministry from the stigma of the two previous ones. "Our government . . . has no right to deal with any political questions," he declared upon taking office, "or to commit itself in any undertakings or new pacts." That refrain, "no new pacts," was the cornerstone of the government's strategy to deflect the popular antagonism that continued to simmer against the monarchy and the most glaring symbol of Jordan's British connection, Glubb Pasha. In what was perhaps a calculated indiscretion, al-Rifaʻi went so far as to tell a Reuters correspondent that the "damage" caused by the Templer mission "set back the question of Jordan's joining the Pact not for one year, but for years."[3] The government's sole task, the ministers repeatedly stated, was to supervise elections tentatively scheduled for April.

Four months seemed a very long time away, and in the days following Hashim's appointment, the regime was engaged in more pressing matters than registering voters and printing ballots. Foremost among these was the Nasser-led attempt to exploit the rift in Anglo-Jordanian relations by offering Egyptian-Syrian-Saudi financial aid in place of the British subsidy. At first, Hussein's intended riposte was to "pitch his price beyond [the] reach" of the Arab allies by asking for the full amount of five years worth of assistance deposited into an escrow account. But the Arab aid offer took an ominous turn in late December when it was backed up by a Soviet offer to provide "any sort of financial or military aid [Jordan] might require with a view to establishing good relations."[4] When Hussein received an invitation from Nasser to attend a meeting of Arab heads of state in Cairo or Jeddah, he parried, offering instead to meet the Egyptian leader one on one or to host the summit meeting in Jordan. In the post-Templer environment, an open rejection of Arab aid in favor of continued dependence on British assistance would have been highly embarrassing, if not actually damaging, to the regime. Therefore, Hussein's gambit was to "play for time," trying to figure out a graceful way to avoid meeting with Nasser and having to deal directly with the Arab aid offer.[5] But by early January, Hussein had far more urgent problems to face.

Less than five days after Hashim's government took office, a group of deputies filed suit challenging the validity of the royal decree dissolving parliament. Their argument, based on a strict reading of the constitution, was motivated more by the prospect of losing their seats in a general election than by their interest in constitutional law.[6] Inside the government, however, their parochial concerns prompted a reexamination of the election issue. Already, opposition groups were marshaling their forces to prepare manifestos, recruit support, and otherwise exploit the regime's weak posture in anticipation of the upcoming vote. Hashemite loyalists viewed with trepidation the prospect of a sweeping opposition victory and began themselves to question the wisdom of new elections. Elections, they argued, could only spell trouble for the regime: If free, the opposition would dominate parliament; if rigged, the opposition would take to the streets. Moreover, with the government itself no longer actively supporting Jordan's membership in the Baghdad Pact, there was virtually no one in the country (other than al-Majali's dwindling coterie) arguing in its favor. Therefore, the original logic behind holding elections—to have a plebiscite on accession—was no longer valid.

The sitting parliament, though timorous and fainthearted despite its overwhelmingly conservative composition, was almost certainly less dangerous than one dominated by the opposition. Therefore, Hussein and the government decided to reverse its dissolution.[7] On December 29, Hussein took Hashim's suggestion and referred the deputies' petition to the Diwan khass, Jordan's Supreme Council for the Interpretation of the Law. One week later, the council, as expected, invalidated the dissolution decree, and Hashim resigned immediately.[8] In the meantime, Glubb had taken several steps to bolster internal security so as to prevent a repetition of the calamitous anti-Majali riots. At his urgent request, Britain approved the speedy supply of special riot gear (tear gas, "kicker shields," etc.) and an "experienced police adviser," and both arrived by the first days of January.[9] The only party that seemed not to take steps to prepare for the expected protests was the government itself. Upon the revocation of the dissolution decree, the caretaker government would cease to exist, and none of its ministers wanted to take responsibility for ordering the sort of security measures for which Glubb pressed in the hours before the court's decision.

In the murky constitutional void following the dissolution's revocation, a decree was issued banning a mass opposition meeting scheduled in Amman for January 6.[10] In response, large-scale protests broke out throughout the kingdom, with violence even more menacing than what had shaken Jordan just three weeks earlier. Again, foreign missions bore the brunt of the attacks, with American interests inexplicably singled out over British, French, or Turkish.[11] The British chargé, R. H. Mason, pleaded with the powers that be to "take the country firmly in hand" and crush the "rapid growth of mob rule." Otherwise, he warned, "everything that Jordan had built since 1918 would crash upon their heads."[12]

This time, Hussein and Glubb were determined to have the upper hand. On January 7, the government—a caretaker of a caretaker—ordered army troops into the towns and cities to quell the demonstrations. The ensuing confrontations were the bloodiest in the kingdom's history. In Jerusalem, Amman, Bethlehem, Jericho, Zerqa, and even as far away as Kerak and Aqaba, the army used tear gas and then live fire to restore order and enforce an around-the-clock curfew. Both Hussein and Glubb feared that the Arab Legion, "fully extended" with internal security and with manning the Israeli frontier, might not be up to the job. On the evening of January 9, the king received word of still more trouble: Three thousand Saudi troops were reported moving toward Aqaba in what army intelligence believed was a feint to divert Jordanian troops from their riot-control duties.[13]

The previous day, Hussein had named al-Rifa'i to succeed Hashim. Declaring himself committed to a policy of "no new pacts," al-Rifa'i proceeded to form a ministry in the midst of the bedlam. Meanwhile, though, Hussein readied a backup plan should either al-Rifa'i or the Arab Legion prove inadequate to their tasks. His strategy, he told Mason, was to "suspend the constitution and introduce a military government at the earliest possible moment." Hussein asked Mason to pass an urgent message to Baghdad invoking the Jordan–Iraq Treaty of Friendship and requesting that an Iraqi division stand by "at immediate readiness to enter Jordan" to help enforce martial law. Secrecy and speed, the king told Mason, were vital. In response, Mason warmly praised Hussein's "stand against anarchy," but he and his London superiors pointedly avoided endorsing the king's plan.[14]

The Iraqis, however, accepted Jordan's request with startling alacrity. "Iraq is ready to do her utmost within her resources to help Jordan," Nuri replied on January 10. Baghdad's response was not wholly selfless. As British envoy Michael Wright noted, the Iraqi leadership viewed the possibility of sending troops into Jordan as a historic opportunity to humble Nasser and finally succeed in forging a Hashemite union. To that end, Nuri told Hussein that "if obliged to send help it would not be a half measure. It would be better not to send help at all than for it to end in failure." Interestingly, Wright reported that the Iraqis "would not necessarily be opposed" to sending a "reassuring message" to the Israelis to the effect that any deployment in Jordan was not targeted against them.[15]

Meanwhile, inside Jordan, the security situation was still shaky. Despite the curfew and the total deployment of army troops, riots continued to flare on both the East and the West Bank. In London, the cabinet met to discuss Jordan for the second time in twenty-four hours and ordered two paratroop battalions airlifted immediately to Cyprus for possible redeployment inside Jordan.[16] In the month since General Templer arrived in Amman, the Jordan connection had changed radically in British eyes from a political asset to a potential military drain of immense proportions. In the words of American Central Intelligence Agency director Allen Dulles, rampant instability in Jordan was, for Britain, "the most humiliating diplomatic defeat in modern history."[17]

The worst, however, did not happen. Tottering on the edge of anarchy with Saudi forces massed on the kingdom's borders, Jordan climbed back just in time, and a semblance of order was restored without resort to foreign troops. That Jordan did not collapse completely in the second week of January 1956 was due to a combination of factors. Chief of them were the subtle scheming of Samir al-Rifa'i, the resolve of the king, and the conclusion reached by Jordan's rivals that the regime's destruction was not a worthy, immediate, or practical objective after all.

Outside Jordan, the chief provocateurs—Nasser and, to a lesser extent, King Saud—were genuinely surprised at the relative ease with which their incitement propelled Jordan to the brink of total collapse. Their goal all along, it seems, was not to destroy the kingdom but to cow the king and his advisers into political deference.[18] When it looked as though their efforts were leading too quickly to something far more serious and irrevocable—for Egypt, perhaps the full burden of responsibility for dismembered Jordan, and for Saudi Arabia, perhaps open hostilities with Great Britain—they wisely pulled back.

On January 10, Egypt's ambassador to Jordan returned to Cairo carrying a letter from Ibrahim Hashim imploring Nasser to call off his campaign (media and otherwise) to subvert the kingdom. The following day, his entreaties were seconded by British ambassador Humphrey Trevelyan. Nasser was in an expansive mood, and he explained to the British envoy that having outdueled Britain over the issue of Jordan's accession in the Baghdad Pact, he had no wish to destroy the kingdom altogether. Al-Rifaʻi's reaffirmation of Hashim's "no new pacts" policy was enough for the time being, Nasser said, and he was therefore ordering a suspension of propaganda attacks. (On January 14, Trevelyan reported a "distinct change" in Sawt al-ʻArab broadcasts.) But Nasser put Trevelyan on notice: If Britain again tried to threaten his interests in Jordan, he would not hesitate to "start his counter action again."[19]

Against Saudi Arabia's military challenge, Britain had more resources at its disposal and, no less important, the will to employ them. Thanks to the Buraymi dispute and the Saudis' general mischief making, London was spoiling for a fight. Nuri, for one, suggested that the Saudi threat provided a handy excuse for Iraqi forces to strike at Saudi oil fields. On January 12, the British envoy in Jeddah warned the Saudis to be under "no misapprehension" that Britain would fulfill its treaty obligations to Jordan. In the meantime, London ordered that if Saudi forces should cross into Jordan, "all means should be employed to ensure that Saudi columns are destroyed and their remnants driven back" to Saudi territory. Eden wanted prisoners to be taken "so as to have tangible proof" of Saudi aggression. Britain's warnings and military moves persuaded King Saud to pull his troops back; his comparative advantage was financial, not military, and he saw the folly of a military adventure that could easily go awry. The truculent Saudi posture turned pacific almost overnight. "We have every affection and friendship for the people of Jordan and their king," beamed Saudi radio, and Saud himself sent "a rather apologetic explanation" to Hussein. The Jordanians were not taken in by Saudi expressions of goodwill, but they preferred to have the Saudis engaged in their traditional form of influence peddling rather than have the Arab Legion engaged on still another front.[20]

One of the factors that convinced Cairo and Riyadh to rein in their respective forces was the extent of Hussein's personal determination to defend his throne. Until January 1956, Hussein had shown neither the tenacity nor the resolve necessary to decide for himself what was best for his kingdom and to fight for it. Although he had steadily assumed the mantle of the kingship, he had yet to display the mettle of a king. That changed with the Baghdad Pact crisis. Mob violence, the incendiary broadcasts from Cairo, and the political demise of three successive regime stalwarts (al-Mufti, al-Majali, and Hashim) had matured the young Hussein in a way that no advice from his mother, uncle, or British patrons possibly could have done. The shy, unassertive king had turned bold and forceful virtually overnight.

"King Hussein's blood is up," Mason reported on January 9. "He is determined to put an end to the instability and mob rule."[21] But at the same time, Hussein was neither precipitate nor hasty. Although preparations were made for the deployment of Iraqi troops on the East Bank, he insisted on giving al-Rifaʻi's civilian effort a chance to succeed, and he refused to undermine it by letting himself be coaxed into impulsive actions by the Iraqis. When he, Glubb, and Bahjat al-Talhuni flew secretly to Habbaniya on January 12 to confer with the Iraqi leadership (so clan-destinely that even the queen mother was not informed) Hussein got exactly what he wanted, firm agreement from the Iraqis to support Jordan and to start joint military planning toward that end without actually having to commit Jordan to any unnecessary provocation.[22] It was a plan both conceived and executed by the king alone, without the political cover of a member of the sitting government. With few able "king's men" to turn to, the king was forced to be his own man. Having rapidly out-grown the indecision that marked his actions in the Baghdad Pact crisis, the January emergency showed Hussein determined to control the pace of events for the first time in his nearly three years on the throne. Although the direction was not particular clear, the January emergency showed him intent on charting his own course.[23]

Whereas the king summoned up the firmness that few thought he had, Samir al-Rifa'i relied on the finesse and subtlety that Jordanians knew only too well. Al-Rifa'i's approach to politics was to avoid confrontation when circumnavigation was possible and to view adversaries as potential allies, not inevitable enemies. In his mind, post-1948 Jordan was an inherently fragile entity that could survive in the brutish world of Arab politics only if it accepted its lot and swam unmenacingly with the regional tide. Critics charged al-Rifa'i with an almost preening delight in com-promising on principle to avoid conflict, and to be sure, throughout the often confusing mid-1950s, al-Rifa'i proved himself a master at keeping his options open. To describe his politics as expedient, however, is not to malign his stalwart loyalty. Banished from power since the death of Abdullah, al-Rifa'i's dexterous pragmatism was sorely missed.

Al-Rifa'i's cabinet, formed with less difficulty than expected, was announced on January 8. It was largely a reshuffle of its predecessor, with six of the retiring ministers—including Hashim himself in the figurehead role of deputy premier—appointed again. Not counting al-Rifa'i and Hashim, only four of the ten ministers were Palestinians, without a polit-ical heavyweight among them. Al-Rifa'i, though, cannot be faulted for not having tried to recruit prominent West Bankers or opposition fig-ures. On the contrary, from the moment of his appointment, al-Rifa'i sought to defuse Jordan's civil strife through a policy of "divide and conquer."

Al-Rifa'i believed that the opposition coalition of National Social-ists, Ba'thists, and Communists was merely an alliance of convenience and that the influence of the latter two groups stemmed from their riding piggyback on the mainstream popularity of the first. He also was con-vinced that an appeal to the enlightened self-interest of the NSP's wealthy, landed leaders would split them from their radical colleagues. Such a nimble policy was in marked contrast with the strong-arm tactics being recommended by Glubb and the British and American embassies. When they pressed al-Rifa'i on January 7 to arrest Sulayman al-Nabulsi and Hikmat al-Masri, they were astounded to learn that the premier-designate proposed instead to enlist the "extremists" into his cabinet. In any event, al-Nabulsi and al-Masri refused his offer, but that was only the beginning of al-Rifa'i's campaign to woo, and thereby neutralize, the NSP leadership.[24]

For example, al-Rifa'i's "no new pacts" pledge, which earned a congratulatory telegram from no less than Nasser himself, was in fact not his idea but Hussein's. Al-Rifa'i wanted a specific promise forswearing membership in the Baghdad Pact, which would have maximum appeal to the opposition, and only when Hussein insisted did he relent and declare his government's opposition to any new alliances, Arab or Western.[25] When al-Rifa'i learned of Hussein's request for Iraqi troops and of the British offer of military support, he was livid; Glubb opined that it was a mistake even to have informed him (the premier, no less). Rather than rely on the army to maintain order, al-Rifa'i bargained for it, trading the release of sixteen persons arrested in the recent rioting for a tenuous peace in Nablus. He often talked strong, repeatedly promising a return to "law and order," but when presented with arrest warrants for several well-known Ba'thists, he repeatedly refused to sign them. His detractors were convinced that his true policy was domestic peace at any price. "I fear he will be forced to make more concessions to the demands of the extremists [and] restore order at the cost of Britain influence in Jordan," Mason reported nervously on the morrow of al-Rifa'i's appointment. Even at that early date, he was afraid that Glubb would be the first to go.[26]

In the short run, at least, the combination of conciliation (al-Rifa'i) and determination (Hussein backed up by Glubb) worked. In the absence of further incitement from Cairo, tensions cooled; at the very least, after a month of violence, the rioters needed a rest. By January 12, Glubb's chief of staff reported a marked improvement and "increasing signs that [the] people wish [a] return to normal life." The Arab Legion itself was said to be in high spirits, having redeemed itself from its December debacle. As Glubb noted:

> Over hundred Communists arrested so far and put in concentration camp. Legion in excellent fettle. They do not enjoy internal security duties. Prefer fight Jews. All have shown excellent discipline combined with firmness in dispersing crowds. They have had to open fire occasionally but always under strict self-control. Morale still seems to be excellent.

On January 14, with calm restored, al-Rifa'i lifted the curfew and censorship restrictions. The crisis had passed.[27]

Three days earlier, Hussein had formally received the Egyptian–Saudi–Syrian offer to replace the British subsidy. By then, a political challenge—one supported by the Soviets, no less—was still a welcome relief from the frontal assault of rebellious rioters and Saudi troops.[28] As a strategy for dealing with the Arab proposal, al-Rifa'i even went further than his old rival Abu'l Huda did in reconciling Jordan with the Arab world's major players. In early February, he embarked on a tour of five Arab capitals, ostensibly to lobby for Hussein's idea of a summit meeting of Arab heads of state. Nasser, of course, never seriously considered ceding the political initiative to the upstart king, and al-Rifa'i used the opportunity to defuse tensions all around. In Baghdad, he lent his grudging support to joint Iraqi–Jordanian staff talks on military coordination and in turn won agreement from Nuri to speed up the delivery of economic aid promised to the al-Majali mission two months earlier. In Cairo, al-Rifa'i scored even more notable success. First, he convinced Nasser that Jordan had no need for the offer of Arab aid because Britain had not linked its own subsidy to Jordan's accession to the Baghdad Pact. Nasser agreed to freeze his proposal. Second, al-Rifa'i declined an Egyptian offer of a bilateral defense agreement, citing his government's policy of "no new pacts." Nasser accepted this, too. Third, al-Rifa'i won Nasser's agreement to a truce in the smoldering propaganda war that had heated up again in early February. On his return home from Cairo, al-Rifa'i did his part to cool tensions by exiling the young, anti-Nasser firebrand Wasfi al-Tall from the directorship of the Government Press Bureau to the Department of Internal Taxation.[29]

That al-Rifa'i proved himself adept at dealing with both Nasser and Nuri raised as many suspicions about his true loyalties as it prompted praise for his diplomatic skill. Indeed, Hussein had sent his personal adviser, Bahjat al-Talhuni, to accompany al-Rifa'i on his Arab tour to keep a watchful eye on his wily premier.[30] (In the course of time, the two became strong political allies, a partnership cemented by the marriage of al-Rifa'i's son to al-Talhuni's daughter.) Whether Samir was artfully snaking his way through an Arab political minefield as Hussein's loyal servant or, alternatively, conniving with the Egyptians behind his sovereign's back remains something of a mystery. Success, though, is perhaps the best judge. Despite some anxiety at the royal court, al-Rifa'i's policies had a much-needed calming effect on the public at large. On February 1, the reinstated parliament awarded al-Rifa'i an overwhelming vote of confidence. The ebullient premier received thirty-five votes, exactly as many as Abu'l Huda had obtained fifteen months earlier. His policy of "divide and conquer" ("capitulation" to his detractors) was vindicated when Hikmat al-Masri, on behalf of the National Socialists, abstained. But al-Rifa'i's accomplishment was soon dwarfed by Hussein's own startling version of the "divide and conquer" strategy.[31]

In a radio address on January 16, King Hussein showered special praise on "our brave army, officers, and soldiers" who, he said, had displayed admirable "self-restraint" during the kingdom's month-long period of uncertainty.[32] Just six weeks later, Hussein ordered the dismissal and immediate expulsion of Glubb, Chief of Staff W. M. Hutton, and Intelligence Chief Patrick Coghill. After having called out the army to suppress the rioting, the king's decision to sack the army's commanders was a grand *volte-face*. Even though it was technically no more than the firing of "hired help," Glubb's ouster assumed immense proportions. It transformed Hussein from an imperialist lackey to an Arab nationalist of the highest order and reverberated throughout the Arab and Western worlds as a bell tolling last rites for the British empire. Glubb's dismissal was reportedly an important contributing factor to the thinking behind both Nasser's decision to seize the Suez Canal in July and Eden's attempt to wrest it back three months later.[33]

The story of Glubb's ouster, retold many times from many angles, has taken on almost mythic dimensions. In its most stylized form, it is a modern version of a medieval morality play or perhaps the first act of a production entitled *Suez*. With Hussein pitted first against Glubb and then, more fatefully, against Eden and the weight of what remained of the British empire, it is a David-and-Goliath confrontation of right versus might. As Hussein later recalled, "We were threatened at that point with the end of the Hashemite dynasty in Jordan."[34] The truth of Glubb's ouster is, of course, more complex.

It is not too retrospective an analysis to state that, as one historian has argued, Britain "should have been prepared."[35] Neither Whitehall nor its Amman embassy adequately appreciated the warning signs of Hussein's deteriorating relationship with Glubb or of the politicization of the Legion's Arab officers. Consider the following appraisal, sent by Duke on the very eve of Glubb's ouster:

> There appears to be little political consciousness among the Arab officers of the Legion, little political organisation, and little or no idea of how the Legion could or would take over the direction of the country. . . . [H]ad there been some ferment of political ideas among the Arab officers, or some crystallisation of discontent around a few leading personalities, we should have heard something of it.[36]

By the same token, Hussein was naive to think that Jordan's relations with Britain would not suffer, at least in the short term, from the dismissal of its foremost local asset. After all, just a few weeks earlier Hussein had been on the verge of joining Britain in the Baghdad Pact. What is truly remarkable is not that London wrongly interpreted the dismissal, as Hussein later contended, but that the bilateral relationship was resilient enough for both sides to bear the costs—for Hussein, political; for Britain, military—of deploying British paratroops in Amman in defense of the Hashemite realm following the Iraqi coup d'état just twenty-eight months later. In the interim, of course, much had happened to soften the hurt of Glubb's ouster.

Glubb was the last of the old triumvirate still holding on in Jordan, a "king's man" to be sure, but no less Britain's man, too.[37] He was not unlike the other political "dinosaurs" left over from King Abdullah's era, men Hussein needed but did not like to need. Their relationship had never been particularly warm, and by mid-1955, almost a full year before his dismissal, it had turned especially frosty. In May 1955, Prime Minister Abu'l Huda told Duke bluntly that "a situation was arising that might lead to [Glubb's] resignation" and anxiously asked whether London would retaliate by reducing the military subsidy. (Duke, acting without instructions, said yes.)[38] The immediate bones of contention were, ostensibly, policy differences regarding the army's deployment strategy for the West Bank, the pace of Arab officer promotions, and the proposed transfer of the police from the Legion's jurisdiction to the Interior Ministry. More fundamental, it seems, was the extent to which men around the king— ranging from Sharif Nasser[39] on the one hand to young army officers on the other—were playing on Hussein's understandable resentment at the commanding role that Glubb played in Jordan. In a letter warning Whitehall to tread carefully on the issue of Arabizing the officer corps, Glubb offered this frank, psychological assessment of the king:

> There is no demand at present from the Jordan Government or the public for the removal of British officers. The demand is a result of a personal complex of the King's. . . . Everything is therefore progressing reasonably favourably . . . if the King can be calmed down and prevented from smashing everything up.[40]

In the end, the May episode passed without further incident, but the fact is that Hussein came within a hair's breath of sacking Glubb with very little provocation.

Five months later, Glubb again found himself on the verge of dismissal. This came as an even greater surprise than the earlier episode had because the intervening months had witnessed something of a honeymoon with the king. This time Hussein focused his complaints on personnel matters: that, as Duke reported, the army was "a rabble," that "incompetent people" were being promoted in place of "good men," and that Glubb himself was "behaving in a manner most calculated to undermine the organisation and discipline of the Legion."[41]

During Hussein's October visit to London, the subject of his relations with Glubb did arise, but on this point, there is some discrepancy. In his memoirs, Hussein contends that he "warned British officials frankly that Jordanians had to be given more opportunities in the Legion. I was fobbed off with promises that the matter would be considered," Hussein recalled, "but nothing was ever done." According to Shuckburgh's account of his October 24 "private talk" with Hussein, Shuckburgh mentioned that he "had heard rumors that the King was not pleased with the General" and asked whether there was "anything we could do to help." Hussein then spoke of the "great affection . . . and confidence" he had in Glubb, adding that "there were those who thought [Glubb's] methods were becoming a little out of date." Then, a bit ominously, Hussein observed that "he was bound to regard this with concern since neighboring states were only too quick to say that the British connection was holding Jordan back." Shuckburgh concluded the meeting by asking the king to "let us know" if he ever decided he could not give

Glubb his full confidence; "Of course," Hussein answered. To Shuck-burgh, it was clear that Hussein still had "considerable reservations" about Glubb, most of which he believed derived from "the poison which Sharif Nasser and others are continually pouring into the king's ear," and he was determined that "we [Whitehall] must do our best to clear them up." In Shuckburgh's account, neither Hussein nor Whitehall emerges unblemished. On the one hand, nothing that Hussein told Shuckburgh could rightly be described as a "frank warning"; on the other hand, Shuckburgh's "let us know" hardly reflected the gravity of the situation. But before long, the Baghdad Pact imbroglio intervened, and the matter was shelved.[42]

The army's role in stamping out the second wave of antipact rioting in January 1956 was the critical turning point in Glubb's relationship with the king. With civilian governments falling on an almost weekly basis, the Arab Legion emerged as the only strong institution capable of safeguarding the regime. It was a lesson not lost on any of the key players, but they each drew different conclusions from it.

Delighted by the army's success in quelling the January riots, the British viewed the period after the riots as a time of vast opportunity. "One good result of the recent crisis," reported Duke in February 1956, "is that it seems to have helped to draw the king and Glubb much closer together." He went on to report with unabashed optimism that neither Hussein nor local politicians would oppose the nomination of a British successor to Glubb when the situation arose and that even the king had "drawn up a 'short list' of British generals from whom he will choose Glubb's successor."[43]

Meanwhile, flushed with enthusiasm, Glubb and his senior officers were taking matters into their own hands. They resented what they viewed as al-Rifa'i's accommodationist policy and continually pressed for blanket arrests of "extremists." At one point, Glubb's chief of staff threatened to prevent al-Rifa'i from releasing internees prematurely, by joining with "other responsible British officers" and "'forming up' to the Government and protest." The Legion also put in motion plans to silence lingering antigovernment sentiment. Army units, for example, occupied the northern border town of Ramtha in mid-January, where they arrested opposition "ringleaders," confiscated weapons, imposed heavy compensatory fines for the riot damage, forced the townspeople to supply food, accommodation and fuel, and then demanded payment for the costs of transporting the troops from Zerqa to Ramtha and back again. "I gather that the troops were not particularly gentle," reported Mason. The army also readied plans for the forced relocation of large numbers of Palestinian refugees, including the transfer of "the Jericho refugee population en bloc to the Ma'an district."[44] A special task force was set up under pro-British Colonel Sadiq al-Shar'a in late January "to deal specifically with the rioting in the refugee camps in the Jordan Valley and Hebron." According to Glubb's biographer, it was composed of "bedouin units that stood no nonsense from the rioters."[45] And it was in February 1956 that Glubb raised the specter of transforming the Arab Legion into an avowedly political, almost praetorian, army (albeit without British officers): "The army is the only decent, honest, practically minded body in the country, and it resents pulling chestnuts out of the fire for corrupt politicians," Glubb wrote Templer.[46]

These were not the only lessons drawn from the January riots. In Cairo, the puppeteers who had orchestrated the anti-Jordan propaganda campaign shifted their target from the diabolical yet intangible Baghdad Pact to Glubb, the flesh-and-blood symbol of Western imperialism. As the architect of the army's crackdown against the rioters, Glubb—far more than Hussein—became the chief villain of anti-Jordan broadcasts. "Glubb must go," implored Ahmad al-Sa'id on Sawt al-'Arab. "The authorities in Jordan should understand that the gap between them and the people is created by Glubb's influence." In this way, focusing on the need to oust Glubb while forswearing any intention to subvert the existing regime complemented the offer to replace the British subsidy with Arab aid.[47]

For Hussein, the January riots left his relationship with the army in an uneasy position. The only strong institution in the country was viewed by many as a foreign occupying power bent on quashing the legitimate national aspirations of the Jordanian people. As one historian cogently noted: "The important thing was to gain complete control of the Legion, to identify it as a 'national' army, i.e., an Arab-officered army, and thus hamstring opposition charges against it. It is in this context that Glubb's dismissal in March 1956 makes sense."[48] Hussein's urgent need was to transform the army from a singularly military asset into a political asset as well, though in not quite the same way that Glubb may have envisioned. A swift, decisive, and irreversible blow against Glubb, so soon after Glubb had salvaged the regime from near-anarchy, was what Hussein had in mind.

In that respect, Hussein's thinking had meshed with that of the Arab Legion's young nationalists, the self-styled Jordanian "Free Officers movement." If there is any aspect of Jordanian politics in this period that remains clouded in mystery, it is the role of the Free Officers. For different reasons, both Hussein and Glubb in their memoirs either belittle the role, or completely deny the existence, of any such group. For Glubb, to admit otherwise would have raised all sorts of awkward questions about his own internal security apparatus; for Hussein, to share the spotlight with others would have deflated the "lonely-at-the-top" image in which the entire episode had to be characterized in the wake of the 1957 Zerqa incident.

In tracing the history of the Free Officers, separating fact from fiction is especially tricky: "The sands of such conspiratorial alignments shift normally anywhere in the world, but perilously so in Jordan."[49] Individual army officers had dabbled with politics at least as far back as the

Palestine war, but it was not until 1952 that a group coalesced under that name.[50] Over the previous two years, a small group of junior officers—captains and lieutenants, almost all of whom were East Bank *hadari* (town and city dwellers)—had outgrown a flirtation with the Jordanian Ba'th party and formed what was called the Secret Organization of Nationalist Officers. The twin goals of this "protoparty" grew out of Ba'thist ideology, to Arabize the army and to forge military union with Syria.[51] With the natural burst of enthusiasm following the Egyptian coup d'état, the group changed its name in 1952 to the Jordanian Free Officers movement.

According to the memoirs of Shahir Yusef Abu Shahut, an artillery officer who reputedly served as chairman of the movement's executive committee, the idea of establishing contact with Egypt's Revolutionary Command Council was considered and rejected as too risky. Instead, the movement tried to recruit "honorary members and advisors" from among the senior ranks of the army, perhaps as an effort to find a Jordanian Neguib. The officer most receptive to the group's aims, and apparently most willing to accept the limited role that the movement had in store for its "honorary member," was Major 'Ali Abu Nuwar.[52] The movement's connection with Abu Nuwar, however, was frozen by his appointment to Paris as military attaché in 1952.[53] At the time, the Free Officers had reportedly extended their membership to include artillery, armor, infantry, and engineering officers. But unless Glubb and Coghill were fantastically inept, it is difficult to believe that the movement could have numbered more than a couple of dozen. In a late-life autobiography, Glubb said that there were just six.[54] In any case, it was in February 1953 that Glubb informed Furlonge for the first time of anti-British and anti-Glubb "murmurings" among army officers. Winston Churchill himself read the report and asked to be kept informed, but Whitehall heard nothing more on the subject for more than a year.[55]

In the interim, the movement's leadership was said to have made its first tenuous contact with King Hussein. Posted to Britain for an artillery training course, Abu Shahut struck up his old relationship with 'Ali Abu Nuwar, who was then accompanying the king as the latter wiled away his time after Sandhurst.[56] Abu Nuwar reportedly told Abu Shahut that Hussein shared the movement's goal of Arabizing the army and arranged for Hussein to pass a word of encouragement to Abu Shahut at a party at the Legion Officers Club. According to Abu Shahut, Hussein told him that once he returned to Amman, he would be in touch.[57]

Nothing happened. Indeed, not until mid-1955, about the time of Hussein's confrontation with Glubb, does Abu Shahut claim to have had any direct contact with the king. Over Glubb's objections, Hussein had pushed through Abu Nuwar's reassignment as his principal aide-de-camp. Based on their old London ties, the Free Officers finally had a direct link with Hussein, and Abu Nuwar allegedly arranged a meeting between some of the movement's leaders and the king. It was then that Hussein was said to have promised to prevent Glubb from purging the army of its nationalist officers and to name Abu Nuwar as his official liaison to the Free Officers. Hussein also appointed two more military aides (Mazin al-'Ajluni and Munthir 'Innab) who were reported to be Free Officers, too.

It was in the wake of the January 1956 rioting that Hussein's disenchantment with Glubb and his ties with the Free Officers take on operational importance and, from a historian's point of view, grow vague. According to Abu Shahut, the king met periodically in January and February with members of the movement's executive committee; he himself was never present because he had been posted to the West Bank. Sometime in February, fellow Free Officer Mahmud al-Mu'ayta told Abu Shahut that "the operation to Arabize the army was imminent" and that, most important, Hussein himself would lead the operation and accept responsibility for it. No date was yet set for its execution.[58]

Although it is the subject of some dispute, the question of whether Glubb's dismissal was Hussein's idea or an initiative of the Free Officers that Hussein adopted as his own is not particularly relevant.[59] After all, the idea of rendering the army "Glubbless" had been around for some time. What is more important is that with the option hanging in the air, Hussein grabbed it. At a time when the young monarch was striking out on his own, the enthusiastic comradeship of like-minded officers of his own generation was, no doubt, a considerable, perhaps critical, boost to his confidence. Neither he, nor they, however, had a clear idea of what future their bold step would bring.

Perhaps an even more vexing question is "why March 1?" After all, Hussein could have used the fact that Glubb's three-year contract was due to expire on March 31, just a month away, as a convenient excuse to terminate the general's services.[60] Instead, he acted on what might have been the worst possible day, the very day that Selwyn Lloyd was in Cairo for his fateful and highly publicized meeting with Nasser. Given Hussein's earnest desire not to let Glubb's ouster sour Jordan's bilateral relationship with Britain, there must surely have been an overpowering reason for the king to act when he did.

According to Hussein, two "events" led him to fix "the exact time" for his action against Glubb. On February 28, he later claimed, al-Rifa'i shrugged off his request to transfer control of the police to the Interior Ministry by citing the potential for "serious repercussion" with the British; the king was "really very angry." This was nothing new; the police proposal had been tabled many months earlier,[61] and there was little immediate need to make the change. Then, on February 29, Glubb requested that Hussein confirm the dismissal of about twenty officers—most likely Free Officers—accused of dabbling in politics. "That night," the king wrote, "I decided Glubb Pasha would have to go immediately," and Hussein evidently passed the word to Abu Nuwar to execute a preventive operation, code-named DUNLOP, to surround Glubb's house, place senior British officers under surveillance, and cut their telephone lines. The next morning, March 1, the king presented his cabinet with a decree ordering Glubb's immediate dismissal. But unless Hussein had acted in a fit of pique,[62] there was no particular urgency to dismiss him on that day. Instead, he could have—as Duke had in the past thought he might—simply overruled Glubb and stayed the dismissals.[63]

A collage of secret and top secret telegrams suggests another reason that Hussein may have acted when he did. Late January and February was a period of intense anxiety on the military front, with widespread fears of impending hostilities. On January 24, al-Rifa'i formally asked Duke for a statement of London's position should Jordan be "forced" by the "pressure of internal public opinion" to join its sister Arab states in a war with Israel "not of its choosing." Although he recognized that the circumstances were not covered by the Anglo-Jordanian treaty, al-Rifa'i said that he still hoped Britain would come to Jordan's aid.[64] Ten days later, Glubb and Duke discussed the details of a possible deployment of British paratroops "in event of further riots" with a liaison officer from the Cyprus-based Middle East Land Forces (MELF). Citing the need for coordination in time of crisis, Glubb implored his interlocutor to participate directly in the joint planning then under way with the Iraqis.[65] This placed London in a quandary. For political reasons, tripartite planning with the Iraqis was a nonstarter, but Whitehall was intrigued with the possibility of bilateral planning with the Arab Legion. But for security reasons, London insisted on keeping advanced planning on the same basis as the Iraqi–Jordanian talks, namely, British officers only. The Foreign Office urgently cabled Duke for his views on two explosive questions:

1. How far would our relations with the king and Glubb's position in Jordan suffer if the king discovered that we have been having military talks with [the] British officers of the Legion behind his back?

2. What chances would there be of keeping such talks secret if the king alone were informed of them, and whether he would agree to [the] exclusion of Arab officers?

On February 15, Duke responded, stating that Anglo-Jordanian relations, and specifically Glubb's position, would suffer "considerably" should Hussein find out what was going on "behind his back" and that secrecy could not be maintained for long. Another week went by before London finally decided that holding military talks "without [the] knowledge of the King of Jordan" was not "politically acceptable" and ordered that "action to initiate planning talks with the Arab Legion should therefore be suspended for the present."[66]

The implication is that "action to initiate planning" was by then already under way. Indeed, during the previous week, the aggressive pursuit of secret planning between MELF and the Arab Legion had become

Glubb's top priority. Britain had stalled on al-Rifaʿi's request for a statement of its position, and in the interim Hussein had committed Jordan
to attack Israel should hostilities break out on either the Egyptian or the
Syrian front. "The only way to avoid this," Glubb cabled Templer, "would
be for me and British officers to refuse. This would lead to chaos and
possibly the massacre of the British community." He pleaded with
Templer not to let Jordan float aimlessly any longer without a lead from
London.

> We are drifting toward disaster with no plan and no (repeat no) advice from
> HMG. If we obey the king's orders, the Legion will be destroyed and Israel
> will occupy the West Bank of Jordan. If we refuse, the British community
> will be in danger and the Legion will be ordered to attack without British
> officers. . . . [I]t is absolutely essential for HMG to take action now (repeat)
> now both to prevent war, if possible, and to prepare joint plan with us in
> case war comes.[67]

On February 21, Glubb went one step further, laying down a final deadline by which he needed to receive instructions regarding the role of
British officers in wartime. His deadline was the date on which Israel
reserved the right to start work on the controversial B'not Yaʿacov Bridge
canal, a date when he feared that hostilities would break out on the Israeli–
Syrian frontier. The date was March 1.[68]

A conversation that al-Rifaʿi had with Duke on February 23 showed
that the Jordan government shared Glubb's anxiety about what might
happen on March 1. In light of the B'not Yaʿacov crisis, the prime minister told Duke that "it was a matter of urgency for the Jordan Government to know where they stood." Al-Rifaʿi added, "somewhat apologeti-
cally," that London's failure to give a prompt reply to his January 24
request gave "rise to an impression . . . that in fact HMG do not intend
to prevent the Israelis from seizing the West Bank."[69]

In the end, the Foreign Office's response arrived too late. The final
version of the British government's assurances to Jordan was not sent to
Amman until February 29 and was not relayed to al-Rifaʿi until the
morning of March 1. "It was an ironical coincidence," Duke later noted,
"that as I left the Prime Minister's office, King Hussein was on his way
to it to instruct the Prime Minister to dismiss General Glubb and the
other British officers forthwith."[70]

Had Hussein gotten wind of Glubb's evangelizing for secret military talks "behind his back"? Was Hussein truly afraid that London had
connived with Israel at the expense of the West Bank? Did Hussein fear
that Glubb might sabotage the army's fighting capability by withdraw-
ing its British officers at the last minute? The only answer to these questions is "perhaps," which might have given Hussein enough cause to fix
the date for Glubb's dismissal for March 1. Glubb certainly did not have
as tight a grip on the army's internal security as he may have thought,
evidenced not least by the existence of the Free Officers movement for

the previous four years.[71] And given Glubb's own statements regarding the withdrawal of the British officers, any fears that Hussein might have had about a reenactment of London's Palestine war policy vis-à-vis the officers would certainly have been legitimate.[72] "News came that the enemy was preparing to attack," Hussein explained to Duke a few days later. "We remembered 1948."[73] Perhaps most important, in Amman's swirl of rumor, intrigue, and conspiracy, it was not too great a leap of faith for Hussein to believe that London might finally want to get out of the commitment made to King Abdullah to support the "union of the two banks." As Hussein hinted in his memoirs, Glubb "was well aware that behind the many influences that brought the clash between us to a head lay the ghost of my grandfather."[74]

9

The Kingdom Unraveled

Ironically, Glubb's ouster did not signal Hussein's consolidation of power at the top of the Jordanian pyramid. By mid-March, the paroxysm of nationalist praise for Hussein's "personal coup"[1] had died down, and the old political tests returned with a vengeance. Only this time, the traditional centers of influence—palace, government, and army—faced challenges from newcomers who believed that the future of a Glubbless Jordan was theirs. To the political opposition and to the ambitious nationalists in the Arab Legion, Glubb's dismissal was as much their victory as Hussein's, and over the subsequent months they proceeded to chip away inexorably at the edifice of the state.

This year was not Hussein's finest. With mild understatement, he himself called it a year of "uneasy experiment."[2] Although at times he showed signs of the maturity that helped him weather the Baghdad Pact riots, more often than not the king wavered, ceding almost indifferently the political initiative to men and ideas that were fundamentally at odds with the Hashemites' core principles. With no clear lead from their sovereign, the "king's men" drifted apart from the palace, or perhaps more accurately, they were set adrift by Hussein himself. It was to be a tense ten months before Hussein's minuet with the radical nationalists came to an end and he was able to discern where his, his family's, and his kingdom's most basic interests lay. When the moment of crisis came, it was the old formula of personal fortitude and the commitment of the "king's men" that was able to make the year following Glubb's dismissal an aberration in Jordanian history and not its final chapter.

* * *

Inside Jordan, Glubb's ouster turned upside down the coalition of forces that had pulled the kingdom back from anarchy during the December–January rioting. Specifically, it had the triple effect of undercutting the al-Rifa'i government, emboldening the opposition, and boosting the influence of the Arabized officer corps.

The prime minister, taken by surprise by the king's abrupt order to sack Glubb, felt he had no option but to comply.[3] With that precedent set, he and the cabinet stood lamely aside as the army's upper ranks were filled with men of junior status, substandard experience, and questionable loyalty to the idea of an independent Jordan. Accordingly, the government contented itself with attending to purely political issues, chief of which was the renewal of the aid offer by the Egyptian–Syrian–Saudi axis. The Cairo-led alliance sought to capitalize on Glubb's ouster by repeating its offer to replace the British subsidy, hoping to strip away Jordan from Britain's orbit once and for all. It was al-Rifa'i's task to deflect the Arab offer without in the process tarnishing the king's newfound nationalist credentials, and his strategy was a rerun of Jordan's response to the earlier offer of Arab aid and a four-power meeting in Cairo. This time, the Arab states were told that the kingdom would welcome "any unconditional aid" in addition to the British subsidy and that Hussein insisted on a meeting of all Arab heads of state in Amman. Again, when Jordan upped the ante, Egypt and its allies balked.[4]

After dismissing Glubb, Hussein said he still wanted to follow the middle path between the Arab world's two opposing camps. But as he began that journey, he found this path was growing narrower day by day. His response to the Arab aid offer kept the Egypt-led alliance at arm's length, but his subsequent agreement, at Britain's urging, to meet Iraq's King Feisal on March 14 almost neutralized the political bonanza of sacking Glubb. Little more came out of those H4 talks beyond a vague acceptance of the need to concert military plans, but their symbolism outweighed their substance. Cairo's *al-Ahram* published news of the supposedly secret meeting on the very day that it was held, and Hussein's critics highlighted the fact that Jordan would turn to its Baghdad Pact neighbor before it would accept the assistance of fraternal, "liberated" Arab states. Two days later, representatives of all opposition groups in Jordan—from the Muslim Brotherhood to the National Front—met to press for new elections as a means to "put an end to unconstitutional interference from the Palace." In just two weeks, Hussein's vacillation—sacking Glubb one day and conferring with Nuri the next—raised doubts about the sincerity of his nationalist commitment.[5]

Hussein's go-it-alone policy also strained his relationship with his premier. Although al-Rifa'i may, in fact, have been relieved that the king had not consulted him on Glubb's dismissal, he was unnerved by Hussein's penchant for acting independently and presenting him with *faits accompli*. Al-Rifa'i differed with Hussein on form, not fundamentals; the *way* that Glubb's ouster and the H4 meeting were handled, he argued, were amateurish and needlessly provoked those countries—Britain and Egypt, respectively—on whose goodwill Jordan relied for its survival. Rather than swing abruptly from one extreme to the other, al-Rifaʻi preferred a more measured approach, and the two engaged in a tug-of-war of sorts over the semantics of Jordan's foreign policy. Excluded from the H4 talks, al-Rifaʻi was beside himself when he learned that archrival Nuri had accompanied Feisal, and he retaliated by issuing a statement reaffirming his government's neutrality in inter-Arab disputes. He reportedly had to threaten resignation in order to win Hussein's consent for him to mute Jordan's propaganda volleys against Nasser and to vet palace political communiqués. For several weeks, al-Rifaʻi and Hussein seemed to reconcile themselves to an uneasy truce, but it did not last. By the end of May, Hussein was so intent on adopting a more forceful foreign policy that he found himself no longer able to work with his more restrained prime minister.[6]

The specific issue over which Hussein and al-Rifaʻi parted ways was, of all things, Algeria. Hussein was genuinely moved by the violence in the French colony and was particularly irked that Nasser had "gained kudos as the champion of the Algerian nationalists" without providing the rebels with much material support. By exposing what he considered Nasser's two-faced Algerian policy, Hussein hoped to exploit an issue peripheral to Palestine on which he could score propaganda points against Egypt. Also, the king may have wanted to capitalize on the mass appeal of the Algerian cause to boost his own flagging popularity. Al-Rifaʻi, however, was always fearful that Hussein's headstrong policy might cause a rupture in his own propaganda truce with Nasser. This time, Hussein was bent on having his way. The final straw was in May, when al-Rifaʻi spurned Hussein's direct order to press for effective Arab League action on Algeria as a way to upstage Nasser and highlight Egypt's alleged duplicity. Whereas their different approaches had complemented each other in January, in the post-Glubb environment, the king was determined to have the upper hand over his prime minister. Angered that al-Rifaʻi would consciously sabotage his policy, Hussein demanded his resignation within days of his return from the league's meeting in Damascus.[7]

Al-Rifaʻi's eclipse was matched by the emergence of the army as an alternative center of political power. Radi ʻInnab, an elderly, portly, lifetime police officer, had been appointed—"to his private horror," Coghill wrote—as Glubb's successor. He knew nothing about the coup against Glubb and little more about the military side of the Arab Legion. This left, by both default and design, the group of Arab officers who had been catapulted into executive command positions suddenly in control of what was the state's strongest institution. By no means, though, were they a cohesive group.[8]

Although the Free Officer clique all received hefty promotions, most of the army's top jobs went to higher-ranking officers who were not themselves party to the conspiracy against Glubb. The dozen or so officers who filled the vacated slots of British commanders included an array of Ba'thists, Nasserites, Anglophiles, Iraqi sympathizers, and Hashemite hawks.[9] Some jumped several notches on the promotion ladder and others, like 'Innab, were shuffled across services—from police to artillery, for example—and were woefully ill prepared for their new tasks. Still others were professional soldiers whose sympathy for the idea of Arabization did not mask their fear at the overnight slump in the army's preparedness. Throughout the ranks, quarrels over the tribal and geographic division of spoils were perhaps an even more fundamental cause of antagonism.

Given these fissures, it was little surprise that reports of serious and sometimes violent dissension inside the army began to emerge within days of Glubb's departure. Although the terms are at best suggestive, there seems to have been an early split between what might be called the "political" officers, led by 'Ali Abu Nuwar, now commanding a Jerusalem-based brigade, and their more "professional" counterparts, most notable of whom was National Guard commander Sadiq al-Shar'a. At one point, al-Shar'a was held "virtually under house arrest" by Abu Nuwar's men to prevent a delegation of "professionals" from petitioning the king to replace the political appointments with "more competent officers."[10] Soon thereafter, petty jealousy led to a shooting incident that left the Legion's artillery commander with a bullet wound in the head and resulted in the exile of an armored brigade commander to Washington as military attaché. Whether the root cause of the confrontation was political (Nasserites versus royalists) or tribal (Irbid partisans versus Keraki and Salti loyalists) or a combination of the two is not clear.[11]

The king consistently put the best face on the army's internal troubles—he was at most "5 percent uneasy," he once told Duke—but the need to deal with the dissension was a constant drain. Hussein found himself issuing orders directly to unit commanders and pleading with bedouin soldiers, the backbone of the Legion's fighting troops, not to desert the army now that it had become "a true Arab Army with an Arab leadership." Many left anyway, unimpressed with the improvement. There were simply too few experienced officers to go around for the king to apply a loyalty test in order to weed out potential troublemakers so soon after Glubb's dismissal. At the heart of Hussein's quandary was a more gnawing question: loyalty to what? Other than Arabization, the king did not seem to have much of a political strategy other than to avoid entanglement in either of the alliances that polarized the Arab world, a position that did not win much support among many of the young, zealous officers now commanding his army.[12]

In May, Hussein ordered a series of promotions and reassignments that he hoped would set the military command on a surer footing. 'Innab, never more than a figurehead, was pensioned off and replaced by 'Ali Abu Nuwar, whose friendship with the king had propelled him from major to major general in a matter of months. Six colonels were promoted to brigadier: two ultraloyalists (Habis al-Majali and Circassian Fawwaz Mahir), two Abu Nuwar supporters (Muhammad al-Mu'ayta and Radi al-Hindawi), and the army's two most experienced officers, Sadiq al-Shar'a (the new chief of staff) and 'Ali al-Hiyari (the new divisional commander). An informal military council of top officers was formed that essentially ran the army by committee.[13] It was, however, an uneasy arrangement:

> The position at present in the Legion seems to be a triangle of power represented by the King, 'Ali Abu Nuwar and the senior officers of the Legion. No component of the triangle can stand against the other two. . . . With the possibility of regional and tribal feeling being intermixed with the personal intrigues, rivalries and jealousies among the officers however, the danger [of further internal dissension] will be present for the foreseeable future in the Legion.[14]

In such a precariously politicized environment, commanders relied almost as much on the weight of their particular constituency as on their rank to enforce orders and discipline. At the top of the heap was Abu Nuwar, who depended on Hussein's good graces to compensate for his almost complete lack of field command. In his memoirs, Abu Shahut highlights the fact that although Abu Nuwar may have considered himself the Jordanian Nasser, the Free Officers never considered him one of their own. But whatever their role in Glubb's ouster, no Free Officer was admitted to the army's highest ranks. The most senior among them was Mahmud Musa, the Free Officers' only full colonel, promoted to chief of military intelligence in May.[15]

For his part, Abu Nuwar's first few months on the job showed him to be less of a republican conspirator than an ambitious officer overwhelmed by the enormity of a task for which he was both unschooled and unprepared. The abrupt shake-up of the officers corps, the assignment of *hadari* commanders to tribal units, and the disgruntled departure of hundreds of bedouin soldiers was a sharp blow to the army's readiness, and beneath the bluster, Abu Nuwar knew that his army was no match for the Israelis. Even though he certainly maintained some links of his own with the Egyptian military,[16] he was prudent enough to take help wherever he could find it with as few strings attached as possible. This meant keeping all options open. As Duke noted in April 1956:

> As far as I can judge, [Abu Nuwar] is no great admirer either of Egypt or of ourselves, but he seems to see the practical advantage of the British connexion. I do not think that he is anxious to quarrel with Gamal Abdul Nasser but he seems to look upon him with a certain healthy skepticism.[17]

When he was short of ammunition or wanted help in establishing a military staff college, for example, Abu Nuwar turned first to Iraq, knowing that London and Baghdad were eager to retain whatever links they could with the Jordanian military.[18] Indeed, time and time again, Abu Nuwar returned to the same ruse, dangling the threat of accepting Egyptian—or, worse, Soviet—arms as a way to blackmail Britain and Iraq into giving him what he needed to strengthen his own position.[19] And he usually got his way. During a June 1956 visit to Baghdad, for example, Abu Nuwar negotiated a military aid agreement that he said "envisaged closer association between Iraqi and Jordanian forces than those with any Arab state." Even the hard-bitten Nuri admitted that Abu Nuwar made a "fairly good impression."[20] Because he often told his interlocutors precisely what they wanted to hear, Abu Nuwar's pragmatism was sometimes mistaken for political moderation. Such was the case when he discussed arms purchases with American intelligence officer Wilbur Crane Eveland and when he convinced the British military attaché in Amman that he was "first and foremost a Jordanian nationalist [and] not unfriendly to Iraq, Britain or the West."[21] In a telling note to British Foreign Secretary Selwyn Lloyd, Eden went so far as to suggest that it was Abu Nuwar "we should see . . . rather than Hussein."[22] To Abu Nuwar's credit, he had successfully marketed his mix of brinkmanship and bargain hunting as a political strategy, when in fact, he was only trying to secure his own weak flanks.

The spring and summer of 1956 was a period of great drift in Jordanian politics. From the end of al-Mulqi's ministry to Glubb's dismissal, the old condominium of king, government, and army had again been functioning, if fitfully and not altogether harmoniously. Each party needed the others and was, in some sense, a check on the others. Even though their relative strength fluctuated and crises sometimes erupted, the three partners shared a common understanding of the fragility of Hashemite rule and the requirements for its survival. The opposition, meanwhile, could influence government policy but never control it. With the Baghdad Pact crisis, the condominium began to crumble; the government parted ways with the king; and Glubb began to lose touch with vital elements in the army. Hussein, al-Rifa'i, and Glubb each contributed his own particular strengths to keeping the country from collapse in early 1956, but the foundation of their institutional relationship—king, government, and army—had eroded.

Glubb's ouster finally set it adrift. Although "king's men" still filled the cabinet, they could no longer rely on the palace's confidence and the army's backing. Since they rarely cultivated popular support, they were virtually powerless. In the meantime, the popular opposition had amassed such a long string of political successes that it had acquired its own veto power over the weakened government. And the other two legs of the triad—Hussein and the Arab Legion—had embarked on new paths with no clear strategy. Among the men who now effectively ruled Jordan was lost the common understanding about Hashemite survival that had kept the old condominium together.

On May 22, Hussein appointed Sa'id al-Mufti to replace Samir al-Rifa'i, and two days later, Abu Nuwar succeeded 'Innab as chief of the general staff. Together, these changes highlighted the new balance of power inside the kingdom. As a political leader, al-Mufti was a spent force, but his refusal to sign on to the Baghdad Pact had made him a popular figure. Six of the new cabinet's ten members had served in al-Mufti's previous government, including three of its five Palestinian ministers.[23] By chartering a cabinet so composed, Hussein was, in a sense, admitting his error in pushing for accession to the pact six months earlier. Indeed, immediately on taking office, al-Mufti picked up the anti-British theme on which his previous government foundered. The first order of business, he announced, was to revise the Anglo-Jordanian treaty to replace the military subsidy with a fixed rent for British base rights to be paid directly to the Jordanian government.[24]

By the summer of 1956, however, the cry of treaty revision had lost the thunder and novelty it had previously enjoyed. On the eve of delivering his ministerial statement outlining his plans to seek revision, al-Mufti was outflanked by the opposition National Socialist and Ba'th parties. They sent a joint note to the premier demanding new elections to choose a parliament able to "draw up an Arab liberation policy for the country"; treaty revision, they declared, could wait.[25] Given al-Mufti's well-publicized antagonism to the sitting parliament, whose rigged election in 1954 still rankled, the opposition demand struck a sensitive chord. Mass demonstrations began to press for both parliament's dissolution and outright abrogation of the Anglo-Jordanian treaty. Parliament itself, perhaps out of sympathy with public opinion or maybe as a way to save its members' own political careers, was poised to take the unprecedented step of denying the government a vote of confidence. Returning from a visit to Egypt, the spokesmen for a group of deputies announced that a majority of the chamber was likely to support abrogation and vote against the government.[26] Rather than have his government so quickly and ignominiously collapse, Hussein bowed to the opposition and ordered parliament's dissolution. Al-Mufti's cabinet resigned on the same day and a caretaker government was formed under Ibrahim Hashim; elections were scheduled for October 21. Everything seemed to be going the opposition's way.

King Hussein wanted the coming election to be different from its predecessors. Abu'l Huda's handling of the 1954 vote had shackled him with the worst of all possible parliaments: one neither legitimate in the eyes of the people nor decisively loyalist in the crunch. Therefore, he early on committed himself to an election "with a view to producing a genuinely representative parliament." Whether Hussein was prompted by a desire to tweak Nasser's democratic protestations, to redress the political drawbacks of the sitting chamber, or to try one last go at establishing a liberal, constitutional government—or perhaps all three—he sincerely believed there was a "fair chance" that a "reasonable parliament" (i.e., one with not more than "two or three extremists") would be returned. In July, it was formally announced that members of the armed forces—now styled in the post-Glubb era as the "Jordan Arab Army"—would not, as they had in 1954, take part in the voting, and Hussein himself issued a royal decree tightening up the election laws.[27] Despite some petty interference in the voting, the October election was truly the "freest that Jordan had ever experienced."[28]

Egypt's seizure of the Suez Canal and its attendant tensions electrified the election campaign. Jordanians of all political persuasions, including Hussein himself, warmly applauded Nasser's gambit. "There is no doubt," Duke reported, "that public opinion in Jordan strongly and wholeheartedly supports Nasser."[29] Abu Nuwar confirmed privately what popular pressure had already forced Hashim's government to state publicly: If Britain took military measures against Egypt, Jordan would have "no choice" but to come to Egypt's aid.[30] Behind the scenes, the specter of war propelled Abu Nuwar (and, to a lesser degree, Hussein) into an almost apoplectic effort to secure commitments of armaments, money, and support from any available source—Britain, Russia, America, Egypt, Saudi Arabia, Syria, and Iraq—and the Jordanians were at least partially successful with everyone they approached. At about this time, Britain and Jordan also held their first-ever discussions about the timing and extent of British military assistance under the terms of the Anglo-Jordanian treaty.[31] Abu Nuwar was especially anxious that London confirm its intention to honor its treaty commitments, and he was willing to bargain away some aspects of those commitments for a public assurance of support in time of war.[32] Abu Nuwar got some of what he wanted, most notably an October 12 warning to Israel—following its devastating attack on the West Bank town of Qalqilya—that affirmed Britain's intention to side with Jordan in the face of Israeli aggression. But at the same time, London refused to accept two key Jordanian requests: that Qalqilya-scale retaliatory raids constituted an act of war; and that RAF commanders in Amman, and not the Foreign Office in London, be empowered to commit British air forces to Jordan's defense.[33] Hussein also turned to his Hashemite cousins for help, but last-minute quarreling between the Jordanian and Iraqi high commands stalled the entry of Iraqi troops into Jordan.[34] As the threat of war escalated, Hussein gave way to unremitting political pressure from both his Arab neighbors and domestic politicians to accede to the Egyptian–Syrian military pact. On the eve of the Suez war, Jordan found itself in the anomalous position of being formally bound to both Britain and Egypt.[35]

When elections were first called, the border situation was anxious but controlled; by the third week of October, however, the prospects of an Israeli attack on Jordan looked imminent, with the chances of an Anglo-French strike against Egypt not far behind. That, in turn, raised the temperature level of the election campaign. Six different groups—the term *party* does not apply to all—competed in the election. They included two religious groups (the Muslim Brotherhood, technically a "charitable organization," and the Liberation party), the National Front, the Ba'th party, the National Socialist party (NSP), and the Arab Constitutional party, "more a parliamentary pressure group than a political party." A handful of independents comprised the rest of 142 registered candidates.[36] Nationalist parties capitalized on the Suez crisis handsomely. The canal's nationalization was announced just days after efforts broke down to form an electoral coalition among the Ba'th, National Front, and NSP. Together, the three parties were then able to exploit Nasser's popularity to organize a nationwide general strike that was "almost 100 percent effective" and that provided a timely boost to their electoral spirits.[37] The frenzied political atmosphere produced a lowest-common denominator campaign. Conservative candidates were forced by public opinion either to vie with their radical opponents for the most extreme nationalist positions or to drop out of the election altogether. As a result, such divisive topics as the difference between "termination" (the moderate view) and "abrogation" (the radical view) of the Anglo-Jordanian treaty was the sum of the campaign's substantive content.

As with all Jordanian parliamentary campaigns, before and since, the 1956 vote was marked by the striking absence of a centrist political voice. Shunted to the wings of the political stage, the "king's men" did not even make such feeble efforts as they had in the past (e.g., al-Rifa'i's Nation party) to enter the electoral fray. Hussein had told Duke in July that he hoped "to organise a Jordan Party in the course of the elections," but nothing came of it.[38] Tawfiq Abu'l Huda, the patriarch of the Arab Constitutionalists, died in July 1956, and the party to which he had lent his prestige four months earlier subsequently degenerated into a motley collection of conservative ex-deputies trying to retain their parliamentary seats by masquerading as aggressive nationalists. By the end of September, the British embassy reported that the party had "more or less disintegrated."[39] Although its nominees did surprisingly well in the election, winning eight seats, the party itself ceased to function corporately, and most of its candidates showed themselves perfectly willing to swim with the nationalist tide.

On paper, at least, the National Socialists could have occupied the political middle. Among their leaders were men from some of the oldest, wealthiest, and most prominent families in the kingdom: Hikmat al-Masri, reputed to be the richest man in Nablus; 'Abd al-Halim al-Nimr, a onetime member of Abdullah's consultative council; and Sulayman al-Nabulsi, remembered by Kirkbride as a "staunch conservative" when he served as finance minister in two of al-Rifa'i's earlier governments. The NSP, it seems, was less a "popular party" than, as al-Nabulsi's son recalled, "a group of friends" that had some popularity. Indeed, the party's political platform was surprisingly tame. According to al-Nimr's son, party leaders were at most "socialists in thought and style"; one should emphasize the "'social' in socialism," cautioned one its founding members. What political philosophy the party espoused was nationalist but mildly so, unionist but in moderation, reformist but not revolutionary, royalist but within constitutional limits. The party, it must be recalled, gave its tacit approval to al-Rifa'i in the February 1956 parliamentary vote of confidence, and despite his son's vehement denial, Sulayman al-Nabulsi was at one time sympathetic to the Baghdad Pact. Among British observers, it was hoped the NSP could wind up "rather as the Congress Party did in India."[40]

Ambition pulled the NSP into alignment with the radical left. In the new age of "street politics" in Jordan, the NSP's aristocratic leaders were swept up in the maelstrom of mass rallies, public demonstrations, and general strikes. They had popular appeal, but only as individuals with little real popular base, so they linked up with the better organized Ba'th and National Front to maximize their electoral attraction. In return, the NSP offered the radical parties a sort of legitimacy—and, by extension, protection from last-minute proscription—that they could not muster for themselves.[41] The contrast between the NSP's "upper class, big, rich men" and the Ba'th's cadres of students, teachers, and government functionaries was sharp: NSP leaders were ill at ease when they took to the hustings and reportedly "remained rather in the background" throughout much of the campaign.[42] But in the end, the NSP's electoral gambit worked.

Despite the high state of tension, the elections went off calmly, without incident and with a respectable, though not overwhelming, voter turnout.[43] At first glance, the returns seemed to indicate a victory for the moderates and a rebuff to the radicals. The National Socialists won a plurality, twelve of the chamber's forty seats, and the Arab Constitutionalists and independents (most, but not all, of whom were Hashemite loyalists) claimed eight and ten seats, respectively. For all the hoopla, the Ba'th put in an embarrassingly poor showing, taking just two seats, one fewer than the National Front. For their part, Islamic parties did moderately well, winning five seats among them.[44]

Although neither the opposition nor the loyalist camps were cohesive groups, the latter was in a sorrier state. Among those defeated were prominent moderates with well-earned nationalist reputations, like Anwar Nusaybah, Hussein Fakhri al-Khalidi, and Khulusi al-Khayri. Some of the nominal independents who did win lacked any strong political convictions and were, it was alleged, "available to the highest bidder"; at least two others were die-hard supporters of Hajj Amin al-Husayni.[45] Even though a theoretical coalition of moderates could have been formed, the NSP instead preferred the formula that had worked so well in the elections. But whereas its electoral alliance with the left had worked in its favor, its decision to retain that alliance after the elections tilted the scales in the other direction, rewarding its coalition partners with political power far in excess of their electoral strength.

For nearly a week after the vote, Hussein mulled over his choice of prime minister. In the meantime, the new parliament convened and, with the Egyptian and Syrian army chiefs-of-staff in attendance, unanimously approved resolutions in support of the Arab struggle against "imperialism" and the severance of diplomatic relations with France. The chamber also elected its own five-man executive, without a "king's man" in sight.[46] The Arab Constitutionalists showed their true colors when spokesman Mustafa Khalifa came out in favor of abrogating the Anglo-Jordanian treaty. When Ibrahim Hashim and Samir al-Rifa'i, neither of whom had had a role in the elections, wanted no part of a new government, Hussein had nowhere to turn but to the party politicians, and so he picked what looked like the most moderate of the lot.[47] On October 27, Sulayman al-Nabulsi, the NSP leader who himself had failed in his own bid for parliament, was asked to form a government.[48] His eleven-man coalition cabinet announced two days later included six members of his party, three independents (none of whom had before served in ministerial posts), and one representative each of the Ba'th (Abdullah al-Rimawi) and the National Front ('Abd al-Qadir al-Salih).[49] For the first, and almost assuredly last, time in the kingdom's history, a government was formed without a single, unabashed "king's man."

A Jordanian historian who has written one of the very few biographical sketches of al-Nabulsi opened his chapter with the following line: "It is not easy to write about Sulayman al-Nabulsi and to evaluate the role he played in the political life of Jordan."[50] This is indeed the case. To this day, the legacy of al-Nabulsi and the government he headed remain a symbol for both the best and the worst of Jordanian political life. To some, al-Nabulsi represents the promise of constitutional democracy and the rule of law; to others, al-Nabulsi is held up as the man who pandered to the jungle politics of the "street" and nearly presided over the very dismemberment of the kingdom. There are, in fact, elements of truth in both characterizations, for al-Nabulsi was a complex and perhaps confused man.

Despite his name, Sulayman al-Nabulsi was a Salti, born in 1908 into a wealthy, landowning family that had migrated from the West Bank more than a century earlier.[51] After graduating from the American University of Beirut, he went directly into government service, rising quickly to cabinet secretary. In 1945, he left government for the financial world and was before long appointed director of an Amman bank. But all the while, al-Nabulsi's conventional exterior masked an intensely political animal; "politics," wrote his biographer, "was in his blood." Al-Nabulsi was an early disciple of Subhi Abu Ghanima, the "godfather" of Transjordanian Arab nationalists, and he was active in local and national political controversies from his early twenties.[52] Indeed, the reason he left government in 1945 was over his opposition to the awarding of a concession to a company with reputed Zionist links, and when he began to stir up trouble, he was banished to town arrest. But financial acumen was such a rare commodity in Jordan at the time that al-Nabulsi never stayed out of favor for long, and he could claim the distinction of being released from prison one day only to be appointed a minister the next. A 1953 personality report spoke of him as "intelligent financially" but suffering from "a streak of left-wing fanaticism." Thus he led a dual life, servant-cum-opponent of the monarchy, and thanks to his good connections— including al-Rifaʿi's patronage, al-Mufti's friendship, and Abu'l Huda's respect—he was able to maintain that uneasy balance for an unusually long time. Part of his secret might have been that he kept his true political loyalties hidden from view. Over the years, he was variously described as "progressive," "nationalist," Iraqi "federalist," "anti-Abu'l Huda without being anti-West," and a proponent of "Jordan for the Jordanians without Palestinian interference." No one, maybe not even al-Nabulsi himself, knew for sure which, if any, were accurate.[53]

Political courage, though, seems not to have been one of al-Nabulsi's strong points. Time and time again, in both opposition and government, when al-Nabulsi was faced with the alternatives of holding fast to an unpopular position or giving way to the often intemperate demands of the "street," he almost invariably opted for the latter. By his own admission, he felt himself powerless to buck popular opinion. Although he disclaimed "love for any of the extremists," there was "little he could do," he said, to avert an electoral alliance with them.[54] Charles Johnston, the "unashamed imperialist"[55] who succeeded Duke as British ambassador in November 1956, recognized al-Nabulsi's weakness from the outset. After crediting al-Nabulsi with maintaining public order during the Suez crisis, he quickly added that "the Nabulsi Government were only able to keep the mob quiet by doing what the mob wanted."[56] One of al-Nabulsi's contemporaries suggested that because he had failed in his own parliamentary election, the prime minister lacked the authority to impose his will on his colleagues.[57] What is clear is that despite his popularity, al-Nabulsi was never a true leader, and this, more than anything else, suggests that he was not the mastermind of the "clique to abolish the monarchy and finish Jordan as an entity," as Hussein charged in his memoirs. Rather, with the passage of time, Hussein gave a more subdued, sympathetic, and probably more accurate picture of the kingdom's only democratically elected prime minister: "I really believe he was 'middle of the road,' not an extremist," the king said. "He just rode the tide. He didn't control his government, [and] he didn't control his colleagues."[58]

As leader of the largest party in parliament, al-Nabulsi took office wielding a strong hand. His first moves were encouraging. His appointment coincided with the beginning of Israel's Sinai campaign, and al-Nabulsi was immediately faced with the decision of whether or not to fulfill Jordan's treaty obligations to Egypt and enter the war on its behalf. Despite warlike sounds from his cabinet colleagues, al-Nabulsi recognized the gravity of London's warning that it would not come to Jordan's aid should it attack Israel.[59] Together, he and Abu Nuwar, who was aware of Jordan's military weakness, urged Hussein to reject pleas for intervention from Egypt's 'Abd al-Hakim Amer and to limit his response to requesting Iraqi, Syrian, and Saudi reinforcements and ordering high-profile gestures like air raid warnings, curfews, and electricity blackouts. Hussein—"furious if not hysterical" for military action—gave way, perhaps as a result of a telegram from Nasser himself overruling Amer and counseling restraint. By the time Arab troops arrived in Jordan, the danger of an Israeli attack had passed, and there was little doubt that al-Nabulsi's prudence—hesitance, perhaps—had saved Jordan from a strategic blunder.[60] As Duke noted: "It is now the present Jordan Government in spite of a strongly nationalistic composition which is making every effort to avoid a break with us or the commitment of Jordan to an attack on Israel and is trying to restrain the King."[61]

The political fallout from the Suez war proved more difficult to handle. Although public opinion accepted Jordan's noninvolvement, it was infuriated by Britain's suspected collusion with France and Israel and demanded retribution. The fact that London had not employed its Jordanian air bases in operations against Egypt made little impression. On November 1, parliament ordered the severance of relations with France; the only reason it did not break ties with Britain too was because a unilateral abrogation of the Anglo-Jordanian treaty would have been an expensive proposition. Jordan's exchequer was reported to be hovering perilously close to bankruptcy, with bank reserves of only £700,000, just about a month's worth of the British subsidy. Al-Nabulsi therefore tried to keep his domestic wolves at bay while exacting what he could, when he could, from London. Specifically, he wanted Britain to make subsidy payments on a monthly basis, rather than wait for an end-of-year payment of the £2.5 million remaining for the fiscal year. London, in turn, sought to use its financial leverage to extract the best deal it could from a bad situation.[62]

In the meantime, a secret initiative was under way to solicit American patronage in place of British. On November 9, 'Ali Abu Nuwar told the American military attaché that in exchange for military and economic aid of "sufficient volume," he would "guarantee" a crackdown on Jordan's communists, dissolution of the parliament, and the imposition of strict martial law. "I and the people of Jordan will follow U.S. policies," he modestly offered, adding his willingness to fly to Washington to seal the deal personally with President Dwight Eisenhower. At the same time, he warned that without American support, Jordan would be forced to accept repeated Soviet offers of aid.[63] About a week later, King Hussein himself made a personal appeal for American assistance. Jordan preferred Western support, he stated, but would turn to Cairo and Moscow if necessary. Washington's immediate response was cool and noncommittal, merely urging Hussein against "jumping from [the] frying pan into [the] fire."[64]

Al-Nabulsi, who knew nothing of the demarche to Washington, had his hands full with the extreme members of his coalition, especially his Baʿthist minister of state for foreign affairs, Abdullah al-Rimawi. Demagogic and conspiratorial, al-Rimawi was one of the most consistent politicians in Jordan. He vowed allegiance to the Baʿth during his university days in Beirut and never wavered, despite periodic spells in jail, throughout the rest of his life. His wife was a Baʿth activist, too.[65] In contrast with al-Nabulsi, there was nothing vague about where al-Rimawi stood: He opposed the very existence of an independent Jordan and was committed to substantive Arab unity under the banner of Syria. Everything—tactics, friendship, democracy—was subordinate to those strategic goals. His widow summed up al-Rimawi's philosophy as follows: "The reason isn't important," she said. "The result is what matters—unity and Arabism."[66]

Once the immediate danger of war abated, al-Rimawi and his colleagues took to the streets to whip up public opinion. His immediate objectives were threefold: to replace the British subsidy with Arab aid, to evict suspect Iraqi troops from Jordanian territory, and to press for the heavily symbolic moves of establishing diplomatic relations with the Soviet Union and the People's Republic of China. His goal was to damage Jordan's relations with the West beyond repair, giving the kingdom no other choice but to turn for support to the Arab states. That would be the important first step toward abolishing Jordan's sovereign independence altogether. When on November 20, parliament unanimously approved resolutions recommending the abrogation of the Anglo-Jordanian treaty and the establishment of direct ties with Moscow and Beijing, his strategy seemed to be working.[67]

November, therefore, heard the starting gun of a race to see whether the palace's feverish efforts to secure American support would bear fruit before the radicals could demolish Jordan's remaining links with the West. Al-Nabulsi and most of his National Socialist colleagues were caught in the middle. They both wanted change and were fearful of its consequences; they had high regard for the ideal of Arab unity but less so for the sincerity of Arab leaders. Therefore, al-Nabulsi adopted a policy designed to hold on as long as possible to the British connection, not out of any lingering affection for Britain but more out of fear of what might (or what might not) replace it. Moreover, he was adamant that the British connection not be severed until a firm agreement had been signed with the Egyptian-led alliance to provide aid in its place. All this would take time, and al-Nabulsi was a master at manipulating the government machinery to strip his vehemently anti-West public rhetoric of any operational significance. But as time passed, al-Nabulsi found it virtually impossible to distinguish, both to himself and to his listeners, between what he said and what he meant.

On November 27, the Jordanian cabinet accepted in principle parliament's two resolutions but approved several time-consuming procedures that delayed their implementation. First, it supported the negotiated termination, not the unilateral abrogation, of the Anglo-Jordanian treaty;[68] second, it conditioned that termination on the prior "guaranteeing" of Arab aid; and third, it accepted the principle of establishing diplomatic relations on the basis of national interest but insisted on the need to "study the recommendation" about extending formal recognition to the Communist states. Given the highly charged atmosphere of the day, this was a platform of laudable restraint. At the same time, there were several items on the radicals' political agenda that al-Nabulsi either did not feel he could oppose or actually supported, such as securing the early withdrawal of Iraqi troops[69] and the sacking of a number of Anglophilic government functionaries.[70] Meanwhile, the palace kept him and the cabinet in the dark about renewed Soviet offers of arms and money. According to Abu Nuwar, Hussein was apparently convinced that the offers would invariably be leaked to the press and that public clamoring in their favor would make them irresistible.[71]

Even though radicals in Jordan's government wanted to goad Britain into a speedy abrogation of the treaty, cooler heads prevailed. Instead, Whitehall and its new man on the ground, Charles Johnston, took advantage of the interlude that al-Nabulsi provided to try to arrange for the Americans to assume the burden of the British commitment to Jordan. That was the only way, London concluded, to prevent the Jordanians from falling prey to the Soviets and, more important, to bolster Nuri's position in Iraq, the real objective of British policy at the time.[72] Accordingly, London swallowed its pride and acquiesced in al-Nabulsi's idea of paying the subsidy in monthly allotments. "I agree that this is humiliating," Johnston counseled. "The only alternative seems to be humiliating and dangerous as well."[73]

Both Britain's and Hussein's strategies converged on the need to secure an American commitment to Jordan. The problem, though, was that Washington was not eager to take over London's burden. On December 10, Selwyn Lloyd told U.S. Secretary of State John Foster Dulles quite candidly that he believed Jordan was doomed as an independent country. What is its future? Dulles asked. "I don't think it's got one," Lloyd replied. If Lloyd's bluntness was meant to shock Dulles into action, he was sorely mistaken. Surprisingly, the prospect of losing Jordan to the Soviets did not alarm the brinkman Dulles at all. He told Lloyd that satellites not contiguous to the Soviet Union's own territory could easily be "pinched off"; moreover, he observed that because Moscow knew this too, it was unlikely to "make a big investment in areas which they could not hold." The tenor of his response to Lloyd and to subsequent British demarches throughout January was clear: Pouring too much money into Jordan would be a waste; the "brutal fact," Dulles later explained, was that "Jordan had no justification as a State." For him, it was better to target American support where it could make a real difference in the contest between East and West.[74]

Hussein was "greatly disappointed" when he was told in late December 1956 that Washington had turned down his request for aid. With the radicals in parliament and in his own government calling for immediate economic union with Syria as a first step toward political integration, he took little solace in the U.S. ambassador's suggestion that the best course for Jordan would be to patch up its tattered ties with Britain.[75] But as London itself had recognized, it was too late for that sort of reconciliation. The king, therefore, was forced to go along with al-Nabulsi's efforts to secure Arab aid in place of the British subsidy. On January 19, 1957, Hussein, Nasser, King Saud, and Syrian Premier Sabri al-'Asali signed the Arab Solidarity Agreement in Cairo, according to which the three Arab states promised to provide Jordan with 12.5 million Egyptian pounds per year for ten years to replace the British subsidy.[76] In public, Hussein extended his "utmost gratitude and appreciation" to his Arab patrons; in private, he admitted he "had no choice." Three days later, Johnston officially requested that negotiations be convened "as soon as possible" to terminate the Anglo-Jordanian treaty.[77]

One month earlier, al-Nabulsi had brashly told an interviewer that real Arab union—military, economic, and political—was necessary and imminent. "Jordan cannot live forever as Jordan," he had declared. After the kingdom formally signed away its financial autonomy to Arab states that a year earlier had been fomenting internal rebellion, al-Nabulsi's idealistic dream, and Hussein's real-life nightmare, seemed on the verge of coming true.[78]

10

The Kingdom Restored

The first weeks of 1957 were the nadir of King Hussein's young reign. One by one, the essential elements of the Hashemite system—a loyalist government; a strong, formidable, and cohesive army; a dependable and faithful patron—were slipping away. "People were convinced that the country didn't have any potential for surviving," Hussein later recalled. "Everything was falling apart."[1] But before all was lost, Hussein summoned up the courage and resources to arrest what looked like an inexorable slide toward extinction and to patch together an alliance of royalist forces unseen in Jordan since the days of Abdullah.

In retrospect, Hussein was excruciatingly slow to respond to the fateful challenges facing his regime. There were at least three reasons to account for that. First, it was Hussein's nature to tarry long before deciding to act but then to act swiftly once the decision was made. Such was the case, for example, with his sacking of al-Mulqi in 1954 and with the buildup to the Baghdad Pact crisis in 1955, and he remained true to form in 1957, too.* Second, for a dangerously long time, Hussein underestimated the magnitude of those challenges. He continued to retain confidence in the loyalty of the army's command, and especially in 'Ali

---

*This pattern, long deliberation before swift action, remains Hussein's *modus operandi.* It describes, as he readily admits, his behavior in 1970 and also, perhaps, his disengagement from the West Bank in 1988. It may also explain his reluctance to go to war in 1973 or to join the peacemaking effort five years later. Far from being impulsive, the record shows him to have a streak of hesitation bordering on indecision. The starkest exception to this rule was, of course, 1967.

Abu Nuwar, long after he had lost faith in the integrity of the al-Nabulsi government, and it came as a rude surprise that the "liberated" Jordan Arab Army posed as much a danger to the regime as did the perfidy of elected politicians. Third, even when he finally recognized the enormity of the threat, he had few assets with which to confront it. Given his internal vulnerabilities, Hussein apparently felt too feeble and too isolated to respond until he was sure of tangible outside support.

The first signal of such outside support came from the weak link in the Arab nationalist alliance, Saudi Arabia. Relations between Jordan and Saudi Arabia, and especially between the two royal families, had long been ambivalent; on regional matters, the Saudis also vacillated between their historic American connection and their alignment with the Egyptian–Syrian axis. Toward the end of 1956, King Saud became the focus of American efforts to check the spread of Arab radicalism, and as one historian noted, "Saudi Arabia seemed to hold the balance" between the success of neutralism and the survival of the Arab world's remaining pro-West regimes.[2] When Washington offered to build Saud up as a conservative alternative to Nasser, the king responded, and nowhere was his response more deeply felt than in Jordan.[3]

As early as late November 1956, Saud warned Hussein against terminating the British treaty prematurely and urged him not to establish diplomatic ties with China and the Soviet Union. At about the same time, a measure of amity was restored between the Houses of Saud and Hashim during an anxious visit to Saudi Arabia by Queen Zayn. With Washington's behind-the-scenes encouragement, an understanding began to emerge in Jeddah and Amman on the common dangers facing the two monarchies. Hussein led a government delegation to Saudi Arabia in mid-January, and while Saudi and Jordanian ministers conferred in Riyadh, he set off for a private audience with Saud in Medina. When Saud came to Washington soon after signing the Arab Solidarity Agreement, the contours of the new Saudi–Jordanian relationship were apparently confirmed. Buoyed by the knowledge that a wedge had been driven in the Egypt-led alliance and that Jordan's financial health was not solely in the hands of suspect radicals, Hussein could begin the slow process of piecing together the fragments of his regime.[4]

The issue on which Hussein built his case against the al-Nabulsi government was its alleged softness toward Communism and, specifically, its apparently blunt dismissal of the Eisenhower Doctrine.[5] Though Hussein was a committed anti-Communist and took seriously the religious responsibility of his Hashemite lineage, domestic politics—not Communism—was the real issue. Even before Eisenhower formally presented his plan, Jordan's press had lambasted any suggestion of America filling what *al-Urdunn* (Amman) termed the "so-called 'vacuum'" in the Middle East. As Jerusalem's *Falastin* noted caustically, "The Arabs have never been attacked by Russia, but they have been attacked many times by Western states."[6] A statement by al-Rimawi that Jordan would forever remain neutral in the East–West conflict amounted to a formal government rejection of the Eisenhower Doctrine. Although al-Rimawi later vowed never to "change the pound for the ruble," 1957 was a time when only "fellow travelers" championed neutrality.[7]

Such a policy gave Hussein a pretext to strike out on his own. In a series of pronouncements culminating in a stunning message to al-Nabulsi on February 2, Hussein was bold, blunt, and clear: "We want this country to be inaccessible to Communist propaganda and Bolshevik theories, and we should resist anyone who objects to our tendencies and beliefs," he declared. Even though the message was technically just a letter from the sovereign urging his premier to take measures against the spread of Soviet propaganda, it was both meant and taken as a direct challenge of wills between king and government. "We will be friendly to those who are friendly to us and hostile to those who choose to be hostile to us," said Hussein. "We believe in the right of this country to live a free life." The king reportedly followed up this directive with a demand that al-Nabulsi sack al-Rimawi but, interesting given the context, not the more avowedly pro-Communist National Front minister, 'Abd al-Qadir al-Salih.[8]

For the first time since Glubb's ouster, Hussein had taken a political gamble. But if he thought al-Nabulsi would meekly submit to a new order of royal absolutism, he was mistaken. The prime minister proved quite adept at deflecting the king's bombast. His public denunciations of the Eisenhower Doctrine were belied by a private message he sent to the State Department offering a tepid welcome to the plan and agreeing to receive special emissary James Richards to discuss "mutual problems." Al-Nabulsi was no ideologue, and he had little compunction in shutting down Communist bookstores and newspapers and banning the circulation of Soviet movies and news reports.[9] Although he refused to unsettle his coalition by firing al-Rimawi, he went one step better, appointing both al-Rimawi and al-Salih to the ministerial committee charged with negotiating the termination of the Anglo-Jordanian treaty, thereby implicating them in what he hoped would be the amicable end of the British connection. (Those negotiations opened on February 4.) All the while, al-Nabulsi kept his eye firmly on his strategic objective, to terminate the treaty. Once that was accomplished, al-Nabulsi believed that he would be hailed as the true champion of Jordan's fight against imperialism, with enough popular support to construct a real constitutional monarchy—complete with a powerless, ornamental monarch—as a first step toward what he termed "the establishment of a Federal Union with Syria."[10]

Hussein followed up his attack on Communism with a series of direct interventions in government policymaking. At a cabinet meeting on February 18, the king issued instructions that the press should not attack the Eisenhower Doctrine; that the government should shelve plans to reorganize the diplomatic service; and that no action should be taken regarding establishing relations with Communist states. Again Hussein was trying to force the government's hand, and again the ministers responded with cautious restraint. Al-Rimawi argued convincingly that it would be best not to resign but to remain in office and force the king to dismiss them if he so wished. For al-Nabulsi, it was imperative that nothing be allowed to upset the treaty termination negotiations, which eventually concluded on a friendly note on March 13.[11] In the meantime, the NSP–Ba'th–National Front alliance organized a series of popular conferences whose goal, according to Samir al-Rifa'i, was to "line up behind [the government] such a formidable array of public support as to intimidate the king and deprive him of any real influence and authority." Despite the surface civility that defined relations between king and government, "the battle," Mallory reported, "was now joined."[12]

So far, Hussein still considered the army part of his solution, not part of his problem. Although reports of political machinations inside the officer corps filtered up to the palace, he had no idea whether disaffection had deteriorated to disloyalty. As one royalist officer put it, "Becoming aware is one thing; being sure is another."[13] Moreover, the king had no real reason to question 'Ali Abu Nuwar's goodwill or the loyalty of the army's high command. Indeed, diplomatic reports suggest that as the confrontation with al-Nabulsi escalated, Abu Nuwar remained firmly in the king's "good graces."[14] To be sure, some of the king's informal advisers raised doubts about him. Al-Rifa'i, for example, believed that Abu Nuwar "was playing a double game" and was "almost certainly a Baathi," and his friendship with al-Rimawi was certainly well known.[15] By Hussein's admission, these and other warning signs may have made his confidence in Abu Nuwar "a little shakier than it was before," but there were still too many unknowns for him to believe that his longtime friend was conspiring against him.[16] As a result, it was not until early April, when the contest between king and government came to a head, that a second contest between king and army emerged as well.

After two months of sparring, the political confrontation finally broke into the open. On March 29, Mallory reported the growing likelihood of a "sort of '*coup de palais*,'"[17] and the first move was indeed Hussein's. In the last week of March, he dispatched Bahjat al-Talhuni to Syria, Egypt, and Saudi Arabia to relay a personal message to his fellow heads of state. Although the text of the written message was anodyne, al-Nabulsi's ministers feared that it was accompanied by an oral communication giving advance warning of a plan by the king to sack al-Nabulsi. (Their fears may indeed have been justified.) They also took as a deliberate provocation the fact that Hussein had failed to let them vet the message. (This too may have been the case.) Faced with a direct, if only perceived, affront, al-Nabulsi vacillated; various options, ranging from resignation to the sacking of al-Rimawi, were considered and rejected. Instead, al-Nabulsi was won over by arguments from al-Rimawi and some of the more extremist NSP ministers, most notably Justice Minister Shafiq al-Rushaydat, that the government ought to exploit the popularity it had gained from terminating the treaty to force a showdown with the king.[18] Their strategy was to present Hussein with formal requests to establish relations with the Soviet Union and to retire several senior public servants. If the king acceded, the cabinet's imprimatur would be confirmed; if he refused, the cabinet would resign and take to the streets.[19]

The first round went to al-Nabulsi. On April 2, he petitioned Hussein to establish relations with Moscow, and when the king did not dissent, al-Rimawi announced the government's decision the following day. (It was not, in fact, executed.) Then on April 7, the cabinet forwarded to the palace the names of twenty-seven proposed retirees, including that of Hussein's director of security, Bahjat Tabara. Beirut born, Turkish trained, and holder of an OBE (Order of the British Empire), Tabara was one of the Hashemites' most loyal and trusted servants. He had been, in fact, "present at the creation"—the historic Abdullah–Churchill meeting that led to the founding of the amirate—and had been a pillar of the regime ever since.[20] For Hussein to acquiesce in Tabara's dismissal would be a sure sign that al-Nabulsi had gained the upper hand. The king nevertheless let Tabara go, and he was replaced by Muhammad al-Mu'ayta, a close confidant of Abu Nuwar.[21] For seventy-two hours, April 7 to 10, it looked as though al-Nabulsi had carried the day. The British embassy reported news of an "official detente" and of Hussein's preparation for a "grand reconciliation dinner party" that he planned to hold in the government's honor.[22]

In fact, the king had merely used that time to prepare a counterstrike against al-Nabulsi, and the government played into Hussein's hand by overplaying its own. On April 10, al-Nabulsi proposed a fresh list of retirees that included Chief of Diwan Bahjat al-Talhuni. If Hussein had any lingering doubts about al-Nabulsi's intentions, they were erased by this bald attempt to interfere in his personal appointments. He sent al-Talhuni back to the premier's office with two letters in his pocket: one, a request for al-Nabulsi's immediate resignation and the other, an outright decree of dismissal should al-Nabulsi have refused. Confident of a sympathetic hearing in the court of public opinion, the cabinet resigned.[23]

Even more unnerving to Hussein than the submission of the government's second pension list was proof positive that the army's loyalty was suspect. This was the enigmatic "Operation Hashim" incident of April 8, in which troops from the First Armored Car Regiment were deployed at four key intersections controlling Amman's main roads. When Hussein learned that the capital was, in effect, encircled and choked off, he personally ordered the regiment back to its base. The crisis passed when the regiment's commander, Captain Nadhir Rashid, apparently lost his nerve and withdrew. According to Rashid, Operation Hashim was harmless—"a pre-planned exercise" to take a "census of cars coming in and out of Amman" undertaken with the full approval of Divisional Commander 'Ali al-Hiyari. But not everyone agreed with his innocuous explanation, least of all Hussein. Enraged, the king accused al-Nabulsi of conniving in a plot against the throne, which, it seems, was not the case. More significantly, Operation Hashim raised profound doubts in Hussein's mind about Abu Nuwar's competence, if not his loyalty, too.[24]

In his memoirs, Abu Shahut offers the most complete explanation of Hashim. By early April, he wrote, the Free Officers, including Rashid, were convinced that Hussein had firm knowledge of their clandestine contacts with radical cabinet members, the Ba'th party, and the Syrian army, and they believed that the king was preparing a preemptive strike against the government and against them.[25] Operation Hashim, Abu Shahut claimed, was intended as a warning to the king's allies not to underestimate the Free Officers' strength. The goal, he wrote, was "to flex our muscles to those who might conspire against us." In its aftermath, the Free Officers were more convinced than ever that the royalists were gaining the upper hand. Three options, Abu Shahut explained, were then considered: to stage a military coup against the king; to force "the conspirators" out of government with, they hoped, Hussein's acquiescence; or to resign en masse from the army. They decided on the second option and relayed it to their ministerial accomplices (al-Rimawi and Justice Minister al-Rushaydat). Hence the second list of proposed retirements on April 10.[26]

Whatever the rationale, Operation Hashim certainly backfired. Instead of being cowed by the show of strength, Hashim alerted the king to the real magnitude of the conspiracy he faced. The time for the *coup de palais* had arrived. Hence al-Nabulsi's dismissal.

Sacking al-Nabulsi removed one problem but brought on a host of others. Out of government, al-Nabulsi was reported to be "in a confident mood," confident, that is, that Hussein would be unable to cobble together a cabinet without his party's support.[27] Events nearly proved al-Nabulsi right. Hussein's first choice for prime minister was Hussein Fakhri al-Khalidi, the sixty-four-year-old Palestinian ex–foreign minister. Within twenty-four hours, al-Khalidi gave up the commission, unable to recruit a cabinet acceptable to both king and parliament. Then in a surprising shift, the king asked 'Abd al-Halim al-Nimr, the outgoing NSP minister of interior and defense, to form a government. Unlike most of his colleagues, al-Nimr had a "name for relative moderation": If al-Nabulsi had been a brake on the Ba'thists, al-Nimr had been a brake on al-Nabulsi. Even Johnston conceded that an al-Nimr government "would not necessarily be a bad compromise situation."[28] Al-Nimr made some progress toward accommodating the king, but his efforts, too, foundered on the inability to balance his party's demand for Ba'thist representation in the cabinet with Hussein's adamant rejection of it.[29]

Other disconcerting developments further complicated matters for the king. Sawt al-'Arab's Ahmad al-Sa'id, notorious for his inflammatory anti-imperialist, anti-Western radio broadcasts, arrived in Amman, thereby suggesting an imminent shift in Nasser's policy of noninvolvement in Jordan's internal situation. Furthermore, an additional brigade of Syrian troops was reported to have arrived in the Irbid–Mafraq area. On the positive side for Hussein, Kings Feisal and Saud sent messages of support; four thousand armed bedouin irregulars set up camp outside Amman; and Baghdad dispatched substantial reinforcements to its battalion stationed near the frontier. The Jordanian situation, noted Allen Dulles, "had reached the ultimate anticipated crisis."[30]

This crisis, like the enigmatic Operation Hashim, was another military confrontation, the obscure Zerqa events of the night of April 13. In Jordanian lore, "Zerqa" is a catchword for conspiracy, insurrection, disloyalty, and, as far as Hussein's image is concerned, intense personal courage. But even though lore usually contains fact, the two are not normally synonymous.[31]

Earlier that day, a third attempt to form a government had been undertaken by Sa'id al-Mufti. That the king might name a royalist as prime minister, and not the NSP's al-Nimr, provoked the army's commanders—this time with 'Ali Abu Nuwar in the lead—to take matters in their own hands. Al-Mufti was summoned to the Zerqa military barracks where Abu Nuwar, with 'Ali al-Hiyari and Muhammad al-Mu'ayta at his side, delivered an ultimatum through him to Hussein: Unless the king appointed a cabinet "satisfactory to the people and all parties," the army "will not be responsible for anything that happens." Though shocked by the officers' temerity, the king did, in fact, relent, and al-Nimr was again asked to try to recruit an acceptable cabinet. Exactly why Hussein acquiesced at that moment is not clear. Perhaps by April 13, he was not yet confident enough of his own support among the largely bedouin ground forces in the army to force a final showdown. Or maybe the fact that Abu Nuwar had himself felt confident enough to be so candid in his insubordination gave the king pause. In any case, accommodation, not confrontation, seemed to be in the offing.[32]

But it was not to be. While al-Nimr was busy contacting prospective ministers, information reached Hussein suggesting that Rashid's armored car regiment had been ordered to surround the palace and kidnap the king and that Abu Nuwar had taken preventive measures to ensure that loyalist bedouin soldiers would be nowhere near Amman when the attack arrived. According to the king's sources, however, troops of the respective units were refusing to carry out their orders and had instead mutinied against their officers.[33] Why the conspirators preferred a risky (and, in retrospect, clumsy) military plot to what looked like the king's imminent political submission in not known; in any case, it proved to be a fatal error. Hussein happened to be in the room when an urgent telephone call came from 'Ali Abu Nuwar's cousin Ma'an reporting bedlam at Zerqa, with loyalist and rebellious troops firing at each other, and the army commander was caught red-handed. The king immediately sent one of his aides-de-camp, Zayd bin Shakir, and a member of his personal guard to Zerqa to check on the situation, while he, Sharif Nasser, another aide-de-camp, and a disconsolate 'Ali Abu Nuwar set out for Zerqa themselves. Along the way, the king's car met a group of bewildered but loyalist bedouin troops. Abu Nuwar, frightened for his life, asked Hussein for permission to return to Amman, and the king, now confident of success, let him go.[34] Meanwhile, Bin Shakir found utter anarchy at Zerqa. Rumors were rife that the king had been assassinated, and nobody was sure who was loyal to whom, but most of the shooting had stopped.[35] In the darkness and confusion, the arrival of the king's car provoked a new round of gunfire. It was at that moment that Hussein displayed the attribute of personal courage with which he has been associated ever since. By all accounts, the king did indeed risk his life by wading into the pandemonium to disprove the rumors. His bold action heartened loyalists and broke the spirit of any lingering rebels.

The "Zerqa affair" ended later that evening. Abu Nuwar had returned directly to the palace, in the mistaken belief that if Rashid's troops had followed the original plan, he might be able to salvage the debacle after all. There he found the First Armored Regiment deployed on the palace grounds, but it was under the command of loyalist NCOs; with the conspiracy unraveling, Rashid and other Free Officers had already begun their escape to Syria. For Abu Nuwar, all was lost. When Hussein finally arrived at the palace, he found his former friend whimpering and begging for mercy. Their encounter, Hussein recalled, was an "anticlimax." The king permitted Abu Nuwar to leave the country—ostensibly to Italy, of all places—and the following day he and his family departed for Damascus.[36]

That a conspiracy was afoot is borne out by the evidence; whether or not a veritable coup was attempted on the night of April 13 remains the stuff of historical debate. After the fact, most of the plotters argued that it was Hussein, not them, who undertook the "coup," with the Ba'thists ascribing to the American embassy in Amman an important supporting role.[37] Just as the Free Officers had assisted the king in evicting Glubb in 1956, so the argument goes, the king relied on bedouin and American support to weed out troublemakers from the army in 1957. The most generous among them, Nadhir Rashid, admits that Hussein was "very smart":

> He took the initiative by getting us all out and he did it at the right time. If things had had more time [to develop], a coup could have happened. But at the time, there was no plan for it. I can't say that His Majesty was wrong [in thinking that a coup was being planned]. What I can say is that if he didn't take the matter into his own hands, it could have developed. . . . Things were moving in that direction.[38]

Even among royalists, there is some disagreement. According to Bin Shakir, for example, Operation Hashim was the closest that the conspirators came to effecting a coup; the events of Zerqa, he maintained, resulted

from the conspirators' premature plans gone awry. In a May 1957 interview, Hussein himself suggested that the plot against him was only "in
the preparatory stage," but this was a passing remark later excised from
his official account.[39] British Ambassador Johnston may have offered the
most accurate appraisal of Zerqa:

> [Zerqa] was no case of plot and counter-plot by two well-knit teams led
> respectively by masterminds. On the contrary, it was a confused triangular
> affair, a game of blind-man's-bluff with three contestants [Hussein,
> al-Nabulsi, and Abu Nuwar, according to Johnston] bumping into each other
> in the dark and none knowing clearly what was happening or what he ought
> to do next.

Why did Hussein win out in the end? Because, Johnston suggested, Abu
Nuwar "proved himself still an amateur conspirator, while the king was
moving towards professional status."[40]

Two aspects of the "Zerqa affair" should be underscored. First, as
Johnston noted, is the multiplicity of conspiracies. There were, it seems,
at least two distinct elements in the plot: a scheme among junior officers, like Rashid, that might have led to a direct assault on the palace; and
a more cunning conspiracy among the army's commanders, perhaps in
concert with radical politicians, to coerce the king into submission. Zerqa
is the story of how these separate though complementary plots got
entangled, bringing the entire house down on the plotters.

Second is the role of the bedouin. It is important to note Hussein
did not make his first public appeal to bedouin troops until *after* it was
clear that most of them were prepared to mutiny against their disloyal
commanding officers. Given many of the signals emitted from the palace
in the days before Zerqa, including the king's apparently indulgent attitude toward the prospect of an al-Nimr government, there was certainly
reason to believe that the king might have opted for capitulation over
confrontation. Although Sharif Nasser and other loyalists kept channels
of communication open to bedouin units, those private messages could
not have fully countered the impact of the king's sometimes submissive
public posture. Nevertheless, the bedouin showed themselves willing to
fight for the throne without even knowing if its occupant were still alive.
Such loyalty left an indelible mark on Hussein, who thereafter never over-
looked the bedouin's bedrock role in maintaining the army and the
Hashemite system in general.[41]

Zerqa brought an end to the military conspiracy against the king, but
that was only one of the problems he faced and, as events turned out,
the least onerous one at that. Far more complicated was his handling of
the domestic political vacuum that still bedeviled Jordan five days after
the fall of the al-Nabulsi government. Even though the secret plotting
was over, popular feeling, especially on the West Bank, was sympathetic
to the ousted cabinet. For Hussein, managing the potential hostility of

thousands of enraged rioters was far trickier than outmaneuvering a few dozen novice conspirators.

On the morning of April 15, Sa'id al-Mufti gave up his efforts to form a ministry, and Hussein turned a second time to al-Khalidi. The premier-designate caught the NSP in a moment of irresolution, shaken by the events of Zerqa. Evidently believing the tide had turned for the king, the party accepted al-Khalidi's offer to join the government with just a single cabinet portfolio, and al-Khalidi was finally able to announce his cabinet that afternoon. It had just seven members, including al-Khalidi himself, all Hashemite loyalists save for Sulayman al-Nabulsi as foreign minister. But none of them was a particularly strong personality—al-Mufti, for example, was ensconced as deputy prime minister—and the cabinet had no intention of embarking on purges of political troublemakers like the ones that had already begun inside the army. Indeed, al-Khalidi reportedly told an interviewer that his government's policy would not be substantially different from that of the previous one.[42] That the king would accept al-Nabulsi in the government underscored his hesitance both to resort to extraconstitutional means to assert his control and to rely too quickly on an army so recently racked by dissension.

Over the next seven days, every element in this equation changed. Al-Nabulsi and his NSP colleagues reverted to form, joined forces with the more radical opposition, and deliberately laid down a direct challenge to the authority of the king. In the face of that challenge, the conciliatory posture of the al-Khalidi government proved untenable. At the same time, the situation inside the army clarified, and whatever qualms Hussein may have had about the army's loyalty and cohesion evaporated. With them went whatever misgivings he may have about the demise of Jordan's democratic experiment as well.

Reorganization of the army began in earnest on April 14, the day after Zerqa. As chief of the general staff, Hussein appointed 'Ali al-Hiyari. Although he was said to be "a Hussein favorite," al-Hiyari was suspect from the start. Not only was al-Hiyari a distant relative of Abu Nuwar, but he had been present when Abu Nuwar delivered his ultimatum to al-Mufti. In addition, his brother, Kamil, was implicated in the Zerqa affair and had already defected to Syria.[43] Perhaps the king had al-Hiyari's questionable background in mind when he named Habis al-Majali as al-Hiyari's deputy. Despite having commanded the Hashemite Regiment under King Abdullah, al-Majali was a career policeman, "not a serious soldier," but since atoning for his futile putsch on Nayif's behalf in 1951, he had shown himself firmly loyal to the king. Al-Hiyari, al-Majali, and Sadiq al-Shar'a (still army chief of staff) formed an administrative committee to reform the officer corps, and the no-nonsense Circassian brigadier 'Izzat Hassan was appointed to take charge of the Zerqa investigation.[44] When Hassan's inquiry provoked speculation about al-Hiyari's loyalty, the army chief folded. On April 19, al-Hiyari went to Damascus with the king's permission for talks with Syrian army leaders on the deployment of their troops still in Jordan since the Suez war.[45] The following day, he defected. Although al-Hiyari warned at an April 20 press conference of "a great plot being launched against Jordan [by] palace officials and military attachés of certain non-Arab countries [i.e., the United States]," he himself was no stealthy conspirator. By most accounts, al-Hiyari simply could not stand up to the emotional strain of the post-Zerqa investigations, and—perhaps out of fear that he had himself been compromised—he took the easiest way out.[46] In any event, al-Majali was appointed to succeed al-Hiyari, and the army purges proceeded with a vengeance.[47]

While the situation in the army was settling, the political situation was building toward a climax. Although the NSP had uneasily joined the government, its former coalition partners went firmly into opposition. They inveighed against Hussein for allegedly turning on his own patriotic army and struck a particularly sensitive chord among Palestinians by highlighting the king's reliance on bedouin troops. This effort culminated in the convening of a National Congress in Nablus on April 22, attended by representatives of all secular parties and opposition trends inside Jordan, including the NSP. Its moment of irresolution now passed, the NSP leadership concluded that it could have no real influence inside a royalist government. With its participation in the congress, any substantive distinction between the NSP and its more radical allies disappeared.

The congress's resolutions, noted Johnston, comprised "the complete extremist programme." They included calls for the dissolution of al-Khalidi's government and its replacement by a NSP–Ba'th–National Front coalition; rejection of the Eisenhower Doctrine and the establishment of federal union with Syria and Egypt; and the dismissal of Bahjat al-Talhuni and Sharif Nasser, the expulsion of the American ambassador and military attaché, and the reinstatement of purged officers. The congress also set up a sixteen-member executive committee under Hikmat al-Masri that was heavily weighted toward Communists and National Front figures. Thus the seeds of a "separatist provisional government," Johnston reported, had begun to take shape. On April 24, al-Nabulsi formally resigned from the cabinet, and a delegation from the congress presented its demands to al-Khalidi. In the meantime, strikes and demonstrations had broken out in Jerusalem, Nablus, and, to a lesser extent, Amman, in accordance with other conference resolutions. That the congress represented the final challenge to Hussein and the existing democratic experiment was underscored by the endorsement of its resolutions by nearly two dozen deputies, a parliamentary majority. It was this fact—the lack of parliamentary confidence—that al-Khalidi cited in his letter of resignation to the king later that evening.[48]

A decisive confrontation could no longer be postponed. The disintegration of the king–government–army condominium had been primarily a political issue, and its reconstruction would come only with a clear victor in the political contest between loyalists and opponents of the regime. As Mallory observed, Hussein's alternatives were "rapidly narrowing down to a choice of military rule or abdication, unless he [was] assassinated first."[49] On April 24, the king opted for military rule.

Just as Hussein did not begin this process without some sign of outside backing, so too he did not take this fateful step without an assurance of outside support. This Washington ultimately decided to give, despite its earlier coolness to the idea. During an April 23 press conference, Dulles spoke of his government's "great confidence in and regard for King Hussein" and offered assistance "to the extent that he [Hussein] thinks that we can be helpful."[50] The king, however, needed a more tangible commitment. Early on the evening of April 24, he passed a message "through intelligence channels" to the U.S. government, in which he outlined his plan to impose martial law and asked for American support should either Israel or the Soviet Union intervene in the situation. About three hours later, the king had his response. In a hastily convened press conference at Eisenhower's Georgia retreat, the White House press secretary announced that both the president and his secretary of state regarded "the independence and integrity of Jordan as vital." It was as explicit an application of the Eisenhower Doctrine as was ever made regarding Jordan. (Amman itself never formally ascribed to the doctrine.) In the meantime, Dulles had already called in Israeli Ambassador Abba Eban, who assured him that his country would "avoid anything that played into Nasser's hands." And as a warning to the Soviets, ships from the U.S. Sixth Fleet set sail for the Lebanese coast, technically at the request of Lebanese President Camille Chamoun. American military planners gave urgent consideration to the airlift of paratroops into Mafraq and Amman, but Hussein's April 24 declaration—"I think we can handle the situation ourselves"—made that move unnecessary.[51]

On the evening of April 24, just after he passed the message to his American contact, Hussein called to the palace the handful of men that had held the kingdom together in the aftermath of his grandfather's murder and asked them to sustain the regime in its time of trouble once again. With the exception of the late Abu'l Huda, virtually all of them were there: Ibrahim Hashim, former head of the Regency Council; Samir al-Rifa'i, credited with ensuring a smooth transfer of power after Abdullah's death; Felah al-Madadha, who had handled internal security in the first post-Abdullah government; Anastas Hanania, the only Palestinian to serve in Abdullah's last cabinet and Talal's first; Sulayman al-Tuqan, the former regent and Nablus strongman; and Khulusi al-Khayri, the Palestinian refugee who had frequently been asked to quiet his compatriots' fears during that tense and anxious period. Conversely, the two former prime ministers who had proved timid in previous crises, Fawzi al-Mulqi and Sa'id al-Mufti, had not been summoned. The only man present who was not a member of the old guard was 'Akif al-Fa'iz, whose participation was in recognition of the king's reliance on bedouin sup-port.[52] Just as in Hussein's early days, critical roles were played by Sharif Nasser and, especially, the queen mother. She later told Johnston that April 24 was "the worst night of the whole prolonged crisis." When the magnitude of the step they were about to take unnerved several of the would-be ministers, Zayn reportedly declared that no one would be allowed to leave the palace until they all had taken the oath of office. "On this not altogether encouraging basis," Johnston reported, "the new Government was eventually formed."[53]

Late that night, curfews were imposed in Amman, Irbid, and throughout much of the West Bank. Bedouin troops, their faces black-ened to prevent reprisals, roamed the streets of the capital. The next morning, the palace announced al-Khalidi's resignation and the appoint-ment of a new cabinet under Hashim, with al-Rifa'i as deputy premier and foreign minister. Martial law (technically, "emergency administration") was declared, and political parties were banned. Hussein went on radio to brand "international communism" as the root of Jordan's troubles. In a nimble twist, he turned the nationalist tables on al-Nabulsi by charg-ing him with softness toward Israel (i.e., his refusal to go to war over Suez) and with connivance with Western imperialism (i.e., his apparent willingness to receive the Richards mission).[54] Two days later, six staunch loyalists were named district military governors under the supervision of the military governor-general, Sulayman Tuqan. They were given wide latitude to arrest and imprison any suspected violators of the martial law regime, and Tuqan himself was granted "all the power and authority vested in the king or the premier." Hundreds were detained, including almost all members of the al-Nabulsi government and the National Congress's executive committee, and most of those not arrested either fled the country or went into hiding. On April 28, parliament was pro-rogued by royal decree. All measures were taken under the appropriate constitutional articles, but it was the survival of the regime, not legal pro-priety, that was at the heart of martial law.[55]

Thus began the Hashemite restoration, a process that involved several elements.

On the external front, restoration entailed renewed dependence—political, financial, military, and moral—on a Western power. From 1957 on, this was normally the United States. Buoyed at Hussein's robust posture, Washington bent over backward over the next few days to sup-port the king, which included making unsolicited offers of military aid and economic assistance. On April 29, the new alliance was cemented with the approval of a $10 million aid program, the most quickly nego-tiated in U.S. history, designed to ensure Jordan's "freedom" and main-tain its "economic and political stability." Why did Washington change tack and actively support Jordan in April 1957? Although many factors were involved, two considerations, one philosophical, and one tangible, were paramount. First, the Americans were clearly impressed with Hussein's efforts on his own behalf. "The young king was certainly showing spunk," Eisenhower told Dulles on April 25, and this sort of self-help was at the core of what the Eisenhower Doctrine was trying to encourage. Second, and no less important, was the realization among U.S. officials that in Jordan, a small investment could have far-reaching results. What might have seemed to be paltry amounts in American terms—as little as $2.5 million in a financial crisis in June 1957, for example—could make all the difference to the Jordanians. Samir al-Rifa'i was not too far off when he quipped that "£10 million to [the Americans] was like 10 piastres."[56]

In some ways, the American relationship proved to be a better bargain than the old British connection, because Washington did not condition its support on any particular Jordanian policy stance.[57] But the fact that King Hussein asked for, and the British government acceded to, the speedy deployment of paratroops to Jordan in July 1958 (Operation FORTITUDE) proved that the termination of the Anglo-Jordanian treaty did not in itself sever the strategic and historic ties that bound the two kingdoms. As Johnston noted, Jordanian leaders had "a genuine affection for Britain which is certainly more than cupboard love."[58] Moreover, despite their mutuality of interest, U.S.–Jordanian relations were not always smooth. Hussein more than once threatened to throw in his hand when military shipments were slow in arriving or when Washington seemed, to him anyway, niggardly with its assistance. "Does the U.S. trust and believe in Jordan or not?" the king asked Mallory in exasperation in November 1957.[59] Such outbursts, though perhaps genuine, were mostly bluster, because Hussein had nowhere else to turn, a predicament that he normally accepted with the same equanimity with which his grandfather had viewed the British connection.

Restoration also meant a shift away from the Egyptian–Syrian bloc and toward the pro-West monarchies of Iraq and Saudi Arabia. Executing this shift was not easy. Both Egypt and Syria had formidable resources at their disposal with which to rattle—if not actually topple—Jordan, should they have taken a firm decision to do so. Therefore, in his April 25 address, Hussein took pains to reaffirm his "effort to preserve our brotherhood and solidarity with sister Egypt," and it was not until the end of May 1957 that he requested, ever so gently, the final withdrawal of Syrian troops from Jordanian territory. Over time, though, as the king's grip on the situation grew firmer and the provocations from Cairo and Damascus grew more brazen, the breach widened until it finally ruptured in July 1958.[60] But until then and after, Hussein should have been gratified that Nasser was besieged with more pressing demands to ever personally set his sights on the overthrow of Hashemite Jordan.[61]

Similarly, the move toward Iraq and Saudi Arabia was not without difficulty. Despite the convergence of macrostrategic interests, the relationship among the three monarchies never grew very warm. There were a variety of reasons for this, ranging from squabbling over the relative size of Baghdad's and Riyadh's subventions to Jordan; to Iraqi and Saudi preoccupation (for very different reasons) with Egypt; to the reemergence of old rivalries inside Jordan, pro-Iraqis versus pro-Saudis, that militated against the creation of a strong, tripartite alliance.[62] But as far as Hussein was concerned, the realignment toward his two fellow monarchies was real and firm.[63]

Restoration also meant a return to Abdullah's studied ambivalence toward Israel. This meant balancing the Jordanians' (and, indeed, Hussein's) genuine support for Arab nationalist aims with a realistic appreciation of where Israel fit in the hierarchy of threats to the Hashemite regime. In this regard, actions mattered more than words, and pragmatism, not dogmatism, reigned. Hussein, however, never risked his grandfather's fate by enmeshing himself too deeply in peacemaking efforts that could rebound against him. Moreover, not too much should be made of whatever tacit understandings were reached between Amman and Jerusalem. At most, the two regimes benefited from a commonality of interests, but even then, there was often less than meets the eye. For example, it was only because of Saudi spinelessness that Hussein was forced to accept the transit of British troops and American supplies over Israel in July 1958, and for its part, Israel's actual role in the crisis was not nearly as sympathetic as it seemed at first glance.[64]

(It is interesting to note that the gulf between Hussein's and al-Nabulsi's attitude toward Israel was narrower than on all other foreign policy issues. For all their rhetoric, neither al-Nabulsi nor 'Ali Abu Nuwar was ever willing to challenge Israel militarily or even to respond to retaliatory raids more forcefully than previous governments had.)[65]

These external shifts were the consequence of fundamental changes in Jordan's internal organization that were at the core of the Hashemite restoration. The two key elements in that process were the reassertion of royal primacy and the resurrection of the king–government–army condominium. Both were essential. Without Hussein's (and his family's) leadership and tenacity, loyalist politicians would never have risked flouting public opinion on April 24, and loyalist troops would not have taken to the streets so zealously the following morning. Conversely, without men to administer martial law and soldiers to enforce it, Hussein's heroics would have been for naught. To be sure, the king's will to survive and prevail was indispensable, but no amount of outside assistance could have compensated for the absence of a group of men willing (if only reluctantly) to respond to his call. Pedestrian as it may sound, the affirmation of royal prerogative in 1957 was not, as Johnston once feared, "a one-man show."[66]

In the years after 1957, neither government nor army was ever again permitted to slide into opposition to the regime. Similarly, not parliament, democracy, or even some abstract and well-meaning notion of constitutionalism was ever again permitted to conflict with the royal "we." This is not to suggest that the years following 1957 were trouble free; they were not, by any means. Hussein and the "king's men" did not always see eye to eye, and the latter sometimes trifled with policies and positions that bordered on the disloyal. This ranged from Samir al-Rifa'i's alleged attempts to "run a reinsurance policy with Egypt" behind Hussein's back; to Hazza' al-Majali's naive flirtation with down-and-out National Socialists to replace al-Rifa'i with a more progressive ministry; to the successful scheming by "Beni Sakhr colonels"—led by that old conspirator Habis al-Majali—to ease al-Rifa'i and Chief of Staff Sadiq al-Shar'a out of office in 1959. In no instance, though, did the principals suffer more than a passing eclipse from royal favor (if that), and al-Rifa'i and both al-Majalis have gone down in Hashemite history as pillars—in the case of Hazza', as a martyr—of the regime.[67]

As for the experiment in parliamentary supremacy, it ended abruptly with al-Nabulsi's fall, its place filled by the sort of benign toleration for constitutional mechanisms that was Abdullah's stock-in-trade. From time to time, parliament attempted robust challenges, but they were handled with deft swiftness. When the NSP, still parliament's largest party, tried to manipulate the chamber after it reconvened in October 1957, the government speedily and unmercifully neutralized the effort. And when, for example, parliament was on the verge of denying the government a vote of confidence in 1963, it was dissolved before the regime suffered further indignity. (The premier at the time, again al-Rifa'i, resigned in the process.)[68] Both the spirit and the rule of law reverted to their proper place in the Hashemite system, as means to an end and never, as Fawzi al-Mulqi had learned, ends in themselves.

In sum, after 1957, the contours of Hussein's monarchy bore a strong resemblance to the regime built up by Abdullah, Kirkbride, and Glubb in the years before the 1948 war. There were, of course, important differences, the two most glaring of which were the departure of a permanent British military presence in August 1957 and the emergence of the emotive call for a "Palestinian entity" in March 1959.[69] But the two eras of Hashemite history, pre-1948 and post-1957, were built on similar foundations and sustained on similar principles. What connected them were the politics and the personalities of the "king's men." They kept the kingdom intact in its period of uncertainty and provided the bridge that permitted Hussein to mature fully into his grandfather's heir. Though among one another they often competed viciously for power and differed wildly on tactics, they were, as a group, intrinsically bound up with the fate of the regime; like it or not, its destiny was theirs. Recognition by Hussein of that organic link set his reign back on course.

Notes

AIR	Air Ministry (UK)
AUB	American University of Beirut
CAB	Cabinet papers (UK)
CGS	Chief of the General Staff
CIA	Central Intelligence Agency (US)
CO	Colonial Office (UK)
COS	Chief(s) of Staff
DOS	Department of State (US)
EMMEA	Eastern Mediterranean/Middle East Area (US)
FAO	Food and Agriculture Organization (UN)
FO	Foreign Office (UK)
FRUS	*Foreign Relations of the United States* (documents series)
GAA	General Armistice Agreement
HC	High Commissioner for Palestine and Transjordan (UK)
HMG	Her (His) Majesty's Government
ISA	Israel State Archives
JCP	Jordanian Communist Party
JCS	Joint Chiefs of Staff (US)
JNA	Jordanian National Archives
MAC	Jordan-Israel Mixed Armistice Commission
MEAF	Middle East Air Force (UK)
MELF	Middle East Land Forces (UK)

177

MOD	Ministry of Defence (UK)
NA/RG	National Archives/Record Group (US)
NEA	Bureau of Near East Affairs, State Department (US)
NSC	National Security Council (US)
NSP	National Socialist Party (Jordan)
PREM	Prime Minister's papers (UK)
PRO	Public Record Office (UK)
RAF	Royal Air Force (UK)
SOS	Secretary of State (US; sometimes UK)
TJL	Transjordan Legation (Arab Legion office in London)
UNRWA	United National Relief and Works Agency for Palestine Refugees
UNSC	United Nations Security Council
UNSCOP	United Nations Special Committee on Palestine
UNTSO	United Nations Truce Supervisory Organization
WHO	World Health Organization (UN)
WO	War Office (UK)

PREFACE

1. These include Aqil Hyder Hasan Abidi, *Jordan: A Political Study, 1948–1957* (London: Asia Publishing House, 1965); Naseer H. Aruri, *Jordan: A Study in Political Development (1921–1965)* (The Hague: Nijhoff, 1972); Ann Dearden, *Jordan* (London: Robert Hale, 1958); George L. Harris, *Jordan, Its People, Its Society, Its Culture* (New York: Grove Press, 1958); James Lunt, *Hussein of Jordan: Searching for a Just and Lasting Peace, a Political Biography* (London: Macmillan, 1989); and James Morris, *The Hashemite Kings* (London: Faber & Faber, 1959). Abidi remains valuable because of its emphasis on detail.

2. The only one that remains useful today is Munib al-Madi and Sulayman Musa, *Tarikh al-urdunn fi al-qarn al-'ashreen* [The history of Jordan in the twentieth century] (1959; Amman: Maktaba al-muhtasab, 1988).

3. Syed Ali el-Edroos, *The Hashemite Arab Army: An Appreciation and Analysis of Military Operations* (Amman: Publishing Committee, 1980). This was written under the patronage of Crown Prince Hassan.

4. The best of these works are by Uriel Dann, *King Hussein and the Challenge of Arab Radicalism: Jordan, 1955–1967* (New York: Oxford University Press, 1989), which was the first to employ the new resources for scholarly research; Benjamin Shwadran, *Jordan: State of Tension* (New York: Council for Middle Eastern Affairs Press, 1959); and P. J. Vatikiotis, *Politics and the Military in Jordan: A Study of the Arab League, 1921–1957* (London: Cass, 1967). The last two rely heavily on personal sources of information; Vatikiotis had some special access.

INTRODUCTION

1. On al-Sulh's assassination, see National Archives and Records Administration, Washington, Amman to DOS, July 19, 1951, DOS 785.00/7-1951.

2. The vague warning by American Minister Gerald Drew centered on the one al-Sulh assassin still at large. Later, Drew tried to distance himself from this warning. Interview with A. David Fritzlan; Drew to SOS, July 24, 1951, DOS 785.11/7-2451.

3. Hazza' al-Majali, *Mudhakkarati* [My memoirs] (Beirut: Dar al-'ilm lil-malayeen, 1960) 102–3.

4. Interview with Moshe Sasson, one of his intended interlocutors. Also see Avi Shlaim, *Collusion Across the Jordan: King Abdullah, the Zionist Movement and the Partition of Palestine* (New York: Columbia University Press, 1988), 606.

5. Interview with Sadiq al-Shar'a.

6. Philip Robins, "The Consolidation of Hashimite Power in Jordan, 1921–1946" (Ph.D. diss., University of Exeter, 1988), 166; Abdullah Hamid A. Khatib, "The Jordanian Legislature in Political Development Perspective" (Ph.D. diss., State University of New York at Albany, 1975), 149.

7. Patrick Coghill, "Before I Forget," mimeograph (copy in the Private Papers Collection, Middle East Centre, St. Antony's College, Oxford, 1960), 105. Coghill was chief of the Arab Legion's Criminal Investigation Division in the mid-1950s.

8. "Annual Report on Transjordan for 1946," Kirkbride to Bevin, January 13, 1947, Public Record Office, London, FO 371.62202/E 417.

9. "Annual Report on Transjordan for 1947," Kirkbride to Bevin, January 1, 1948, FO 371.68844/E 2010.

10. On the "ultimatum" of 1924, see Uriel Dann, "The Political Confrontation of Summer 1924 in Transjordan," in Uriel Dann, *Studies in the History of Transjordan, 1920–1949: The Making of a State* (Boulder, CO: Westview Press, 1984), 81–92; and Mary C. Wilson, *King Abdullah, Britain and the Making of Jordan* (Cambridge: Cambridge University Press, 1987), 81–87. On the 1928 agreement, see Benjamin Shwadran, *Jordan: A State of Tension* (New York: Council for Middle Eastern Affairs Press, 1959), 167–75.

11. See especially Major C. S. Jarvis, *Arab Command: The Biography of Lieutenant Colonel F. W. Peake Pasha* (London: Hutchinson and Co., 1942); and John Bagot Glubb, *The Story of the Arab Legion* (London: Hodder & Stoughton, 1946).

12. Macmichael to Cranbourne, November 23, 1942, CO 831/59 [secret].

13. In August 1952, Britain and the United States raised the status of their missions in Jordan from legations to embassies.

14. See William Roger Louis, *The British Empire in the Middle East, 1945–1951* (Oxford: Clarendon Press, 1984), 345–79.

15. James Morris, *The Hashemite Kings* (London: Faber & Faber, 1959), 107. On Kirkbride, see Ilan Pappé, "Sir Alec Kirkbride and the Making of Greater Transjordan," *Asian and African Studies* 23 (1989): 42–70; and Itamar Rabinovich, *The Road Not Taken: Early Arab–Israeli Negotiations* (New York: Oxford University Press, 1991), 161–63.

16. See Abdullah's Greater Syria manifesto, *Suriya al-kubra: al-kitab al-urdunni al-abyadh* [Greater Syria: The Jordanian white paper] (Amman: al-Matba' al-Wataniyya, 1947); and Munib al-Madi and Sulayman Musa, *Tarikh al-urdunn fi al-qarn al 'ashreen* [The history of Jordan in the twentieth century] (1959; Amman: Maktaba al-muhtasab, 1988), 439–48.

17. On Abdullah's Greater Syria aspirations and the British reaction to them, see Shwadran, *Jordan*, 221–44; Patrick Seale, *The Struggle for Syria: A Study of Post-War Arab Politics, 1945-1958* (London: I. B. Tauris, 1965), 11–15; and Daniel Pipes, *Greater Syria: The Making of an Ambition* (New York: Oxford University Press, 1990), 71–82.

18. Transjordanians provided only one member of Abdullah's first seven cabi-

nets and just seventeen of the seventy-five total appointments to the Executive, or Ministerial, Council from 1926 to 1946. See Robins, "The Consolidation of Hashimite Power," 174, 241–44.

19. Even Jordan's East Bank–born premiers had roots outside Transjordan: Fawzi al-Mulqi, born in Irbid, was of Damascene stock, and the family of Sulayman al-Nabulsi, a Salti, heralded from Palestine. Moreover, even the al-Majalis of Kerak trace their roots to Hebron.

20. See Patai's description of the 1947 parliamentary election, the first held under the monarchy: Raphael Patai, *The Kingdom of Jordan* (Princeton, NJ: Princeton University Press, 1958), 46. More generally, see the Central Intelligence Agency's analysis of Abdullah's salad days in Report SR-13, September 27, 1949, Harry S Truman Presidential Library.

21. Kirkbride to HC, May 19, 1945, FO 371.45415/E 4962 [secret].

22. In 1945, Abdullah outraged the local citizenry by insisting on the registration of the Jewish-owned "Jordan Exploration Company." This precipitated a rare ministerial crisis and provoked "a dangerous situation . . . of demonstrations and strikes." Transjordan to SOS/Colonies, August 31, 1945, FO 371.45415/E 6772 [secret]. Also see Wilson, *King Abdullah*, 115; and Shlaim, *Collusion Across the Jordan*, 52.

23. Pinpointing the right admixture of these three ingredients is the subject of considerable historical debate and revisionism.

24. For parliament's resolution of union, April 24, 1950, see Helen Miller Davis, *Constitutions, Electoral Laws, Treaties of States in the Near and Middle East* (Durham, NC: Duke University Press, 1953), 265–66.

25. Additional Law No. 56 (December 1949) amended the original Citizenship Ordinance of 1928 and extended Jordanian nationality to "all habitual residents . . . in Transjordan or in the Western Bank which is administered by the Hashimite Kingdom of Jordan, who hold Palestinian nationality." For details, see Aqil Hyder Hasan Abidi, *Jordan: A Political Study, 1948–1957* (London: Asia Publishing House, 1965), 66–67.

26. Kirkbride to McNeil, "Jordan: Annual Review for 1949," January 2, 1950, FO 371.82702/ET 1011/1 [secret].

27. See Avi Plascov, *The Palestinian Refugees in Jordan, 1948–1957* (London: Cass, 1981); and Amnon Cohen, *Political Parties in the West Bank Under the Jordanian Regime, 1949–1967* (Ithaca, NY: Cornell University Press, 1982).

28. See Aaron David Miller, *The Arab States and the Palestine Question: Between Ideology and Self-Interest* (New York: Praeger, 1986).

29. Abdullah ceded a ten-mile strip along the Jenin–Tulkarm front lest he face a renewed Israeli offensive when he undertook to replace Iraqi troops with Arab Legion forces. See Wilson, *King Abdullah*, 188.

30. Amman's population grew from 33,110 in 1947 to 108,000 by 1952. The city absorbed 42,000 refugees in 1948 alone. See Nurit Kliot and Arnon Soffer, "The Emergence of a Metropolitan Core Area in a New State—The Case of Jordan," *Asian and African Studies* 20 (1986): 222–24.

31. Kirkbride to FO, April 1, 1950, FO 371.82703 [secret]; Kirkbride to Bevin, March 6, 1950, FO 371.82705/ET 1016.

32. In June 1950, al-Mufti's cabinet had unanimously rejected a royal summons to "get on with negotiations with Israel," but Abdullah shied away from a confrontation, apparently because he "realized that it would be next to impossible . . . to find any worthwhile politician willing or able to form a Cabinet com-

mitted to making peace with Israel." Amman to DOS, June 27, 1950, DOS 785.00/6-2750.

33. Amman to DOS, October 18, 1950, DOS 785.13/10-1850; Kirkbride to FO, November 1, 1950, FO 371.82793 [secret].

34. One factor that might have given al-Rifa'i special standing with the Zionists was that one of his brothers-in-law, Suhayl Shukri, was married to a Jewish woman and continued to live in Haifa after 1948. There is evidence that Shukri on occasion may have been an intermediary with the Israeli Foreign Ministry: ISA 2565/11, August 31, 1951; enclosure in letter from Latymer to Shuckburgh, April 19, 1956, FO 371.121466/VJ 1015/163.

35. Jerusalem to DOS, December 13, 1950, DOS 785.13/12-1350.

36. Kirkbride to Furlonge, May 16, 1951, FO 371.91364/EE 1041/35.

37. The opposition of local Jordanian political figures toward a negotiated peace with Israel in 1950/51 is not the only reason that peace efforts failed, but it is the one least explored in a historical debate that usually focuses on apportioning blame among Ben-Gurion, Abdullah, and the British. Rabinovich touches on this theme in *The Road Not Taken*, chap. 4; as does Shlaim, *Collusion Across the Jordan*, 513–49, 622.

38. On March 9, 1950, President Truman accepted Secretary of State Dean Acheson's advice not to send a personal message to Abdullah because the latter's "primary difficulty was with his own Cabinet." Dean Acheson Papers, Truman Library; also see Shlaim, *Collusion Across the Jordan*, 546.

39. Plascov noted that for the refugees, "most demonstrations centred around the issue of relief." Plascov, *The Palestinian Refugees*, 148–49.

40. Kirkbride to FO, May 1, 1950, FO 371.82703 [secret]; also see Plascov, *The Palestinian Refugees*, 159.

41. Amman to DOS, March 24, 1950, DOS 785.00/3-2450; Kirkbride to Bevin, March 22, 1950, FO 371.82705/ET 1016/5.

42. Kirkbride to Attlee, October 5, 1950, FO 371.82705/ET 1016/21.

43. West Bank representation was dropped in the wake of King Hussein's disengagement decision of July 1988. The term *parliament* is used throughout the text, usually in reference to the lower house.

44. See reportage in Jerusalem to DOS, May 12, 1950, DOS 785.21/5-1250.

45. Contrast American Minister Gerald Drew's comments with Kirkbride's curt dismissal of parliament as "a thoroughly irresponsible body of men in which the more reasonable East Bank elements were led astray by West Bank troublemakers." Amman to DOS, June 21, 1950, DOS 785.21/6-2150; Kirkbride to Morrison, May 5, 1951, FO 371.91789.

46. Amman to DOS, August 8, 1950, DOS 785.21/8-850.

47. *Daily Telegraph* (London), May 3, 1951; *al-Difa'* (Jerusalem), May 4, 1951; Kirkbride to Morrison, May 5, 1951, FO 371.91789; Amman to DOS, May 29, 1951, DOS 885.10/5-2951. Also, Abidi, *Jordan*, 73–75.

48. Abidi, *Jordan*, 70; also see Shlaim, *Collusion Across the Jordan*, 622.

49. As a result of Jordan's role in World War II, the Arab Legion's manpower had been increased from 1,350 in 1941 to 8,000 in 1945; by 1948, it was back down to 6,000, of whom only 4,500 were available for combat. See P. J. Vatikiotis, *Politics and the Military in Jordan: A Study of the Arab Legion, 1921–1957* (London: Cass, 1967), 75–78; and Shwadran, *Jordan*, 255.

1. This paragraph is based on Jerusalem to SOS, July 20, 1951, DOS 785.11/7-2051; Amman to SOS, DOS 785.00/7-2051; Jerusalem to SOS, DOS 785.11/7-2151; Walmsley to FO, July 7, 1951, FO 371.91838; Walker to FO, July 20, 1951, FO 371.91838; and interviews with Sadiq al-Shar'a and Walid Salah.

2. John Bagot Glubb, *A Soldier with the Arabs* (London: Hodder & Stoughton, 1957), 278. On several occasions, Glubb's recollection of events is blurred by his animosity toward al-Rifa'i borne of their respective roles in Glubb's dismissal five years later. This episode is corroborated in Hazza' al-Majali, *Mudhakkarati* [My memoirs] (Beirut: Dar al-'ilm lil-malayeen, 1960), 104.

3. The last two were Farhan al-Shubaylat and Muhammad al-Shurayqi, respectively. See al-Majali, *Mudhakkarati*.

4. Talal's mother was Sharifa Misbah, Abdullah's first wife and first cousin.

5. Shuckburgh to Parkinson, December 12, 1939, CO 831/54.

6. Ibid.

7. Translation of a letter from Abdullah to Kirkbride, March 23, 1939, CO 831/54.

8. On Talal's near-enrollment at Cambridge, see CO 831/27/10.37741.

9. Pirie-Gordon to Burrows, July 12, 1949, FO 371.75316/E 8782 [secret].

10. She was Princess Mihrimah, granddaughter of Sultan Mehmed V. I am grateful to Bernard Lewis for bringing this to my attention.

11. Bowman to Mayhew, April 14, 1929, CO 831/6.

12. Pirie-Gordon to Shuckburgh, December 11, 1929, CO 831/6; Chancellor to SOS/Colonies, March 1, 1930, CO 831/9.

13. Translation of a letter from Abdullah to Kirkbride, March 23, 1939, CO 831/54.

14. Macmichael to Shuckburgh, March 28, 1939, CO 831/54.

15. HC to SOS/Colonies, December 11, 1939, CO 831/54 [secret].

16. Kirkbride to HC, October 20, 1939, CO 831/54 [most secret].

17. Macmichael to Shuckburgh, November 5, 1940; HC to CO, December 13, 1940, and January 19, 1941, CO 831/57 [secret]; also, see Mary C. Wilson, *King Abdullah: Britain and the Making of Jordan* (Cambridge: Cambridge University Press, 1987), 132.

18. Pirie-Gordon to Burrows, July 12, 1949, FO 371.75316/E 8782 [secret].

19. Macmichael to SOS/Colonies, December 4, 1942, CO 831/59 [secret].

20. Kirkbride to Baxter, March 25, 1947, FO 371.62220/E 2873; Kirkbride to Burrows, October 21, 1948, FO 371.68864/E 13842 [secret and personal]; and Pirie-Gordon to Burrows, July 12, 1949, FO 371.75316/E 8782 [secret].

21. The recitation of Talal's exploits as an officer with a frontline artillery unit in the 1948 war, published in a panegyric after his death, should not be taken at face value. See Muhammad Taysir Dhubyan, *al-Malak Talal* [King Talal] (Amman: Majallat al-shari'a, 1972), 14–15.

22. Pirie-Gordon to Burrows, July 12, 1949, FO 371.75316/E 8782 [secret].

23. "Extract from the Report on the Political Situation in Transjordan—October 1932," November 3, 1932, CO 831/19.

24. Shuckburgh to Parkinson, December 19, 1939, CO 831/54.

25. Kirkbride to Burrows, October 21, 1948, FO 371.68864/E 13842 [secret and personal]; Pirie-Gordon to Burrows, July 12, 1949, FO 371.75316/E 8782 [secret]; and Amman to DOS, January 17, 1950, DOS 785.11/1-1750.

26. Fritzlan to SOS, May 17, 1951, DOS 785.11/5-1751.

27. Fritzlan to DOS, May 23, 1951, DOS 785.11/5-2351.

28. Drew to DOS, July 12, 1951, DOS 785.11/7-1251.

29. Only after Talal left Amman was Abdullah informed of his son's illness and subsequent departure. Despite the ruckus at home, Abdullah continued with his visit to Turkey. Fritzlan to SOS, May 17, 1951, DOS 785.11/5-1751. Fritzlan to DOS, May 23, 1951, DOS 785.11/5-2351; also see *New York Times,* May 17, 1951.

30. Press release, June 23, 1951, enclosed in Drew to DOS, July 5, 1951, DOS 785.11/7-551; also see Aqil Hyder Hasan Abidi, *Jordan: A Political Study, 1948–1957* (London: Asia Publishing House, 1965), 87.

31. Bruce Maddy-Weitzman, "Jordan and Iraq: Efforts at Intra-Hashemite Unity," *Middle Eastern Studies* 26 (January 1990): 65–66.

32. Mack to Wright, June 29, 1950, FO 371.82779/ET 1944/1 [personal and top secret].

33. Kirkbride to Wright, July 4, 1950, FO 371.82779/ET 1944/4g [top secret].

34. Trevelyan to Furlonge, July 20, 1950, FO 371.82779/ET 1944/3g [top secret]; Kirkbride to Wright, July 5, 1950, FO 371.82779/ET 1944/5g [top secret].

35. Beeley to Eastern Department, May 5, 1951, FO 371.91797/ET 10393/1.

36. See Abdullah's federation plan and Abdul Ilah's counterproposal in Kirkbride to Morrison, July 26, 1951, FO 371.91797/ET 10393/19.

37. *New York Times,* June 2, 1951.

38. After Abdullah's death, Abdul Ilah claimed that the late king had given him a draft of a declaration announcing his intention to name Feisal as his heir. Younger's minute, July 21, 1951, FO 371.91797/ET 10393/3.

39. "He loved me very much, that I know, and I in my turn loved him. . . . To me he was more than a grandfather, and to him I think I was a son." Hussein bin Talal, *Uneasy Lies the Head* (New York: Bernard Geis Associates, 1962), 13–14.

40. Drew to DOS, July 5, 1951, DOS 785.00/7-551 in United States, *Foreign Relations of the United States (FRUS)*, Near East and Africa, 1951, 5:981.

41. Amman to SOS, July 20, 1951, DOS 785.00/7-2051.

42. Drew to DOS, July 20, 1951, DOS 785.11/7-2051; Kirkbride to FO, July 22, 1951, FO 371.92838.

43. Tyler to SOS, July 22, 1951, DOS 785.11/7-2251.

44. Walker to FO, July 21, 1951, FO 371.91838.

45. This Solomonic decision provoked much anxiety in London and Washington. No. 10 Downing Street addressed its official message of condolence to Nayif as regent; the White House sent its telegram to Talal, then in hospital, in his capacity as crown prince. When word leaked to the press, it was opined (by, among others, Moshe Dayan) that backing different horses in the royal race was illustrative of the deep divisions in British and American Middle East policy. Tyler to SOS, July 22, 1951, DOS 785.11/7-2251; also see al-Majali, *Mudhakkarati,* 104.

46. Al-Majali, *Mudhakkarati*, 108.

47. Israeli Foreign Ministry biographic data referred to such men as either "Palestinian" or, interestingly enough, "Men of the Land of Israel" (Eretz Yisra'eliyim). For the latter, see ISA, "Skirat Reka'" intelligence file S/265, December 23, 1955.

48. Al-Rifa'i's son recalled that his "father was never really Palestinian [and] never worked as a Palestinian. When the Allies met in Lausanne to give nationalities to all the citizens of the area . . . my father was already in Jordan so that the only citizenship he ever had other than Ottoman was Jordanian." Interview with Zayd al-Rifa'i.

49. For a complete listing of the composition of Jordanian governments, see Ministry of Information, *al-Wath'iq al-urdunniyya: al-wazarat al-urdunniyya, 1921–1984* [Jordanian documents: Jordanian ministries, 1921–1984] (Amman: Directorate of Press and Publications, 1984).

50. Tawfiq's birth date is obscure; he may have been older. According to Zayd al-Rifa'i, Samir was proud of the fact that at the time he was the youngest man ever named prime minister. On birth dates, see Epiphan (Bernard) Zacharia Sabella, "External Events and Circulation of Political Elites: Cabinet Turnover in Jordan, 1946–1980," (Ph.D. diss., University of Virginia, 1982), 243; and ISA 2477/11, September 4, 1951.

51. Wilson, *King Abdullah*, 1–2.

52. Uriel Dann, "The United States and the Recognition of Jordan, 1946–1949," in Uriel Dann, *Studies in the History of Transjordan* (Boulder, CO: Westview Press, 1984), 111.

53. Interview with Walid Salah.

54. For example, Abu'l Huda opposed the immediate annexation of the West Bank in 1948, opposed a generous exchange of territory with Israel in 1952, and opposed the expansion of the British military presence in Jordan as a deterrent to Israeli retaliatory raids in 1953.

55. Al-Rifa'i's policy on peace with Israel is the most obvious example of this strategy in action. Others included his shrewd request in 1947 that Britain suspend its lobbying for Jordan's membership in the United Nations, lest the kingdom be forced to associate itself with the other Arab states' "thoroughly foolish lines of policy" on Palestine. See Pirie-Gordon to Garran, July 11, 1947, FO 818.110.

56. From an unsigned letter from the American embassy in London to NEA Director Satterthwaite, January 3, 1949 [secret], NA/RG 84, Box 1, 350.

57. Charles Johnston, *The Brink of Jordan* (London: Hamish Hamilton, 1972), 69.

58. Interview with Hamad al-Farhan.

59. Al-Majali, *Mudhakkarati*, 107.

60. Interviews with Anwar al-Khatib; 'Abd al-Rahman Shuqayr; and a close family friend of Abu'l Huda's who prefers to remain anonymous.

61. Glubb, *A Soldier*, 72–73.

62. Despondency over cancer is how most historians have accounted for Tawfiq's suicide. See Sabella, "External Events," 243. Interviews with family associates account for the claim that it might have been family troubles that led to his suicide. Shuqayr, among others, alleged that Abu'l Huda was murdered, ostensibly to prevent the publication of his memoirs.

63. Interview with Sami Judeh.

64. Interview with Zayd al-Rifaʻi.

65. Tyler to SOS, July 22, 1951, DOS 785.11/7-2251; also *New York Herald Tribune,* July 22, 1951.

66. Al-Majali, *Mudhakkarati,* 108.

67. Kirkbride to FO, July 22 and 23, 1951, FO 371.91789 [secret].

68. Interview with Zayd al-Rifaʻi.

69. Kirkbride to FO, July 24, 1951, FO 371.91789 [particular secrecy].

70. Kirkbride to Furlonge, July 25, 1951, FO 816.172 [secret].

71. Drew to SOS, July 25, 1951, DOS 785.00/7-2551.

72. They were Shaykh Muhammad al-Shanqiti and Minister of Court Muhammad al-Shurayqi.

73. Kirkbride to FO, July 24, 1951, FO 371.91789 [particular secrecy]; Kirkbride to Furlonge, July 25, 1951, FO 816.172 [secret].

74. "I think he expected to be asked to form the government again," son Zayd later said. "Though he never spoke about it, I think he was disappointed that he wasn't allowed to continue. I think the change was a shock to him."

75. Kirkbride to Furlonge, July 25, 1951, FO 816.172 [secret].

76. Al-Shanqiti and Felah al-Madadha were Nayif's men; al-Tutunji, Anastas Hanania, and Hashim Jayyousi, if not "Samir's men," had served in al-Rifaʻi's previous government.

77. As Drew wrote about Justice Minister al-Madadha, "The less said about his habits and morals the better." Drew to DOS, July 26, 1951, DOS 785.13/7-2651.

78. Kirkbride to Furlonge, July 27, 1951, FO 816.172 [secret].

79. Younger's memorandum, July 21, 1951, FO 371.91797/ET 10393/3.

80. According to al-Majali, they began lobbying for union while Abdullah "was still a corpse in our hands that we had not yet buried." See al-Majali, *Mudhakkarati,* 108.

81. Kirkbride to FO, July 25, 1951, FO 371.91797/ET 10393/8; Kirkbride to FO, July 24, 1951, FO 371.91789 [particular secrecy].

82. Kirkbride to FO, July 25, 1951, FO 371.91789 [particular secrecy].

83. Kirkbride to Furlonge, July 27, 1951, FO 816.172 [secret].

84. Kirkbride to Furlonge, July 25, 1951, FO 816.172 [secret]; Kirkbride to Rapp, August 2, 1951, FO 371.91839 [secret]; Drew to SOS, July 31, 1951, DOS 785.00/7-3151.

CHAPTER 2

1. *New York Times,* July 25, 1951.

2. Drew to DOS, July 21, 1951, DOS 785.11/7-2151.

3. Tyler to DOS, July 27, 1951, DOS 785.11/7-2751; Drew to SOS, July 31, 1951, DOS 785.00/7-3151.

4. Walker to Morrison, September 3, 1951, FO 816.172.

5. United Press report, August 20, 1951, FO 778.34; interview with Walid Salah, from which subsequent quotations in this chapter are taken.

6. One of Wilson's main charges against the propriety of the trial was the dual role of Salah as prosecutor and judicial adviser. According to Salah, Hashim served in the latter role. Technically, both did. See Mary C. Wilson, *King Abdullah, Britain and the Making of Jordan* (Cambridge: Cambridge University

Press, 1987), 211–12; Salah interview; and Abu'l Huda's letter to the Royal Court, August 8, 1951, JNA file 95/156-15/679-157-15.

7. S. G. T., "King Abdullah's Assassins," *The World Today*, October 1951, pp. 411–12. One or two errors notwithstanding, this article provides a useful description and analysis of the investigation and trial of the assassins. Also see Munib al-Madi and Sulayman Musa, *Tarikh al-urdunn fi al-qarn al-'ashreen* [The history of Jordan in the twentieth century] (1959; Amman: Maktaba al-muhtasab, 1988), 550–58.

8. Members of the tribunal were Brigadier 'Abd al-Qadir al-Jundi and Colonels Habis al-Majali and 'Ali al-Hiyari. Technically, the tribunal was styled "the special court to prosecute those who break the peace of the state whether internally or externally" and was created with the expressed purpose of adjudicating the murders of Abdullah and Riyadh al-Sulh. The latter's case closed with the conviction and the sentencing to death *in absentia* of the one remaining suspect in November 1951. See Kirkbride to Furlonge, July 27, 1951, FO 816.172 [secret]; Walker to Beirut, December 18, 1951, FO 816.172; Drew to DOS, November 26, 1951, DOS 785.00/11-2651; *al-Urdunn* (Amman), November 18, 1951; and Aqil Hyder Hasan Abidi, *Jordan: A Political Study, 1948–1957* (London: Asia Publishing House, 1965), 86.

9. S. G. T., "King Abdullah's Assassins," 418.

10. Drew to DOS, August 9, 1951, DOS 785.00/8-951 [secret].

11. Salah blamed Sam'an Da'ud, his successor as Jerusalem's attorney-general and one of the authors of the indictments, for wrongly accusing three of those eventually acquitted. But, he maintained, Iyad "definitely knew about the conspiracy."

12. In contrast with other unsuccessful Palestinian candidates in the 1950 elections, Musa went out of his way to explain to British diplomats that he had no complaints about government heavy-handedness, only criticism of his own "errors of judgment." Dow to Younger, April 19, 1950, FO 371.82705/ET 1016/14. In general, see S. G. T., "King Abdullah's Assassins," 413–14.

13. See P. J. Vatikiotis, *Politics and the Military in Jordan: A Study of the Arab Legion, 1921–1957* (London: Cass, 1967), 99–108. Also see Abdullah al-Tall, *Karithat Filastin: Mudhakkarat Abdullah al-Tall* [The Palestine disaster: Memoirs of Abdullah al-Tall] (Cairo: Dar al-Qalm Press, 1959).

14. In some quarters, the question continues to rage. See Nasr al-din al-Nashashibi, *Man qatala al-malak Abdullah?* [Who killed King Abdullah?] (Kuwait: Manshurat al-anba', 1980).

15. Glubb to Melville (TJL), August 6, 1951, FO 371.91839/ET 1942/ 60 [secret].

16. Wilson, *King Abdullah*, 212. There are similar intimations in Avi Shlaim, *Collusion Across the Jordan: King Abdullah, the Zionist Movement and the Partition of Palestine* (New York: Columbia University Press, 1988), 606; and Barry Rubin, *The Arab States and the Palestine Conflict* (Syracuse, NY: Syracuse University Press, 1981), 213.

17. Kirkbride to Younger, September 17, 1951, FO 816.172.

18. Soviet complicity was mentioned by a Jerusalem-based European diplomat citing Jordanian government officials; ISA 2565/39154, July 23, 1951. And in a Cold War analysis, one Soviet writer termed Abdullah's assassins members of "a pro-American terrorist organization." Perhaps the Soviet archives will

shed some light on this. See Y. A. Lebedev, "Soviet Writing on Jordan," *The Mizan Newsletter* 2 (November 1960): 5.

19. Testimony of Muhammad Hasan Salman, head of the mission, to the Iraqi revolutionary court, October 13, 1958; cited in Abidi, *Jordan*, 88-89.

20. The delegation met with Sulayman al-Nabulsi, Hikmat al-Masri, Abdullah al-Rimawi, Anwar al-Khatib, and Akram Zu'aytar, as well as Abu'l Huda. See Abidi, *Jordan*.

21. Kirkbride confirmed as "relevant" the Israeli intelligence reports of this "secret campaign of vote purchasing." Chadwick to FO, August 24, 1951, and Kirkbride to Younger, September 19, 1951, FO 371.91798/ET 10393/28, 39; ISA 2408/11/a, August 21 and 24, 1951.

22. Kirkbride to Younger, September 19, 1951, FO 371.91798/ET 10393/28, 39.

23. Ibn Saud could not have been too pleased with the American response, which spoke of the "right of peoples freely to choose their own form of government." Hare to SOS, August 5, 1951, DOS 785.00/8-551; Acheson to Jeddah, August 7, 1951, DOS 785.00/8-551.

24. Abidi, *Jordan*, 89; *New York Times,* August 29, 1951.

25. Kirkbride to FO, August 3, 1951, FO 816.172; Leonard to DOS, August 6, 1951, DOS 683.85/8-651.

26. Kirkbride to Rapp, August 2, 1951, FO 371.91839 [secret]; Drew to DOS, August 10, 1951, DOS 785.00/8-1051 [secret].

27. Drew to SOS, August 10, 1951, DOS 785.00/8-1051 [secret]; Kirkbride to FO, August 3, 1951, FO 816.172.

28. Kirkbride to FO, August 3, 1951, FO 816.172.

29. Jordan radio, July 26, 1951; cited in FO 371.91789.

30. These alliances sometimes made odd bedfellows. Hazem Nusaybah recalled that his Cambridge-educated brother Anwar routinely welcomed endorsements by the radical Islamist Shaykh Taqi' al-Din Nabahani of the Tahrir [Liberation] party.

31. The blacklisted candidate was Shafiq al-Rushaydat of Irbid, described as "the central figure in Hashemite Jordan's pro-Mufti faction." See *Christian Science Monitor* (Boston), July 21, 1951. Also see Drew to DOS, August 9, 1951, DOS 785.00/8-951 [secret]; Kirkbride to Morrison, September 5, 1951, FO 371.91789.

32. Al-Rimawi ran under the banner of the fictitious "Popular Constitutional Front"; Na'was claimed to be an "independent." Both were, in fact, Ba'thists. See Abidi, *Jordan*, 90.

33. Kirkbride to FO, August 1, 1951, FO 816.172; Drew to SOS, August 15, 1951, DOS 685.86/8-1551 [secret]; Kirkbride to Furlonge, August 25, 1951, FO 371.91798/ET 10393/31 [secret]; Abidi, *Jordan*, 88.

34. See, for example, *Christian Science Monitor,* September 1, 1951. Also, Aruri's account smacks of overstatement; see Nasser H. Aruri, *Jordan: A Study in Political Development (1921–1965)* (The Hague: Nijhoff, 1972), 102-3.

35. Abidi, *Jordan*, 90.

36. Dann offers a useful corrective when he states that "it is an impermissible generalization that [the Palestinians] were, because of their background, 'more progressive' politically than the Transjordanians." Uriel Dann, "Regime and Opposition in Jordan Since 1949," in *Society and Political Structures in*

the Arab World, ed. Menachem Milson (New York: Humanities Press, 1973), 148.

37. See the British embassy's preelection forecast in Walker to Eastern Department, August 27, 1951, FO 371.91789. Complete election results were published in *al-Urdunn*, August 30, 1951.

38. The official figures of registered voters were East Bank, 147,308 (1950), 181,628 (1951); West Bank, 160,205 (1950), 161,086 (1951). The American embassy's "rough estimates" for voter participation ("somewhat less than 50 percent on the East Bank; somewhat above 50 percent on the West Bank") differ markedly from Kirkbride's. Kirkbride to Morrison, September 5, 1951, FO 371.91789; Drew to DOS, September 6, 1951, DOS 785.00/9-651; also see Abidi, *Jordan*, 89–90.

39. ISA 2408/11/a, August 21 and 31, 1951.

40. For this paragraph, see Geneva to SOS, July 21 and 23, 1951, DOS 785.11/7-2151 and DOS 785.11/7-2351 [secret]; Kirkbride to FO, July 24, 1951, FO 371.91789 [particular secrecy]; the Foreign Office's Swiss consular file on Talal, FO 778.34; also *Journal de Genève*, July 26, 1951; and *New York Herald Tribune*, July 22, 1951.

41. Drew to SOS, July 31, 1951, DOS 785.00/7-3151; Kirkbride to Furlonge, July 25 and 27, 1951, FO 816.172 [secret].

42. United Press report, July 29, 1951, cited in FO 778.34.

43. Interview with United Press correspondent, Amman, July 24, 1951, cited in FO 778.34; Kirkbride to Furlonge, July 25, 1951, FO 816.172 [secret]; ISA, 2408/11/a, August 21, 1951.

44. Robertson to Barrett, July 30, 1951, FO 778.34.

45. Kirkbride to FO, August 8, 1951, FO 816.172.

46. Drew to DOS, August 23, 1951, DOS 785.00/8-2351 [secret]; Kirkbride to FO, August 15, 1951, FO 816.172.

47. Kirkbride to FO, August 15, 1951, FO 816.172; Drew to DOS, August 23, 1951, DOS 785.00/8-2351 [secret].

48. Ibid. Stymied by Kirkbride, several of Nayif's backers beat a track to Drew's door, but the American was no more sympathetic than his British counterpart had been.

49. Drew to DOS, August 23, 1951, DOS 785.00/8-2351 [secret].

50. Specifically, they claimed that Talal suffered from an "acute inflammation of the lymphatic glands . . . accompanied by a high fever [during which] he was liable to violent fits, accompanied by 'symptoms of a schizophrenic nature.'" *The Observer* (London), August 26, 1951, in FO 778.34.

51. *La Suisse* (Geneva), August 25, 1951, in FO 778.34; Drew to SOS, August 28, 1951, DOS 785.11/8-2851; *al-Urdunn*, August 24, 1951.

52. As outlined earlier, the first two were his attempt to entice Samir al-Rifa'i into conspiracy and his ultimatum to Kirkbride.

53. Drew to SOS, September 4, 1951, DOS 785.00/9-451.

54. Drew to SOS, September 4, 1951, DOS 785.00/9-451; Drew to SOS, September 6, 1951, DOS 785.00/9-651; Furlonge to Strong, October 25, 1951, FO 371.91822/ET 1201/74. Also see *al-Misri* (Cairo), September 11, 1951, cited in DOS 785.00/9-2751.

55. Peter Snow, *Hussein: A Biography* (London: Barrie & Jenkins, 1972) 38; Benjamin Shwadran, *Jordan: State of Tension* (New York: Council for Middle Eastern Affairs Press, 1959), 313; and Drew to DOS, October 26, 1951, DOS

785.11/10-2651 [secret]. For a slightly different version, see Patrick Coghill, "Before I Forget," mimeograph (Oxford, 1960), 108.

56. There is considerable contradiction on this point. According to Drew, Nayif signed the death warrants on September 3 and left the country before the sentences were carried out the following morning. In his first volume of memoirs, Kirkbride spoke of his efforts to "bolster up the determination" of Nayif and his relevant ministers "to hang the killers." But in his second volume, published two decades later, he told a different story. Nayif refused to approve the executions, Kirkbride wrote, but "then made the mistake of going for a week's holiday to Lebanon, and left the Council of Regency in charge of the administration. Almost as soon as he was across the frontier, the members of the Council . . . signed the death warrants of the condemned." Kirkbride's first explanation and Drew's are, I believe, correct. See Alec Kirkbride, *A Crackle of Thorns: Experiences in the Middle East* (London: Murray, 1956), 167; and Alec Kirkbride, *From the Wings: Amman Memoirs, 1947–1951* (London: Cass, 1976), 138–39; also see Drew to SOS, September 4, 1951, DOS 785.00/90-451.

One further note: On August 29, the cabinet ordered the executions to be carried out in Jerusalem (ministerial decision 84). The next day, however, a substitute recommendation omitted the reference to Jerusalem (ministerial decision 85). Whether it was Nayif, Kirkbride, or a third party that convinced Abu'l Huda to change his mind is not known. The assassins were hanged in Amman. See JNA file 95/156-15.

57. ISA, 2408/11/a, August 2, 1951.

58. The Glubb story, first reported in the *Jerusalem Post,* May 22, 1951, was hotly denied by Glubb; see *New York Times,* May 24, 1951.

59. Kirkbride to Furlonge, September 4, 1951, FO 371.91789.

60. Abdul Ilah had himself visited Geneva and pronounced Talal fit. Baghdad to SOS, September 19, 1951, DOS 685.87/9-1951; Kirkbride to Younger, September 19, 1951, FO 371.91789; Amman to Eastern Department, October 10, 1951, FO 371.91789.

61. Kirkbride to Rapp, August 2, 1951, FO 371.91839 [secret].

62. Among those present at the July 23 meeting were Foreign Minister Moshe Sharett, Foreign Ministry Director-General Walter Eytan, and Israel's chief interlocutor with Abdullah, Reuven Shiloah. ISA, 2410/9, July 29, 1951.

63. Drew to DOS, August 23, 1951, DOS 785.00/8-2351 [secret].

CHAPTER 3

1. Al-Madadha, a Keraki, was vilified by many Palestinians for his role as governor-general of Palestine in 1949. See Amman to DOS, October 18, 1950, 785.13/10-1850.

2. Most notable among those dropped was chief plotter Muhammad al-Shurayqi. See Munib al-Madi and Sulayman Musa, *Tarikh al-urdunn fi al-qarn al-ʿashreen* [The history of Jordan in the twentieth century] (1959; Amman: Maktaba al-muhtasab, 1988), 561, 565; Muhammad Taysir Dhubyan, *al-Malak Talal* [King Talal] (Amman: Majallat al-shariʿa, 1972), 52; and Aqil Hyder Hasan Abidi, *Jordan: A Political Study, 1948–1957* (London: Asia Publishing House, 1965), 96.

3. Sixteen of them, however, remained under town arrest. Drew to DOS, October 17, 1951, DOS 785.00/10-1751.

4. *New York Times*, October 3, 1951; Drew to DOS, November 16, 1951, DOS 785.00/11-1651.

5. Parliament had gone so far as to appoint its own constitutional revision committee, under the energetic chairmanship of Hazza' al-Majali. Hazza' al-Majali, *Mudhakkarati* [My memoirs] (Beirut: Dar al-'ilm lil-malayeen, 1960), 111–17. On Talal, see Drew to DOS, October 26, 1951, DOS 785.11/10-2651 [secret]; and Drew to DOS, November 16, 1951, DOS 785.00/11-1651. More generally, see Furlonge to Eden, February 21, 1952, enclosing Kirkbride's note on parliamentary developments, FO 371.98859/ET 1015/1.

6. All citations are taken from *The Constitution of the Hashemite Kingdom of Jordan* [English and Arabic] (Amman, n.d.).

7. George L. Harris, *Jordan, Its People, Its Society, Its Culture* (New York: Grove Press, 1958), 94.

8. Kirkbride's note, cited in Furlonge to Eden, February 21, 1952, FO 371.98859/ET 1015/1. Also see Uriel Dann, "Regime and Opposition in Jordan Since 1949," in *Society and Political Structures in the Arab World*, ed. Menachem Milson (New York: Humanities Press, 1973), 155.

9. Ibid.

10. The Talal constitution, with several significant amendments, remains in force today.

11. Drew to DOS, November 16, 1951, DOS 785.00/11-1651; Abidi, *Jordan*, 100.

12. Walker to Eden, February 2, 1952, FO 371.98857/ET 1013/2.

13. "Annual Report for 1951," Walker to Eden, January 26, 1952, FO 371.98836/ET 1011/1.

14. Al-Majali's claim that Abu'l Huda compelled Talal to improve ties with Saudi Arabia does not stand up. See al-Majali, *Mudhakkarati*, 117. Also see Kirkbride to FO, November 9, 1951, FO 371.91798/ET 10393/43; and Jeddah to DOS, November 29, 1951, DOS 785.11/11-2951.

15. On relations with Egypt, see Mary C. Wilson, *King Abdullah, Britain and the Making of Jordan* (Cambridge: Cambridge University Press, 1987), 142; also see *al-Misri* (Cairo), February 1, 1951, and the accompanying notation in FO 371.91205/E 1072/5.

16. Abu'l Huda reportedly soothed Syria's nationalist sentiments by describing Glubb as a government employee who could be fired "at any time." Montagu-Pollock to FO, November 7, 1951, FO 371.91798/ET 10389/7.

17. Dudgeon's minute, January 15, 1951; and Walker to Wardrop, January 21, 1952, FO 371.98262/E 1071/1, 4.

18. For example, a treaty demarcating Jordan's frontier with Saudi Arabia, negotiated by Abu'l Huda and Ibn Saud in 1932, remained unratified. Not until 1965 was their border finally fixed. Drew to DOS, October 3, 1951, DOS 685.86a/10-351; Uriel Dann, *King Hussein and the Challenge of Arab Radicalism: Jordan, 1955–1967* (New York: Oxford University Press, 1989), 144–45.

19. Troutbeck to FO, November 7, 1951, FO 371.91798/ET 10393/422 [secret].

20. Crocker to SOS, January 8, 1952, DOS 785.00/10-852; Troutbeck to Bowker, December 31, 1951, FO 371.98865/ET 10393/1 [secret].

21. Unwelcome in Amman, Nayif found refuge in Baghdad, again arousing Talal's suspicions of Abdul Ilah. Nayif, though, proved to be as much a burden to his host as he had been to his half-brother and before long was convinced to move on to Beirut. Acheson to Amman, October 19, 1951, DOS 785.00/10-1951; Drew to SOS; October 22, 1951, DOS 785.00/10-2251; Crocker to SOS, February 11, 1952, DOS 785.00/2-1152; Fritzlan to SOS, May 14, 1952, DOS 785.13/5-1452; Gifford to SOS, June 18, 1952, DOS 785.11/6-1852 [all secret].

22. A Hashemite union figured prominently in the political program of some-time Iraqi premier Fadhil al-Jamali. See Selwyn Lloyd's conversation with al-Jamali, May 22, 1952, FO 371.98245/E 1027/5.

23. Furlonge to Bowker, May 2, 1952, FO 371.98866/ET 10393/17.

24. At one point, however, Abu'l Huda's strategy might have gone too far. Abdul Ilah was evidently so incensed at Talal's trip to the Hijaz that he considered sending the Iraqi army into Jordan to settle his dynastic troubles once and for all. Troutbeck to Bowker, November 17, 1951, FO 371.98898/ET 1941/6.

25. Although he refused to initiate any retaliatory reaction against West Germany, he did bow to the Arab League's decisions on the matter. Green to SOS, September 17, 1952, DOS 684a.86/9-1752.

26. Rapp to Furlonge, May 2, 1952, FO 816.177/10103.

27. Implicated in the attempt were relatives of 'Abd al-Qadir Farhat, one of those convicted in Abdullah's assassination. Tyler to SOS, October 30, 1951, DOS 785.11/10-3051.

28. See Fritzlan's memorandum of conversation with Anastas Hanania, September 17, 1951, in NA/RG 84, Box 2, 350.

29. Amman to DOS, March 5, 1954, DOS 785.13/3-354.

30. Tyler to SOS, December 13, 1951, DOS 684a.12-1351.

31. Walmsley to Walker, January 9, 1952, FO 371.98490/EE 1091/40.

32. Davis to DOS, February 27, 1952, DOS 784a.5 MSP/2-2752 [secret], in *Foreign Relations of the United States (FRUS)*, 1952–54, 9:898–99.

33. Fritzlan to DOS, February 29, 1952, DOS 684a.85/2-2952 [secret], in *FRUS*, 9:899–900.

34. Fritzlan's assessment that the proposed was "procedural rather than substantive" was, in my opinion, shortsighted. Fritzlan to DOS, March 7, 1952, DOS 684a.86/3-752, in *FRUS*, 9:905; also Furlonge to Eden, April 7, 1952, FO 371.98857/ET 1013/4; and *New York Times*, June 5, 1952.

35. See reportage in Fritzlan to DOS, March 7, 1952, DOS 684a.86/3-752, in *FRUS*, 9:905.

36. Fritzlan to SOS, May 21, 1952, DOS 785.00/5-2152; Kopper to Waller, June 2, 1951, DOS 785.00/6-251 [secret]; Wakefield to Eden, June 17, 1952, FO 371.98857/ET 1013/6; Abu'l Huda's statement in *al-Urdunn* (Amman), May 30, 1952; *New York Times*, June 5, 1952.

37. For an American analysis of British influence in Jordan, see Drew to DOS, August 30, 1951, DOS 641.85/8-3051 [secret].

38. Abu'l Huda did not, however, proscribe the export of vegetables to British forces at Suez, which he viewed as vital to the Jordanian economy. Walker to Eden, February 4, 1952, FO 371.98857/ET 1013/2.

39. Furlonge to Bowker, March 17, 1952, FO 371.98862/ET 1022/1.

40. Walker to Eden, January 5, 1952, FO 371.98857/ET 1013/1.

41. On Furlonge's "less agreeable side," see a letter from Bayard Dodge to

Joseph C. Green, May 8, 1952; Green Papers, John Foster Dulles Library, Princeton University, Princeton, NJ.

42. See his defense of Abu'l Huda's coolness toward Britain and the subsequent FO rebuke for his "complaisance," in correspondence with Bowker, March 17 and 29, 1952, FO 371.98862/ET 1022/1.

43. Although the date of the quotation is one year after the failure of Tuqan's plan, it accurately reflects Furlonge's overall disposition toward the possibility of Aran–Israeli peace, as related by the then-American ambassador. See Joseph C. Green, "Jordan Journal," manuscript, 3 vols. (copy in the Green Papers, Dulles Library, Princeton, NJ), May 10, 1953, 2:408.

44. See his analysis of Anglo-Jordanian relations in Furlonge to Eden, December 24, 1952, FO 371.98857/ET 1013/14.

45. To a similar, though lesser extent, the departure of American Minister Drew in early 1952 and his replacement by Joseph Coy Green further lightened Abu'l Huda's diplomatic burden. Shortly after leaving Jordan, the highly regarded Drew was promoted to career minister and subsequently served as director-general of the Foreign Service. In contrast, Green proved to be one of America's least auspicious diplomatic envoys. Even though he was a Republican, he had been named minister (and, as of August 27, 1952, ambassador) through a recess appointment by the Truman administration. When Eisenhower took office, the State Department never sent Green's name to the Senate for formal confirmation, despite (or perhaps because of) the fact that Green was a Princeton classmate of John Foster Dulles. Green was forced to leave Amman after just one year, his career ending on the ignominious note of never having been accorded recognition as his country's official representative. Given his anti-Zionist paranoia and anti-Semitic innuendo (e.g., his memoirs are replete with references to Jewish control and censorship of the media; to "the sinister influence" of men like "Messrs. Gross, Cohen and other Zionists"; to "obnoxious Jews"; and to the "ghetto traditions" that explain the "horrible, sordid" Israeli kibbutzim), his departure was not a significant loss. See his voluminous "Jordan Journal."

46. Furlonge to Bowker, March 3, 1952, FO 371.98859/ET 1015/2; also Drew to DOS, September 20, 1951, DOS 785.00/9-2051; Drew to DOS, November 14, 1951, DOS 785.00/11-1451; Fritzlan to DOS, February 29, 1952, DOS 785/00/2-2952.

47. Hunter margin note, FO 371.98898/ET 1941/1.

48. Furlonge to FO, March 22, 1952; and Furlonge to Eden, May 22, 1952, FO 371.98898-98900/ET 1941/12, 49 [secret].

49. Fritzlan to DOS, April 21, 1952, DOS 785.13/4-2152 [secret]; Furlonge to Eden, May 5, 1952, FO 371.98860/ET 1016/2.

50. Furlonge to Eden, May 22, 1952, FO 371.98900/ET 1941/49 [secret].

51. Ibid.; Furlonge to FO, May 13, 1952, FO 371.98899/ET 1941/33 [secret]; Fritzlan to SOS, May 13, 1952, DOS 785.11/5-1352 [top secret security].

52. Whitehall was a full partner in the effort to "get [Talal] away at the earliest possible moment," going so far as to ready an RAF backup airplane. See FO 371.98899-98900/ET 1941/25-26, 30, 61.

53. Furlonge to Eden, May 22, 1952, FO 371.98900/ET 1941/49 [secret]; medical report in Furlonge to Bowker, May 19, 1952, FO 371.98900/ET 1941/48; cabinet decision in Furlonge to Bowker, May 22, 1952, FO 371.98901/ET 1941/64 [secret].

54. Fritzlan to SOS, May 25, 1952, DOS 785.11/5-2552 [secret].

55. Why Zayn did not seek refuge with the Jordanian minister to Paris, a distant relative, is not known. Furlonge to FO, May 26 and 30, 1952; FO to Amman, May 29, 1952; and Ross minute, May 30, 1952, in FO 371.98900/ ET 1941/42, 47 [emergency secret]; Dunn to SOS, May 29, 1952, DOS 785.11/5-2952 [secret]; Fritzlan to SOS, May 30, 1952, DOS 785.11/5-3052 [secret].

56. Fritzlan to SOS, May 21, 1952, DOS 785.00/5-2152.

57. Anastas Hanania, quoted in Fritzlan to SOS, May 16, 1952, DOS 785.11/5-1652 [top secret].

58. What seems to have been an important factor in Abu'l Huda's thinking was information that British law forbade ministers from serving as counsellors of state. Another Palestinian, Ruhi 'Abd al-Hadi, was later appointed as Tuqan's interim replacement. Fritzlan to SOS, June 4, 1952, DOS 785.11/6-452; Fritzlan to SOS, June 4, 1952, DOS 785.00/6-452; FO 816.177.

59. Troutbeck to FO, June 2, 1952, FO 271.98900-98901/ET 1941/59, 67 [secret].

60. Zayd was the half-brother of the elder three sons. Troutbeck to FO and FO to Amman, June 3, 1952, FO 371.98900/ET 1941/59 [secret]; al-Majali, *Mudhakkarati*, 120.

61. Furlonge to FO, June 3, 1952, FO 371.98901/ET 1941/66 [secret].

62. In the meantime, Abu'l Huda took steps to assure Syria, Saudi Arabia, and Egypt about Jordan's dynastic troubles. Whitehall was left to allay Israeli fears. See Furlonge to Bowker, June 5, 1952, FO 371.98866/ET 10393/29 [secret]; Eagleton to DOS, June 9, 1952, DOS 785.00/6-952; Wardrop to Tel Aviv, June 10, 1952, and Furlonge to FO, June 12, 1952, FO 371.98901-98902/ ET 1941/81, 114; Troutbeck to FO, June 6 and 10, 1952, FO 371.98866/ET 10393/20, 27; Fritzlan to SOS, June 6, 1952, DOS 785.11/6-652; Ireland to SOS, June 7, 1952, DOS 685.87/6-752 [secret]; Fritzlan to DOS, June 9, 1952, DOS 785.11/6-952; *Falastin* (Jerusalem), June 6–8, 1952.

63. Fritzlan to SOS, May 25, 1952, DOS 785.11/5-2552 [secret].

64. BBC monitoring Jordan Radio, June 6, 1952, FO 371.98859/ET 1015/4; Furlonge to FO, June 6, 1952, FO 371.98901/ET 1941/78; *Le Figaro* (Paris), June 4, 1952.

65. Bowker was referring to the *Evening Standard*'s (London) headline "Lost Queen Hunt." See FO 371.98902/ET 1941/96, June 9, 1952. See also "Jordan Queen, Crown Prince Hide from King in Switzerland," *New York Herald Tribune*, June 10, 1952; and "Queen of Jordan Hides from Ailing King with Crown Prince Under Swiss Police Guard," *New York Times*, June 10, 1952.

66. See FO files 371.98902/ET 1941/99, 100, 108, 119; Fritzlan to SOS, June 14, 1952, DOS 785.11/6-1452.

67. Apparently Abdul Ilah had not bothered to ask Zayd about all this. When queried by the British embassy in Baghdad, Zayd said that he "would not dream of going to live in Jordan" and that in his opinion, the regent "ought to leave Jordan alone." He and his family eventually did take up residence in Amman after the 1958 Iraqi revolution. Eastern Department to Amman, July 3, 1952, FO 371.98867/ET 10393/45.

68. Gifford to SOS, June 14, 1952, DOS 785.11/6-1452 [secret]; Beeley to FO, June 16, 1952, FO 371.98866/ET 10393/35; Gifford to SOS, June 18, 1952, DOS 785.11/6-1852 [secret].

69. Berne to FO, June 20, 1952, FO 371.98903/ET 1941/131.

70. See Abu'l Huda's memorandum to the Foreign Office in Wakefield to FO, June 18, 1952, FO 371.98867/ET 10393/40.

71. "Many exploit Your Majesty's absence to attack the Government," the telegram read. "Your Majesty has no doubt read in the newspapers the serious criticisms and accusations made by His Highness Prince Abdul Ilah against the Government. . . . The Government begs Your Majesty to accept its request to undergo medical treatment or to return immediately to your capital. . . . We are still awaiting Your Majesty's arrival. The Government is afraid that in case of Your Majesty's refusing the appeal it may find itself unable to bear any more responsibilities." Wakefield to FO, June 17, 1952, FO 371.98902/ET 1941/116.

72. Gifford to SOS, June 20, 1952, DOS 785.11/6-2052 [secret].

73. Geneva to FO, June 16, 1952, FO 371.98902/ET 1941/105 [secret]; Wakefield to FO, June 19, and Geneva to FO, June 20, 1952, FO 371.98903/ET 1941/129.

74. Berne to FO, June 25, 1952, FO 371.98903/ET 1941/135.

75. Nuri's account was viewed "with some reserve." Bowker's memorandum of conversation with Nuri, June 27, 1952, FO 371.98867/ET 10393/47; Troutbeck minute, July 2, 1952, FO 371.98747/EQ 1055/4; Gifford to SOS, July 2, 1952, DOS 785.00/7-252 [secret].

76. Geneva to FO and MacDermot to Wardrop, June 25, 1952, FO 371.98903/ET 1941/136, 140 [secret].

77. Fritzlan to DOS, July 1952, DOS 785.00/7-952; *The Times* (London), July 4, 1952.

78. They were Dr. Muhammad Kamil al-Khuli, director of the Department of Mental Health, Ministry of Public of Health, and Dr. Yusef Barrada, professor of neurology, Fu'ad al-Awal University. Their full report remains closed in FO 371.98907/ET 1941/215; also see *New York Times*, July 11, 1952.

79. The previous three paragraphs are based on FO 371.98903-9805/ET 1941.

80. Hunter's margin note on Furlonge to FO, July 30, 1952, FO 371.98905/ET 1941/188 [secret]; Green to SOS, July 31, 1952, DOS 785.11/7-3152 [top secret security].

81. Furlonge to FO, August 5, 1952, FO 371.98906/ET 1941/190 [secret]; Furlonge to Bowker, August 7, 1952, FO 371.98907/ET 1941/213 [secret].

82. Green, "Jordan Journal," August 11, 1952, 1:82; Green to SOS, August 9, 1952, DOS 785.00-8-952; memorandum from Jordan's Directorate of General Intelligence, August 13, 1952, FO 816.177; *New York Herald Tribune*, August 12, 1952.

83. Green, "Jordan Journal," August 11, 1952, 1:82.

84. The committee included former regent Abdullah al-Kulaib, a tribal deputy, three moderate government critics (Hikmat al-Masri, Hazza' al-Majali, and Anwar al-Khatib), one Sa'id al-Mufti man (Sa'id 'Ala' al-Din), three Abu'l Huda loyalists (Wasfi Mirza, Felah al-Madadha, and Muhammad 'Ali Bdeir), and Muhammad al-Shanqiti, who had been present at the final day of Abdullah's reign, too. See al-Madi and Musa, *Tarikh al-urdunn*, 569; interview with Anwar al-Khatib.

85. Green, "Jordan Journal," August 11, 1952, 1:85.

86. In September 1952, Muhammad bin Talal, Hussein's brother, was confirmed as crown prince but was later replaced by Abdullah, Hussein's firstborn son, in 1962. Three years later, Abdullah himself was replaced by Hussein's youngest brother, Hassan.

87. Abidi, I believe, is incorrect in suggesting the vote was not unanimous. See Furlonge to FO, August 11, 1952, FO 371.98906/ET 1941/196-197; Green, "Jordan Journal"; John Bagot Glubb, *A Soldier with the Arabs* (London: Hodder & Stoughton, 1957), 292–95; and Abidi, *Jordan*, 106–7.

88. The new regime, however, declined to pay all of Talal's expenses, as Faruq had previously offered to do. Ibn Saud graciously picked up the tab, giving him the final riposte in his game of one-upmanship with Abdul Ilah. Furlonge to Bowker, September 29, 1952, FO 371.98909/ET 1941/252 [secret].

89. Furlonge to FO, August 14, August 22, and September 16, 1952, FO 371.98906-98909/ET 1941/202, 209, and 240; Green to DOS, August 26, 1952, DOS 785.1/8-2652; Beeley to FO, August 22, 1952, FO 371.98907/ET 1941/218 [secret].

90. Walker to FO, August 5, 1953, and Furlonge to FO, September 3, 1953, FO 371.104887/ET 1013/9, 10; Frank C. Roberts, ed., *Obituaries from the Times, 1971–1975* (London: Newspaper Archive Developments, 1976), 276.

CHAPTER 4

1. Drew to DOS, November 14, 1951, DOS 785.00/11-1451.

2. Fritzlan to SOS, March 14, 1952, DOS 785.00/3-1452 [secret]; Fritzlan to DOS, March 18, 1952, DOS 785.00/3-1852 [secret]; Acheson to Amman, March 28, 1952, DOS 785.00/3-2852 [seret]. On the JCP arrest, see *al-Urdunn* (Amman), December 30, 1951; Walker to Eden, January 5, 1952, FO 371.98857/ET 1013/1; Amnon Cohen, *Political Parties in the West Bank Under the Jordanian Regime, 1949–1967* (Ithaca, NY: Cornell University Press, 1982), 31; and WZL [Walter Z. Laqueur], "Communism in Jordan," *The World Today* 12 (1956): 109–19.

3. Defense Regulations nos. 1 and 2, respectively, April 24, 1952, translations in FO 816.177.

4. Drew to DOS, December 17, 1952, DOS 785.00/12-1752.

5. Furlonge to Bowker, March 3, 1952, FO 371.98859/ET 1015/2; Fritzlan to DOS, February 29, 1952, DOS 785.00/2-2952.

6. Naseer H. Aruri, *Jordan: A Study in Political Development* (1921–1965) (The Hague: Nijhoff, 1972), 97.

7. Walker to Morrison, June 14, 1951, FO 371.01802/ET 1102/74. More generally, see Department of Statistics, Hashemite Kingdom of Jordan, *Annual Statistical Bulletin* (Amman: Department of Statistics, 1952); Department of Statistics and U.S. Technical Cooperation Service for Jordan, *1952 Census of Housing: Statistics for Districts, Subdistricts, Nahiyas and Principal Towns* (Amman: n.p., n.d.); James Baster, "The Economic Problems of Jordan," *International Affairs* 31 (1955); International Bank for Reconstruction and Development, *The Economic Development of Jordan* (Baltimore: Johns Hopkins University Press, 1957); and Raphael Patai, *Jordan, Lebanon and Syria: An Annotated Bibliography* (New Haven, CT: Yale University Press, 1957), 96–135.

8. Walmsley's "Review of Economic Conditions in Arab Palestine," Janu-

ary 1952, cited in FO 371.98494/EE 1102/1. For similar conclusions, see the UNRWA report (March 1952) and the joint FAO/WHO report (April 1952), cited in FO 371.98516/EE 1827/7, 16.

9. See Bassam Khalil Saket, "Foreign Aid to Jordan, 1924/25–1972/73: Its Magnitude, Composition and Effect" (Ph.D. diss., University of Keele, 1976).

10. Fritzlan to DOS, April 30, 1952, DOS 885.10/4-3052; municipal budget in JNA file 907-13/a/2/25.

11. Fritzlan to DOS, April 23, 1952, DOS 885.10/4-2352; Green to DOS, August 26, 1952, DOS 885.10/8-2652.

12. Dearden's conversation with al-Rifaʻi, May 16, 1952, FO 816.177.

13. Although the leadership of Jordan's Baʻth party was a healthy mix of East and West Bankers, its popular support was principally Palestinian. Interview with Sulayman al-Hadidi.

14. Furlonge to Eden, May 5, 1952, FO 371.98860/ET 1016/2; Fritzlan to DOS, July 9, 1952, DOS 785.00/7-952; Walmsley to Wakefield, July 24 and August 3, 1952, FO 816.177. Also see Aqil Hyder Hasan Abidi, *Jordan: A Political Study, 1948–1957* (London: Asia Publishing House, 1965), 191–212; Avi Plascov, *The Palestinian Refugees in Jordan, 1948–1957* (London: Cass, 1981), 123–47; and Cohen, *Political Parties.*

15. See Naim Sofer, "The Political Status of Jerusalem in the Hashemite Kingdom of Jordan: 1946–67," *Middle Eastern Studies* 12 (1976): 73–94.

16. See Plascov, *The Palestinian Refugees*, 92–103; and P. J. Vatikiotis, *Politics and the Military in Jordan: A Study of the Arab Legion, 1921–1957* (London: Cass, 1967), 75–93.

17. For a list of attendees and a translation of the petition, see FO 816.177; Green to DOS, August 13, 1952, DOS 785.00/8-1352; Dearden minute to Furlonge, July 30, 1952, FO 816.177.

18. Drew to DOS, July 26, 1951, DOS 785.13/7-2651.

19. Tuqan was one of the foremost Hashemite partisans on the West Bank. He refused a ministerial post in the All-Palestine Government, and he was one of the leading lights of the September 1948 Amman Congress, the precursor to the celebrated Jericho Conference, which was one of the first Palestinian conclaves to empower Abdullah to speak on their behalf. In addition, he chaired the subsequent Nablus Conference in December 1949. See Plascov, *The Palestinian Refugees*, 11–14.

20. Dearden minute to Furlonge, August 4, 1952, FO 816.177.

21. Furlonge to Bowker, September 17, 1952, FO 371, 98859/ET 1015/9.

22. Green to DOS, August 29, 1952, DOS 785.00/8-2952.

23. Furlonge to Bowker, September 17, 1952, FO 371.98859/ET 1015/9; Green to DOS, September 19, 1952, DOS 785.00/9-1952.

24. Fritzlan to DOS, January 5, 1950, DOS 785.521/1-550.

25. Tyler to SOS, July 26, 1952, DOS 684a.85/7-2652 [secret].

26. Plascov, *The Palestinian Refugees*, 40; Green to DOS, October 6, 1952, DOS 785.00/10-652; Seelye to DOS, May 10, 1954, DOS 785.13/5-1054; Furlonge to FO, September 30, 1952, FO 371.98859/ET 1015/11.

27. On the day of their release, a group of former detainees promptly "started a minor pro-Stalin demonstration" in Amman and were "equally promptly locked up again by Tawfiq." Furlonge to Bowker, October 16, 1952, FO 371.98859/ET 1015/18.

28. Amman to Eastern Department, December 9, 1952, FO 371.98859/

ET 1015/30; Dearden to Walker, October 13, 1952, FO 816.177; Green to DOS, October 14, 1952, DOS 785.00/10-1452.

29. Furlonge to Bowker, September 17, 1952, FO 372.98859/ET 1015/9; Furlonge to Bowker, October 9, 1952, FO 371.98859/ET 1015/1.

30. Furlonge to Bowker, October 9, 1952, FO 371.98859/ET 1015/1. Dearden's memorandum of conversation with Tuqan, October 9, 1952, FO 816.177.

31. Dearden's memorandum, October 9, 1952, FO 816.177; Furlonge to Bowker, October 9, 1952, FO 371.98859/ET 1015/1.

32. See the ministerial statement in FO 816.177; also Green to SOS, November 1, 1952, Dos 785.00/11-152 [secret]; Dearden minutes, November 3 and 5, 1952, FO 816.177.

33. See Furlonge's memorandum of conversation with Abu'l Huda, November 4, 1952, and Dearden's minute to Furlonge, November 11, 1952, FO 816.177; also, Furlonge to Eden, November 6, 1952, FO 371.98859/ET 1015/19.

34. Joseph C. Green, "Jordan Journal," manuscript, 3 vols. (copy in the Green Papers, Dulles Library, Princeton University, Princeton, NJ), August 28, 1952, 1:133.

35. Dearden's memorandum of converstion with Hashim, November 6, 1952, FO 816.177.

36. The bureau included Hazza' al-Majali, 'Abd al-Qadir al-Salih, Anwar al-Khatib, Yusef 'Abbas 'Umru, Abdullah al-Rimawi, and 'Abd al-Fattah Darwish. According to al-Majali, who served as secretary, the bureau was not a skeleton political party, just a group of individuals united in their desire to oust Abu'l Huda. See Hazza' al-Majali, *Mudhakkarati* [My memoirs] (Beirut: Dar al-'ilm lil-malayeen, 1960), 124–27; and Munib al-Madi and Sulayman Musa, *Tarikh al-urdunn fi al-qarn al-'ashreen* [The history of Jordan in the twentieth century] (1959; Amman: Maktaba al-muhtasab, 1988), 572.

37. See FO 816.177; Furlonge to FO, November 13, 1952, FO 371.98859/ET 1015/24; al-Majali, *Mudhakkarati*, 125.

38. Furlonge to FO, November 13, 1952, FO 371.98859/ET 1015/24.

39. The Emergency Laws, as distinct from Defense Regulations, were a package of three statutes: the Law for the Prevention of Crimes, the Law of Collective Penalties, and the Law of Banishment and Deportations. See Green to DOS, March 12, 1953, DOS 785.21/3-1253.

40. Furlonge to FO, November 12, 1952, FO 371.98859/ET 1015/21; Green to SOS, November 24, 1952, DOS 785.00/11-2452 [secret]/

41. Green to SOS, November 15, 1952, DOS 785.00/11-1552 [secret]; Monypenny to Furlonge, November 19, 1952, FO 816.177; Furlonge to FO, November 20, 1952, FO 371.98859/ET 1015/27.

42. Dearden's memorandum of conversation with Hashim, November 16, 1952, FO 816.177; al-Majali, *Mudhakkarati*, 128.

43. Dearden minute, November 19, 1952, and Furlonge's memorandum of conversation with Abu'l Huda, November 22, 1952, FO 816.177; Furlonge to FO, November 23, 1952, and Furlonge to Bowker, November 20, November 27, and December 12, 1952, FO 371.98859/ET 10105/25, 27, 29, and 32.

44. This was evident, for example, in his vendetta against Farhan al-Shubaylat, the popular Amman mayor and former chief of the royal court whom Abu'l Huda sacked, was forced to reinstate on court order, and then sacked again. See Green

to DOS, April 2, 1953, DOS 785.00/4-253, and al-Shubaylat's unpublished memoirs.

45. Green to SOS, December 15, 1952, DOS 785.00/12-1552.

46. Green to DOS, March 12, 1953, DOS 785.21/3-1253; Walker to Eastern Department, January 1, 1953, FO 371.104890/ET 1017/3.

47. Lynch to DOS, February 16, 1952, DOS 885.561/2-1653.

48. Walker to Eastern Department, January 29, 1953, and Furlonge to Eden, February 5, 1953, FO 371.104890/ET 1017/3, 4 [secret]; Green to SOS, January 21, 1953, DOS 785.14/1-2153.

49. For details, see Plascov, *The Palestinian Refugees*, 75–79.

50. Furlonge to FO, February 3, 1953, FO 371.104893/ET 1051/2.

51. BBC monitoring Arab News Agency, November 16, 1952, and Walker to FO, December 18, 1952, FO 371.98881/ET 1198/1, 2.

52. *New York Times*, January 2, 4, 17, and 30, 1952; Tyler to SOS, January 21, 1953, DOS 684a.85/1-2153 [secret]; Green to SOS, February 1, 1953, DOS 684a.85/2-153; *Foreign Relations of the United States* (*FRUS*), 9:1110–83; FO 371.104778-104780; and John Bagot Glubb, *A Soldier with the Arabs* (London: Hodder & Stoughton, 1957), 302–7.

53. London's policy of exploiting Jordanian fears to the benefit of Britain's own imperial defense interests was a continuing theme of Anglo-Jordanian relations in the 1950s. See FO 371.104231-104233 and especially Lloyd to Eden, April 14, 1953, FO 800.808 [top secret].

54. Green to DOS, April 30, 1953, DOS 785.00/4-3053.

55. Furlonge to Bowker, March 19, 1953, FO 371.104890/ET 1017/7.

56. Whitehall, though, was tempted. Eden himself penciled in the margin of a relevant file, "Why should he not stay on?" But in the end, London deferred to the wishes of Hussein and the queen mother. Bowker minute, January 19, 1953, and Furlonge to Bowker, March 5, 1953, FO 371.104890/ET 1017/2, 5 [secret]; Green to SOS, March 7, 1953, DOS 785.11/3-753.

57. On the origins and membership of the "Mau Mau," see Amman to DOS, May 11, 1955, NA/RG 85, Box 7, 350; and Jarallah to Mallory, May 18, 1955, RG 84, Box 9, 350.

58. Furlonge to FO, May 5, 1953, FO 371.104887/ET 1013/6; Furlonge to Eden, January 25, 1954, "Political Review of Jordan for 1953," FO 371.110873/VF 1011/1.

59. Glubb letter to James Lunt, February 13, 1980, in James Lunt, *Glubb Pasha: A Biography* (London: Harvill Press, 1984), 169.

60. See FO 816.177.

61. Furlonge to FO, November 23, 1952, FO 371.98859/ET 1015/25.

62. Uriel Dann, "Regime and Opposition in Jordan Since 1949," in *Society and Political Structures in the Arab World*, ed. Menachem Milson (New York: Humanities Press, 1973), 157.

63. *Christian Science Monitor*, October 18, 1952.

64. Dearden minute to Furlonge, November 16, 1952, FO 816.177.

CHAPTER 5

1. The most useful works on King Hussein's life in the 1950s are his own memoirs, *Uneasy Lies the Head* (New York: Bernard Geiss Associates, 1962); Peter

Snow, *Hussein: A Biography* (London: Barrie & Jenkins, 1972); and Uriel Dann, *King Hussein and the Challenge of Arab Radicalism: Jordan, 1955–1967* (New York: Oxford University Press, 1989). James Lunt's recent *Hussein of Jordan: Searching for a Just and Lasting Peace, a Political Biography* (London: Macmillan, 1989) is less accurate and less exacting. King Hussein's autobiographical discussions with a French journalist in his *Mon métier de roi* (Paris: Editions Robert Laffont, 1975) add little to his 1962 memoirs.

2. Bowker minute, June 11, 1952, FO 371.98902/ET 1941/97; also FO 371.98904/ET 1941/171, 173, and 184; *The Times,* August 15, 1952; also Furlonge to FO, August 20 and 28, 1952, FO 371.98907-98908/ET 1941/211, 225. Hussein's account is substantially different; see his *Uneasy Lies the Head,* 43–44.

3. Wardrop to Furlonge, September 2, 1952, FO 371.98908/ET 1942/229 [secret and personal]; Hunter minute, September 8, 1952, and Bowker to Dawney, February 4, 1953, FO 371.98909/ET 1941/238.

4. Hussein, *Uneasy Lies the Head,* 25.

5. Ibid., 11.

6. Several persons that I interviewed mentioned that the memoir was ghostwritten by *Daily Mail* (London) foreign correspondent Noel Barber.

7. John Bagot Glubb, A *Soldier with the Arabs* (London: Hodder & Stoughton, 1957), 349.

8. Interview with King Hussein.

9. See Hussein's Independence Day speech, May 25, 1954, in Ministry of Information, *al-Majmuʿa al-kamila l'khutub jalalat al-malak al-Hussein bin Talal al-muʿazm, 1952–1985* [Complete collection of the speeches of His Majesty King Hussein bin Talal the Great, 1952–1985], vol. 1 (Amman: Directorate of Press and Publications, n.d. [1986?]), 40; Furlonge to Bowker, April 14, 1953, FO 371.104890/ET 1017/8.

10. Asked when he became Jordan's "preeminent political actor," Hussein replied, "I suppose the period just before the Arabization of the army [in 1956]." Of all those interviewed, only one (Sharif Zayd bin Shakir) believed that Hussein achieved that status before the end of 1954.

11. Instead of returning home for Sandhurst's winter break, Hussein and his mother spent three weeks in Switzerland, where the young king spent much of his time in the company of a distant cousin, Sharifa Dina bint ʿAbd al-Hamid al-ʿAwn. The two were eventually married in April 1955 and divorced the following year. See Ross's minute, January 15, 1952, FO 371.104959/ET 1941/5; and Furlonge to Bowker, February 10, 1953, FO 371.104960/ET 1941/27 [secret].

12. Joseph C. Green, "Jordan Journal," manuscript, 3 vols. (copy in the Green Papers, Dulles Library, Princeton University, Princeton, NJ), April 10, 1953, 2:298.

13. Green to DOS, September 8, 1952, DOS 785.00/9-852; Dearden to Furlonge, September 2, 1952, FO 816.177.

14. Furlonge was ordered to deny to his American colleague "that he has ever met with the Queen privately." See margin notes by Ross and Strange on Furlonge to Bowker, November 20, 1952, FO 371.98859/ET 1015/28; also Ross to Vincent, December 5, 1952, FO 371.98912/ET 1941/296; Furlonge to Bowker, October 16, 1952, FO 371.98859/ET 1015/18.

15. Memorandum on "Jordan," FO 371.104961/ET 1941/51.

16. In an Israeli analysis of the Zayn–Hussein relationship, Moshe Sasson, citing an Arab interlocutor, noted: "We should attribute to her much of his personality and many of his decisions. But at the same time, the more he leaves her fold, she is sorry to see him create for himself his own identity and to see that others succeed in influencing him contrary to her opinion." ISA 2531/9/a, June 22, 1953 [secret].

17. This paragraph is based on interviews with King Hussein and Hani al-Mulqi, Fawzi's son; Green to DOS, May 7, 1953, DOS 785.13/5-753 [secret]; Jarallah's memorandum to U.S. Ambassador Lester Mallory, May 18, 1955, NA/RG 84, Box 9, 350; and Bowker's minute, January 19, 1953, FO 371.104890/ET 1017/2.

18. Green, "Jordan Journal," May 5, 1953, 2:387–88.

19. Paraphrasing a line from al-Majali's memoirs, one of them described al-Mulqi's government as a cabinet of "ten prime ministers and one minister—al-Mulqi himself." Interview with Anwar al-Khatib; Hazza' al-Majali, *Mudhakkarati* [My memoirs] (Beirut: Dar al-'ilm lil-malayeen, 1960), 140.

20. Bowker to Furlonge, January 31, 1953, FO 371.104890/ET 1017/2 [secret and personal]; Bowker's minute, January 19, 1953, FO 371.104890/ET 1017/2.

21. See Naseer H. Aruri, *Jordan: A Study in Political Development (1921–1965)* (The Hague: Nijhoff, 1972), 106; and Glubb, *A Soldier,* 349.

22. Interview with King Hussein.

23. Green to DOS, June 2, 1953, DOS 885.561/6-253; Furlonge to Falla, September 8, 1953, FO 371.104888/ET 1015/5 [secret].

24. For details, see al-Majali, *Mudhakkarati,* 130–31.

25. Anwar Nusaybah was sorely missed, but he had been blackballed from the cabinet by al-Khatib, who refused to serve with his Jerusalem rival, and then by al-Mulqi himself, who feared losing his monopoly on the king's ear and rejected Nusaybah's appointment as minister of the court. Al-Mulqi was his own defense minister. Furlonge to FO, May 18, 1953, FO 371.104890/ET 1017/15; Green, "Jordan Journal," May 7–11, 1953, 2:393–410.

26. In the interim, al-Mulqi issued at least one directive of lasting importance. On May 23, 1953, he officially changed the English designation of the country from the "Hashemite Kingdom of the Jordan" to the "Hashemite Kingdom of Jordan." JNA 548/1-2.

27. Ministerial statement in FO 371.104890/ET 1017/17; also Green to DOS, May 28, 1953, DOS 785.135-2853; Furlonge to FO, May 18, 1953, FO 371.104890/ET 1017/25.

28. For excerpts from a wide spectrum of Jordanian newspapers targeting, among others, Abu'l Huda, Anwar Nusaybah, Winston Churchill, John Foster Dulles, and Eleanor Roosevelt, see Green to DOS, June 4, 1953, DOS 985.61/6-453.

29. Green to DOS, June 23, 1953, DOS 785.00/6-2353.

30. Al-Mulqi's compromise budget was approved unanimously on July 22. See FO 371.104908/ET 1114; Furlonge's monthly reports for March, June and July 1953, FO 371.104887/ET 1013/4, 8, and 9; and Green to DOS, July 22, 1953, DOS 785.00/7-2253.

31. Green to DOS, July 22, 1953, DOS 785.00/7-2253.

32. Bergus to Green, July 2, 1953, NA/RG 84, Box 4, 312.3.

33. Lynch to DOS, September 16, 1953, DOS 785.00/9-1653.

34. Furlonge to Bowker, September 9, 1953, FO 371.104887/ET 1013/11.

35. During his May visit, Saud passed out gifts reportedly worth £115,000, including two cars for Hussein, gold swords and gold watches for each member of the cabinet, and up to £500 in gold for "more or less everyone else with whom the party were in contact." Six weeks later, Saud turned down Jordan's request for an industrial development loan, on the grounds that Saudi Arabia was already in debt. Furlonge to FO, May 18, 1953, FO 371.104892/ET 10393/2; Furlonge to FO, June 27, 1953, FO 371.104912/ET 1117/7 [secret].

36. Furlonge to Bowker, April 28, 1953, FO 371.104890/ET 1017/9; Evans to FO, April 22, 1953, FO 371.104233/E 1194/46 [top secret].

37. Furlonge to FO, May 6, 1953; FO to Amman, May 8, 1953; and Furlonge to Bowker, May 12, 19531 FO 371.104233/E 1194/48, 81 [top secret].

38. Damascus to SOS, May 16, 1953, DOS 683.85/5-1553 [secret]; memorandum of conversation between Dulles and al-Mulqi, May 15, 1953, Lot 59 D 95, in *Foreign Relations of the United States* (*FRUS*), 9:41–43; Furlonge to FO, May 15 and 18, 1953, FO 371.104781/ER 1091/149, 153; also see *The Times* and *Jerusalem Post,* June 30, 1953.

39. The economic benefit of deploying seven thousand to eight thousand men (including dependents) was estimated to "be equivalent to a pessimistic estimate of the employment possibilities likely to be opened up by the Yarmuk scheme." Rapp to Bowker, March 5, 1953, FO 371.104900/ET 1105/19 [top secret].

40. The institutional history of the "O" Force, named after its first commanding officer, Lieutenant Colonel R. H. L. Oulton, may be found in WO 106.6009.

41. Furlonge to FO, June 25 and 27, 1953, FO 371.104925/ET 1192/12, 14 [top secret].

42. Al-Mulqi to Walker, August 25, 1953, and Furlonge to FO, September 1, 1953, FO 371.104925/ET 1192/18, 20 [secret, top secret].

43. Walker to Ross, August 17, 1953, FO 371.104787/ER 1091/329.

44. Walmsley to FO, August 28, 1953, FO 371.104787/ER 1091/332.

45. Furlonge to FO, September 22, 1953, FO 371.104925/ET 1192/25 [top secret].

46. Furlonge to FO, September 16, 1953, FO 371.104925/ET 1192/24 [top secret].

47. Furlonge to FO, September 29, 1953, FO 371.104925/ET 1192/27 [top secret]; and FO 371.104926/ET 1192/31 [top secret].

48. Throughout this period, King Hussein was vacationing and seeking medical care in England and played no active role in these developments. He did not return to Jordan until mid-October.

49. On the Ben Gurion–Sharett clash during this period, see, for example, Michael Brecher, *The Foreign Policy System of Israel: Setting, Images, Process* (Oxford: Oxford University Press, 1972), 379–91; and Avi Shlaim, "Conflicting Approaches to Israel's Relations with the Arabs: Ben Gurion and Sharett, 1953–1956," *Middle East Journal,* 37 (Spring 1983): 180–201.

50. At first, the Israeli government claimed that "frontier settlers" were responsible for the attack. See FO 371.104789/ER 1091/387; and *The Times,* October 18, 1953.

51. Glubb to Cruickshank (TJL) to FO/WO, October 15, 1953, FO 371.104783/ER 1091/352 [secret]; Seelye to DOS, October 15, 1953, DOS 684a.85/10-1553 [secret]; *New York Times,* October 14 and 16, 1953; also see John Bagot Glubb, *The Changing Scenes of Life: An Autobiography* (London: Quartet Books, 1983), 171–72; and more generally, John Bagot Glubb, "Violence on the Jordan–Israel Border: A Jordanian View," *Foreign Affairs* 32 (July 1954): 552–62.

52. Furlonge to Allen, October 21, 1953, FO 371.104890/ET 1017/24.

53. Glubb considered opposing the order but rejected the notion on the faulty information that "the whole Jewish army is just across the border *fully mobilized.*" This was not true (emphasis in the original). Glubb to Furlonge, FO 8l6.189; MELF to WO, October 16, 1953, FO 371.104788/ER 1091/352 [top secret flash]; Amman to DOS, October 21, 1953, DOS 785.00(w)/10-2153 [secret].

54. Evans to FO, October 31, 1953, FO 371.104790/ER 1091/441.

55. Better late than never, Furlonge took the opportunity to press for the deployment of British troops in Jordan. A British tank squadron was finally relocated from Suez to Ma'an in February 1954. Furlonge to FO, October 15 and 16, 1953, FO 371.104788/ER 1091/354, 365; Furlonge to FO, October 20, 1953, FO 371.104926/ET 1192/34 [secret].

56. The Tripartite Declaration committed Britain, France, and America to take action, individually or collectively, to preserve the territorial status quo in the Middle East. There was never, however, any military contingency planning among the three powers to lend teeth to the declaration.

57. Lynch to DOS, October 27, 1953, NA/RG 84, Box 3, 310.

58. Completed in early November, the investigation found Third Brigade Commander J. O. M. Ashton and three Arab subordinates guilty of "negligence." Glubb's confidential report, however, exonerated Ashton and instead laid blame on the commander of the border regiment. In the end, Ashton was relieved of his command. Of the three Arab officers, one was imprisoned, another was pensioned off, and the third was demoted. See the handwritten testimonies given to the investigation board, including that of Ashton himself, in JNA 96/160/15; Furlonge to Allen, October 21, 1953, FO 371.104890/ET 1017/24; Glubb to Melville (TJL) to FO/WO, October 28, 1953, FO 371.104790/ER 1091/430 [secret]; Furlonge to FO, November 1, 1953, FO 371.104890/ET 1017/25; Glubb's confidential report in FO 371.104890/ET 1017/31; James Lunt, *Glubb Pasha. A Biography* (London: Harvill Press, 1984), 178–80; and *Daily Telegraph,* November 9, 1953.

59. Glubb to Melville (TJL) to FO/WO, October 20, 1953, FO 371.104790/ER 1091/430 [secret personal]; *The Observer,* November 8, 1953.

60. Lynch to SOS, October 21, 1953, DOS 785.00/10-2153; Furlonge to Eden, October 27, 1953, FO 371.104890/ET 1017/27; Lynch to DOS, October 31, 1953, DOS 785.00/10-3153; also FO 371.104789/ER 1091/395–96.

61. Other resolutions called for the deployment of troops as close as possible to the Jordanian border; the "immediate" commitment of military forces in event of an Israeli attack; the refusal to participate in the U.S.-backed Jordan Valley Plan; and a rather ironic promise to provide Jordan with weapons belonging to the Arab League, in a Syrian depot, left over from the Palestine war. See Lynch

to DOS, October 27, 1953, NA/RG 84, Box 3, 310; Gardener to FO, October 23, 1953, FO 371.104789/ER 1091/413 [secret].

62. One footnote of the Qibya affair was the impetus it gave to Hussein's desire to equip Jordan with a modern air force. See the fascinating account by the king's close friend, RAF officer John "Jock" Dalgleish, in FO 371.104933/ET 1223/15; also see Hussein, *Mon métier de roi*, 74–77.

63. Lynch to DOS, October 31, 1953, DOS 785.00/10-3153; Glubb to Melville (TJL) to FO/WO, October 22, 1953, FO 371.104790/ER 1091/430 [secret].

64. The suspension remained in effect until November 30. In 1953, total U.S. assistance to Israel was $73.6 million, all of which was grant aid. The United States offered no military assistance (loans or grants) until 1959. See *FRUS*, 9:1369; and DOS press release, October 18, 1953, in *FRUS*, 9:1367. Also see Steven L. Spiegel, *The Other Arab–Israeli Conflict: Making America's Middle East Policy, from Truman to Reagan* (Chicago: University of Chicago Press, 1984); and Gabriel Sheffer, *Dynamics of Dependence* (Boulder, CO: Westview Press, 1987), App. A, Table 4.1.

65. There is some evidence to support such skepticism. As a complement to its suspension of economic aid, Washington tabled a motion before the Near East Arms Coordinating Committee—the secret Anglo-Franco-American body managing the flow of weaponry into the Middle East—suspending arms deliveries to Israel pending the outcome of the Security Council session. Two weeks later, the motion was withdrawn, and according to British diplomats, the United States adopted instead a "go slow" arms supply policy to both Israel and the Arab states. See Makins to FO, October 29, 1953, FO 371.104228/E 1192/328 [secret]; also Lynch to DOS, November 4, 1953, DOS 611.85/11-453 [secret]; Furlonge to FO, November 2, 1953, FO 371.104890/ET 1017/26.

66. This paragraph is based on FO 371.104890/ET 1017/29, 33, 35, and 36; Seelye to DOS, September 8, 1953, NA/RG 84, Box 3, 301; Lynch to DOS, November 10, 1953, DOS 785.13/11-1053; and *al-Difaʿ* (Jerusalem), November 9, 1953.

67. UNSC Resolution 101 (UN doc. S/3139/Rev 2) was approved 9 to 0 with two abstentions (USSR and Lebanon). For text of the resolution, see *FRUS*, 9:1436–37; also SOS to Amman, November 24, 1953, DOS 684a.85/11-2453 [secret]; Lynch to DOS, November 30, 1953, DOS 684a.85/11-3053 [secret].

68. Amman to DOS, March 12, 1954, DOS 785.00(w)/3-1254.

69. Richmond to Eden, May 5, 1954, FO 371.110875/VJ 1015; Green, "Jordan Journal," May 13, 1953, 2:417–18.

70. Furlonge to Eden, February 22, 1954, and Furlonge to Falla, February 1, 1954, FO 371.110878/VJ 1017/2, 11; memorandum of conversation between Seelye and Egyptian diplomat ʿAbd al-Aziz Mustafa, March 10, 1954, NA/RG 84, Box 6, 350; Mallory to SOS, March 11, 1954, DOS 641.85/3-1154; Aldrich to SOS, March 16, 1954, DOS 641.85/3-1654; and Seelye to DOS, May 11, 1954, DOS 785.00/5 1154.

71. One amendment that did pass and come into effect in 1955 lowered the threshold for no-confidence motions from two-thirds to a simple majority. Seelye to DOS, February 12, 1954, DOS 785.03/2-1254; Furlonge to Eden, February 1, 1954, FO 371.110878/VJ 1017/1.

72. Mallory to DOS, December 2, 1953, DOS 684a.85/12-253 [secret];

Furlonge to FO, January 8 and February 25, 1954, FO 371.111068/VR 1071/ 8; also see *al-Difa'*, December 31, 1953, and *Falastin*, (Jerusalem), January 1, 1954.

73. Seelye to DOS, December 21, 1953, DOS 785.11/12-2153.

74. Both Hussein and Glubb relate the story of the king's flouting Jordanian cabinet decisions regarding flight training. What they failed to mention was that all such decisions were secretly passed on by Glubb and the British commander of the infant Arab Legion Air Force to Britain's Middle East Air Force in Ismailia and, ultimately, to the Air Ministry and the Foreign Office in London. See Hussein, *Uneasy Lies the Head*, 71–78; Glubb, *The Changing Scenes of Life*, 170; and, for example, AIR to MEAF, September 25, 1953, FO 371.104969/ET 1941/147.

75. See his role in the Jordanian rejection of the Jordan Valley Plan. Lynch to DOS, November 11, 1953, DOS 684a.85/11-1153.

76. Hussein signaled this displeasure by excluding al-Mulqi from meetings with King Saud in Badna in January 1954. See FO 371.110883/VJ 10325/1, 3.

77. Seelye to DOS, February 12, 1954, DOS 785.03/2-1254.

78. Interview with King Hussein.

79. Furlonge to Falla, February 22, 1954, FO 371.110878/VJ 1017/2.

80. Seelye to DOS, December 5, 1953, DOS 785.34/12-553; Furlonge to FO, December 2, 1953, FO 371.104888/ET 1015/7.

81. This idea was the brainchild of Hamad al-Farhan, al-Khatib's undersecretary at the Ministry of Economy and leader of Jordan's infant "East Bank first" school of thought. The relationship between al-Khatib and al-Farhan was peculiar. Al-Khatib was one of Jordan's leading Palestinians; al-Farhan, his deputy, was a founder of what was at the time termed "East Bank 'vigilantes.'" But both men were among Jordan's few able administrators and that, plus the common antipathy West and East Bank chauvinists each had toward British and American influence in Jordan was evidently the glue that kept their relationship together. Seelye to DOS, March 5, 1954, DOS 785.13/3-554; Seelye to DOS, March 11, 1954, DOS 785.00/3-1154; Mallory to DOS, April 24, 1954, NA/RG 84, Box 7, 350 [secret]; Mallory to DOS, April 29, 1954, DOS 785.00/4-2954 [secret]; interviews with al-Khatib and al-Farhan.

82. Furlonge to Allen, March 24, 1954, FO 371.110875/VJ 1015/1.

83. See the memorandum of conversation between Glubb and the American military attaché, March 18, 1954, NA/RG 84, Box 7, 350; and *FRUS*, 9:1504.

84. The proposal was entirely Lloyd's idea; Eden expressed serious reservations. Lloyd's minute, March 23, 1954, and Eden's margin note, March 24, 1954, FO 371.111069/VR 1072/17, 20.

85. Furlonge to FO, March 25, 1954, FO 371.111069/VR 1072/22 [secret].

86. Davis's memorandum, March 29, 1954, NA/RG 84/Box 7, 350; Furlonge to Eden, April 5, 1954, FO 371.110874/VJ 1013/4.

87. Richmond to Levant Department, March 31, 1954, FO 371.110875/ VJ 1015/2.

88. Richmond to Eden, May 4, 1954, F0 371.110874/VJ 1013/5; *New York Times*, April 21, 1954.

89. Mallory to DOS, April 29, 1954, DOS 785.00/4-2954 [secret].

90. Appropriately, Furlonge's departure from Jordan came less than a week

before al-Mulqi's departure from the premiership. See his farewell message, Furlonge to Eden, April 27, 1954, FO 371.110875/VJ 1015/6.

91. For details of al-Mulqi's demise, see Mallory to SOS, May 3, 1954, DOS 785.00/5-354; Falla's minute, May 4, 1954, and Richmond to Eden, May 11, 1954, FO 371.110875/VJ 1015/4, 12; Seelye to DOS, May 11, 1954, DOS 785.00/5-1154; also see Aqil Hyder Hasan Ahidi, *Jordan: A Political Study, 1948–1957* (London: Asia Publishing House, 1965), 115; al-Majali, *Mudhakkarati*, 141–42; *The Times* and *New York Times*, May 3, 1954.

92. Ann Dearden, *Jordan* (London: Robert Hale, 1958), 107. Dearden, a special correspondent for the *Manchester Guardian*, was married to the British embassy's political officer.

CHAPTER 6

1. Hussein bin Talal, *Uneasy Lies the Head* (New York: Bernard Geiss Associates, 1962), 25.

2. He called him "Abdul Huda," ibid., 38.

3. And not, interestingly, to Samir al-Rifa'i, on whom Zayn had particularly soured. Seelye to DOS, May 11, 1954, DOS 785.00/5-1154.

4. Interview with King Hussein.

5. Seelye to DOS, May 10, 1954, DOS 785.13/5-1054.

6. *The Times* and *New York Times*, May 5, 1954.

7. See Glubb's assessment in Duke to FO, May 19, 1954, FO 371.111071/VR 1072/85.

8. Furlonge's successor was a marked improvement. The American embassy's personality report on Duke described him in near glowing terms: a "hard worker but at the same time popular with his staff. . . . [H]e is not inhibited with the clichés and prejudices so often found among career British Foreign Service Officers who have spent a great deal of time in the Middle East." Jones's report, May 6, 1954, NA/RG 84, Box 3, 301.

9. At Eden's urging, the Foreign Office drafted a list of thirteen suggestions to improve border security. Most dealt with ways to bolster the MAC (Mixed Armistice Commission) machinery; two were dropped at the urging of Washington and Paris. The most controversial proposal was for the formal demarcation of the frontier and the erection of physical barriers along the armistice line. See FO to Geneva Conference, May 5, 1954, FO 371.111071/VR 1072/76; more generally, FO 371.111071/VR 1072 and *Foreign Relations of the United States* (*FRUS*), 9:1547–66.

10. After receiving Jordan's response, an approach was made to Israel, but the initiative was compromised by a leak to the press to the effect that the plan had originally called for the dismissal of the incumbent UNTSO (United Nations Truce Supervisory Organization) chief. London blamed the leak on the French. See details in FO 371.111072/VR 1072.

11. A standard clause obligating both parties to reduce barriers to international trade was waived, because Amman argued it would have conflicted with its commitment to the Arab economic boycott of Israel. Memorandum of conversation between Mallory and al-Khalidi, April 19, 1954, and Geren to DOS, May 15, 1954, DOS 785.00/5-1554.

12. Seelye to DOS, May 10, 1954, DOS 785.13/5-1054.

13. Ministerial statement in FO 371.110876/VJ 1015/24; Duke to Shuckburgh, June 29, 1954, FO 371.110876/VJ 1015/25.

14. Prominent in this group were former palace chamberlain Subhi Zayd al-Kilani, Senators 'Umar Matar and 'Umar al-Bargouti, former chief prosecutor Walid Salah, and Amman merchants Kamal Mango and Isma'il Belbeisi. See Cassin to DOS, May 20, 1954, DOS 785.00/5-2054; Seelye to DOS, July 6, 1954, DOS 785.00/7-654 [secret].

15. Founders included former East Bank Ministers Hazza' al-Majali, 'Abd al-Halim al-Nimr, Shafiq al-Rushaydat, and Sulayman al-Nabulsi (who resigned as ambassador to Britain in early June) and West Bankers Anwar al-Khatib and Hikmat al-Masri. During its early days, Sa'id al-Mufti and Fawzi al-Mulqi were unofficial "friends" of the party. Al-Majali stated that the party was formed in response to Abu'l Huda's appointment as prime minister. See Hazza' al-Majali, *Mudhakkarati* [My memoirs] (Beirut: Dar al-'ilm lil-malayeen, 1960), 143–44.

16. Shuqayr denied that the front was Communist but admitted that Communists (including Ya'qub Ziyadin) were the front's prime movers. The Soviet news agency TASS acknowledged the front's formation on June 1. Duke to Eden, June 8, 1954, FO 371.110879/VJ 1018/3; Mallory to DOS, September 15, 1954, DOS 785.001/9-1554 [secret]; Amnon Cohen, *Political Parties in the West Bank Under the Jordanian Regime, 1949–1967* (Ithaca, NY: Cornell University Press, 1982), 31–32; interview with Shuqayr.

17. See FO 371.110879/VJ 1018/2; also Avraham Sela, *Ha'ba'th ha'filistini* [The Palestinian Ba'th] (Jerusalem: Magnes Press, Hebrew University, 1984).

18. See party platforms in FO 371.110879/VJ 1018/3; Aqil Hyder Hasan Abidi, *Jordan: A Political Study, 1948–1957* (London: Asia Publishing House, 1965), 200–12; on the Islamic parties, see Cohen, *Political Parties*; Jacob M. Landau, "Political Tenets of the Liberation Party in Jordan," in *Man, State and Society in the Contemporary Middle East*, ed. Jacob M. Landau (London: Pall Mall Press, 1972), 183–88; and Musa Zayd al-Kilani, *al-Harakat al-islamiyya fi al-urdunn* [Islamic movements in Jordan] (Amman: General Directorate of Press and Publications, 1990).

19. Duke to Eden, June 8, 1954, FO 371.110879/VJ 1018/3; Duke to Shuckburgh, June 29, 1954, FO 371.110876/VJ 1015/25; *al-Difa'* (Jerusalem), June 22, 1954.

20. Al-Majali, *Mudhakkarati*, 144–45; Duke to Shuckburgh, June 29, 1954, FO 371.110876/VJ 1015/25; Seelye to DOS, June 24, 1954, DOS 785.00/6-2454.

21. Seelye to DOS, June 29, 1954, DOS 785.00/6-2954.

22. Duke to Shuckburgh, June 29, 1954, FO 371.110876/VJ 1015/25.

23. See Seelye to DOS, June 29, 1954, DOS 785.00/6-2954; FO 371.110876/VJ 1015/11, 22.

24. Richmond to Levant Department, June 26, 1954, FO 371.110879/VJ 1018/5; Geren to DOS, July 10, 1954, DOS 985.64/7-1054.

25. Duke to Shuckburgh, June 29, 1954, FO 371.110876/VJ 1015/25.

26. Hussein had originally intended to depart on July 3 but postponed his trip because of frontier incidents in the Jerusalem area between June 30 and July 2. See Amman's weekly political reports to DOS, June/July 1954; Duke to Shuckburgh, June 29, 1954, FO 371.110876/VJ 1015/25; Dodds-Parker's minute, July 27, 1954, FO 371.110831/V 1199/4.

27. Al-Majali, *Mudhakkarati*, 143.

28. Geren to DOS, July 10, 1954, DOS 985.64/7-1054.

29. Cassin to DOS, July 22, 1954, DOS 785.00/7-2254; Mallory to SOS, July 30, 1954, DOS 785.00/7-3054; Seelye to DOS, August 7, 1954, DOS 785.00/8-754; Duke to Eden, August 16, 1954, FO 371.110876/VJ 1015/28.

30. Hussein reportedly intimated that the British embassy had weighed in on Abu'l Huda's behalf. Also, Zayn was known to have supported Abu'l Huda. See Mallory to SOS, July 30, 1954, DOS 785.00/7-3054; Duke to Eden, August 16, 1954, FO 371.110876/VJ 1015/28; Mallory to SOS, August 17, 1954, DOS 785.00/8-1754; Seelye to DOS, August 21, 1954, DOS 785.00/8-2154.

31. Like Drew, Mallory was a Latin American expert by training and experience. Mallory to SOS August 17, 1954, DOS 785.00/8-1754; Duke to SOS, August 27, 1954, FO 371.110876/VJ 1015/30.

32. The ministry was not very subtle. Its tabulation of 445,978 registered voters amounted to a phenomenal 30 percent increase over that of the 1951 election. Seelye to DOS, October 8, 1954, DOS 785.00/10-854; al-Majali, *Mudhakkarati*, 148.

33. In his memoirs, Glubb played down both Abu'l Huda's efforts to "rig" the elections and his own role in support of the government. See John Bagot Glubb, *A Soldier with the Arabs* (London: Hodder & Stoughton, 1957), 350–51; Cole to DOS, October 20, 1954, DOS 785.00/10-2054; Geren to DOS, October 16, 1954, DOS 785.00/10-1654.

34. Seelye to DOS, October 8, 1954, DOS 785.00/10-854.

35. Ba'thist and Front candidates ran as independents; see ibid. and also Mallory's memorandum of conversation with Hanania, August 19, 1954, NA/RG 94, Box 9, 350; interviews with Hazem Nusaybah and Jamal al-Sha'ir.

36. See FO 371.110876/VJ 1015; Mallory to DOS, October 19, 1954, DOS 785.00/10-1954; Mallory to DOS, October 23, 1954, DOS 785.00/10-2354; Geren to DOS, October 30, 1954, DOS 785.00/10-3054; *New York Times,* October 17, 1954.

37. Translation of the al-Nabulsi/al-Mufti telegram in NA/RG 84, Box 9, 350; see also Geren to DOS, October 21, 1954, DOS 785.00/10-2154.

38. Because candidates ran as individuals, there is some confusion in ascribing party affiliations. For example, al-Majali states that he and Hikmat al-Masri were the only NSP winners, but in fact, both 'Abd al-Fattah Darwish and Walid Shak'a were associated with the party. The National Front's lone winner was 'Abd al-Qadir al-Salih of Nablus; Rashad Maswadeh had been affiliated with the front but accepted an offer of electoral support from Abu'l Huda and changed sides. Surprisingly, the two seats won by al-Rif'i's Nation party were on the West Bank. See Geren to DOS, November 10, 1954, DOS 785.00/11-1054; and Geren to DOS, November 15, 1954, DOS 785.00/11-1554.

39. Duke to Eden, Octoher 18, 1954, FO 371.110876/VJ 1015/40.

40. His brother explained that Nusaybah "knew of and condoned" interference in the election in order to gain revenge on al-Khatib. Nusaybah's margin of victory was so great that he most likely would have won without the army's support. Interview with Hazem Nusaybah; Cole to DOS, October 20, 1954, DOS 785.00/10-2054.

41. Duke to Falla, October 23, 1954, FO 371.110876/VJ 1015/47.

42. Duke to FO, October 19, 1954, FO 371.110876/VJ 1015/39.

43. Duke to Falla, October 23, 1954, FO 371.110876/VJ 1015/47.

44. Geren to DOS, November 15, 1954, DOS 785.00/11-1554.

45. This led to al-Majali's estrangement from the NSP. Although he claimed to have resigned from the party when he entered the cabinet, there is evidence that the party forced him out. On this point, al-Nabulsi's son Faris is quite adamant. See al-Majali, *Mudhakkarati*, 149–51; Duke to Falla, October 25, 1954, FO 371.110876/VJ 1015/48; Sulayman Musa, *A'lam min al-urdunni safahat min tarikh al-'arab al-hadith* [Luminaries from Jordan: Pages from modern Arab history] (Amman: Dar al-sha'b, 1986), 21; Munib al-Madi and Sulayman Musa, *Tankh al-urdunn fi al-qarn al-'ashreen* [The history of Jordan in the twentieth century] (1959; Amman: Maktaba al-muhtasab, 1988), 600; and interview with Faris al-Nabulsi.

46. Salah's appointment was somewhat surprising. Since 1951, he and Abu'l Huda had been on bad terms, and Salah had gravitated to the camp of Abu'l Huda's main rival. He was appointed to fill the post left vacant by the departure of Jamal Tuqan, who requested a transfer to the embassy in Beirut where he could more readily receive cancer treatment. Salah was the sixth Palestinian (not counting al-Rifa'i and Abu'l Huda) since 1950 to serve as foreign minister. See Seelye's memorandum of conversation with Salah, March 25, 1954, NA/RG 84, Box 11; Richmond to Levant Department, September 27, 1954, FO 371.110876/VJ 1015/31; interview with Salah.

47. The petition was signed by eleven National Socialists, seven Ba'thists, five members of the National Front, two Nation party candidates, and fifteen independents. Sa'id al-Mufti signed, too; Samir al-Rifa'i and Fawzi al-Mulqi did not. The government censored press references to the petition, but a copy reached the king. Al-Nabulsi earned Hussein's ire for sending copies to Arab embassies in Amman and was, for a short while, jailed. See Geren to DOS, November 23, 1954, DOS 785.00/11-2354; Geren to DOS, November 28, 1954, DOS 785.00/11-2854.

48. Duke to Falla, November 15, 1954, FO 371.110887/VJ 1052/12 [secret]; ministerial statement in FO 371.110876/VJ 1015/50.

49. See "Treaty of Alliance Between His Majesty in Respect of the United Kingdom of Great Britain and Northern Ireland and His Majesty the King of the Hashemite Kingdom of Transjordan," March 15, 1948, Treaty Series No. 26) (1948), in Helen Miller Davis, *Constitutions, Electoral Laws, Treaties of States in the Near and Middle East* (Durham, NC: Duke University Press, 1953), 267–76.

50. The relevant letter, no. 5, spoke of "arrangements to be agreed upon annually" for the payment of the British subsidy. See Davis, *Constitutions*, 274.

51. Emmett (WO) to Henley (Treasury), May 27, 1954, FO 371.110924/VJ 1201/21. Also FO 371.104928/ET 1202/24, 31 [secret].

52. In fact, the Jordanians were never informed of the British assessment that withdrawal from Suez would render "inoperative [the] existing plan for coming to Jordan's aid if she is engaged in war." Falla's brief for Harding, November 13, 1954, FO 371.110832/V 1202/15 [top secret].

53. Duke to Shuckburgh, September 27, 1954, FO 371.110887/VJ 1052/2 [secret].

54. Lloyd later claimed to have "no recollection" of the treaty's being "specifically mentioned." Memorandum of conversation with Lloyd, December 20, 1954, FO 371.110887/VJ 1052/21; Evelyn Shuckburgh, *Descent to Suez: Diaries, 1951–56* (London: Weidenfeld and Nicholson, 1986), 227.

55. Duke to Shuckburgh, September 27, 1954, FO 371.110887/VJ 1052/2 [secret].

56. This showed how poorly Duke understood Abu'l Huda. The prime minister was not a social animal and never once took a vacation outside the Arab world. Duke to FO, October 30, 1954, FO 371.110887/VJ 1052/4 [secret].

57. FO to Duke, October 21, 1954, and Eden's note in FO to Amman, November 6, 1954, FO 371.110887/VJ 1052/3, 5 [secret].

58. Ministerial statement in FO 371.110876/VJ 1015/50.

59. *The Times*, November 12, 1954.

60. Kirkpatrick to Levant Department, November 8, 1954; and Duke to Falla, November 15, 1954, FO 371.110887/VJ 1052/10, 12 [secret].

61. The following paragraphs are drawn from Foreign Office minutes of the talks in FO 371.110886/VJ 1051/14. A general (though not altogether accurate) Jordanian account can be found in al-Madi and Musa, *Tarikh al-urdunn*, 606–10.

62. The minutes of the talks do not bear out Shwadran's claim that a request to reassign or retire Glubb was on the agenda of the Jordanians. See Benjamin Shwadran, *Jordan: State of Tension* (New York: Council for Middle Eastern Affairs Press, 1959), 324.

63. Peter Snow, *Hussein: A Biography* (London: Barrie & Jenkins, 1972), 62.

64. This was not dissembling. Overnight, the Foreign Office discussed the "rent suggestion" with the Treasury, War Office, and Air Ministry and concluded that the most they could give Amman was "a greater appearance of control." Falla's minute, December 22, 1954, FO 371.110924/VJ 1201/8 [secret].

65. Only Evelyn Shuckburgh, Sir John's son and assistant undersecretary of the Foreign Office with responsibility for the Levant, seemed to have had second thoughts. "I do not feel very happy about the way we have left this," he minuted. "The Jordanians will never be satisfied with the present method of payment and we shall have recurrent trouble on it. Are we really sure that we have been into their case thoroughly and that there is nothing more we can do?" See Shuckburgh's note and the Jordanian aide-mémoire in FO 371.115670/VJ 1192/2; also Eden's private papers, FO 800.808, December 23, 1954 [secret].

66. Falla's brief for Churchill, FO 371.110952/VJ 1941/37.

67. Hussein's own attitude toward Abu'l Huda in this period is unclear. The king remained in Europe until February, when the announcement of the Baghdad Pact overshadowed Jordan's own embarrassment in the London talks. He made no reference to the talks in his memoirs. See Richmond to FO, January 6, 1955, and Richmond to Falla, January 10, 1955, FO 371.115638/VJ 1015/1, 2 [secret]; Geren to DOS, January 10, 1955, and Mallory to DOS, January 17, 1955, NA/RG 84, Box 9, 360; also al-Majali, *Mudhakkarati*, 152.

68. FO to Amman, January 8, 1955, and Richmond to FO, January 10, 1955, FO 371.115671/VJ 1193/1, 2

69. Eden was miffed that Abu'l Huda had not adequately recognized British generosity and instructed the Amman embassy to "inform Abu'l Huda that his omission . . . did not pass unnoticed." Richmond to FO, February 2, 1955, FO 371.115671/VJ 1193/8 [secret]; Richmond to FO, February 10, 1955, and FO to Amman, February 11, 1955, FO 371.115652/VJ 1051/6, 7.

70. Hussein, *Uneasy Lies the Head*, 101.

71. At the Arab League meeting in February, Foreign Minister Salah adopted

a militantly anti-Iraq stance in contravention of Jordan's official policy. He "out-Egyptianed the Egyptians," Mallory quipped. Al-Majali claimed that Salah later told him privately that Abu'l Huda had personally instructed him to criticize Iraq. This, al-Majali said, was a function of Abu'l Huda's close ties with the Saudis. See al-Majali, *Mudhakkarati*, 154; Geren to DOS, March 7, 1955, NA/RG 84, Box 9, 361.2.

72. See Mallory to DOS, February 18, 1955, DOS 033.8587/2-1855 [secret], in *FRUS*, 1955–57, 13:2–3; Mallory to DOS, February 24, 1955, NA/ RG 84, Box 5, 320.1; Stevenson to Eden, March 4, 1955, FO 371.115714/VJ 1941/10; Byroade to DOS, March 7, 1955, NA/RG 84, Box 6, 320.1; and Uriel Dann, *King Hussein and the Challenge of Arab Radicalism: Jordan, 1955– 1967* (New York: Oxford University Press, 1989), 22.

73. Geren to SOS, March 2, 1955, NA/RG 84, Box 5, 320.1.

74. Mallory to DOS, March 16, 1955, DOS 682.87/3-1655; and Mallory to DOS, March 19, 1955, DOS 682.87/3-1955, in *FRUS*, 13:4–5.

75. Mallory to DOS, February 7, 1955, DOS 780.5/2-755 [secret].

76. Mallory to SOS, February 3, 1955, NA/RG 84, Box 5, 320.1 [secret].

77. Geren to DOS, March 9, 1955, DOS 682.87/3-955; and Mallory to DOS, March 19, 1955, DOS 682.87/3-1955, in *FRUS*, 13:4–5.

78. Mallory to SOS, March 22, 1955, NA/RG 84, Box 5, 320.1.

79. Geren to DOS, June 28, 1955, NA/RG 84, Box 6, 320.1.

80. Ibid. In this regard, Dann's statement that Abu'l Huda "opposed accession" does not adequately describe the situation. See Dann, *King Hussein*, 25.

81. Parker to DOS, April 5, 1955, NA/RG 84, Box 5, 320.1.

82. See Wilbur Crane Eveland, *Ropes of Sand: America's Failure in the Middle East* (London, 1980); and *FRUS*, 14:1–401.

83. See the editorial note in *FRUS*, 13:5–6; and Dulles to London, April 6, 1955, NA/RG 84, Box 5, 320.1 [secret].

84. A less generous appraisal would be that once revision was no longer possible, Abu'l Huda's second loyalty was to his Saudi patrons. But as the Foreign Office noted, Abu'l Huda's acceptance of Saudi largesse should not "count against him when the King himself is receiving a very much larger subvention from the same source." Memorandum of conversation between Mallory and the Turkish minister, February 15, 1955, NA/RG 84, Box 9, 361.2; Duke to Macmillan, May 27, 1955, FO 371.115638/VJ 1015/11 [secret], margin notes by Summerhayes and Hadow therein.

85. Mallory to SOS, May 31, 1955, NA/RG 84, Box 7, 350.

86. See al-Nabulsi's comment in Geren to DOS, May 20, 1955, NA/RG 84, Box 7, 350.

87. Al-Majali stated that Abu'l Huda offered to make him his political heir apparent should he withdraw his resignation, but he refused. It is likely that al-Majali thought the time ripe to put some distance between Abu'l Huda and himself in anticipation of the prime minister's dismissal. See al-Majali, *Mudhakkarati*, 156–58; also Geren to DOS, May 5, 1955, NA/RG 84, Box 3, 310; Geren to DOS, May 24, 1955, NA/RG 84, Box 3, 310; and Jarallah's memo to Mallory, May 18, 1955, NA/RG Box 9, 350.

88. Also figuring in Abu'l Huda's resignation were his frequent clashes with Sharif Nasser, which culminated in the premier's refusal to issue a license for the establishment of Jordan International Airlines, reported to have been set up as a

conduit for the sharif's lucrative trade in contraband. When the matter came to a head, Hussein sided with his uncle. See Geren's memorandum of conversation with al-Khayri, June 15, 1955, NA/RG 84, Box 7, 350; Geren's memorandum of conversation with al-Rifa'i, July 15, 1955, NA/RG 84, 350; and Duke to Macmillan, June 3, 1955, FO 371.115638/VJ 1015/12; also see Duke to FO, May 29, 1955, FO 371.115638/VJ 1015/8.

89. The first discussion of a potential "showdown" between Glubb and Hussein was in May 1955. See FO 371.115674/VJ 1201; and Chapter 8 of this book.

90. Interview with Sharif Zayd bin Shakir.

91. In fact, Abu'l Huda was on one of his rare trips out of Amman, seeking medical care in Beirut, when Sir Gerald Templer arrived for his fateful visit. During his final months, Abu'l Huda lived in virtual seclusion, which, according to al-Majali, might have been the result of a mental breakdown ("neurasthenia," he called it) that he claimed Abu'l Huda suffered in the summer of 1956. Although some of his former friends claim he was murdered, it seems likely that Abu'l Huda did commit suicide in July 1956. See Chapter 1 of this book; minutes of the upper house of Parliament, November 21, 1955, JNA 575; and al-Majali, *Mudhakkarati*, 158.

CHAPTER 7

1. In 1921, Abdullah's headquarters was set up in al-Mufti's home. In 1928, al-Mufti suffered a temporary lapse from the amir's favor for his opposition to the Anglo-Transjordan agreement, which provided the amirate with significantly less than full constitutional government. See Mary C. Wilson, *King Abdullah, Britain and the Making of Jordan* (Cambridge: Cambridge University Press, 1987), 69 and 238, n. 48.

2. Seelye to DOS, March 5, 1954, DOS 785.13/3-554.

3. See Glubb's portrayal of al-Mufti in his *A Soldier with the Arabs* (London: Hodder & Stoughton, 1957), 384.

4. Parker to DOS, May 24, 1955, NA/RG 84, Box 7, 350.

5. Hussein bin Talal, *Uneasy Lies the Head* (New York: Bernard Geis Associates, 1962), 111.

6. Duke to Rose, July 18, 1955, FO 371.115638/VJ 1015/18.

7. These included Hussein Fakhri al-Khalidi and several National Socialists. The king, however, rejected anyone who opposed the Baghdad Pact or demanded parliament's dissolution. See Jarallah's memorandum to Mallory, no date, NA/RG Box 9, 350; Amman to Millett, June 1, 1955, NA/RG 84, Box 9, 361.2 [secret]; Duke to BO, June 1, 1955, FO 371.115638/VJ 1015/8.

8. Duke to Macmillan, August 18, 1955, and Duke to Levant Department, August 25, 1955, FO 371.115638/VJ 1015/21, 22.

9. Al-Mufti kept the portfolio for himself, and the administration of the ministry was left to Undersecretary Baha' al-Din Tuqan, a Palestinian and King Hussein's future father-in-law.

10. Mallory to SOS, June 7, 1955, NA/RG 84, Box 7, 350.

11. Duke to FO, September 3–6, 1955, FO 371.115904/VR 1092/249–270 [secret].

12. *Al-Urdunn* (Amman), October 1 and 5, 1955; Mallory to SOS, October 5, 1955, NA/RG 84, Box 6, 350; and Mallory to DOS, October 25, 1955, NA/RG 84, Box 7, 350.

13. Hussein, *Uneasy Lies the Head,* 106.

14. Uriel Dann, "The Foreign Office, the Baghdad Pact and Jordan," *Asian and African Studies* 21 (1987): 250.

15. There is little evidence for the claim that al-Mufti was a "strong advocate of the pact," made in Michael B. Oren's "A Winter of Discontent: Britain's Crisis in Jordan, December 1955–March 1956," *International Journal of Middle East Studies* 22 (1990): 174–75; see Wilson to Mallory, July 1, 1955, NA/RG 84, Box 6, 320.1 [secret].

16. "As a government," said 'Ali al-Hindawi, al-Mufti's justice minister, in an interview, "we never discussed the issue until late 1955." Also see Geren to Wilson, July 12, 1955, NA/RG 84, Box 6, 320.1 [secret].

17. Duke to Rose, June 1, 1955, FO 371.115717/VJ 1941/69.

18. Nutting to Eden, June 18, 1955, FO 800.678 [secret]; also see Nutting's memorandum, June 24, 1955, FO 371.115718/VJ 1941/89.

19. Also discussed was the deterioration in Hussein's relationship with Glubb. See FO 371.115683/VJ 12011/4; Evelyn Shuckburgh, *Descent to Suez: Diaries, 1951–56* (London: Weidenfeld and Nicholson, 1986), 292; and Chapter 8 of this book. Also see Hadow's minute, October 21, 1955, FO 371.115687/VJ 1223/64; in general, FO 371.115686-115687/VJ 1223/39-66.

20. Warren to DOS, October 7, 1955, NA/RG 84, Box 5, 320.1 [secret].

21. Snow contends that Britain enlisted Turkey to lobby Jordan on its behalf, but in fact, Ankara, not London, was the prime mover. Peter Snow, *Hussein: A Biography* (London: Barrie & Jenkins, 1972), 75. See the memorandum of conversation between the Turkish ambassador, Haydar Gork, and the U.S. assistant secretary, George V. Allen, October 24, 1955, NA/RG 84, Box 7, 350 [secret]; also see Macmillan's conversation with Foreign Minister Fatin Zorlu, in Macmillan to Bowker, October 24, 1955, FO 800.678/V 1025/1 [secret].

22. Duke to FO, October 15, 1955, FO 371/115523; cited in Dann, "The Foreign Office," 251.

23. Union with Iraq, Mallory concluded, was the "logical way" for the West to overcome Jordan's political and structural weaknesses. Mallory to DOS, October 22, 1955, DOS 785.00/10-2255, in *Foreign Relations of the United States* (*FRUS*), 13:6–7; Duke to Shuckburgh, October 27, 1955, FO 371.115653/VJ 1051/22 [secret].

24. Bowker to FO, November 1, 1955, FO 371.115526/V 1073/1206; also, the Gork–Allen memorandum, October 24, 1955, NA/RG 84, Box 7, 350 [secret].

25. Glubb to Melville to MELF, October 6, 1955 [secret], and Tel Aviv to Levant Department, October 10, 1955, FO 371.115905/VR 1092/324, 326.

26. For details of the cooling of Saudi–Jordanian relations, including the Saudi decision to suspend its "regular stipend" to Sharif Nasser, see Richmond to Hadow, June 17, 1955, FO 371.115647/VJ 10325/2; and Parker to DOS, July 5, 1955, NA/RG 84, Box 7, 350.

27. They may have also boosted their private subventions to Jordan's royal family. In general, see references in Phillips to FO, September 28, 1955, FO 371.115719/VJ 1941/130 [secret]; and Dudgeon to Hadow, Octoher 12, 1955,

FO 371.115645/VJ 10316/1 [secret]. Reportage on the royal visits remains closed in FO 371.115719/VJ 1941.

28. Reportage of the Soviet initiative is closed in FO 371.115719/VJ 1941/150, but clear reference is made in Duke to Shuckburgh, November 10, 1955, FO 371.115653/VJ 1051/27 [secret]. Snow refers obscurely to a visit paid to Hussein by the Soviet ambassador in Beirut. See Snow, *Hussein,* 76.

29. Snow, *Hussein,* 76; Cairo to African Department, November 5, 1955, FO 371.115648/VJ 10338/1.

30. See *al-Urdunn,* October 21 and 22, 1955.

31. On the leaflets, see NA/RG 84, Box 9, 350 and FO 371.115684; also Duke to FO, November 4, 1955, FO 371.115649/VJ 10344/4; Duke to Macmillan, November 16, 1955, FO 371.115649/VJ 10344/6; Shuckburgh's minute to Caccia, November 7, 1955, FO 371.115528/V 1073/1251; Cole to DOS, November 7, 1955, NA/RG 84, Box 7, 350; *al-Urdunn,* November 3, 1955.

32. Duke to FO, November 4, 1955, FO 371.115527/V 1073/1218.

33. At the same time, Turkey courted Israel, too. Five days after his return from Amman, Zorlu told Israel's ambassador to Ankara that Turkey intended to preserve its friendly relations with Israel, and he urged Israel to support Jordan's accession to the pact. ISA, 2457/3 [secret personal]; also see Aqil Hyder Hasan Abidi, *Jordan: A Political Study, 1948–1957* (London: Asia Publishing House, 1965), 127; Duke to Shuckburgh, November 10, 1955, FO 371.115653/VJ 1051/27 [secret].

34. Duke to FO, November 6–8, 1955, FO 371.115527/V 1073/1224-1234; Glubb's memorandum, November 9, 1955, FO 371.115653/VJ 1051/27 [top secret].

35. FO to Amman, November 7, 1955, FO 371.115527/V 1073/1224 [emergency secret].

36. Emphasis in the original. Eden to Macmillan, November 6, 1955, FO 800.678; Shuckburgh's minute to Caccia, November 7, 1955, FO 371.115528/V 1073/1251.

37. Duke to FO, November 8, 1955, FO 371.115527/V 1073/1234; Duke to FO, November 8, 1955, FO 371.115682/VJ 12010/2 [secret]; Glubb's memorandum, November 9, 1955, FO 371.115653/VJ 1051/27 [top secret].

38. Duke to FO, November 8, 1955, FO 371.115527/V 1073/1235 [secret].

39. Duke to Shuckburgh, November 10, 1955, FO 371.115653/VJ 1051/27 [secret]; Duke to FO, November 10, 1955, FO 371.115653/VJ 1051/24.

40. Dulles reportedly said that "unless Lebanon, Syria and Jordan were ready to make peace with Israel [which Dulles doubted, the rapporteur noted], he [Dulles] rather wondered whether it was wise to bring them in." Memorandum of conversation between Macmillan and Dulles, November 9, 1955, FO 800.678/V 1023/25g [secret].

41. FO to Amman, November 9, 1955, FO 371.115653/VJ 1051/29.

42. Glubb to Melville (TJL), November 15, 1955 FO 371.115653/VJ 1051/33 [top secret].

43. Cairo to Amman, November 16, 1955, FO 371.115713/VJ 1911/5; Glubb to Melville, (TJL), November 15, 1955, FO 371.115653/VJ 1051/33 [top secret].

44. The aide-mémoire defined the following *additional* units as the "mini-

mum to defend Jordan": two infantry divisions; one armored division; heavy artillery; one brigade of paratroops; a commando group; an air force of bombers and fighters; gradual provision of air bases; and a small naval force to patrol the Dead Sea and Aqaba. Duke to FO, November 16, 1955, FO 371.115653/VJ 1051/30-31 [secret]; Mason to Rose, November 17, 1955, FO 371.115654/ VJ 1051/40 [secret]; on parliament, see Duke to FO, November 18, 1955, FO 371.115683/VJ 11051/34 [secret].

45. FO to Amman, November 19, 1955, FO 371.115654/VJ 1051/39 [secret].

46. Memorandum of conversation among Macmillan, Menderes, and Zorlu, November 22, 1955, FO 800.678/VJ 1051/42 [secret]; Harold Macmillan, *Tides of Fortune, 1945–1955* (London: Macmillan, 1969), 652–55.

47. They included a "definite promise" to replace the Anglo–Jordanian treaty with a Special Agreement, like the one between Iraq and Britain; reequipment of an armored regiment with Comet tanks; the "free gift" of ten Vampire jets; and a "definite promise" to augment the Arab Legion's strength "to the order of a division with ancillary and support troops." Shuckburgh claimed authorship of this "package offer," but records indicate that the honor was Duke's. See Duke's memo, November 22, 1955, FO 371.115654/VJ IOSI/46; Shuckburgh, *Descent to Suez*, 304.

48. Shuckburgh, *Descent to Suez*, 308; Duke's memo, November 22, 1955, FO 371.115654/VJ 1051/46; Macmillan's minute to Eden, November 25, 1955, FO 371.115532/V 1073/1336 [top secret]; Macmillan, *Tides of Fortune*, 653–54.

49. Shuckburgh's brief, December 1, 1955, FO 371.115654/VJ 1051/49; Duke's memo, November 22, 1955, FO 371.115654/VJ 1051/46.

50. Shuckburgh's minute, November 30, 1955, and FO minute, December 1, 1955, FO 371.115655/VJ 1051/54a, 57; Shuckburgh, *Descent to Suez*, 306.

51. See FO 371 115720/VJ 1941/143, 159.

52. On the eve of Templer's departure, Duke "confessed" his "doubt [that] it will be possible to secure a public commitment from the Jordan Government in the course of a few days, *whatever we do*" [emphasis added]. Duke to FO, December 4, 1955, FO 371.115655/VJ 1051/54 [secret].

53. Duke to Lloyd (who succeeded Macmillan in late December 1955), July 25, 1956, FO 371.121461/VJ 1011/1 [secret].

54. Duke to FO, November 25, 1955, FO 371.115639/VJ 1015/29; Rifa't al-Mufti quoted in Parker to DOS, November 29, 1955, NA/RG 84, Box 9, 360; Duke to Rose, December 1, 1955, Fo 371.115639/VJ 1015/39; Mallory's memorandum of conversation with Rifa't, December 2, 1955, NA/RG, 84, Box 9, 350.

55. *Al-Urdunn*, December 1, 1955; Cole to DOS, December 5, 1955, NA/ RG 84, Box 6, 320; Mallory to SOS, December 5, 1955, NA/RG 84, Box 5, 320.1 [secret]; P. J. Vatikiotis, *Politics and the Military in Jordan: A Study of the Arab Legion, 1921–1957* (London: Cass, 1967), 122.

56. Several accounts (Hussein, Snow, and Oren) suggest that Amer's visit was coterminous with Templer's. This was not the case. Amer left Jordan on December 3, three days before Templer's arrival. Oren implies that Amer's visit was meant to undercut Templer's; if anything, the choice of Templer as the British representative was meant as an antidote to Amer. Oren, "A Winter of Discon-

tent," 176; Snow, *Hussein*, 76; Hussein, *Uneasy Lies the Head*, 108–9; also see Uriel Dann, *King Hussein and the Challenge of Arab Radicalism: Jordan, 1955–1967* (New York: Oxford University Press, 1989), 26.

57. Hussein's story, however, is not altogether clear. In his memoirs, he stated that he sent a memo to Nasser outlining Jordan's rationale and that Nasser "immediately sent one of his top officials to Amman to discuss the matter with me." When this memo was sent and who this Egyptian official was remain obscure. See Hussein, *Uneasy Lies the Head*, 110.

When this episode was recalled in 1957, the Foreign Office could find no confirmation that Jordan had ever "obtained the agreement of the Egyptian Government" to discuss accession to the pact. See FO 371.127909/VJ 1072/1.

For his part, Nasser believed Britain had promised him not to enlarge the pact without prior consultations. See Humphrey Trevelyan, *Middle East in Revolution* (London: Macmillan, 1970), 56.

Text quotations from Hussein, *Uneasy Lies the Head*, 112 and 101, respectively.

58. Duke to FO, December 3, 1955, and Templer to FO, December 7, 1955, FO 371.115655/VJ 1051/53, 68 [secret].

59. Present at the meeting were Hussein, al-Mufti, al-Shubaylat, al-Mulqi, al-Talhuni, and Glubb. Templer to FO, December 7, 1955, FO 371.115655/VJ 1051/69 [secret]. On Templer's written and oral orders, see FO 371.115655/VJ 1051/61g [top secret]; and Shuckburgh, *Descent to Suez*, 307–8.

60. Treasury officials complemented Templer by offering the Jordanians an extra £500,000 in development loans and £250,000 in budget subsidy. FO 371.115655/VJ 1051/74.

61. On their acrimonious negotiations in Baghdad, see Duncan to DOS, December 17, 1955, NA/RG 84, Box 11, 500; Templer to FO, December 8, 1955, FO 371.115656/VJ 1051/76 [secret]; also see Sulayman Musa, *A'lam min al-urdunn: safahat min tarikh al-'arab al-hadith* [Luminaries from Jordan: Pages from modern Arab history] (Amman: Dar al-sha'b, 1986), 24.

62. Templer to FO, December 10, 1955, FO 371.115656/VJ 1051/81 [emergency secret].

63. Templer implied that these "personalities" were Jordanians (i.e., members of parliament's Foreign Affairs Committee). In an interview, 'Abd al-Hadi said that the Palestinian ministers wanted to consult with Egypt and Syria. Templer to FO, December 10, 1955, FO 371.115656/VJ 1051/82 [secret].

64. Templer to FO, December 11, 1955, and FO to Templer, December 12, 1955, FO 371.115656/VJ 1051/84 [emergency secret].

65. Templer to FO and FO to Templer, December 13, 1955, FO 371.115675/VJ 1051/93, 94 [emergency secret].

66. Templer's report to Macmillan, December 16, 1955, FO 371.115658/VJ 1051/127g [secret].

67. To which Macmillan replied, "I should like to congratulate you. I think you have had a great triumph." Such was the state of the empire in 1955. FO to Templer, December 14, 1955, FO 371.115657/VJ 1051/96 [emergency secret].

68. Templer to FO, December 13, 1955, and Templer to al-Majali, December 14, 1955, FO 371.115657/VJ 1015/95, 96 [emergency, top secret].

69. Farid Irshayd's son Mahir recalled that al-Majali's stock was so low on the West Bank that King Hussein himself had to telephone his father to per-

suade him to join the cabinet. See Duke to FO, December 14, 1955, Duke to FO, December 16, 1955, and Turton's memo, December 15, 1955, FO 371.115657-115658/VJ 1051/105, 109, 123 [secret]; Mallory to SOS, December 16, 1955, NA/RG 84, Box 7, 350; Duke to FO, December 16, 1955, FO 371.115639/VJ 1015/40; Hazza' al-Majali, *Mudhakkarati* [My memoires] (Beirut: Dar al-'ilm lil-malayeen, 1960); interviews with Yusef Haykal and Mahir Irshayd.

70. Cited in Duke to FO, December 16, 1955, FO 371.115639/VJ 1015/40.

71. Dann, *King Hussein,* 28; on refugees, see Avi Plascov, *The Palestinian Refugees in Jordan, 1948–1957* (London: Cass, 1981), 156.

72. Mallory to SOS, December 20, 1955, and Parker to DOS, December 31, 1955, NA/RG 84, Box 7, 350 [secret].

73. A Jerusalem editor quoted in Cole to DOS, December 30, 1955, NA/RG 84, Box 5, 320.1.

74. Duke to FO, December 17, 1955, FO 371.115657/VJ 1051/112 [secret]; Duke to FO, December 18, 1955, FO 371.115639/VJ 1015/43 [emergency].

75. For Hussein's December 18 address, see Ministry of Information, *al-Majmu'a al-kamila l'khutub jalalat al-malak al-Hussein bin Talal al-mu'athm, 1952–1985* [Complete collection of the speeches of His Majesty King Hussein bin Talal the Great, 1952–1985], 3 vols. (Amman: Directorate of Press and Publications, n.d. [1986?]), 1: 65.

76. Duke to FO, December 19, 1955, FO 371.115658/VJ 1051/121 [emergency secret]; Barbour to DOS, December 19, 1955, NA/RG 84, Box 7, 350.

77. Mallory to SOS, December 21, 1955, NA/RG 84, Box 7, 350; Parker to DOS, December 31, 1955, NA/RG 84, Box 7, 350 [secret].

78. In his postmortem, Templer had nothing but praise for Hussein. See Templer's report to Macmillan, December 16, 1955, FO 371.115658/VJ 1051/127g [secret].

79. Hazza' al-Majali, *Qissat muhadathat Templer* [Story of the Templer talks] (Amman: n.p., 1956); English translation in FO 371.121492.

80. This allegation first appeared December 28 in the pro-Western Damascus newspaper, *al-Ittihad*; its source was Bahjat al-Talhuni. The bribery charges were hotly denied by the Palestinian ministers, and in al-Sadat's defense, it is noteworthy that he was feted during his visit by both King Hussein and Prime Minister al-Mufti. The *al-Ittihad* story is cited in Strong to DOS, December 29, 1955, NA/RG 84, Box 7, 350; Mason to Rose, December 31, 1955, FO 371.121476/VJ 10316/3 [secret]; Mason to FO, January 5, 1956, FO 371.121462/VJ 1015/9 [secret]; Eilts to Baghdad, December 6, 1955, NA/RG 84 Box 3, 310; interview with 'Abd al-Hadi.

81. FO to Washington, December 12, 1955, FO 371.115656/VJ 1051/87 [secret]; Makins to FO, December 14, 1955, FO 371.115657/VJ 1051/98 [secret]; interview with Makins, Dulles Oral History Project, Dulles Library, Princeton University, Princeton, NJ.

82. Interview with 'Abd al-Hadi. These themes were expounded by 'Abd al-Hadi in a series of newspaper articles in early 1956 and were hinted at in Templer's report to Macmillan, December 16, 1955, FO 371.115658/VJ 1051/127g [secret]. This story is generally supported by Musa, *A'lam min al-urdunn,* 25.

83. See Musa, *A'lam min al-urdunn*; and Mohammad Ibrahim Faddah, *The Middle East in Transition: A Study in Jordan's Foreign Policy* (London: Asia Publishing House, 1974), 243, n. 90.

84. As late as December 10, the Government Press Bureau was still encouraging editors "neither to oppose nor support" the pact. Amman to Levant Department, December 15, 1955, FO 371.115533/V 1073/1396.

85. Interview with al-Hindawi.

CHAPTER 8

1. Hashim twice resigned the prime ministry on matters of principle, in 1938 and 1947. See Ya'acov Shimoni and Evyatar Levine, *Political Dictionary of the Middle East in the Twentieth Century* (Jerusalem: G. A. Jerusalem Publishing House, 1974), 151.

2. Interview with Hani Hashim.

3. Duke to FO, December 22, 1955, FO 371.115641/VJ 1015/83; Reuters report, December 26, 1955, quoted in FO to Amman, December 28, 1955, FO 371.115641/VJ 1015/87 [emergency].

4. When queried, Britain's embassy in Cairo reported "no evidence" that Moscow "initiated or [was] directly concerned" with the Arab aid offer. Ironically, the Soviet offer was relayed to the Jordanian chargé in Cairo, Hani Hashim, the prime minister's son. Interview with Hashim; Duke to FO, December 29, 1955, FO 371.115659/VJ 1051/146 [secret]; Murphy to FO, January 2, 1956, FO 371.121491/VJ 1051/7 [secret].

5. Duke to FO, December 29, 1955, FO 371.115534/V 1073/1431.

6. The constitution requires the sitting prime minister and interior minister to sign dissolution decrees. The deputies contended that because Interior Minister 'Abbas Mirza had already resigned, the absence of his signature invalidated the decree.

7. There are hints that the deputies' petition may have been prompted by the government to provide a pretext to rescind the dissolution decree. At the very least, it was welcomed by the government. Duke to FO, December 27, 1955, FO 371.115641/VJ 1015/86; Uriel Dann, *King Hussein and the Challenge of Arab Radicalism: Jordan, 1955–1967* (New York: Oxford University Press, 1989), 29, n. 28.

8. Duke to FO, December 28 and 29, 1955, FO 371.115641/VJ 1015/91, 93 [secret]; Duke to FO, January 2, 1956, FO 371.121462/VJ 1015/1 [secret].

9. Duke to FO, December 29, 1955, FO 371.115659/VJ 1051/150 [top secret]; Mideast Main to Hutton, December 30, 1955, FO 371.115641/VJ 1015/92 [secret]; Patrick Coghill, "Before I Forget," mimeograph (Oxford, 1960), 124.

10. Hussein asked Hashim to remain in office until a successor government was formed. The Interior Ministry's decree banning the opposition assembly contained the following tortured logic: "I have studied . . . the present disturbed situation and found that the matter does not come under the responsibility of the present Government on the one hand and on the other hand that this meeting is not in the public interest." Mason to FO, January 5, 1956, FO 371.121462/VJ 1015/11.

11. Ironically, just hours before the U.S. consulate in Jerusalem was attacked, Mallory telegraphed Washington his suggestion that the United States ought to bow to Nasser's role as regional strongman, acquiesce in the dismemberment of Jordan, and support the creation of a "new independent Arab Palestine" as a "buffer state." Mallory to DOS, January 5, 1956, DOS 785.00/1-556 [secret], in *Foreign Relations of the United States (FRUS)*, 13:12–15.

12. Mason to FO, January 7, 1956, FO 371.121462/VJ 1015/16 [emergency].

13. First reports of Saudi troops movement reached Glubb on or about January 1. By the second week of January, there were sizable Saudi forces deployed across the border from Aqaba and in Saudi territory southeast of Amman, just a few hours' drive from the capital. Glubb to Melville (TJL), January 2, 1956, FO 371.121510/VJ 1092/1 [secret]; Duke to FO, January 10, 1956, FO 371.121463/VJ 1015/44 [secret]; Anthony Eden, *Full Circle* (London: Cassell, 1960), 346.

14. Hussein also said he had considered, but rejected, requesting the assistance of British troops. Glubb, who was present, suggested having British troops stand by in case the situation deteriorated further; Hussein did not dissent. That night, the British cabinet ordered two paratroop battalions ready to move to Cyprus and asked for Hussein's approval for the redeployment to Amman of a 250-man RAF regiment from Habbaniya, Iraq, and of the armored regiment stationed in Aqaba. It also agreed to pass on Hussein's request to Nuri al-Sa'id but "to offer no advice on the question of Iraqi troops." Mason to FO, January 9, 1956, FO 371.121462/VJ 1015/27, 32 [emergency top secret]; CAB 130.111/GEN 513, January 9, 1956.

15. Wright to FO, January 10, 1956, FO 371.121462/VJ 1015/33 [emergency top secret].

16. Also, Hussein approved the move of the RAF regiment but counseled against moving the armored regiment. London respected his wishes. Two weeks later, the cabinet formally defined the paratroops' prospective mission as both to evacuate Britons and to "assist King Hussein to restore order." CAB 130.111/GEN 513, January 10 and 23, 1956.

17. Minutes of NSC meeting 272, January 12, 1956, in *FRUS*, 13:19.

18. This is a central theme of Dann's book: "The critical point is that Hussein was never remotely as important to Abdel Nasser as Abdel Nasser was to Hussein. This was understandable: Egypt, or the UAR, under Abdel Nasser was of vital consequence to Hussein, but Jordan under Hussein was to Abdel Nasser only an irritant and a reproach." Dann, *King Hussein*, 168–69.

19. Duke to DO, January 10, 1956, FO 371.121476/VJ 10316/2 [secret]; Trevelyan to FO, January 11, 1956, FO 371.121241/V 1071/19; Trevelyan to FO, January 14, 1956, FO 371.121241/V 1071/32.

20. FO to Jeddah, January 11, 1956, and MOD to MELF, January 14–15, 1956, FO 371.121463/VJ 1015/44 [top secret]; Wright to FO, January 19, 1956, and Duke to Rose, January 26, 1956, FO 371.121510/VJ 1092/3, 7 [top secret]; Jeddah to FO, January 15, 1956, FO 371.121465/VJ 1015/97.

21. Mason to FO, January 9, 1956, FO 371.121462/VJ 1015/27.

22. Glubb to Melville (TJL), January 13, 1956, Duke to FO, January 19, 1956, and Beirut to FO, January 18, 1956, in FO 371.121465/VJ 1015/94, 99, and 106 [secret].

23. Duke to FO, January 10, 1956, and FO to Amman, January 11, 1956, FO 371.121463-121464/VJ 1015/46, 66 [secret].

24. Mason to FO, January 8, 1956, and Duke to Lloyd, January 12, 1956, FO 371.121462, 121464/VJ 1015/17, 92.

25. Mason to FO, January 9, 1956, and Trevelyan to FO, January 11, 1956, FO 371.12-1462-121463/VJ 1015/32, 83 [emergency secret]; Mason to FO, Janllary 8, 1956, and FO to Amman, January 9, 1956, FO 371.121491/VJ 1051/13 [secret].

26. Mason to FO, January 9, 1956, FO 371.121462/VJ 1015/27 [emergency top secret]; Duke to FO, January 11, 1956, FO 371.121464/VJ 1015/62 [secret].

27. Hutton to Melville (TJL), January 12, 1956, FO 371.121464/VJ 1015/90; Glubb to Templer, January 11, 1956, FO 371.121464/VJ 1015/93 [personal and private].

28. The Arab proposal was again complemented by a Soviet offer to "supply everything Jordan needs, including arms." Hani Hashim noted that the Soviet ambassador "kept repeating the word 'everything.'" Glubb to Melville, January 13, 1956, FO 371.121465/VJ 1015/94, 96 [top secret].

29. See FO 371.121591-121592/VJ 1671; and Mason to Hadow, March 1, 1956, FO 371.121466/VJ 1015/145 [secret].

30. Such fears were not totally unfounded. See the anti-British, pro-Egyptian account of the Baghdad Pact riots by Samir's brother, 'Abd al-Mun'im, Jordan's ambassador to Washington. Memorandum of conversation between Allen and al-Rifa'i, January 28, 1956, DOS 785.00/1 2856, in *FRUS*, 13:23–26. On Salmir's tour, see Duke to Lloyd, March 1, 1956, FO 371.121473/VJ 1022/4; *The Times*, February 17, 1956.

31. Duke to Lloyd, February 2, 1956, FO 371.121465/VJ 1015/123.

32. Ministry of Information, *al-Majmu'a al-kamila l'khutub jalalat al-malak al-Hussein bin Talal al-mu'athm, 1952–1985* [Complete collection of the speeches of His Majesty King Hussein bin Talal the Great, 1952–1985], 3 vols. (Amman: Directorate of Press and Publications, n.d. [1986?]), 1: 79.

33. Forty-eight hours after Glubb's dismissal, Eden ordered Shuckburgh "seriously to consider reoccupation of [the] Suez [base] as a move to counteract the blow to our prestige which Glubb's dismissal means." Evelyn Shuckburgh, *Descent to Suez: Diaries, 1951–56* (London: Weidenfeld and Nicholson, 1986), 341; Anthony Nutting, *I Saw for Myself: The Aftermath of Suez* (London: Hollis and Carter, 1958), 1.

34. Interview with King Hussein.

35. Dann, *King Hussein*, 31.

36. Duke to Rose, February 29, 1956, FO 371.121563/VJ 1208/3 [top secret].

37. Throughout his life, Glubb stressed his absolute loyalty to Jordan, but his protestations do not stand up under inspection. Through his direct communications with Cyprus and London, he maintained a backdoor link to a foreign power outside the purview of his civilian superiors. Glubb repeatedly divulged top secret Jordanian and even inter-Arab planning documents to London, kept conversations and initiatives secret from the Jordan government, and disparaged the politics and personalities of ministers and members of the royal family that in any other context would be labeled as clear insubordination. After expelling

Glubb, Hussein normally took the high road in extolling the former's devotion, but his pique periodically filtered out. Indeed, he once summed up Glubb's performance as "the general only transmitted Whitehall's orders." See Hussein bin Talal, *Mon métier de roi* (Paris: Editions Robert Laffont, 1975), 108.

38. Duke to FO, May 3, 1955, FO 371.115674/VJ 1201/12 [top secret].

39. Most of the information about Sharif Nasser's role remains in closed files, though Duke does refer to the "intrigues of Sharif Nasser among Arab officers of the Arab Legion against Glubb and the British officers." Also topping Mallory's list of "contributory" reasons to Glubb's ouster was "dislike of Glubb by certain family elements." Duke to FO, May 3, 1955, FO 371.115674/VJ 1201/12 [top secret]; Mallory to DOS, March 16, 1956, DOS 785.00/3-1656, in *FRUS*, 13:32.

40. Glubb to Duke, June 5, 1955, FO 371.115674/VJ 1201/21 [top secret]; see also John Bagot Glubb, *A Soldier with the Arabs* (London: Hodder & Stoughton, 1957), 364–69.

41. This outburst may have been partly due to Hussein's anger over the imminent reassignment of Dalgleish, his close friend and commander of the Arab Legion's air force. Duke to Shuckburgh, October 6, 1955, FO 371.115683/VJ 12011/1 [secret].

42. At the time, Shuckburgh's lone suggestion was to "bring about [the sharif's] removal." In his memoirs, Selwyn Lloyd also recalled discussing Glubb with the king in "the autumn of 1955," and Hussein saying that he "was completely satisfied with the existing state of affairs." Hussein bin Talal, *Uneasy Lies the Head* (New York: Bernard Geis Associates, 1962), 139; Shuckburgh, *Descent to Suez*, 292; Shuckburgh to Duke, November 5, 1955, FO 371.115683/VJ 12011/4 [secret]; Selwyn Lloyd, *Suez 1956: A Personal Account* (London: Jonathan Cape, 1978), 48.

43. Duke to Rose, February 1, 1956, FO 371.121560/VJ 1206/4 [secret].

44. Mason to Hadow, January 19, 1956, FO 371.121564/VJ 1015/105; see also Peter Young, *Bedouin Command: With the Arab Legion, 1953–1956* (London: William Kimber, 1956), 158.

45. James Lunt, *Glubb Pasha: A Biography* (London: Harvill Press, 1984), 201; interview with al-Shar'a.

46. Glubb to Templer February 2, 1956, FO 371/121563/VJ 1208/1 [top secret]; see Uriel Dann, "Glubb and the Politization of the Arab Legion: An Annotated Document," *Asian and African Studies* 21 (1987): 213–20.

47. For details of anti-Glubb broadcasts, see FO 371.121560/VJ 1206/6.

48. Vatikiotis goes too far, however, in labeling as "nothing short of ingenious" Hussein's insistence than Glubb's ouster should have no effect on Jordan's relations with Britain. Hussein could not have known at the time that Eden would decide not to seek retribution for Glubb's dismissal. See P. J. Vatikiotis, *Politics and the Military in Jordan: A Study of the Arab Legion, 1921–1957* (London: Cass, 1967), 124.

49. Ibid., 133. When not otherwise noted, the following paragraphs are based on interviews with King Hussein, 'Ali Abu Nuwar, Sadiq al-Shar'a, Mahmud al-Mu'ayta, Nadhir Rashid, and Zayd bin Shakir, as well as on the following authors: Dann, Glubb, Vatikiotis, Young, and Shahir Yusef Abu Shahut, *al-Jaysh wa'l-siyasa fi al-urdunn: dhikriyat 'an harakat al-dhubat al-urdunniyeen al-ahrar* [Army and politics in Jordan: Memories of the Jordanian Free Officers movement] (n.p.: al-Qabas, 1985).

50. Abdullah al-Tall claimed to have plotted a coup in late 1948 with "Free Officers," but it was most likely an anachronistic use of the term. See al-Tall, *Karithat Filastin*, cited in Vatikiotis, *Politics and the Military*, 100.

51. Interview with Mahmud al-Mu'ayta.

52. Other approaches were allegedly made to Habis al-Majali, Muhammad al-Mu'ayta, 'Ali al-Hiyari, Radi al-Hindawi, and Mahmud al-Rusan—but not to Sadiq al-Shar'a. Abu Shahut, *al-Jaysh wa'l-siyasa*, 9–11.

53. Abu Nuwar reportedly proposed a coup against Abu'l Huda to avert Talal's deposition, which was most likely the cause of Abu Nuwar's banishment to France. Also, Abu Shahut claimed that the Free Officers later tried to contact Talal in order "to save the monarchy from conspiracy"—the background to deposition-eve plotting referred to in Chapter 3. Abu Shahut, *al-Jaysh wa'l-siyasa*, 11; also see Vatikiotis, *Politics and the Military*, 127, n. 33.

54. John Bagot Glubb, *The Changing Scenes of Life: An Autobiography* (London: Quartet Books, 1983), 180.

55. Furlonge to FO, February 3, 1953, FO 371.104893/ET 1051/2, 4. Glubb's reference to the 1952 "Free Officer" activities of an "officer in the Supply and Transport Corps" was evidently viewed as a one-man aberration. Glubb, *A Soldier*, 412.

56. On this period, see Peter Snow, *Hussein: A Biography* (London: Barrie & Jenkins, 1972), 62–63.

57. Abu Shahut, *al-Jaysh wa'l-siyasa*, 11–12.

58. Ibid., 15–16.

59. Nadhir Rashid and Abu Nuwar claimed that the initiative came from the officers. Hussein himself acknowledged some role for them when he said in an interview that "what brought it [the urgency of Glubb's dismissal] about even more was that just a couple of days before, some officers came to meet me who shared the same feelings as I had." Khulusi al-Khayri's accusation that Hussein was forced to sack Glubb under threat from "a group of officers" is difficult to sustain. Duke to FO, March 5, 15356, FO 371.121541/VJ 1201/37 [secret].

60. Memorandum of conversation between Hadow and Melville, March 3, 1956, FO 371.121542/VJ 1201/60.

61. See Duke to Shuckburgh, June 3, 1955, FO 371.115706/VJ 1641/2 [secret].

62. The "fit of pique" explanation, favored by Glubb, is bolstered by Hussein's admission to Duke that "he had been upset by constant articles in the Press, even in England, representing Glubb as everything that mattered in Jordan," evidently including the celebrated tabloid story depicting Glubb as "the uncrowned king of Jordan." However, this was just one of several explanations Hussein offered and, from the historical context, appears less to have determined his actions than to have been useful in justifying them. Duke to FO, March 1, 1956, FO 71.121540/VJ 1201/6 [emergency]; Glubb, *A Soldier*, 426.

63. Hussein had intimated as much to Duke once before. Duke to Shuckburgh, November 28, 1955, FO 371.115683/VJ 12011/4 [secret]; Hussein, *Uneasy Lies the Head*, 140–41; interviews with Abu Nuwar and Mahmud al-Mu'ayta.

64. Duke to FO, January 25, 1956, FO 371.121723/VR 1073/27 [secret].

65. MELF to MOD, February 6, 1956, FO 371.121531/VJ 1192/16 [top secret].

66. FO to Amman, February 9, 1956, Duke to FO, February 15, 1956,

and MOD to MELF, February 22, 1956, FO 371.121531/VJ 1192/16, 17 [top secret].

67. Glubb to Templer, February 17, 1956, FO 371.121724/VR 1073/63 [top secret].

68. Glubb to Templer, February 21, 1956, FO 371.121724/VR 1073/68 [top secret].

69. Duke to FO, February 23, 1956, FO 371.121725/VR 1073/109 [secret].

70. Duke informed Glubb of "the gist" of the message on February 29 but waited until the next morning to see al-Rifa'i. Duke to FO, March 3, 1956, and FO to Amman, March 6, 1956, FO 371.121725/VR 1073/85 [top secret]; Shuckburgh, *Descent to Suez*, 337.

71. For details of Glubb's questionable control of internal security, see Coghill, "Before I Forget," 121, and Vatikiotis, *Politics and the Military*, 101.

72. Hussein had already been shown files pilfered from brigade headquarters outlining plans for a redeployment alway from the armistice line in case of hostilities with Israel. This might have led the king to believe that London would prevent British officers from serving on the West Bank, as was the case in 1944. Interview with Nadhir Rashid.

73. Duke to FO, March 4, 1956, FO 371.121492/VJ 1051/50.

74. Hussein, *Uneasy Lies the Head*, 130. Incidentally, the assurances Duke belatedly passed to al-Rifa'i were decidedly equivocal. Only in the case of an unprovoked Israeli attack on Egypt or Syria would Britain consider military cooperation under the Anglo-Jordanian treaty. Glubb was informed that there had to be "no reasonable doubt" about Israel's aggression for the Arab Legion's British officers to remain in their posts. And if the Syrians (or the Egyptians) started the fighting and Jordan joined on their behalf, "it would be impossible for [Britain] to support Jordan." FO to Amman, February 28, 1956, and March 1, 1956, FO 371.121724/VR 1073/77 [top secret].

CHAPTER 9

1. London to DOS, March 9, 1956, DOS 641.85/3-956, in *Foreign Relations of the United States* (*FRUS*), 13:29.

2. Hussein bin Talal, *Uneasy Lies the Head* (New York: Bernard Geis Associates, 1962), 151.

3. Al-Rifa'i's reaction to the dismissal order has been disputed. According to Duke, the premier "maintained that [the dismissal] was not final but was the only way to handle the situation for the moment and said he hoped to see Glubb back in his place after a week or so." Zayd al-Rifa'i maintained that his father never expressed the hope that Glubb would return. Duke to FO, March 1, 1956, FO 371.121540/VJ 1201/9 [emergency secret]; interview with Zayd al-Rifa'i; Peter Snow, *Hussein: A Biography* (London: Barrie & Jenkins, 1972), 85.

4. See FO 371.121243/V 1071/113.

5. *Al-Ahram* (Cairo), March 14, 1956; FO files 371.121492-121493/VJ 1051/54, 55, 71; FO 371.121494/VJ 10393/7-24; FO 371.121466/VJ 1051/151.

6. Duke to FO, March 6, 1956, FO 371.121492/VJ 1051/57-58, [secret];

Duke to FO, March 19, 1956, FO 371.121484/VJ 10393/20; Duke to Rose, March 29, 1956, FO 371.121466/VJ 1015/157.

7. See Amman to Levant Department, May 16, 1956, FO 371.121475/VJ 1024/18; Duke to FO, May 21 and 24, 1956, FO 371.121407/VJ 1015/180, 191; also FO 371.121475/VJ 1024/20.

8. Patrick Coghill, "Before I Forget," mimeograph (Oxford, 1960), 127; Duke to FO, March 1, 1956, FO 371.121540/VJ 1201/9 [emergency secret].

9. In addition to those dismissed, nine senior British officers were relieved of their commands on March 1. In response, Eden demanded the withdrawal of all British officers still in executive positions. Anthony Eden, *Full Circle* (London: Cassell, 1960), 350.

10. Duke to FO, March 7 and 10, 1956, FO 371.121564/VJ 1209/6, 10 [secret]; Duke to FO, March 9, 1956, FO 371.121493/VJ 1051/71 [secret].

11. The shooting incident pitted the Rusans of Irbid against the al-Mu'aytas of Kerak and the Abu Nuwars of Salt. After his acquittal, Colonel Mahmud Rusan was bundled off to Washington. There were also reports of an Iraqi-backed conspiracy, hatched by Brigade Commander Radi Abdullah with support from Nuri al-Sa'id, foiled later that spring. Amman to Levant Department, April 26, 1956, FO 371.121547/VJ 1201/176; *New York Times,* July 26, 1956; Shahir Yusef Abu Shahut, *al-Jaysh wa'l-siyasa fi al-urdunn: dhikriyat 'an harakat al-dhubat al-urdunniyeen al-ahrar* [Army and politics in Jordan: Memories of the Jordanian Free Officers movement] (n.p.: al-Qabas, 1985), 16.

12. Duke to FO, April 5, 1956, FO 371.121545/VJ 1201/136 [secret]; Gardener to FO, March 7, 1956, FO 371.121564/VJ 1209/7; Duke to FO, March 9, 1956, FO 371.121493/VJ 1051/71 [secret]; Duke to Rose, March 29, 1956, FO 371.121466/VJ 1015/ 157.

13. Also included on the council were two other Hashemite hawks, Circassian brigade commander Colonel 'Izzat Hassan and bedouin tank commander Colonel 'Akkash al-Zabn. Also see Duke to Rose, March 28, 1956, WO 216.912 [top secret].

14. Duke to Lloyd, April 28, 1956, FO 371.121565/VJ 1209/19 [secret].

15. Abu Shahut, *al-Jaysh wa'l-siyasa,* 17; interview with al-Mu'ayta; Duke to FO, May 24, 1956, FO 371.121548/VJ 1201/204.

16. Snow, *Hussein,* 88; Uriel Dann, *King Hussein and the Challenge of Arab Radicalism: Jordan, 1955–1967* (New York: Oxford University Press, 1989), 179, n. 6; Jerusalem to Levant Department, March 7, 1956, FO 371.121542/VJ 1201/70.

17. Duke to Shuckburgh, April 29, 1956, FO 371.121485/VJ 10393/42 [secret].

18. On ammunition, see FO 371.121485/VJ 110393/28 [top secret] and FO 371.121544/VJ 1201/118 [top secret]; on the staff college, see FO 371.121567/VJ 12012/3 [secret].

19. On the potential for Soviet aid, see Duke to FO, May 11, 1956, FO 371.121466/VJ 1015/173; DOS to Baghdad, May 12, 1956, DOS 785.00/5-1256 [secret]; Duke to FO, June 16 and July 24, 1956, FO 371.121553-121554/VJ 1203/7, 25; also see *The Times,* June 6, 1956.

20. Duke to FO, June 24, 1956, and Ross's minute, June 21, 1956, FO 371.121485/VJ 10393/45, 50 [secret].

21. Wilbur Crane Eveland, *Ropes of Sand: America's Failure in the Middle*

East (London: Norton, 1980), 183–84, 188; also see *New York Times,* May 25, 1956; Amman to Levant Department, June 21, 1956, FO 371.121475/VJ 1024/21 [secret].

22. Eden's note, June 12, 1956, FO 371.121495/VJ 1051/139.

23. The most intriguing appointment was that of newcomer Muhammad 'Ali al-'Ajluni as minister of defense and interior. He was the father of Mazin al-'Ajluni, one of Hussein's aides-de-camp and a leading figure in the plan to oust Glubb.

24. Al-Mufti's *Daily Telegraph* interview, cited in FO 371.121494/VJ 1051/123.

25. BBC monitor of an Arab News Agency broadcast, June 19, 1956, in FO 371.121495/VJ 1051/144.

26. Duke to FO, June 26–27, 1956, FO 371.121469/VJ 1015/214–215.

27. Duke to FO, July 3, 1956; BBC monitoring Arab News Agency report, July 30, 1956; and Amman to Levant Department, August 2, 1956, FO 371.121468/VJ 1015/221, 231, and 236.

28. Conversations with Lieutenant Colonel Ma'an Abu Nuwar and Jerusalem Governor Hassan al-Khatib in Wikeley to Duke, August 13 and September 19, 1956, FO 371.121469/VJ 1015/242, 258 [secret]; Amman to Levant Department, September 29, 1956, and Duke to Lloyd, October 26, 1956, FO 371.121469-121470/VJ 1015/260, 292; *New York Times,* October 19, 1956; Dann, *King Hussein,* 38; and Aqil Hyder Hasan Abidi, *Jordan: A Political Study, 1948–1957* (London: Asia Publishing House, 1965), 134.

29. Duke to FO, August 11, 1956, FO 371.121497/VJ 1051/180 [secret].

30. Duke to FO, August 13, 1956, FO 371.121497/VJ 1051/183 [secret].

31. "We have never yet discussed with the Jordanians military plans for collaboration against Israel under the Anglo-Jordanian Treaty. So long as General Glubb was in command of the Arab Legion, we were able to get away with this." Rose's minute, April 12, 1956, FO 371.121531/VJ 1192/30.

32. Abu Nuwar freed Britain from having to provide any ground troops other than Aqaba's "O" Force. The participation of British land forces, he said, would be "inadvisable for sound political reasons." Instead, he chose to rely solely on British air and naval support. See reportage on the Anglo-Jordan Joint Defense Board, July 23–24, 1956, and Abu Nuwar's memorandum to Benson, July 30, 1956, in FO 371.121534/VJ 1192/91g [top secret].

33. London never admitted to Amman its view that British air and naval support "cannot possibly of itself halt the Israeli army and save Jordan if a full-scale war breaks out." See FO–Amman–Tel Aviv correspondence in FO 371.121780-121781/VR 1091/303–315 [secret].

34. The widely held belief that it was Israeli complaints that prevented Iraqi troops from moving into Jordan prior to the outbreak of the Suez war is incorrect. In fact, Israel was willing to acquiesce in the move, given Nuri's numerous assurances of "no aggressive intent." Rather, it was a combination of Iraqi–Jordanian disagreement over the command structure of the expeditionary force, protests from Jordan's opposition parties, and an emergency appeal from Eden that convinced King Hussein to retract his request for the immediate deployment of Iraqi forces. For details, see FO 371.121486-121489/VJ 10393/56-173 [top secret and secret]; FO 371.121499/VJ 1051/205; FO 371.121780, 121782/VR 1091/297, 350 [secret]; DOS to Baghdad, September 27, 1956, DOS 685.87/9-2756 [secret]; Baghdad to DOS, September 29, 1956, DOS

685.87/9-2956 [secret]; various telegrams in ISA 2453/10; *New York Times,* October 11 and 14, 1956.

35. Britain's military strategy was no less schizophrenic. As late as October 18, three days before the Sèvres meeting to concert plans with Israel, the plan to attack Israel (Operation CORDAGE) still took priority over the plan to attack Egypt (Operation MUSKETEER). See W. Scott Lucas, "Redefining the Suez 'Collusion'," *Middle Eastern Studies* 26 (January 1990): 88–112; Dann, *King Hussein,* 37; also see MOD to MELF, October 18, 1956, FO 371.121535/VJ 1192/118 [operational top secret].

The Jordanian–Egyptian–Syrian military pact was signed on October 24, after Jordan's election but before the installation of the al-Nabulsi government. Jordan was, of course, already bound to Egypt by the Arab League Collective Security Pact.

36. Amman to Levant Department, August 4, 1956, FO 371.121468/VJ 1015/236. In general, see Amnon Cohen, *Political Parties in the West Bank Under the Jordanian Regime, 1949–1967* (Ithaca, NY: Cornell University Press, 1982).

37. Duke to FO and Amman to Levant Department, August 18, 1956, FO 371.121469/VJ 1015/239, 243; also see Cohen, *Political Parties,* 35.

38. Duke to FO, July 3, 1956, FO 371.121468/VJ 1015/221; Amman to Levant Department, August 4, 1956, FO 371.121468/VJ 1015/236.

39. The party was led by an eight-man executive headed by Abu'l Huda loyalists Riyadh al-Mifleh and Ahmad al-Tawarneh. See Amman to Levant Department, March 24, 1956, FO 371.121471/VJ 1017/1; also Amman to Levant Department, September 29, 1956, FO 371.121469/VJ 1015/260.

40. Quotations in this paragraph are from Kirkbride, cited in Snow, *Hussein,* 100; interviews with Faris al-Nabulsi, Marwan 'Abd al-Halim al-Nimr, and Na'im 'Abd al-Hadi; and Charles Johnston, *The Brink of Jordan* (London: Hamish Hamilton, 1972) 66–67.

41. Amman to Levant Department, August 4, 1956, FO 371.121468/VJ 1015/236.

42. Interview with Sulayman al-Hadidi; Amman to Levant Department, September 29, 1956, FO 371.121469/VJ 1015/260.

43. Estimates put the voter turnout at 50 to 60 percent nationwide, but at only 20 to 30 percent in Amman itself. Duke to Lloyd, October 26, 1956, FO 371.121470/VJ 1015/292.

Duke was instructed to urge Hussein to cancel the elections, but he evidently never had the chance to relay the message to the king. Hussein later stated that the idea of canceling the vote never even occurred to him. See Rose's margin note, October 16, 1956, FO 371.121469/VJ 1015/272. Also see Hussein, *Uneasy Lies the Head,* 153; Dann, *King Hussein,* 38; interview with King Hussein.

44. Abidi's breakdown, *Jordan,* 144, citing *Falastin,* October 23, 1956. Both Vatikiotis and Hussein made curious references to a NSP "majority," which it certainly did not have. See P. J. Vatikiotis, *Politics and the Military in Jordan: A Study of the Arab Legion, 1921–1957* (London: Cass, 1967), 125; Hussein, *Uneasy Lies the Head,* 153.

45. Duke to Lloyd, October 26, 1956, FO 371.121470/VJ 1015/292.

46. Although the bedouin deputy 'Akif al-Fa'iz was elected first deputy president, he had a questionable political past and was not yet viewed as the royalist he would later prove to be. See Duke to FO and Amman to Levant Depart-

ment, October 26, 1956, FO 371.121470/VJ 10151282, 293; Vatikiotis, *Politics and the Military*, 106, n. 12.

47. Duke to FO, October 27, 1956, FO 371.121470/VJ 1015/285 [secret].

48. The king reportedly considered naming al-Nimr, who had won handily in Salt, but al-Nimr insisted that al-Nabulsi, the party's leader, be appointed instead. Al-Nabulsi's son told a different story, that al-Nabulsi wanted al-Nimr to be named premier and accepted the appointment only when Hussein insisted. Hussein himself denied ever having considered anybody but al-Nabulsi. Interviews with Marwan al-Nimr, Faris al-Nabulsi, and King Hussein.

49. There was, it seems, a halfhearted attempt to have the Muslim Brotherhood, or at least a representative, join the coalition, too. Interview with Yusef al-'Athm.

50. Sulayman Musa, *A'lam min al-urdunn: safahat min tarikh al-'arab al-hadith* [Luminaries from Jordan: Pages from modern Arab history] (Amman: Dar al-sha'b, 1986), 57.

51. Lunt erred in describing al-Nabulsi as a "West Bank lawyer." He was neither. James Lunt, *Hussein of Jordan: Searching for a Just and Lasting Peace, a Political Biography* (London: Macmillan, 1989), 32.

52. Musa, *A'lam min al-urdunn*, 59–60; interviews with Marwan al-Nimr and Jamal al-Sha'ir.

53. This paragraph is drawn from Amman to DOS, December 20, 1950, DOS 785.521/12-2050; Amman to DOS, September 8, 1953, in NA/RG 84, Box 3, 301; FO 371.104893/ET 1051/19; Amman to DOS, May 10, 1954, DOS 785.13/5-1054; Amman to DOS, October 16, 1954, DOS 785.00/10-1654; Amman to DOS, May 20, 1955, in NA/RG 84, Box 7, 350; and interviews with Faris al-Nabulsi and Marwan al-Nimr.

54. Memorandum of conversation with al-Nabulsi, September 14, 1955, NA/RG 84, Box 9, 350.2.

55. Interview with Sir Julian Bullard.

56. Johnston, *The Brink of Jordan*, 22–23.

57. Interview with Hamad al-Farhan.

58. Hussein, *Uneasy Lies the Head*, 153; interview with King Hussein.

59. Duke to Rose, November 2, 1956, FO 371.121500/VJ 1051/235.

60. On November 1, Hussein asked King Feisal to move troops immediately into Jordan. Command arrangements were quickly ironed out, and Iraqi troops began to move to Mafraq on November 3. By then, about two Syrian brigades had already been deployed inside the kingdom. Saudi troops crossed into Jordan on November 6. For details, see Wright to FO, November 1–2, 1956, FO 371.121489/VJ 10393/176, 180–182 [emergency secret]; Duke to FO, November 3, 1956, FO 371.121787/VR 1091/544 [secret]; Shattock to FO, December 6, 1956, FO 371.121503/VJ 1072/21 [secret]; Nicholls to Lloyd, December 13, 1956, FO 371.121804/VR 1091/1044 [secret]; also Snow, *Hussein*, 100.

61. Duke to FO, November 3, 1956, FO 371.121787/VR 1091/549 [emergency secret]; interview with King Hussein; Dann, *King Hussein*, 41.

62. Duke to FO, November 8 and 11, 1956, FO 371.121499-121500/VJ 1051/226, 231 [secret]; FO minute, November 19, 1956, FO 371.121559/VJ 1205/57 [secret]; *New York Times*, November 2, 1956.

63. Abu Nuwar repeated these warnings to Mason on November 21.

Johnston to FO, November 21, 1956, FO 371.121731/VR 1073/289 [secret]; Mallory to DOS, November 9, 1956, DOS 684a.86/11-956 [top secret], in *FRUS,* 13:59.

64. Mallory to DOS, November 17, 1956, and DOS to Amman, November 18, 1956, DOS 684a/11-1756 [top secret], in *FRUS,* 13:61–62; Johnston to FO, November 20, 1950, FO 371.121555/VJ 1203/60.

65. In 1946, al-Rimawi had been sacked from his job as chief Arabic translator for the British legation in Jeddah. According to his personnel file, his "inflamed inferiority complex reduced both the career-staff of the Mission and the other native translators to desperation." Extract from Jeddah dispatch, July 3, 1946, FO 371.82705.

66. Interview with Suheilah al-Rimawi; Amman to DOS, November 16, 1951, DOS 785.521/11-1651; Amman to DOS, November 10, 1954, DOS 785.00/11-1054.

67. *New York Times,* November 21, 1956.

68. Although the distinction between termination and abrogation, like that between abdication and deposition in Talal's case, was substantial, it has often been confused. See, for example, Benjamin Shwadran, *Jordan: State of Tension* (New York: Council for Middle Eastern Affairs Press, 1959), 343; and Naseer H. Aruri, *Jordan: A Study in Political Development (1921–1965)* (The Hague: Nijhoff, 1972), 135.

69. See FO 371.121409/VJ 10393/190-194 [secret], FO 371.121503/VJ 1072/19 [secret]; and Dann, *King Hussein,* 44.

70. These included Sa'ad Jum'a and Hassan al-Khatib, governor of Jerusalem. Johnston to FO, December 13, 1956, FO 371.121470/VJ 1015/306-307; Dann, *King Hussein,* 44–45.

71. Ministerial statements in FO 371.121500/VJ 1051/246; FO 371.121522/VJ 1122/1; and FO 371.121480/VJ 10338/1; also see Mohammad Ibrahim Faddah, *The Middle East in Transition: A Study in Jordan's Foreign Policy* (London: Asia Publishing House, 1974) 208–9; *New York Times,* November 28, 1956.

72. Less than one month after Glubb's ouster, the British chiefs of staff formally concluded that the Anglo-Jordanian treaty "was of no further value and was now, in fact, an embarrassment." But the political value of the Jordanian connection, if only as a buffer for Nuri's Iraq, remained as strong as ever. Minutes of COS meeting, May 1, 1956, FO 371.121558/VJ 1205/224 [top secret].

73. Johnston to FO, November 27 and December 1, 1956, FO 371.121500/VJ 1051/247, 254 [secret]; Rose's minute, December 5, 1956, FO 371.121501/VJ 1051/249 [secret]; cabinet minutes, December 7, 1956, in FO 371.121501/VJ 1051/261, and January 3, 1957, in CAB 128/30 [secret].

74. On the Lloyd–Dulles meeting, see FO 371.121501/VJ 1051/262 [top secret] and Lot 62 D 181, CF 814 [secret], in *FRUS,* 13:73–74; also Morris to Hadow, December 22, 1956, FO 371.121482/VJ 10345/2 [secret]; Washington to FO, December 24, 1956, FO 371.121525/VJ 11345/7 [secret]; and the memorandum of Dulles's meeting with Makins, January 17, 1957, DOS 785.5/1-1757 [secret], in *FRUS,* 13:81–83.

75. DOS to Amman, December 24, 1956, DOS 685.00/12-2456 [top secret]; and Mallory to DOS, December 27, 1956, DOS 685.00/12-2756 [top secret], in *FRUS,* 13:77–79; Johnston to FO, January 1, 1957, FO 371.121525/VJ 11345/10a [secret].

76. For details of the agreement, see Johnston to FO, January 22, 1957, FO 371.127915/VJ 1121/10 [secret]; Shwadran, *Jordan*, 343–44.

77. Hussein's speech, January 23, 1957, in Ministry of Information, *al-Majmu'a al-kamila l'khutub jalalat al-malak al-Hussein bin Talal al-mu'athm, 1952–1985* [Complete collection of the speeches of His Majesty King Hussein bin Talal the Great, 1952–1985], 3 vols. (Amman: Directorate of Press and Publications, n.d. [1986?]), 1: 123–24; Johnston to FO, January 22, 1957, FO 371.127901/VJ 1051/28–29 [secret].

78. *New York Times,* December 17, 1956; Dann, *King Hussein,* 45.

CHAPTER 10

1. Interview with King Hussein.

2. Mohammad Ibrahim Faddah, *The Middle East in Transition: A Study in Jordan's Foreign Policy* (London: Asia Publishing House, 1974), 212.

3. Uriel Dann, *King Hussein and the Challenge of Arab Radicalism: Jordan, 1955–1967* (New York: Oxford University Press, 1989), 180, n. 15; and Benjamin Shwadran, *Jordan: State of Tension* (New York: Council for Middle Eastern Affairs Press, 1959), 344–46.

4. Johnston to FO, November 29, 1956, FO 371.121500/VJ 1051/251 [secret]; Middleton to Johnston, December 12, 1956, FO 371.121475/VJ 1024/ 33; DOS to Jeddah, December 24, 1956, DOS 685.00/12-2456 [top secret], in *Foreign Relations of the United States* (*FRUS*), 13:76–77; Johnston to FO, January 16, 1957, FO 371.127892/VJ 10325/2 [secret]; Hussein bin Talal, *Uneasy Lies the Head* (New York: Bernard Geis Associates, 1962), 155.

5. On the Eisenhower Doctrine, see *United States Policy in the Middle East: Documents, September 1956–June 1957* (1957; New York: Greenwood Press, 1969) 15–23.

6. *Al-Urdunn* (Amman), January 4, 1957, and *Falastin* (Jerusalem), January 3, 1957, cited in FO 371.127740/V 10345/52.

7. *New York Times,* January 3, 1957; Johnston to FO, January 31, 1957, FO 371.127989/VJ 1023/5; also, Dann, *King Hussein,* 47.

8. Text of royal message in FO 371.127989/VJ 1941/4; Johnston to FO, February 1, 1957, FO 371.127878/VJ 1015/6 [secret].

9. Johnston to FO, February 25, 1957, FO 371.127889/VJ 1023/6; Caccia to FO, March 15, 1957, FO 371.127742/V 10345/101; Johnston to FO, March 16, 1957, FO 371.127878,/VJ 1015/11 [secret]; *New York Times,* February 6–7, 1957.

10. Johnston to FO, February 25, 1957, FO 371.127889/VJ 1023/6; Charles Johnston, *The Brink of Jordan* (London: Hamish Hamilton, 1972), 40.

11. According to the agreement, Britain undertook to withdraw its forces from Jordan within six months, and Jordan promised to pay £4.25 million over six years in compensation for military stores and facilities. Also, Britain exonerated Jordan of a lingering £1.5 million debt from the Palestine war. As fortunes changed, few of Jordan's payments were ever made. See "Exchange of Notes Terminating the Treaty of Alliance of March 15, 1948, Amman, March 13, 1957." Treaty Series no. 39 (1957); FO 371.127905/VJ 10151/119-121; also Johnston to Lloyd, March 27, 1957, FO 371.127878/VJ 1015/15.

12. Johnston to FO, February 20, 1957, FO 371.127990/VJ 1941/14;

al-Rifa'i quoted in Mason to Hadow, February 20, 1957, FO 371.127878/VJ 1015/8 [secret]; Mallory to DOS, February 13, 1957, DOS 685.00/2-1357 [secret], in *FRUS*, 13:84–86.

13. Interview with Amer Khammash.

14. Johnston to FO, February 20, 1957, FO 371.127990/VJ 1941/14.

15. Mason to Hadow, February 20, 1957, FO 371.127878/VJ 1015/8 [secret].

16. Hussein's later claims to have known very early on of the extent of Abu Nuwar's disloyalty smack of retrospection. See Hussein, *Uneasy Lies the Head*, 156–57; interview with King Hussein.

17. Mallory to DOS, March 29, 1957, DOS 1201590/3-2957 [secret], in *FRUS*, 13: 88–89.

18. Johnston reported that "there is some reason to believe" that in mid-March al-Nabulsi "received a large bribe, perhaps as much as £100,000, from the Russians." Johnston to Lloyd, May 8, 1957, FO 371.127880/VJ 1015/114.

19. Johnston to FO, April 4, 1957, FO 371.127878/VJ 1015/16; Dann, *King Hussein*, 51; Shwadran, *Jordan*, 346–48.

20. See Amman to Levant Department, March 17, 1956, FO 371.121543/VJ 1201/94 [secret].

21. Both al-Mu'ayta and Abu Nuwar had served as members of Jordan's Armistice Delegation in 1949/50. See P. J. Vatikiotis, *Politics and the Military in Jordan: A Study of the Arab Legion, 1921–1957* (London: Cass, 1967), 129, n. 36.

22. Johnston to Lloyd, May 8, 1957, FO 371.127880/VJ 1015/114; Mason to Hadow, April 10, 1957, FO 371.127878/VJ 1015/40.

23. Johnston to Lloyd, May 8, 1957, FO 371.127880/VJ 1015/114; Dann, *King Hussein*, 55–56.

24. Interviews with Nadhir Rashid, Marwan al-Nimr, Zayd Bin Shakir, and Na'im 'Abd al-Hadi; Dann, *King Hussein*, 55–56.

25. In his memoirs, Hussein anachronistically claimed to have information of "infiltration by Soviet or U.A.R. influence." Hussein, *Uneasy Lies the Head*, 156.

26. Shahir Yusef Abu Shahut, *al-Jaysh wa'l-siyasa fi al-urdunn: dhikriyat 'an harakat al-dhubat al-urdunniyeen al-ahrar* [Army and politics in Jordan: Memories of the Jordanian Free Officers movement] (n.p.: al-Qabas, 1985), 21–22.

27. Johnston to FO, April 11, 1957, FO 371.127878/VJ 1015/21 [secret].

28. Johnston to FO, April 12, 1957, FO 371.127878/VJ 1015/23; interview with Marwan al-Nimr.

29. Johnston to Lloyd, May 14, 1957, FO 371.127880/VJ 1015/118; Dann, *King Hussein*, 57.

30. Johnston to Lloyd, May 14, 1957, FO 371.127880/VJ 1015/118; Johnston to FO, April 12, 1957, FO 371.127939/VJ 1194/5 [secret]; Dulles's comments, April 11, 1957, in *FRUS*, 13:89.

31. See Dann, *King Hussein*, 58–59.

32. Hussein, *Uneasy Lies the Head*, 168.

33. This was the infamous "wild-goose chase," Operation THABIT ("constant, enduring"), ordered by Lieutenant Colonel Ma'an Abu Nuwar of the Amira 'Aliya Brigade. In an interview, he refused to comment on the affair. Hussein's

principal sources of information were his uncle Sharif Nasser and 'Akif al-Fa'iz, son of the paramount shaykh of the Bani Sakhr who had now come out firmly for the king. See Johnston to Lloyd, May 14, 1957, FO 371.127880/VJ 1015/118; Dann, *King Hussein*, 59; Vatikiotis, *Politics and the Military*, 106, n. 12, and 130; Hussein, *Uneasy Lies the Head*, 169–70; Munib al-Madi and Sulayman Musa, *Tarikh al-urdunn fi al-qarn al-'ashreen* [The history of Jordan in the twentieth century] (1959; Amman: Maktaba al-muhtasab, 1988), 669–71.

34. Interview with King Hussein.

35. Bin Shakir himself was arrested by loyalist troops believing him to be in league with the conspirators. There may have been some truth to this allegation, as his subsequent reassignment away from the palace and diplomatic reports suggest. However, as with Habis al-Majali's youthful indiscretion, this did not substantially impede Bin Shakir's rise to army chief of staff, field marshal, and prime minister. Johnston to FO, April 21, 1957, and Mason to Hadow, May 22, 1957, FO 371.127879-127880/VJ 1015/54, 117; Uriel Dann, "Regime and Opposition in Jordan Since 1949," in *Society and Political Structures in the Arab World*, ed. Menachem Milson, (New York: Humanities Press, 1973), 171.

36. Hussein, *Uneasy Lies the Head*, 177–80; and Hussein bin Talal, *Mon métier de roi* (Paris: Editions Robert Laffont, 1975), 128–41.

37. Mallory, his military attaché, and Hussein's CIA contacts most likely played no more than a bit part in the Zerqa affair. Early on the evening of April 13, Mallory reported to Washington that "there is little ground for optimism." Mallory to DOS, April 13, 1957, DOS 120.1580/4-1357 [secret], in *FRUS*, 13:90–91; interview with Mahmud al-Mu'ayta.

38. By 1989, when the interview with Rashid took place, he had good reason to be so generous. After having atoned for his participation in the conspiracy, he was pardoned, returned to military service, and eventually rose to become Hussein's chief of intelligence—in other words, a "king's man" through and through.

39. Interview with Bin Shakir; also, Hussein's May 1957 interview cited by the BBC in FO 371.127880/VJ 1015/103.

40. Johnston to Lloyd, May 14, 1957, FO 371.127880/VJ 1015/118.

41. One of Hussein's few previous initiatives toward the bedouin was his February 1955 distribution of eight thousand *dunams* of prime Jordan Valley land to bedouin who had participated in his great-grandfather's Great Arab Revolt. According to Patai, this act cemented bedouin allegiance to the Hashemites, and though "insignificant at the time," it "may have contributed materially to the saving of the throne two years later." See Raphael Patai, *The Kingdom of Jordan* (Princeton, NJ: Princeton University Press, 1958), 57.

42. Aqil Hyder Hasan Abidi, *Jordan: A Political Study, 1948–1957* (London: Asia Publishing House, 1965), 161, n. 74.

43. At first, al-Hiyari was appointed acting chief of general staff and was not confirmed in his post until April 19. See also memorandum from the deputy director for intelligence (JCS) to assistant secretary of defense, April 15, 1957 [secret], in *FRUS*, 13:94–95; Johnston to FO, April 21, 1957, FO 371.127879/VJ 1015/54.

44. Johnston to FO, April 18–20, 1957, FO 371.127879/VJ 1015/51-53.

45. Suspicious maneuvers by these troops on April 14, perhaps in support of the Zerqa conspirators, had already provoked a minor crisis. See Johnston to Lloyd, May 29, 1957, FO 371.127880/VJ 1015/118.

46. Al-Hiyari's statement in Johnston to Lloyd, May 29, 1957, FO 371.127880/VJ 1015/123; Dann, *King Hussein*, 60; interviews with Bin Shakir and Anwar al-Khatib; *New York Times*, April 24, 1957; also Mallory to DOS, April 21, 1957, DOS 785.00/4-2157 [secret], in *FRUS*, 13:100–2. Al-Hiyari refused to be interviewed.

47. In September 1957, a military tribunal sentenced Abu Nuwar, al-Hiyari, al-Rimawi, Rashid, and Lieutenant Karim 'Uqlah to fifteen years imprisonment; twelve other officers, including Abu Shahut and most of the Free Officers' executive committee, received ten years' imprisonment; and five men, including Muhammad al-Mu'ayta, Ma'an Abu Nuwar, and al-Hiyari's brother Kamil, were acquitted. Most of those convicted had already fled the country. See Johnston to Lloyd, October 9, 1957, FO 371.127887/VJ 10110/5; see also *Qarar al-mahkama al-'urfiyya al-'askariyya al-khassa* [Decision of the special military court martial], 1957 (private collection of Mahmud al-Mu'ayta).

48. Abidi, *Jordan*, 161, n. 76; Dann, *King Hussein*, 60–61; Johnston to Lloyd, May 29, 1957, and Mallory to DOS, April 21, 1957, DOS 785.00/4-2157 [secret].

49. Mallory to DOS, April 21, 1957, DOS 785.00/4-2157 [secret].

50. Dulles's press conference extract in *United States Policy in the Middle East*, 68–69.

51. Eisenhower first heard of Hussein's message at 2:40 P.M. local time; Dulles met Eban at 3:30 P.M.; and the press conference was held at 5:30 P.M. In the interim, a message had been relayed back to Hussein, presumably through the same "intelligence channels." According to Eveland, Hussein's CIA contact was Second Secretary Frederick Latrash. This paragraph is based on documents in *FRUS*, 13:103–9; JCS to commander in chief, U.S. Forces/Europe, April 24, 1957, NA/RA JCS 381 EMMEA (11-19-47), sec. 57 [top secret]; Wilbur Crane Eveland, *Ropes of Sand: America's Failure in the Middle East* (London: Norton, 1980), 183; *New York Times*, April 25 and May 6, 1957.

52. Dann, *King Hussein*, 64.

53. Johnston to Lloyd, May 29, 1957, FO 371.127880/VJ 1015/118.

54. Johnston to FO, April 25, 1957, FO 371.127879/VJ 1015/69; Hussein's speech in Ministry of Information, *al-Majmu'a al-kamila l'khutub jalalat al-malak al-Hussein bin Talal al-mu'athm, 1952–1985* [Complete collection of the speeches of His Majesty King Hussein bin Talal the Great, 1952–1985], 3 vols. (Amman: Directorate of Press and Publications, n.d. [1986?]), 1: 147–51; translation in FO 371.127880/VJ 1015/95.

55. Abidi, *Jordan*, 162, n. 78; BBC report of Jordan Radio, April 27, 1957, in FO 371.127879/VJ 1015/92.

56. On the $2.5 million, see internal DOS memoranda in *FRUS*, 13:146–47; al-Rifa'i quoted in Mason to Hadow, December 12, 1956, FO 371.121475/VJ 1024/34; also see Stephen S. Kaplan, "United States and Regime Maintenance in Jordan, 1957–1973," *Public Policy* 23 (Spring 1975): 214–15.

57. Dann, *King Hussein*, 70–72.

58. Johnston to FO, May 14, 1957, FO 371.127889/VJ 1023/13 [secret].

59. In Washington, the answer was not clear-cut. Mallory to DOS, November 25, 1957, DOS 681.85/11-2257 [secret], in *FRUS*, 13:164–66.

60. Johnston to FO, May 6, 1957, FO 371.127880/VJ 1015/107 [secret].

61. As noted earlier, this is one of the principal themes of Dann's book. As for the Syrians, their best-laid plot was foiled in July 1958.

62. Baghdad to DOS, April 24, 1957, DOS 120.1580/4-2457 [secret]; and Baghdad to DOS, June 10, 1957, DOS 885.0086/6-1057 [secret], in *FRUS;* 13:111, 141–43.

63. Until July 1958, when the Iraqi monarchy disappeared and the Saudis timidly turned their backs on Hussein.

64. Israel was less interested in Hussein's survival than in nurturing a strategic relationship with the West. Even so, the first overflights occurred without Israel's permission and were subsequently suspended by an angry David Ben-Gurion. For details of Israel's overflight policy in the 1958 crisis, see FO 371.134038-134045/VJ 1091; FO 371.134313/VR 1093; FO 371.134345-134347/VR 1222; AIR 22/510; PREM 11.2377; PREM 11.2380; Hussein, *Uneasy Lies the Head,* 202–8; interview with King Hussein. Also see Michael B. Oren, "The Test of Suez: Israel and the Middle East Crisis of 1958," *Studies in Zionism* 12 (Spring 1991):55–83.

65. See Abu Nuwar's Special Order of the Day, September 26, 1956, following two Israeli retaliatory raids: "I call upon you to control your temper, keep calm and quiet, as I know you always will, to have patience and remain united until the promised day comes." Translation in FO 371.121782/VR 1091/365.

66. Johnston to FO, April 26, 1957, FO 371.127879/VJ 1015/76.

67. On Samir, see Johnston to FO, May 14, 1957, FO 371.127889/VJ 1023/13 [secret]; on Hazza', see Johnston to Lloyd, November 6, 1957, FO 371.127882/VJ 1015/189; and Johnston, *The Brink of Jordan,* 152–53; on al-Shar'a, see FO 371.142102-142103/VJ 1015; Johnston, *The Brink of Jordan,* 138–39; and interview with al-Shar'a. Al-Shar'a was sentenced to death, and then pardoned, for conspiring against Hussein, but the details of his conspiracy remain obscure.

68. On these episodes, see Johnston to Lloyd, November 6, 1957, FO 371.127882/VJ 1015/189; and Dann, *King Hussein,* 130.

69. Moshe Shemesh, The *Palestinian Entity, 1959–1974: Arab Politics and the PLO* (London: Cass, 1988), 1.

Bibliography

PUBLISHED SOURCES

English and French

Abdullah, ibn al-Hussein. *My Memoirs Completed, "al-Takmilah."* London: Longman Group, 1978.

Abidi, Aqil Hyder Hasan. *Jordan: A Political Study, 1948–1957.* London: Asia Publishing House, 1965.

Abu Jaber, Kamel S. "The Legislature of the Hashemite Kingdom of Jordan: A Study in Political Development." *The Muslim World* 59 (July–October 1969): 220–50.

Alan, Ray. "Jordan: Rise and Fall of a Squirearchy." *Commentary* 23 (March 1957): 242–49.

Almany, Abraham. *Constitutions of the Countries of the World: Jordan.* New York: Oceana Publications, 1972.

An Annotated Bibliography of the United States Government Documents Pertaining to the Hashemite Kingdom of Jordan, 1920–1983. Amman: Royal Foundation for Islamic Civilization Research (Ahl al-bayt Foundation), 1984.

Aruri, Naseer H. *Jordan: A Study in Political Development (1921–1965).* The Hague: Nijhoff, 1972.

Bar-Joseph, Uri. *The Best of Enemies: Israel and Transjordan in the War of 1948.* London: Cass, 1987.

Baster, James. "The Economic Problems of Jordan." *International Affairs* 31 (1955): 26–35.

Birdwood. *Nuri as-Said: A Study in Arab Leadership.* London: Cassell, 1959.

Brecher, Michael. *The Foreign Policy System of Israel: Setting, Images, Process.* Oxford: Oxford University Press, 1972.

Burns, E. L. M. *Between Arab and Israeli*. London: Harrap, 1962.

NC. "Jordan's Frontier Villages." *The World Today* 9 (1953): 467–75.

Campbell, John C. *Defense of the Middle East: Problems of American Policy*. New York: Council of Foreign Relations by Harper Bros., 1958.

Childers, Erskine B. *The Road to Suez: A Study of Western–Arab Relations*. London: MacGibbon & Kee, 1962.

Clarke, John. *Templer, Tiger of Malaya: The Life of Field Marshal Sir Gerald Templer*. London: Harrap, 1985.

Cohen, Amnon. *Political Parties in the West Bank Under the Jordanian Regime, 1949–1967*. Ithaca, NY: Cornell University Press, 1982.

The Constitution of the Hashemite Kingdom of Jordan (English and Arabic). Amman: n.p. (National Assembly?), n.d.

Copeland, Miles. *The Game of Nations: The Amorality of Power Politics*. London: Weidenfeld and Nicolson, 1969.

Dann, Uriel. "Book Review of *Politics and Change in Al-Karak, Jordan: A Study of a Small Arab Town and Its District* by Peter Gubser." *Middle Eastern Studies* 14 (May 1978): 254–56.

————. "The Foreign Office, the Baghdad Pact and Jordan." *Asian and African Studies* 21 (1987): 247–61.

————. "Glubb and the Politicization of the Arab Legion: An Annotated Document." *Asian and African Studies* 21 (1987): 213–20.

————. *King Hussein and the Challenge of Arab Radicalism: Jordan, 1955–1967*. New York: Oxford University Press, 1989.

————. "Regime and Opposition in Jordan Since 1949." In *Society and Political Structures in the Arab World*, ed. Menachem Milson, 145–81. New York: Humanities Press, 1973.

————. *Studies in the History of Transjordan*. Boulder, CO: Westview Press, 1984.

Davis, Helen Miller. *Constitutions, Electoral Laws, Treaties of States in the Near and Middle East*. Durham, NC: Duke University Press, 1953.

Dearden, Ann. *Jordan*. London: Robert Hale, 1958.

Department of Statistics, Hashemite Kingdom of Jordan. *Annual Statistical Bulletin*. Amman: Department of Statistics, various issues from 1952.

———— and U.S. Technical Cooperation Service for Jordan. *1952 Census of Housing: Statistics for Districts, Subdistricts, Nahiyas and Principal Towns*. Amman: n.p., n.d.

Eden, Anthony. *Full Circle*. London: Cassell, 1960.

el-Edroos, Syed Ali. *The Hashemite Arab Army: An Appreciation and Analysis of Military Operations*. Amman: Publishing Committee, 1980.

Eveland, Wilbur Crane. *Ropes of Sand: America's Failure in the Middle East*. London: Norton, 1980.

Faddah, Mohammad Ibrahim. *The Middle East in Transition: A Study in Jordan's Foreign Policy*. London: Asia Publishing House, 1974.

Gallman, Waldemar J. *Iraq Under General Nuri: My Recollections of Nuri al-Said, 1954–1958*. Baltimore: Johns Hopkins University Press, 1964.

Gendizer, Irene L. "The United States, the USSR and the Arab World in NSC Reports of the 1950s." *Arab-American Affairs*, Summer 1989, 22–29.

Gilbar, Gad G. "The Economy of Nablus and the Hashemites: The Early Years, 1949–56." *Middle Eastern Studies* 25 (January 1989): 51–63.

Glubb, John Bagot. *The Changing Scenes of Life: An Autobiography.* London: Quartet Books, 1983.

————. *A Soldier with the Arabs.* London: Hodder & Stoughton, 1957.

————. *The Story of the Arab Legion.* London: Hodder & Stoughton, 1948.

————. "Violence on the Jordan–Israel Border: A Jordanian View." *Foreign Affairs* 32 (July 1954): 552–62.

Goichon, A. M. *Jordanie réelle.* 2 vols. Paris: Desclée de Brouwer, 1967 and 1972.

Graves, Philip R., ed. *Memoirs of King Abdullah of Transjordan.* London: Jonathan Cape, 1950.

Gubser, Peter. *Politics and Change in Al-Karak, Jordan: A Study of a Small Arab Town and Its District.* Oxford: Oxford University Press, 1973.

Hacker, Jane. *Modern Amman: A Social Study.* Durham: University of Durham Press, 1960.

Haddad, George M. *Revolutions and Military Rule in the Middle East: The Arab States, Part 1: Iraq, Syria, Lebanon and Jordan.* Vol. 2. New York: Robert Speller & Sons, 1971.

Harris, George L. *Jordan, Its People, Its Society, Its Culture.* New York: Grove Press, 1958.

Hourani, Albert. *Vision of History: Near Eastern and Other Essays.* Beirut: Khayyats, 1961.

Huntington, Samuel P. *Political Order in Changing Societies.* New Haven, CT: Yale University Press, 1968.

Hussein bin Talal. *Mon métier de roi.* Paris: Editions Robert Laffont, 1975.

————. *Uneasy Lies the Head.* New York: Bernard Geis Associates, 1962.

Ifram, Hala Farhan. *Bibliography of Jordan.* Amman: Royal Scientific Society, 1973.

International Bank for Reconstruction and Development. *The Economic Development of Jordan.* Baltimore: Johns Hopkins University Press, 1957.

Ionides, Michael. *Divide and Lose.* London: Geoffrey Bles, 1960.

J. D. L. "The Jordan Coup d'Etat: March 1st, 1956." *History Today* 7 (January 1957): 3–10.

Jarvis, C. S. *Arab Command: The Biography of Lieutenant Colonel F. W. Peake Pasha.* London: Hutchinson and Co., 1942.

Johnston, Charles. *The Brink of Jordan.* London: Hamish Hamilton, 1972.

Jordan Development Board. *Manpower Study.* Amman: Jordan Development Board, 1960.

Khair, Hani. *Brief Survey of Parliamentary Life in Jordan, 1920–1988.* Amman: n.p., n.d. (1989?).

Khairi, Majduddin Omar. *Jordan and the World System: Development in the Middle East.* Frankfurt am-Main: Peter Lang, 1984.

Kirkbride, Alec Seath. *A Crackle of Thorns: Experiences in the Middle East.* London: Murray, 1956.

————. *From the Wings: Amman Memoirs, 1947–1951.* London: Cass, 1976.

Kliot, Nurit, and Arnon Soffer. "The Emergence of a Metropolitan Core Area in a New State—The Case of Jordan." *Asian and African Studies* 20 (1986): 217–32.

Landau, Jacob M., ed. *Man, State and Society in the Contemporary Middle East.* London: Pall Mall Press, 1972.

WZL (Laqueur, Walter Z.). "Communism in Jordan." *The World Today* 12 (1956): 109–19.

Lebedev, Y. A. "Soviet Writing on Jordan." *The Mizan Newsletter* 2 (November 1960): 2–12.

Lerner, Daniel. *The Passing of Traditional Society: Modernizing the Middle East.* London: Free Press, 1958.

Lias, Godfrey. *Glubb's Legion.* London: Evans Brothers, 1956.

Lloyd, Selwyn. *Suez 1956: A Personal Account.* London: Jonathan Cape, 1978.

Louis, William Roger. *The British Empire in the Middle East, 1945–1951.* Oxford: Clarendon Press, 1984.

Lucas, W. Scott. "Redefining the Suez 'Collusion'." *Middle Eastern Studies* 26 (January 1990): 88–112.

Lunt, James. *Glubb Pasha: A Biography.* London: Harvill Press, 1984.

_____. *Hussein of Jordan: Searching for a Just and Lasting Peace, a Political Biography.* London: Macmillan, 1989.

Macmillan, Harold. *Riding the Storm, 1956–1959.* London: Macmillan, 1971.

_____. *Tides of Fortune, 1945–1955.* (London: Macmillan, 1969).

Maddy-Weitzman, Bruce. "Jordan and Iraq: Efforts at Intra-Hashemite Unity." *Middle Eastern Studies* 26 (January 1990): 65–75.

Ma'oz, Moshe. *Palestinian Leadership on the West Bank: The Changing Role of the Arab Mayors Under Jordan and Israel.* London: Cass, 1984.

Miller, Aaron David. *The Arab States and the Palestine Question: Between Ideology and Self-Interest.* The Washington Papers 120. New York: Praeger, 1986.

_____. "Jordan and the Arab–Israeli Conflict: The Hashemite Predicament." *Orbis* (Winter 1986): 795–820.

_____. "Jordan and the Palestinian Issue: The Legacy of the Past." *Middle East Insight* (4:4–5): 21–29.

Ministry of Foreign Affairs, Hashemite Kingdom of Jordan. *The Rising Tide of Terror or Three Years of an Armistice in the Holy Land.* Amman: General Directorate of Press and Publications, 1952.

Mishal, Shaul. *West Bank/East Bank: The Palestinians in Jordan, 1949–1967.* New Haven, CT: Yale University Press, 1978.

Mogannam, Theodore E. "Developments in the Legal System of Jordan." *Middle East Journal* 6 (Spring 1952): 194–206.

Monroe, Elizabeth. *Britain's Moment in the Middle East.* London: Chatto & Windus, 1963.

Morris, James. *The Hashemite Kings.* London: Faber & Faber, 1959.

Mutawi, Samir. *Jordan and the 1967 War.* Cambridge: Cambridge University Press, 1987.

Neff, Donald. *Warriors at Suez: Eisenhower Takes America into the Middle East.* New York: Linden Press, 1981.

Nisan, Mordechai. "The Palestinian Features of Jordan." In *Judea, Samaria and Gaza: Views of the Present and Future,* ed. Daniel J. Elazar, 191–209. Washington, DC: American Enterprise Institute, 1982.

Nolte, Richard N. "The Arab Solidarity Agreement: The Influence of History and National Attitudes on Jordan's Decision to Break with Britain." *American University Field Staff Report—Southwest Asia,* March 18, 1957.

Nutting, Anthony. *I Saw for Myself: The Aftermath of Suez.* London: Hollis and Carter, 1958.

_____. *No End of a Lesson: The Story of Suez*. London: Constable, 1967.

Oren, Michael B. "The Test of Suez: Israel and the Middle East Crisis of 1958." *Studies in Zionism* 12 (Spring 1991): 55–83.

_____. "A Winter of Discontent: Britain's Crisis in Jordan, December 1955–March 1956." *International Journal of Middle East Studies* 22 (1990): 171–84.

Pappé, Ilan. "Sir Alec Kirkbride and the Making of Greater Transjordan." *Asian and African Studies* 23 (1989): 43–70.

Patai, Raphael. *Jordan, Lebanon and Syria: An Annotated Bibliography*. New Haven, CT: Yale University Press, 1957.

_____. *The Kingdom of Jordan*. Princeton, NJ: Princeton University Press, 1958.

Philby, H. A. R. and Walid Khalidi. "Glubb's *Soldier with the Arabs*: Two Review Articles." *Middle East Forum* 23 (1958): 21–25.

Plascov, Avi. *The Palestinian Refugees in Jordan, 1948–1957*. London: Cass, 1981.

Pipes, Daniel. "Abdallah's 'Pure Joke' and the Greater Syria Plan." *Middle East Review*, Fall 1987: 43–53.

_____. *Greater Syria: The History of an Ambition*. New York: Oxford University Press, 1990.

Rabinovich, Itamar. *The Road Not Taken: Early Arab–Israeli Negotiations*. New York: Oxford University Press, 1991.

Reid, Donald M. *Lawyers and Politics in the Arab World, 1880–1960*. University of Chicago Studies in Middle Eastern History. Chicago: Bibliotheca Islamica, 1981.

Roberts, Frank C., ed. *Obituaries from the Times, 1971–1975*. London: Newspaper Archive Developments, 1976.

Royal Institute of International Affairs. *The Middle East: A Political and Economic Survey*. Oxford: Oxford University Press, various editions under various editors.

Rubin, Barry. *The Arab States and the Palestine Conflict*. Syracuse, NY: Syracuse University Press, 1981.

Safran, Nadav. *From War to War*. New York: Pegasus, 1969.

Sanger, Richard H. *Where the Jordan Flows*. Washington, DC: Middle East Institute, 1963.

Seale, Patrick, ed. *The Shaping of an Arab Statesman: Abd al-Hamid Sharaf and the Modern Arab World*. London: Quartet Books, 1983.

_____. *The Struggle for Syria: A Study of Post-War Arab Politics, 1945–1958*. London: I. B. Tauris, 1965.

Seecombe, Ian J. *Jordan*. World Bibliographic Series. Vol. 55. Oxford: Clio Press, 1984.

SGT. "King Abdullah's Assassins." *The World Today* 7 (1951): 411–19.

Sheffer, Gabriel. *Dynamics of Dependence*. Boulder, CO: Westview Press, 1987.

Shemesh, Moshe. *The Palestinian Entity, 1959–1974: Arab Politics and the PLO*. London: Cass, 1988.

Shimoni, Yaacov, and Evyatar Levine. *Political Dictionary of the Middle East in the Twentieth Century*. Jerusalem: G.A. Jerusalem Publishing House, 1974.

Shlaim, Avi. *Collusion Across the Jordan: King Abdullah, the Zionist Movement and the Partition of Palestine*. New York: Columbia University Press, 1988.

_____. "Conflicting Approaches to Israel's Relations with the Arabs: Ben Gurion and Sharett, 1953–1956." *Middle East Journal* 37 (Spring 1983): 180–201.

Shuckburgh, Evelyn. *Descent to Suez: Diaries, 1951–56*. London: Weidenfeld and Nicolson, 1986.

Shwadran, Benjamin. *Jordan: State of Tension*. New York: Council for Middle Eastern Affairs Press, 1959.

Simon, Reeva S. "The Hashemite 'Conspiracy': Hashemite Unity Attempts, 1921–1958." *International Journal of Middle East Studies* 5 (1974): 314–27.

Sinai, Anne, and Allen Pollack, eds. *The Hashemite Kingdom of Jordan and the West Bank: A Handbook*. New York: American Academic Association for Peace in the Middle East, 1977.

Slonim, Shlomo. "The Origins of the Tripartite Declaration." *Middle Eastern Studies* 23 (1987): 135–49.

Sofer, Naim. "The Political Status of Jerusalem in the Hashemite Kingdom of Jordan: 1946–67." *Middle Eastern Studies* 12 (1976): 73–94.

Snow, Peter. *Hussein: A Biography*. London: Barrie & Jenkins, 1972.

Sparrow, Gerald. *Hussein of Jordan*. London: Harrop, 1960.

Spiegel, Steven L. *The Other Arab–Israeli Conflict: Making America's Middle East Policy, from Truman to Reagan*. Chicago: University of Chicago Press, 1984.

Trevelyan, Humphrey. *Middle East in Revolution*. London: Macmillan, 1970.

Tully, Andrew. *CIA: The Inside Story*. New York: Morrow, 1962.

United Nations Relief and Works Agency (UNRWA). *Special Reports on Jordan. Bulletin of Economic Development*. No. 14. Beirut, July 1956.

United States. Department of State. Historical Office. *Foreign Relations of the United States*. Near East and Africa. Vols. 5 (1951), 9 (1952–54), and 13 (1955–57). Washington, DC: U.S. Government Printing Office.

————. *United States Policy in the Middle East: Documents, September 1956–June 1957*. Washington, DC: U.S. Government Printing Office, 1957. Reprint. New York: Greenwood Press, 1968.

Vatikiotis, P. J. *Politics and the Military in Jordan: A Study of the Arab Legion, 1921–1957*. London: Cass, 1967.

Wilson, Mary C. *King Abdullah, Britain and the Making of Jordan*. Cambridge: Cambridge University Press, 1987.

Wright, Esmond. "Abdullah's Jordan: 1947–1951." *Middle East Journal* 5 (Autumn 1951): 439–60.

Young, Peter. *Bedouin Command: With the Arab Legion, 1953–1956*. London: William Kimber, 1956.

Arabic

Abu Nuwar, Ma'an. *Talal bin Abdullah bin al-Hussein: tarikh al-quwwat al-musallah al-urdunni, II: 1950–52* [Talal bin Abdullah bin al-Hussein: History of the Jordanian armed forces, II: 1950–52]. Amman: Jordanian Armed Forces, 1972.

Abu'l Ragheb, Akram. *Shibl quraysh: tafula wa'siba al-Hussein bin Talal* [The lion cub of Quraysh: Childhood and youth of Hussein bin Talal]. Amman: Madinah Printing Press, n.d.

Abu Shahut, Shahir Yusef. *Al-Jaysh wa'l-siyasa fi al-urdunn: dhikriyat 'an harakat al-dhubat al-urdunniyeen al-ahrar* [Army and politics in Jordan: Memories of the Jordanian Free Officers movement]. N.p.: al-Qabas, 1985.

Al-'Amn al-'amm fi al-urdunn, 1920–1980 [Public security in Jordan, 1920–1980]. Amman: Directorate for Public Security, 1981.

'Ashqar, Mursi al-. *Mashahir al-rijal fi al-mamlaka al-urdunniyya al-hashimiyya,*

1955–1956 [Famous men in the Hashemite Kingdom of Jordan, 1955–1956]. Jerusalem: Roman Orthodox Church, n.d.

Bandaqji, Riyadh Ahmad. *Al-Urdunn fi 'ahd Glubb* [Jordan in the time of Glubb]. Amman: n.p., n.d. (1956?).

Dhubyan, Muhammad Taysir. *Al-Malak Talal* [King Talal]. Amman: Majallat al-shari'a, 1972.

Government of Jordan. *Suriya al-kubra: al-kitab al-urdunni al-abyadh* [Greater Syria: The Jordanian white paper]. Amman: al-Matba' al-Wataniyya, 1947.

Hijazi, Nayif. *Shakhsiyyat urdunniyya* [Jordanian personalities]. Amman: Nayif Hijazi, 1973.

Hussein bin Talal. *Qissa hayati* [The story of my life]. Arabic version of English autobiography serialized in *Daily Mail* (London) and published as *Uneasy Lies the Head*. Amman: General Directorate for Press and Publications, n.d.

Kilani, Subhi Zayd al-, ed. *Al-Urdunn al-yawm* [Jordan today]. Amman: General Directorate of Press and Publications, 1956.

League of Jordanian Students in Cairo. *Sawt al-urdunn* [The voice of Jordan]. Cairo: Dar al-nashr wa'l-thiqafa, 1955.

Madi, Munib al-, and Sulayman Musa. *Tarikh al-urdunn fi al-qarn al-'ashreen* [The history of Jordan in the twentieth century]. Amman: n.p., 1959; 2nd ed., Amman: Maktaba al-muhtasab, 1988.

Majali, Hazza' al-. *Mudhakkarati* [My memoirs]. Beirut: Dar al-'ilm lil-malayeen, 1960.

————. *Qissat muhadathat Templer* [Story of the Templer talks]. Amman: n.p., 1956.

Ministry of Culture and Information. *Al-Urdunn fi khamsin 'aman: 1921–1971* [Jordan in fifty years: 1921–1971]. Amman: Directorate of Press and Publications, 1972.

Ministry of Information. *Al-Majmu'a al-kamila l'khutub jalalat al-malak al-Hussein bin Talal al-mu'athm, 1952–1985* [Complete collection of the speeches of His Majesty King Hussein bin Talal the Great, 1952–1985]. 3 vols. Amman: Directorate of Press and Publications, n.d. (1986?).

————. *Al-Witha'iq al-urdunniyya: Al-wizarat al-urdunniyya, 1921–1984* [Jordanian documents: Jordanian ministries, 1921–1984]. Amman: Directorate of Press and Publications, 1984.

Muhafaza, 'Ali. *Al-'Alaqat al-urdunniyya al-baritaniyya: 1921–1957* [Jordanian-British relations, 1921–1957]. Beirut: Dar al-nahar wa'l-nashr, 1973.

Murad, 'Abbas. *Al-Daur al-siyasi lil-jaysh al-urdunni: 1921–1973* [The political role of the Jordanian army, 1921–1973]. Beirut: Palestine Liberation Organization, Research Department, 1973.

Musa, Sulayman. *A'lam min al-urdunn: safahat min tarikh al-'arab al-hadith* [Luminaries from Jordan: Pages from modern Arab history]. Amman: Dar al-sha'b, 1986.

Nashashibi, Nasir al-din al-. *Man qatala al-malak Abdullah?* [Who killed King Abdullah?] Kuwait: Manshurat al-anba', 1980.

Nasir, Nadim. "Al-Liwa' 'Ali Abu Nuwar yatadhakkar . . ." ["General 'Ali Abu Nuwar Remembers . . ."], Series of interviews in *al-Majalla*, 1983.

Qarar al-mahkama al-'urfiyya al-'askariyya al-khassa [Decision of the special military court martial], 1957. Private collection of Mahmud al-Mu'ayta.

Qa'ush, Abdullah, and Wasif al-Shaykh Yasin. *Al-Mamlaka al-urdunniyya al-hashimiyya fi 'ahd al-muluk al-hashimiyya al-'utham* [The Hashemite Kingdom of Jordan in the time of the great Hashemite kings]. Jerusalem: n.p., n.d. (1953?).

Rida, Mahmud. *Mudhakkarat al-Malak Talal* [Memoirs of King Talal]. Cairo: Ruz al-Yusef Publishers, n.d..

Sha'ir, Jamal al-. *Siyasi yatadhakkir* [A politician remembers]. London: Riyad al-Rayyes, 1987.

Shar'a, Salih al-. *Mudhakkarat jundi* [Memoirs of a soldier]. Amman: n.p., 1985.

Tandawi, Samir al-. *Ila 'ayn yatajih al-urdunn* [Where is Jordan heading?]. Cairo: Al-Dar al-masriyah li'l-tiba'a wa'l-nashr, n.d.

Tall, Abdullah al-. *Karithat Filastin: Mudhakkarat Abdullah al-Tall* [The Palestine disaster: Memoirs of Abdullah al-Tall]. Cairo: Dar al-Qalm Press, 1959.

Wahby, Mustafa al-Tall, and Khalil Nasr. *Talal.* Amman: Hashemite Publications, 1934.

Ziyadin, Ya'qub. *Al-Bidayat* [Beginnings]. N.p.: Salah al-Din Publishers, 1981.

Hebrew

Cohen, Amnon., ed. *Miflagot politiyot b'geda ha'ma'aravit takhat ha'shilton ha'hashimi* [Political parties on the West Bank under the Jordanian regime]. Jerusalem: Hebrew University Press, 1972.

Sela, Avraham. *Ha'ba'th ha'filastini* [The Palestinian Ba'th]. Jerusalem: Magnes Press, Hebrew University, 1984.

DISSERTATIONS

Alberts, Darlene Jean. "King Hussein of Jordan: The Consummate Politician." Ph.D. diss., Ohio State University, 1973.

Bailey, Clinton. "The Participation of the Palestinians in the Politics of Jordan." Ph.D. diss., Columbia University, 1966.

Khatib, Abdullah Hamid A. "The Jordanian Legislature in Political Development Perspective." Ph.D. diss., State University of New York at Albany, 1975.

Lipe, Roseanne Catherine. "Jordan's Foreign Relations, 1953–1978: A Quantitative Description." Ph.D. diss., University of North Carolina at Chapel Hill, 1980.

Obeidate, Khalid Abdullah. "Les Données interieures (socio-politiques) de la politique étrangère jordanienne, 1948–1975." Ph.D diss., University of Paris, Sorbonne, 1978.

Peck, Brian Maclellan. "King Husayn of Jordan: Tradition and Change in Modern Middle East Monarchy." M.A. thesis, University of Arizona, 1985.

Phillips, Paul G. "The Hashemite Kingdom of Jordan: Prolegomena to a Technical Assistance Program." Ph.D. diss., University of Chicago, 1954.

Robins, Philip. "The Consolidation of Hashimite Power in Jordan, 1921–1946." Ph.D. diss., University of Exeter, 1988.

Sabella, Epiphan (Bernard) Zacharia. "External Events and Circulation of Political Elites: Cabinet Turnover in Jordan, 1946–1980." Ph.D. diss., University of Virgina, 1982.

Saket, Bassam Khalil. "Foreign Aid to Jordan, 1924/25–1972/73: Its Magnitude, Composition and Effect." Ph.D. diss., University of Keele, 1976.

ARCHIVES

Public Record Office, London
    FO 371: Political
    FO 624: Baghdad
    FO 778: Geneva
    FO 800: Private Papers
    FO 816: Amman
    FO 953: Information Policy
    CO 831: Transjordan
    WO 106: Intelligence
    WO 216: Chief of the Imperial General Staff
    PREM 11: Prime Minister's Papers
    AIR 22: Periodical returns, summaries, and bulletins, 1936–60
    CAB 130: Ad Hoc Committee: General and Miscellaneous Series, 1945–58

National Archives, Washington, DC, and Suitland, MD
    RG 59: Relating to Jordan
    RG 84: Amman post records
    RG 218: Records of the Joint Chiefs of Staff, including 381, Eastern Mediterranean and Middle East Area; and 092, Palestine
    RG 330: Records of the Secretary of Defense
    Various lot files of the records of the Office of Intelligence Research, Department of State

Harry S Truman Presidential Library, Independence, MO
    Files on Transjordan and Jordan

Dwight D. Eisenhower Presidential Library, Abilene, KS
    Files on Jordan

Jordanian Ministry of Culture and Information, Department of Documentation, Libraries and National Archives, Amman
    N.B.: Classification system is antiquated and not uniform

    9-14-2: Prime Ministry and Foreign Ministry documents, 1951
    907/13-a-2-25: Budgets for Amman municipality, 1951–53
    91/155-15-a: Condolence telegrams on the death of King Abdullah
    95/156-15: Trial of Abdullah's assassins, 1951
    96/160-15: Qibya, 1953
    143/14-146-13: Jordan Development Board, 1959–61
    225: Directives of the Ministry of Interior, 1958–60
    228/12-1: Military file, 1952–57 (all secret)
    230/10-11: Jordan Development Board, 1956–58
    240/12-21: Higher Economic Committee, 1949–51
    292/5-27-3: Press and Publications, 1955–59
    298: Minutes of the Chamber of Deputies, 1951–53
    422: Directives of the Ministry of Interior, 1954–55
    454: Minutes of the Chamber of Deputies, 1955
    483/1-19-3: Economic development, 1953–58
    489: Political affairs, 1929–51
    548/1-2: Directives of the Prime Ministry, 1952–57

575: Minutes of the Senate, 1955

592/2-2: General Security, 1942–57

592/4-2: Directives of the Ministries of Finance and Economy, 1936–56

666/9-11: Directives of the Ministry of Economics, 1953–55

675/6-28-20: Accounting of certain embassies

719/9-18-22: Refugees, 1951–52

771/912: Directives of the Ministry of Defense

812/1-15-2: Regulations of defense organization, 1944–52

1084/6-3: National Guard, 1952–59

1205: Information relating to Saudi Arabia, 1950–52

Israel State Archives, Jerusalem
Files relating to Jordanian domestic and foreign policy:
2408/11; 2408/11/aleph; 2408/12; 2408/12/aleph; 2408/14; 2410/6;
2427/12; 2440/3/aleph; 2448/2; 2450/6; 2453/10; 2457/3; 2459/13;
2477/11; 2474/18; 2477/21/aleph; 2512/22; 2531/9/aleph; 2531/10;
2551/11; 2565/9; 2565/22.

Jerusalem Municipal Archives
Files relating to municipal elections

Moshe Dayan Center for Middle Eastern and African Studies, Tel Aviv University
Newspaper Documentation Center
Benjamin Shwadran Collection

PRIVATE PAPERS

Middle East Centre, St. Antony's College, Oxford
Patrick Coghill. "Before I Forget." Mimeographed memoirs, 1960.
J. B. Slade-Baker, diaries

Liddell Hart Military Archive, King's College, University College, London
Geoffrey Furlonge Papers
Charles Johnston Papers

John Foster Dulles Library, Princeton University, Princeton, NJ
Joseph Coy Green, "Journal Journal," 3 vols. Mimeographed memoirs,
1952–53; and private papers

Farhan al-Shubaylat, unpublished Arabic memoirs

NEWSPAPERS AND PERIODICALS CITED

Al-Ahram (Cairo)

Christian Science Monitor (Boston)

Daily Telegraph (London)

Al-Difaʿ (Jerusalem)

Evening Standard (London)

Falastin (Jerusalem)

Le Figaro (Paris)

Al-Ittihad (Damascus)
Jerusalem Post
Journal de Genève
Al-Misri (Cairo)
New York Times
New York Herald Tribune
Observer (London)
The Times (London)
Al-Urdunn (Amman)

INTERVIEWS (WITH RELEVANT IDENTIFICATIONS
FOR THE 1950s)

King Hussein bin Talal	June 25 and July 1, 1989
Crown Prince Hassan bin Talal	July 20, 1989
Na'im 'Abd al-Hadi minister and NSP politician	July 10, 1989
Adnan Abu Awdah Communist activist	June 25 and July 1, 1989
'Ali Abu Nuwar CGS, JAA; defected, April 1957	July 2, 1989
Ma'an Abu Nuwar Army officer acquitted of complicity in 1957 Zerqa plot	June 1, 1989
Yusef al-'Athm Muslim Brotherhood leader and member of parliament	July 17, 1989
Colin Brant second secretary, British embassy	June 18, 1989
Sir Julian Bullard second secretary, British embassy	May 31, 1989
Hamad al-Farhan undersecretary of the ministry of economics	July 6, 1989
A. David Fritzlan deputy chief of mission and chargé d'affaires, U.S. embassy	April 11, 1989
Sir John Graham third secretary, British embassy	December 13, 1989
Sulaymar al-Hadidi founding member, Jordanian Ba'th party	July 6, 1989
John Halaby former editor, *al-Jihad* (Amman); Reuters correspondent	July 17, 1989
Hani Hashim son of prime minister Ibrahim Hashim; diplomat	July 25, 1989

Yusef Haykal   July 16, 1989
    ambassador to Washington and London

'Ali al-Hindawi   July 1, 1989
    minister

Mahir Irshayd   June 27, 1989
    son of minister Farid Irshayd

Sami Judeh   June 27, 1989
    son-in-law of Samir al-Rifa'i

Amer Khammash   July 18, 1989
    ADC to al-Mulqi, Abu'l Huda, and al-Mufti

Anwar al-Khatib   July 15 and August 14, 1989
    NSP founder and minister

Muhammad Rasul al-Kilani   July 26, 1990
    chief investigator, 1958 al-Shar'a conspiracy

Mahmud al-Mu'ayta   July 23, 1989
    Free Officer and Ba'th party member

'Ali Muhafaza   July 6, 1989
    Jordanian historian

Hani al-Mulqi   June 28, 1989
    son of Fawzi al-Mulqi

Sulayman Musa   June 29, 1989
    Jordanian historian

Faris al-Nabulsi   July 8, 1989
    son of Sulayman al-Nabulsi

Marwan 'Abd al-Halim al-Nimr   July 24, 1989
    son of NSP founder and minister 'Abd al-Halim al-Nimr

Hazem Nusaybah   July 17, 1989
    brother of Defense Minister Anwar Nusaybah

Nadhir Rashid   July 9, 1989
    Free Officer

Sir John Richmond   November 29, 1989
    counselor, British embassy

Dia' al-din al-Rifa'i   July 27, 1990
    brother of Samir al-Rifa'i, diplomat

Zayd al-Rifa'i   June 26, 1989
    son of Samir al-Rifa'i

Zayn al-Rifa'i   December 6, 1989
    daughter of Samir al-Rifa'i

Suheilah al-Rimawi   July 9, 1989
    widow of Ba'th party leader Abdullah al-Rimawi

Walid Salah   July 3, 1989
    prosecutor-general and foreign minister

Moshe Sasson   August 20, 1989
    Israeli diplomat; interlocutor of Abdullah

Jamal al-Sha'ir   July 4, 1989
    Ba'th party activist

Sadiq al-Shar'a   July 3 and July 12, 1989
    COS, JAA; implicated in 1958 conspiracy

Ghayth and Layth al-Shubaylat   July 3, 1989
    sons of Defense Minister Farhan al-Shubaylat

'Abd al-Rahman Shuqayr   July 2 and July 10, 1989
    National Front leader

Raja'i Suqqar   July 5, 1989
    son of Finance Minister Sulayman Suqqar

Bahjat al-Talhuni   June 29, July 2, and July 5, 1989
    chief of the royal court

Sharif Zayd bin Shakir   July 18, 1989
    cousin of and aide-de-camp to King Hussein

Akram Zu'aytar   July 17, 1989
    prominent politician; leader of pro-Iraqi faction

Index